Intercultural Discourse and Communication

This book is due for return on or before the last date shown below.

Linguistics: The Essential Readings

This series consists of comprehensive collections of classic and contemporary reprinted articles in a wide range of fields within linguistics. The primary works presented in each book are complemented by outstanding editorial material by key figures in the field. Each volume stands as an excellent resource on its own, as well as an ideal companion to an introductory text.

Intercultural Discourse and Communication

The Essential Readings

Edited by
Scott F. Kiesling
and
Christina Bratt Paulston

Blackwell
Publishing

BLACKWELL PUBLISHING
350 Main Street, Malden, MA 02148-5020, USA
108 Cowley Road, Oxford OX4 1JF, UK
550 Swanston Street, Carlton, Victoria 3053, Australia

First published 2005 by Blackwell Publishing Ltd

Library of Congress Cataloging-in-Publication Data

Intercultural discourse and communication: the essential readings / edited by
Scott F. Kiesling and Christina Bratt Paulston.
p. cm. – (Linguistics)
Includes bibliographical references and index.
ISBN 0-631-23543-4 (hardcover: alk. paper) – ISBN 0-631-23544-2 (pbk.: alk. paper)
1. Intercultural communication.   2. Identity (Psychology)   I. Kiesling, Scott F.
II. Paulston, Christina Bratt.   III. Series: Linguistics (Malden Mass.)

P94.6.I5825 2005
302.2–dc22
2003025112

A catalogue record for this title is available from the British Library.

Set in 10½/12½pt Ehrhardt
by Graphicraft Limited, Hong Kong

For further information on
Blackwell Publishing, visit our website:
www.blackwellpublishing.com

Contents

Part II: Intercultural Communication: Case Studies

Part III: Cultural Contact: Issues of Identity

Part IV: Implications

Notes on Authors

H. Samy Alim is co-author (with James G. Spady and Charles G. Lee) of *Street Conscious Rap* (1999) and editor of *The Black Arts Quarterly*. He is currently teaching in Duke University's Linguistics Program within the English Department. His research has focused on ethnographic and sociolinguistic approaches to the study of styleshifting in the Black American speech community, anthropological and literary studies of language and language use within the Hip Hop Nation (Hip Hop Nation Language – HHNL), and developing ways to diversify approaches to language and literacy development for linguistically and culturally diverse populations. His most current research takes him to Cairo, Egypt to study youth language and culture in the Arabic-speaking world.

Benjamin Bailey received his PhD in Linguistic Anthropology from UCLA and is currently Assistant Professor in the Department of Communication at the University of Massachusetts-Amherst. His research interests center on ethnic and racial identities in face-to-face interaction in urban, immigrant contexts. He is the author of *Language, Race, and Negotiation of Identity: A Study of Dominican Americans* (2002).

Åke Daun is Professor Emeritus of European Ethnology at Stockholm University. He served as director of the Man–Environment Program at the Royal Institute of Technology in Stockholm from 1975 to 1984 and as director of the Institute of Folk Life Research at the Nordic Museum and Stockholm University from 1981 to 2001. His numerous publications include *Swedish Mentality* (1996) and *Europeans: Essays on Culture and Identity* (1999, edited with Sören Jansson).

Alessandro Duranti is Professor of Anthropology at UCLA and author of a number of books, including *Rethinking Context: Language as an Interactive Phenomenon* (1992, edited with Charles Goodwin), *Linguistic Anthropology* (1997), and *Linguistic Anthropology: A Reader* (Blackwell, 2001, edited).

Diana Eades is Associate Professor in the Department of Second Language Studies at the University of Hawai'i. She has been conducting sociolinguistic research on the participation of Aboriginal English-speakers in the Australian legal system since the mid-1980s. In addition to publishing journal articles and book chapters on this work, she has written a handbook for lawyers, given lectures and workshops to judges and lawyers, and appeared as an expert witness in a number of cases.

John Gumperz is Professor Emeritus of Anthropology at the University of California, Berkeley. He has done linguistic anthropological fieldwork in India, Britain, Norway, Germany, and the urban United States on linguistic representations of social boundaries, communicative practice in polyglossic situations, and theories of discourse interpretation. He is currently working on a follow-up to Gumperz and Hymes's *Directions in Sociolinguistics* (Blackwell, 1971), which will apply ethnography of communication perspectives to today's communicative issues.

Penelope Harvey received her PhD in Social Anthropology from the London School of Economics and is currently head of the Department of Social Anthropology at the University of Manchester. Her research interests include language, politics, gender, representation, nation state, technology, and skilled practice. Her fieldwork has been undertaken in the Peruvian Andes and at the Expo '92 in Seville.

Janet Holmes is Professor of Linguistics at Victoria University of Wellington, where she teaches a variety of sociolinguistics courses. She is director of the Wellington Corpus of Spoken New Zealand English and of the Wellington Language in the Workplace Project. She has published on a wide range of topics including New Zealand English, language and gender, sexist language, pragmatics particles, compliments and apologies, and most recently on workplace discourse. Her publications include *An Introduction to Sociolinguistics* (1992), *Women, Men and Politeness* (1995), and *The Handbook of Language and Gender* (Blackwell, 2003, edited with Miriam Meyerhoff).

Dell Hymes has taught at Harvard, Berkeley, Pennsylvania, and the University of Virginia, where he is now retired as Commonwealth Professor of Anthropology and of English. He has been president of the Linguistic Society of America, the American Anthropological Association and the American Association of Applied Linguistics. He founded the journal *Language in Society* and was its editor for 22 years.

Gabriele Kasper is Professor of Second Language Studies at the University of Hawai'i and currently co-editor of the journal *Applied Linguistics*. Her most recent books are *Misunderstanding in Social Life: Discourse Approaches to Problematic Talk* (2003, with Juliane House and Steven Ross), *Pragmatic Development in a Second Language* (2002, with Kenneth R. Rose), and *Pragmatics in Language Teaching* (2001, with Kenneth R. Rose). Other books include *Communication Strategies* (1997, with Eric Kellerman), *Interlanguage Pragmatics* (1993, with Shoshana Blum-Kulka), and *Cross-cultural Pragmatics* (1989, with Shoshana Blum-Kulka and Juliane House).

Scott F. Kiesling is Assistant Professor of Linguistics at the University of Pittsburgh. His dissertation work (1996) focused on language, power, and masculinity. He is currently working on language variation and change in Australian English, with a focus on ethnicity and gender.

Jayant Lele, PhD (Cornell) was, until his recent retirement, Professor of Political Science and Sociology at Queen's University, Kingston, Canada.

Gita Martohardjono, PhD (Cornell) is Associate Professor of Linguistics at Queen's College, New York. Her main area of research is second language acquisition, a domain in which she has published several papers.

Elinor Ochs is Professor of Anthropology and Applied Linguistics and Director of the Sloan Center on Everyday Lives of Families at UCLA, a Mac Arthur Fellow, and member of the American Academy of Arts and Sciences. Her work examines the role of language, especially narrative practices, in the socialization of children and other novices into social and cultural competence. Selected publications include *Culture and Language Development* (1988), *Constructing Panic* (1995, with Lisa Capps), and *Living Narrative* (2001, with Lisa Capps).

Karen Ogulnick is Associate Professor of Education at Long Island University, C. W. Post Campus. Her publications include *Onna Rashiku (Like a Woman): The Diary of a Language Learner in Japan* (1998) and *Language Crossings: Negotiating the Self in a Multicultural World* (2000).

Christina Bratt Paulston is Professor Emerita of Linguistics at the University of Pittsburgh. She served as chair of the department from 1974 to 1989 and as director of the English Language Institute from 1969 to 1998. Her numerous publications include *Memories and Reflections: The Early Days of Sociolinguistics* (1997, edited with G. Richard Tucker), *Sociolinguistic Perspectives on Bilingual Education* (1992), *Linguistic Minorities in Multilingual Settings* (1994), and *Sociolinguistics: The Essential Readings* (Blackwell, 2003, edited with G. Richard Tucker).

Susan U. Philips is Professor of Anthropology at the University of Arizona. She received her PhD in Anthropology from the University of Pennsylvania. Her current research focuses on diversity in gender ideology in Tongan discourse. Her most recent book, *Ideology in the Language of Judges* (1998), addresses the discourse organization of ideological diversity in American judges' courtroom language use.

Maria Sifianou is Professor of Linguistics at the Faculty of English Studies, University of Athens. She studied in Greece (BA English) and England (MA, PhD Linguistics). Her publications include the books *Politeness Phenomena in England and Greece* (1992), *Discourse Analysis* (2001) and a number of articles in books and journals. She has co-edited *Themes in Greek Linguistics* (1994), *Anatomies of Silence* (1999) and *Linguistic Politeness across Boundaries: The Case of Greek and Turkish* (2001).

Rajendra Singh, PhD (Brown) is Professor of Linguistics at the Université de Montréal. His primary research areas are phonology, morphology, language contact and sociolinguistics. His most recent books are *Towards a Critical Sociolinguistics* (1996), *Trubetzkoy's Orphan* (1996), and *Linguistic Theory, Language Contact, and Modern Hindustani* (1995).

Deborah Tannen is a University Professor and Professor of Linguistics at Georgetown University. She has had nearly one hundred articles published on such topics as cross-cultural communication, modern Greek discourse, the poetics of everyday conversation, workplace interaction, and family interaction. Her many books include *Conversational Style: Analyzing Talk Among Friends* (1984), *That's Not What I Meant!: How Conversational Style Makes or Breaks Relationships* (1986), *You Just Don't Understand: Women and Men in Conversation* (1990), *Talking from 9 to 5: Women and Men at Work* (1994), *The Argument Culture* (1998), and *I Only Say This Because I Love You* (2001).

Suwako Watanabe is Associate Professor of Japanese in the Department of Foreign Languages and Literatures at Portland State University. She received her PhD in Linguistics from Georgetown University. Her research interests are discourse analysis and language assessment, and her major articles include "Analyzing Discourse in Group Discussion" (2001, in *Pragmatics in 2000: Selected papers from the 7th International Pragmatics Conference*) and "Concurrent Validity and Application of the ACTFL Oral Proficiency Interview in A Japanese Program" (1998, in *Journal of the Association of Teachers of Japanese*).

Preface

This reader is offered as a resource for students and instructors for courses in "cross-cultural communication," or "intercultural discourse and communication," as the field is also called. It contains introductory readings for courses that involve the study of how language use varies from culture to culture, and how knowledge of these differences can be put to work to help understand differences and dominance relations between cultures.

The book is organized so that foundational and new theoretical readings are provided in the first part, case studies applying these perspectives in the second, views of cultural contact and identity in the third, and applications to "real world" problems in the fourth. The theoretical approaches are meant to give the student an idea of the ways in which language and discourse is universal across cultures, and how differences among cultures might be usefully compared. The case studies are exemplary of these approaches. They are not necessarily simple applications of the theoretical approaches, but rather in some way enhance or problematize them. Finally, the readings in parts three and four somehow apply a knowledge of intercultural communication to solving problems of society, including problems arising from intercultural contact, and power imbalances between dominant and subordinate cultures in a single society. The chapters can thus be read in order, or a reading in a theoretical approach could be paired with the case study and/or applied reading which it matches.

The reader is, of course, only a sampling of many crucial articles in intercultural discourse, and the title of "essential readings" should be looked upon with some skepticism; the "complete" list of essential readings would fill an entire, ever-expanding bookcase. The readings are designed to be used with an introductory text, such as Bonvillain (2003), Duranti (1997), Foley (1997), or Scollon and Scollon (2001). Asante and Gudykunst (1989) could also provide support for these readings. The readings could also be used on their own, with an instructor providing background discussion and leading discussions about the significance of each reading. Students may also want to search for further readings in journals like *Journal of Linguistic Anthropology*, *Journal of Pragmatics*, *Language in Society*, *Language and Intercultural Communication*, *Multilingua*, and *Pragmatics*.

In the case studies and applied parts, we have tried to include a wide range of cultures, large and small, from around the globe. There were always multiple candidates for each "slot," and once or twice decisions were made to include a reading because it increased the cultural diversity of the readings. This is not to say that all of the world's cultures are present, or even a majority. Because of the places in which the field has grown, there is still no doubt an Anglo-American bias.

There are also some topics related to the study of intercultural discourse that readers will note are not present. We do not have a reading discussing the contentious problem of the nature of culture itself. We have also made no attempt to include readings on linguistic relativity, either in its "classic" sense, or in the newer work being done by Levinson, Lucy, Silverstein, and others. There are excellent discussions of culture in both Duranti's and Foley's texts; the question of universality vs. relativity is the main focus of Foley's text. Bonvillain also has an extensive discussion of linguistic relativity. There is also no reading on language ideology *per se*, although in general language ideology is central to many of the theoretical and practical readings here, and is central to the articles with an applied focus.

We would like to thank a number of people, first and foremost contributors who either wrote new contributions specifically for the reader, or who revised articles significantly: H. Samy Alim, Benjamin Bailey, Diane Eades, and Rajendra Singh. We would also like to thank Roger Freedline in the University of Pittsburgh Department of Linguistics for his tireless support, as well as the great editorial team at Blackwell Publishing, especially Tami Kaplan, Sarah Coleman, and Glynis Baguley.

References

Asante, Molefi Kete and William Gudykunst. 1989. *Handbook of International and Intercultural Communication*. Newbury Park, CA: Sage Publications.

Bonvillain, Nancy. 2003. *Language, Culture, and Communication: The Meaning of Messages*. 4th edn. Upper Saddle River, NJ: Prentice Hall.

Duranti, Alessandro. 1997. *Linguistic Anthropology*. New York: Cambridge University Press.

Foley, William A. 1997. *Anthropological Linguistics*. Malden, MA: Blackwell Publishing.

Scollon, Ronald and Suzanne Wong Scollon. 2001. *Intercultural Communication: A Discourse Approach*. Malden, MA: Blackwell Publishing.

Acknowledgments

The editors and publisher gratefully acknowledge the permission granted to reproduce the copyright material in this book:

1. Dell Hymes, extract from "Models of the interaction of language and social life" in *Directions in Sociolinguistics*, edited by John J. Gumperz and Dell Hymes (Oxford: Basil Blackwell, 1986), pp. 52–65 plus associated references. Reprinted by permission of Blackwell Publishing Ltd.

2. Alessandro Duranti, "Ethnography of speaking: Toward a linguistics of the praxis" from *Linguistics: The Cambridge Survey. Volume IV – Language: The Sociocultural Context*, edited by Frederick J. Newmeyer (Cambridge: Cambridge University Press, 1989), pp. 210–28. © by Cambridge University Press, reproduced with permission of the author and publisher.

3. John J. Gumperz, "Interethnic communication," chapter 8 of Gumperz's *Discourse Strategies* (Cambridge: Cambridge University Press, 1982), pp. 172–86 plus associated references. © by Cambridge University Press, reproduced with permission of the author and publisher.

4. Rajendra Singh, Jayant Lele, and Gita Martohardjono, extract from "Communication in a multilingual society: Some missed opportunities" in *Language in Society* 17:1 (March 1988), pp. 43–59. © by Cambridge University Press, reproduced with permission of the authors and publisher.

5. Gabriele Kasper, "Linguistic etiquette" from *The Handbook of Sociolinguistics*, edited by Florian Coulmas (Oxford: Blackwell, 1997), pp. 374–85 plus associated references. Reprinted by permission of Blackwell Publishing Ltd.

6. Elinor Ochs, "Constructing social identity: A language socialization perspective" from *Research on Language and Social Interaction* 26:3 (1993), pp. 287–306. Reprinted by permission of Lawrence Erlbaum Associates, Inc.

7. Scott Fabius Kiesling, "Norms of sociocultural meaning in language: Indexicality, stance, and cultural models." This is an adapted version of his essay "Prestige, cultural models, and other ways of talking about underlying norms and gender" which appeared in *The Handbook of Language and Gender*, edited by Janet Holmes and

Miriam Meyerhoff (Oxford: Blackwell, 2003), pp. 509–27. Reprinted by permission of Blackwell Publishing Ltd.

8. Janet Holmes, abridged version of "Why tell stories? Contrasting themes and identities in the narratives of Maori and Pakeha women and men" from *Journal of Asian Pacific Communication* 8:1 (1998), pp. 1–7, 9–20, 22–9. Reprinted with kind permission by John Benjamins Publishing Company, Amsterdam/Philadelphia, www.benjamins.com.

9. Deborah Tannen, "New York Jewish conversational style" in *International Journal of the Sociology of Language* 30 (1981), pp. 133–49. Reprinted by permission of the author and Mouton de Gruyter, a division of Walter de Gruyter GmbH & Co publishers.

10. Åke Daun, "Swedishness as an obstacle in cross-cultural interaction" from *Ethnologia Europaea* 14:2 (1984), pp. 95–109. Copenhagen. Reprinted by permission of the author and editor and Museum of Tusculanum Press.

11. Penelope Harvey, "The presence and absence of speech in the communication of gender," chapter 3 in *Bilingual Women: Anthropological Approaches to Second-Language Use*, edited by Pauline Burton, Ketaki Kushari Dyson, and Shirley Ardener (Oxford: Berg, 1994), pp. 44–64. Reprinted with permission of Berg Publishers. All rights reserved.

12. H. Samy Alim, "Hearing what's not said and missing what is: Black language in White public space." © 2004 by Blackwell Publishing Ltd. This essay was specially commissioned for this volume.

13. Christina Bratt Paulston, abridged version of "Pronouns of address in Swedish: Social class semantics and a changing system" in *Language in Society* 5 (1976), pp. 359–60, 362–75, 377–86. © by Cambridge University Press, reproduced with permission.

14. Maria Sifianou, "Off-record indirectness and the notion of imposition" from *Multilingua* 12:1 (1993), pp. 69–79. Reprinted by permission of the author and Mouton de Gruyter, a division of Walter de Gruyter GmbH & Co publishers.

15. Suwako Watanabe, abridged version of "Cultural differences in framing: American and Japanese group discussions," chapter 6 in *Framing in Discourse*, edited by Deborah Tannen (Oxford: Oxford University Press, 1993), pp. 176–86, 191–9, 203–9. © 1993 by Deborah Tannen. Used by permission of Oxford University Press, Inc.

16. Karen Ogulnick, "Learning language/learning self," chapter 25 in *Language Crossings: Negotiating the Self in a Multicultural World*, edited by Karen Ogulnick (New York: Teachers College Press, 2000), pp. 166–70. Reprinted by permission of the publisher. All rights reserved.

17. Benjamin Bailey, "The language of multiple identities among Dominican Americans." This is a shortened version of an article which appeared under the same title in *Journal of Linguistic Anthropology* 10:2 (December 2000), pp. 190–223. Reproduced by permission of the American Anthropological Association. Not for sale or further reproduction.

18. Christina Bratt Paulston, abridged version of "Biculturalism: Some reflections and speculations" which originally appeared as chapter 5 in Paulston's *Sociolinguistic Perspectives on Bilingual Education* (Clevedon, UK: Multilingual Matters, 1992), pp. 116–30.

19. Susan Urmston Philips, "A comparison of Indian and Anglo communicative behavior in classroom interaction" from Philips's *The Invisible Culture: Communication in Classroom and Community on the Warm Springs Indian Reservation* (Long Grove, Ill.: Waveland Press, 1983), pp. 95, 108–25 (from 1993 reissue). Reprinted by permission of Waveland Press, Inc. All rights reserved.

20. Diana Eades, "Beyond difference and domination: Intercultural communication in legal contexts." © 2004 by Blackwell Publishing Ltd. This essay was specially commissioned for this volume.

Every effort has been made to trace copyright holders and to obtain their permission for the use of copyright material. The publisher apologizes for any errors or omissions in the above list and would be grateful to be notified of any corrections that should be incorporated in future reprints or editions of this book.

Part I

Approaches to Intercultural Discourse

Introduction

While studies which compare cultures have been undertaken informally for as long as there have been travelers, it is not until the 1960s that systematic ways of undertaking comparisons of language use, with a view to understanding how language and culture works more generally, appear. We have identified four main ways of viewing these differences and similarities, beginning with Hymes's groundbreaking Ethnography of Speaking, then Interactional Sociolinguistics, Linguistic Etiquette (also known as Politeness), and finally theories of indexicality and syntheses of these approaches.

We begin with a reading by Dell Hymes, who began to develop this field as a response to the Chomskyan notion that what linguists should focus on is the linguistic competence of a speaker of a language. Hymes noted that Chomsky thought of this competence in a fairly restricted way (all and only the grammatical sentences of a language), and that were a man to stand on a street corner and utter all and only the grammatical sentences of English he would likely be institutionalized. Rather, speakers need a whole range of competencies that go with language, specifying not just the sentences of a language, but information about the appropriateness of the form of those sentences, the speakers, and other aspects of context which speakers understand as part of being competent in language. Hymes thus sought to develop a descriptive, etic model that could describe speech events across cultures, and compare them. Hymes's chapter describes the motivations and outlines of this model. The goal is to understand what knowledge a speaker must have in a speech community in order to be a competent speaker of the language of that community. Alessandro Duranti's chapter further outlines the ethnography of speaking and compares this approach to some others, especially Conversation Analysis, as a path to understanding the ways culture and language are intertwined. Although ethnography of speaking was not developed to analyze intercultural encounters, it could be used to do so. Its outlining of specific parts of a speech event are extremely useful for beginning to analyze what might go wrong when two cultures meet, by comparing components of similar speech events across two cultures.

The next two readings focus explicitly on intercultural encounters. John Gumperz's work is often the first mentioned when intercultural communication is taught; his *Discourse Strategies* was pioneering in its analysis of the sources of misunderstanding in intercultural encounters, by focusing on forms of language that are not often explicitly studied, such as intonation. Teachers and students may want to use this chapter in conjunction with a short film made by Gumperz called *Crosstalk*. Gumperz's essential insight is that there are language forms like intonation that tell us how talk is meant to be received by the listener – a cue for the context in which it should be taken. This context can refer to aspects of interpersonal context such as "I am being friendly," as well as aspects of speech event context such as "This is a joke." Gumperz tells us that we are not just following pre-existing rules for situations (as we might expect from the ethnography of speaking), but that we use language to actively signal what our understanding of our stance is – our relationship to our talk and to our interlocutors. Gumperz used this paradigm to show how cultural misunderstandings occur, and suggests that if more people understand these differences in contextualization cues, then discrimination will be lessened.

Rajendra Singh, Jayant Lele, and Gita Martohardjono, however, point out that finding and learning the differences on these levels is only the beginning. They suggest that there are other pre-existing relationships that must be considered when trying to understand intercultural encounters and how discrimination works within them. Most importantly, they point out that people from different cultures rarely meet as equals, and much of this inequality is not personal, but due to power differences in the cultures they come from. So in England, South Asian migrants have less power than native Anglos, and they are expected to accommodate to the dominant culture. This kind of power asymmetry is almost universal in immigrant situations, but also in colonial and post-colonial situations. While Singh et al. are quite critical of Gumperz, they add to rather than subtract from his perspective, by showing that there are other important considerations in intercultural encounters *in addition to* the concerns outlined by Gumperz.

The reading by Gabriele Kasper on linguistic etiquette clearly summarizes and criticizes the work that usually comes under the rubric of "politeness theory," which has been dominated since 1978 by the theoretical perspective of Brown and Levinson. Their theory focuses on universality rather than relativity, and outlines a way of accounting for cross-cultural differences through a small number of universal constructs. As Kasper explains, it is the universality of these constructs that has been criticized. But the idea that something like politeness – linguistic etiquette – is present in all cultures is unquestioned. Kasper presents several ways this etiquette may be thought of, including Brown and Levinson's, and outlines a number of important issues facing politeness theory. Students often find the abstractness of this theory quite difficult, and it is recommended to include a textbook reading in this area (see Bonvillain 2003, Foley 1997, and Holmes 1992, for discussions of politeness theory).

The set of articles in the theoretical approaches is rounded out by two articles that discuss the ways that language encodes and communicates sociocultural information, and the kinds of social information it encodes. Both Ochs and Kiesling view social meaning in language as *indexicality*, which is the meaning process in which linguistic form is related to context. A linguistic form becomes associated with an aspect of the social world, so that the same linguistic form indexes, or "brings to mind" that social aspect whenever used. This view is related to that of Gumperz, but investigates in more depth the relationship between linguistic form and social meaning, noting that people do other things with indexicality in addition to indicating "what is going on": they can call up social identities such as male or female, and even specific cultural models, as suggested by Kiesling. Of course, these indexes must be shared, and significant inter-cultural misunderstanding can occur if they are not shared.

The four parts thus present four different but compatible perspectives on how language and culture are related. We can consider politeness and contextualization cues to be kinds of indexicality, and these ideas can be used in describing speech events in the ethnography of speaking. Students will profit by comparing the approaches and their use in different situations; such a comparison will help illuminate the ways in which discourse differs across cultures.

References

Bonvillain, Nancy. 2003. *Language, Culture, and Communication: The Meaning of Messages*. 4th edn. Upper Saddle River, NJ: Prentice Hall.

Foley, William A. 1997. *Anthropological Linguistics*. Malden, MA: Blackwell Publishing.

Holmes, Janet. 1992. *An Introduction to Sociolinguistics*. New York: Longman.

1

Models of the Interaction of Language and Social Life: Toward a Descriptive Theory

Dell Hymes

[. . .]

1.1   Introduction

The primary concern now must be with descriptive analyses from a variety of communities. Only in relation to actual analysis will it be possible to conduct arguments analogous to those now possible in the study of grammar as to the adequacy, necessity, generality, etc., of concepts and terms. Yet some initial heuristic schema are needed if the descriptive task is to proceed. What is presented here is quite preliminary – if English and its grammarians permitted, one might call it "toward toward a theory." Some of it may survive the empirical and analytical work of the decade ahead.

Only a specific, explicit mode of description can guarantee the maintenance and success of the current interest in sociolinguistics. Such interest is prompted more by practical and theoretical needs, perhaps, than by accomplishment. It was the development of a specific mode of description that ensured the success of linguistics as an autonomous discipline in the United States in the twentieth century, and the lack of it (for motif and tale types are a form of indexing, distributional inference a procedure common to the human sciences) that led to the until recently peripheral status of folklore, although both had started from a similar base, the converging interest of anthropologists, and English scholars, in language and in verbal tradition.

The goal of sociolinguistic description can be put in terms of the disciplines whose interests converge in sociolinguistics. Whatever his questions about language, it is clear to a linguist that there is an enterprise, description of languages, which is central and known. Whatever his questions about society and culture, it is clear to a sociologist or an anthropologist that there is a form of inquiry (survey or ethnography) on which the

Dell Hymes, extract from "Models of the interaction of language and social life" in *Directions in Sociolinguistics*, edited by John J. Gumperz and Dell Hymes (Oxford: Basil Blackwell, 1986), pp. 52–65 plus associated references. Reprinted by permission of Blackwell Publishing Ltd.

answers depend. In both cases, one understands what it means to describe a language, the social relations, or culture of a community. We need to be able to say the same thing about the sociolinguistic system of a community.

Such a goal is of concern to practical work as well as to scientific theory. In a study of bilingual education, e.g., certain components of speaking will be taken into account, and the choice will presuppose a model, implicit if not explicit, of the interaction of language with social life. The significance attached to what is found will depend on understanding what is possible, what universal, what rare, what linked, in comparative perspective. What survey researchers need to know linguistically about a community, in selecting a language variety, and in conducting interviews, is in effect an application of the community's sociolinguistic description (see Hymes 1969). In turn, practical work, if undertaken with its relevance to theory in mind, can make a contribution, for it must deal directly with the interaction of language and social life, and so provides a testing ground and source of new insight.

Sociolinguistic systems may be treated at the level of national states, and indeed, of an emerging world society. My concern here is with the level of individual communities and groups. The interaction of language with social life is viewed as first of all a matter of human action, based on a knowledge, sometimes conscious, often unconscious, that enables persons to use language. Speech events and larger systems indeed have properties not reducible to those of the speaking competence of persons. Such competence, however, underlies communicative conduct, not only within communities but also in encounters between them. The speaking competence of persons may be seen as entering into a series of systems of encounter at levels of different scope.

An adequate descriptive theory would provide for the analysis of individual communities by specifying technical concepts required for such analysis, and by characterizing the forms that analysis should take. Those forms would, as much as possible, be formal, i.e., explicit, general (in the sense of observing general constraints and conventions as to content, order, interrelationship, etc.), economical, and congruent with linguistic modes of statement. Only a good deal of empirical work and experimentation will show what forms of description are required, and of those, which preferable. As with grammar, approximation to a theory for the explicit, standard analysis of individual systems will also be an approximation to part of a theory of explanation.

Among the notions with which such a theory must deal are those of speech community, speech situation, speech event, speech act, fluent speaker, components of speech events, functions of speech, etc.

1.2   Social Units

One must first consider the social unit of analysis. For this I adopt the common expression *speech community*.

1.2.1   Speech community

Speech is here taken as a surrogate for all forms of language, including writing, song and speech-derived whistling, drumming, horn calling, and the like. Speech community is a necessary, primary term in that it postulates the basis of description as a social, rather than a linguistic, entity. One starts with a social group and considers all the linguistic varieties present in it, rather than starting with any one variety.

Bloomfield (1933) and some others have in the past reduced the notion of speech community to the notion of language (or linguistic variety). Those speaking the same language (or same first language, or standard language) were defined as members of the same speech community. This confusion still persists, associated with a quantitative measure of frequency of interaction as a way of describing (in principle) internal variation and change, as speculatively postulated by Bloomfield. The present approach requires a definition that is qualitative and expressed in terms of *norms for the use* of language. It is clear from the work of Gumperz, Labov, Barth, and others that not frequency of interaction but rather definition of situations in which interaction occurs is decisive, particularly identification (or lack of it) with others. [Sociolinguistics here makes contact with the shift in rhetorical theory from expression and persuasion to identification as key concept (see Burke 1950:19–37, 55–9).]

Tentatively, a *speech community* is defined as a community sharing rules for the conduct and interpretation of speech, and rules for the interpretation of at least one linguistic variety. Both conditions are necessary.

The sharing of grammatical (variety) rules is not sufficient. There may be persons whose English I can grammatically identify but whose messages escape me. I may be ignorant of what counts as a coherent sequence, request, statement requiring an answer, requisite or forbidden topic, marking of emphasis or irony, normal duration of silence, normal level of voice, etc., and have no metacommunitative means or opportunity for discovering such things. The difference between knowledge of a variety and knowledge of speaking does not usually become apparent within a single community, where the two are normally acquired together. Communities indeed often mingle what a linguist would distinguish as grammatically and as socially or culturally acceptable. Among the Cochiti of New Mexico J. R. Fox was unable to elicit the first person singular possessive form of "wings," on the grounds that the speaker, not being a bird, could not say "my wings" – only to become the only person in Cochiti able to say it on the grounds that "your name is Robin."

The nonidentity of the two kinds of rules (or norms) is more likely to be noticed when a shared variety is a second language for one or both parties. Sentences that translate each other grammatically may be mistakenly taken as having the same functions in speech, just as words that translate each other may be taken as having the same semantic function. There may be substratum influence or interference (Weinreich 1953) in the one as in the other. The Czech linguist J. Neustupny has coined the term *Sprechbund* "speech area" (parallel to *Sprachbund* "language area") for the phenomenon of speaking rules being shared among contiguous languages. Thus, Czechoslovakia, Hungary, Austria, and southern Germany may be found to share norms as to greetings, acceptable topics, what is said next in a conversation, etc.

Sharing of speaking rules is not sufficient. A Czech who knows no German may belong to the same *Sprechbund*, but not the same speech community, as an Austrian.

The *language field* and *speech field* (akin to the notion of social field) can be defined as the total range of communities within which a person's knowledge of varieties and speaking rules potentially enables him to move communicatively. Within the speech field must be distinguished the *speech network*, the specific linkages of persons through shared varieties and speaking rules across communities. Thus in northern Queensland, Australia, different speakers of the same language (e.g., Yir Yoront) may have quite different networks along geographically different circuits, based on clan membership, and involving different repertoires of mutilingualism. In Vitiaz Strait, New Guinea, the Bilibili islanders (a group of about 200–250 traders and potmakers in Astrolabe Bay) have collectively a knowledge of the languages of all the communities with which they have had economic relations, a few men knowing the language of each particular community in which they have had trading partners.

In sum, one's speech community may be, effectively, a single locality or portion of it; one's language field will be delimited by one's repertoire of varieties; one's speech field by one's repertoire of patterns of speaking. One's speech network is the effective union of these last two.

Part of the work of definition obviously is done here by the notion of community, whose difficulties are bypassed, as are the difficulties of defining boundaries between varieties and between patterns of speaking. Native conceptions of boundaries are but one factor in defining them, essential but sometimes partly misleading (a point stressed by Gumperz on the basis of his work in central India). Self-conceptions, values, role structures, contiguity, purposes of interaction, political history, all may be factors. Clearly, the same degree of linguistic difference may be associated with a boundary in one case and not in another, depending on social factors. The essential thing is that the object of description be an integral social unit. Probably, it will prove most useful to reserve the notion of speech community for the local unit most specifically characterized for a person by common locality and primary interaction (Gumperz 1962:30–2). Here I have drawn distinctions of scale and of kind of linkage within what Gumperz has termed the *linguistic community* (any distinguishable intercommunicating group). Descriptions will make it possible to develop a useful typology and to discover the causes and consequences of the various types.

1.2.2   Speech situation

Within a community one readily detects many situations associated with (or marked by the absence of) speech. Such contexts of situation will often be naturally described as ceremonies, fights, hunts, meals, lovemaking, and the like. It would not be profitable to convert such situations en masse into parts of a sociolinguistic description by the simple expedient of relabeling them in terms of speech. (Notice that the distinctions made with regard to speech community are not identical with the concepts of a general communicative approach, which must note the differential range of communication by speech, film, art object, music.) Such situations may enter as contexts into the statement of rules of speaking as aspects of setting (or of genre). In contrast to speech events, they are not in themselves governed by such rules, or one set of such rules throughout. A hunt, e.g., may comprise both verbal and nonverbal events, and the verbal events may be of more than one type.

In a sociolinguistic description, then, it is necessary to deal with activities which are in some recognizable way bounded or integral. From the standpoint of general social description they may be registered as ceremonies, fishing trips, and the like; from particular standpoints they may be regarded as political, esthetic, etc., situations, which serve as contexts for the manifestation of political, esthetic, etc., activity. From the sociolinguistic standpoint they may be regarded as speech situations.

1.2.3   Speech event

The term *speech event* will be restricted to activities, or aspects of activities, that are directly governed by rules or norms for the use of speech. An event may consist of a single speech act, but will often comprise several. Just as an occurrence of a noun may at the same time be the whole of a noun phrase and the whole of a sentence (e.g., "Fire!"), so a speech act may be the whole of a speech event, and of a speech situation (say, a rite consisting of a single prayer, itself a single invocation). More often, however, one will find a difference in magnitude: a party (speech situation), a conversation during the party (speech event), a joke within the conversation (speech act). It is of speech events and speech acts that one writes formal rules for their occurrence and characteristics. Notice that the same type of speech act may recur in different types of speech event, and the same type of speech event in different contexts of situation. Thus, a joke (speech act) may be embedded in a private conversation, a lecture, a formal introduction. A private conversation may occur in the context of a party, a memorial service, a pause in changing sides in a tennis match.

1.2.4   Speech act

The *speech act* is the minimal term of the set just discussed, as the remarks on speech events have indicated. It represents a level distinct from the sentence, and not identifiable with any single portion of other levels of grammar, nor with segments of any particular size defined in terms of other levels of grammar. That an utterance has the status of a command may depend upon a conventional formula ("I hereby order you to leave this building"), intonation ("Go!" vs. "Go?"), position in a conversational exchange ["Hello" as initiating greeting or as response (perhaps used when answering the telephone)], or the social relationship obtaining between the two parties (as when an utterance that is in the form of a polite question is in effect a command when made by a superior to a subordinate). The level of speech acts mediates immediately between the usual levels of grammar and the rest of a speech event or situation in that it implicates both linguistic form and social norms.

To some extent speech acts may be analyzable by extensions of syntactic and semantic structure. It seems certain, however, that much, if not most, of the knowledge that speakers share as to the status of utterances as acts is immediate and abstract, depending upon an autonomous system of signals from both the various levels of grammar and social settings. To attempt to depict speech acts entirely by postulating an additional segment of underlying grammatical structure (e.g., "I hereby X you to . . .") is cumbersome and counterintuitive. (Consider the case in which "Do you think I might have that last bit of tea?" is to be taken as a command.)

An autonomous level of speech acts is in fact implicated by that logic of linguistic levels according to which the ambiguity of "the shooting of the blacks was terrible" and the commonality of "topping Erv is almost impossible" and "it's almost impossible to top Erv" together requires a further level of structure at which the former has two different structures, the latter one. The relation between sentence forms and their status as speech acts is of the same kind. A sentence interrogative in form may be now a request, now a command, now a statement; a request may be manifested by a sentence that is now interrogative, now declarative, now imperative in form.

Discourse may be viewed in terms of acts both syntagmatically and paradigmatically; i.e., both as a sequence of speech acts and in terms of classes of speech acts among which choice has been made at given points.

1.2.5   Speech styles

Style has often been approached as a matter of statistical frequency of elements already given in linguistic description, or as deviation from some norm given by such description. Statistics and deviations matter, but do not suffice. Styles also depend upon qualitative judgments of appropriateness, and must often be described in terms of selections that apply globally to a discourse, as in the case of honorific usage in Japanese (McCawley 1968:136), i.e., there are consistent patternings of speaking that cut across the components of grammar (phonology, syntax, semantics), or that operate within one independently of the selectional restrictions normally described for it. Whorf adumbrated as much in his conception of "fashions of speaking"; Joos has made and illustrated the point with regard to English; Pike (1967) has considered a wide variety of contextual styles as conditions on the manifestation of phonological and morphological units. Besides the existence of qualitatively defined styles, there are two other points essential to sociolinguistic description. One is that speech styles involve elements and relations that conventionally serve "expressive" or, better, stylistic, as well as referential function (e.g., the contrast in force of aspiration that conventionally signals emphasis in English). The second point is that speech styles are to be considered not only in terms of cooccurrence within each but also in terms of contrastive choice among them. Like speech acts, they have both syntagmatic and paradigmatic dimensions. [...] The coherence, or cohesion, of discourse depends upon the syntagmatic relation of speech acts, and speech styles, as well as of semantic and syntactic features.

1.2.6   Ways of speaking

Ways of speaking is used as the most general, indeed, as a primitive, term. The point of it is the regulative idea that the communicative behavior within a community is analyzable in terms of determinate ways of speaking, that the communicative competence of persons comprises in part a knowledge of determinate ways of speaking. Little more can be said until a certain number of ethnographic descriptions of communities in terms of ways of speaking are available. It is likely that communities differ widely in the features in terms of which their ways of speaking are primarily organized.

1.2.7   Components of speech

A descriptive theory requires some schema of the components of speech acts. At present such a schema can be only an etic, heuristic input to descriptions. Later it may assume the status of a theory of universal features and dimensions.

Long traditional in our culture is the threefold division between speaker, hearer, and something spoken about. It has been elaborated in information theory, linguistics, semiotics, literary criticism, and sociology in various ways. In the hands of some investigators various of these models have proven productive, but their productivity has depended upon not taking them literally, let alone using them precisely. All such schemes, e.g., appear to agree either in taking the standpoint of an individual speaker or in postulating a dyad, speaker–hearer (or source–destination, sender–receiver, addressor–addressee). Even if such a scheme is intended to be a model, for descriptive work it cannot be. Some rules of speaking require specification of *three* participants [addressor, addressee, hearer (audience), source, spokesman, addressees; etc.]; some of but *one*, indifferent as to role in the speech event; some of *two*, but of speaker and audience (e.g., a child); and so on. In short, serious ethnographic work shows that there is one general, or universal, dimension to be postulated, that of *participant*. The common dyadic model of speaker–hearer specifies sometimes too many, sometimes too few, sometimes the wrong participants. Further ethnographic work will enable us to state the range of actual types of participant relations and to see in differential occurrence something to be explained.

Ethnographic material so far investigated indicates that some sixteen or seventeen components have sometimes to be distinguished. No rule has been found that requires specification of all simultaneously. There are always redundancies, and sometimes a rule requires explicit mention of a relation between only two, message form and some other. (It is a general principle that all rules involve message form, if not by affecting its shape, then by governing its interpretation.) Since each of the components may sometimes be a factor, however, each has to be recognized in the general grid.

Psycholinguistic work has indicated that human memory works best with classifications of the magnitude of seven, plus or minus two (Miller 1956). To make the set of components mnemonically convenient, at least in English, the letters of the term SPEAKING can be used. The components can be grouped together in relation to the eight letters without great difficulty. Clearly, the use of SPEAKING as a mnemonic code word has nothing to do with the form of an eventual model and theory.

1.   *Message form.* The form of the message is fundamental, as has just been indicated. The most common, and most serious, defect in most reports of speaking probably is that the message form, and, hence, the rules governing it, cannot be recaptured. A concern for the details of actual form strikes some as picayune, as removed from humanistic or scientific importance. Such a view betrays an impatience that is a disservice to both humanistic and scientific purposes. It is precisely the failure to unite form and content in the scope of a single focus of study that has retarded understanding of the human ability to speak, and that vitiates many attempts to analyze the significance of behavior. Content categories, interpretive categories, alone do not suffice. It is a truism, but one frequently ignored in research, that *how* something is said is part of *what* is said. Nor can one prescribe in advance the gross size of the signal that will be crucial to content and skill. The more a way of speaking has become shared and meaningful within a group, the more likely that crucial cues will be efficient, i.e., slight in scale. If one balks at such detail, perhaps because it requires technical skills in linguistics, musicology, or the like that are hard to command, one should face the fact that the human meaning of one's object of study, and the scientific claims of one's field of inquiry, are not being taken seriously.

Especially when competence, the ability of persons, is of concern, one must recognize that shared ways of speaking acquire a partial autonomy, developing in part in terms of an inner logic of their means of expression. The means of expression condition and sometimes control content. For members of the community, then, "freedom is the recognition of necessity"; mastery of the way of speaking is prerequisite to personal expression. Serious concern for both scientific analysis and human meaning requires one to go beyond content to the explicit statement of rules and features of form.

While such an approach may seem to apply first of all to genres conventionally recognized as esthetic, it also applies to conversation in daily life. Only painstaking analysis of message form – how things are said – of a sort that indeed parallels and can learn from the intensity of literary criticism can disclose the depth and adequacy of the elliptical art that is talk.

2. *Message content.* One context for distinguishing message form from message content would be: "He prayed, saying '. . .'" (quoting message form) vs. "He prayed that he would get well" (reporting content only).

Content enters analysis first of all perhaps as a question of *topic* and of change of topic. Members of a group know what is being talked about and when what is talked about has changed, and manage maintenance and change of topic. These abilities are parts of their communicative competence of particular importance to study of the coherence of discourse.

Message form and message content are central to the speech act and the focus of its "syntactic structure"; they are also tightly interdependent. Thus they can be dubbed jointly as components of "act sequence" (mnemonically, A).

3. *Setting.* Setting refers to the time and place of a speech act and, in general, to the physical circumstances.

4. *Scene.* Scene, which is distinct from setting, designates the "psychological setting," or the cultural definition of an occasion as a certain type of scene. Within a play on the same stage with the same stage set the dramatic time may shift: "ten years later." In daily life the same persons in the same setting may redefine their interaction as a changed type of scene, say, from formal to informal, serious to festive, or the like. [. . .] Speech acts frequently are used to define scenes, and also frequently judged as appropriate or inappropriate in relation to scenes. Settings and scenes themselves, of course, may be judged as appropriate and inappropriate, happy or unhappy, in relation to each other, from the level of complaint about the weather to that of dramatic irony.

Setting and scene may be linked as components of act situation (mnemonically, S). Since scene implies always an analysis of cultural definitions, setting probably is to be preferred as the informal, unmarked term for the two.

5. *Speaker,* or *sender.*

6. *Addressor.*

7. *Hearer,* or *receiver,* or *audience.*

8. *Addressee.*

These four components were discussed in introducing the subject of components of speech. Here are a few illustrations. Among the Abipon of Argentina *-in* is added to the end of each word if any participant (whatever his role) is a member of the Hocheri (warrior class). Among the Wishram Chinook, formal scenes are defined by the relationship between a source (e.g., a chief, or sponsor of a ceremony), a spokesman who repeats the source's words, and others who constitute an audience or public. The source whose words are repeated sometimes is not present; the addressees sometimes are spirits of the surrounding environment. In the presence of a child, adults in Germany often use the term of address which would be appropriate for the child. Sometimes rules for participants are internal to a genre and independent of the participants in the embedding event. Thus male and female actors in Yana myths use the appropriate men's and women's forms of speech, respectively, irrespective of the sex of the narrator. Use of men's speech itself is required when both addressor and addressee are both adult and male, "women's" speech otherwise. Groups differ in their definitions of the participants in speech events in revealing ways, particularly in defining absence (e.g., children, maids) and presence (e.g., supernaturals) of participation. Much of religious conduct can be interpreted as part of a native theory of communication. The various components may be grouped together as participants (mnemonically, P).

9. *Purposes – outcomes.* Conventionally recognized and expected outcomes often enter into the definition of speech events, as among the Waiwai of Venezuela, where the central speech event of the society, the *oho-chant*, has several varieties, according to whether the purpose to be accomplished is a marriage contract, a trade, a communal work task, an invitation to a feast, or a composing of social peace after a death. The rules for participants and settings vary accordingly (Fock 1965). A taxonomy of speech events among the Yakan of the Philippines [. . .] is differentiated into levels according jointly to topic (any topic, an issue, a disagreement, a dispute) and outcome (no particular outcome, a decision, a settlement, a legal ruling).

10. *Purposes – goals.* The purpose of an event from a community standpoint, of course, need not be identical to the purposes of those engaged in it. Presumably, both sides to a Yakan litigation wish to win. In a negotiation the purpose of some may be to obtain a favorable settlement, of others simply that there be a settlement. Among the Waiwai the prospective father-in-law and son-in-law have opposing goals in arriving at a marriage contract. The strategies of participants are an essential determinant of the form of speech events, indeed, to their being performed at all [. . .].

With respect both to outcomes and goals, the conventionally expected or ascribed must be distinguished from the purely situational or personal, and from the latent and unintended. The interactions of a particular speech event may determine its particular quality and whether or not the expected outcome is reached. The actual motives, or some portion of them, of participants may be quite varied. In the first instance, descriptions of speech events seek to describe customary or culturally appropriate behavior. Such description is essential and prerequisite to understanding events in all their individual richness; but the two kinds of account should not be confused (see Sapir 1949:534, 543).

Many approaches to communication and the analysis of speech have not provided a place for either kind of purpose, perhaps because of a conscious or unconsciously lingering behaviorism. [Kenneth Burke's (1945) approach is a notable exception.] Yet communication itself must be differentiated from interaction as a whole in terms of purposiveness (see Hymes 1964). The two aspects of purpose can be grouped together by exploiting an English homonymy, *ends* in view (goals) and *ends* as outcomes (mnemonically, E).

11. *Key.* Key is introduced to provide for the tone, manner, or spirit in which an act is done. It corresponds roughly to modality among grammatical categories. Acts

otherwise the same as regards setting, participants, message form, and the like may differ in key, as, e.g., between *mock: serious* or *perfunctory: painstaking.*

Key is often conventionally ascribed to an instance of some other component as its attribute; seriousness, for example, may be the expected concomitant of a scene, participant, act, code, or genre (say, a church, a judge, a vow, use of Latin, obsequies). Yet there is always the possibility that there is a conventionally understood way of substituting an alternative key. (This possibility corresponds to the general possibility of choosing one speech style or register as against another.) In this respect, ritual remains always informative. Knowing what should happen next, one still can attend to the way in which it happens. (Consider, for example, critics reviewing performances of the classical repertoire for the piano.)

The significance of key is underlined by the fact that, when it is in conflict with the overt content of an act, it often overrides the latter (as in sarcasm). The signaling of key may be nonverbal, as with a wink, gesture, posture, style of dress, musical accompaniment, but it also commonly involves conventional units of speech too often disregarded in ordinary linguistic analysis, such as English aspiration and vowel length to signal emphasis. Such features are often termed *expressive*, but are better dubbed *stylistic* since they need not at all depend on the mood of their user. Revill (1966:251) reports, for instance, that "some forms have been found which *cannot* [emphasis mine] be described as reflecting feelings on the part of the speaker, but they will be used in certain social situations" (for emphasis, clarity, politeness).

12.   *Channels.* By choice of channel is understood choice of oral, written, telegraphic, semaphore, or other medium of transmission of speech. With regard to channels, one must further distinguish modes of use. The oral channel, e.g., may be used to sing, hum, whistle, or chant features of speech as well as to speak them. Two important goals of description are accounts of the interdependence of channels in interaction and the relative hierarchy among them.

13.   *Forms of speech.* A major theoretical and empirical problem is to distinguish the verbal resources of a community. Obviously, it is superficial, indeed misleading, to speak of the language of a community (Ferguson and Gumperz 1960). Even where there is but a single "language" present in a community (no cases are known in the contemporary world), that language will be organized into various forms of speech. Three criteria seem to require recognition at the present time: the historical provenience of the language resources; presence or absence of mutual intelligibility; and specialization in use. The criteria often do not coincide. *Language* and *dialect* are suggested for the first; *codes* for the second; and *varieties* and *registers* for the third. One speaks normally of the English language, and of dialects of English, wherever forms of speech are found whose content is historically derived from the line of linguistic tradition we call "English." The different dialects are not always mutually intelligible (see Yorkshire and Indian English), and their social functions vary considerably around the world, from childhood vernacular to bureaucratic lingua franca. "Code" suggests decoding and the question of intelligibility. Unintelligibility may result when speech is in a language historically unrelated to one's own, but also from use of a simple transformation of one's own speech, e.g., Pig Latin, or "op" talk. In short, some forms of speech derive from others by addition, deletion, substitution, and permutation in various combinations. Finally, forms of speech are commonly specialized to uses of various sorts. *Register* has become familiar in English linguistic

usage for reference to specific situations; varieties, or "functional varieties," has been used in American linguistics in relation to broad domains (e.g., vernacular vs. standard).

For sociolinguistics, *varieties* has priority as a standpoint from which to view the forms of speech of a community. The criteria of provenience and intelligibility have to do with sources and characteristics of the criterion of use with the functional organization, of the forms of speech. Channels and forms of speech can be joined together as means or agencies of speaking and labeled, partly for the sake of the code word, partly with an eye on the use of the term *instrumental* in grammar, as *instrumentalities* (mnemonically, I).

14. *Norms of interaction.* All rules governing speaking, of course, have a normative character. What is intended here are the specific behaviors and proprieties that attach to speaking – that one must not interrupt, for example, or that one may freely do so; that normal voice should not be used except when scheduled in a church service (whisper otherwise); that turns in speaking are to be allocated in a certain way. Norms of interaction obviously implicate analysis of social structure, and social relationships generally, in a community. An illustration follows:

> The next morning during tea with Jikjitsu, a college professor who rents rooms in one of the Sodo buildings came in and talked of koans. "When you understand Zen, you know that the tree is really *there*." – The only time anyone said anything of Zen philosophy or experience the whole week. Zenbos never discuss koans or sanzen experience with each other. (Snyder 1969:52)

15. *Norms of interpretation.* An account of norms of interaction may still leave open the interpretation to be placed upon them, especially when members of different communities are in communication. Thus it is clear that Arabic and American students differ on a series of interactional norms: Arabs confront each other more directly (face to face) when conversing, sit closer to each other, are more likely to touch each other, look each other more squarely in the eye, and converse more loudly (Watson and Graves 1966:976–7). The investigators who report these findings themselves leave open the meanings of these norms to the participants (p. 984).

The problem of norms of interpretation is familiar from the assessment of communications from other governments and national leaders. One often looks for friendliness in lessened degree of overt hostility. Relations between groups within a country are often affected by misunderstandings on this score. For white middle-class Americans, for example, normal hesitation behavior involves "fillers" at the point of hesitation ("uh," etc.). For many blacks, a normal pattern is to recycle to the beginning of the utterance (perhaps more than once). This black norm may be interpreted by whites not as a different norm but as a defect. (I owe this example to David Dalby.)

Norms of interpretation implicate the belief system of a community. The classic precedent in the ethnographic analysis of a language is Malinowski's (1935) treatment of Trobriand magical formulas and ritual under the heading of *dogmatic context.* (Malinowski's other rubrics are roughly related to these presented here in the following way: His *sociological context* and *ritual context* subsume information as to setting, participants, ends in view and outcome, norms of interaction, and higher level aspects of genre; *structure* reports salient patterning of the verbal form of the act or event; *mode of recitation* reports salient characteristics of the vocal aspect of channel use and message form.)

The processes of interpretation discussed by Garfinkel [in Chapter 10 of the publication from which this extract is taken], including "ad hocing" generally, would belong in this category. These two kinds of norms may be grouped together (mnemonically, N) (*ibid.*, p. 984).

16.   *Genres.* By genres are meant categories such as poem, myth, tale, proverb, riddle, curse, prayer, oration, lecture, commercial, form letter, editorial, etc. From one standpoint the analysis of speech into acts is an analysis of speech into instances of genres. The notion of genre implies the possibility of identifying formal characteristics traditionally recognized. It is heuristically important to proceed as though all speech has formal characteristics of some sort as manifestation of genres; and it may well be true (on genres, see Ben-Amos 1969). The common notion of "casual" or unmarked speech, however, points up the fact that there is a great range among genres in the number of and explicitness of formal markers. At least there is a great range in the ease with which such markers have been identified. It remains that "unmarked" casual speech can be recognized as such in a context where it is not expected or where it is being exploited for particular effect. Its lesser visibility may be a function of our own orientations and use of it; its profile may be as sharp as any other, once we succeed in seeing it as strange.

Genres often coincide with speech events, but must be treated as analytically independent of them. They may occur in (or as) different events. The sermon as a genre is typically identical with a certain place in a church service, but its properties may be invoked, for serious or humorous effect, in other situations. Often enough a genre recurs in several events, such as a genre of chanting employed by women in Bihar state in India; it is the prescribed form for a related set of acts, recurring in weddings, family visits, and complaints to one's husband (K. M. Tiwary, personal communication). A great deal of empirical work will be needed to clarify the interrelations of genres, events, acts, and other components (mnemonically, G).

[. . .]

References

Ben-Amos, Dan, 1969, Analytical categories and ethnic genres. *Genre* 2:275–301.

Bloomfield, Leonard, 1933, *Language*. New York: Holt, Rinehart and Winston, Inc.

Burke, Kenneth, 1945, *A grammar of motives*. Englewood Cliffs, N.J.: Prentice-Hall. (Republished by University of California Press, Berkeley, 1969.)

——, 1950, *A rhetoric of motives*. Englewood Cliffs, N.J.: Prentice-Hall. (Republished by University of California Press, Berkeley, 1969.)

Ferguson, Charles A., and John J. Gumperz, 1960, Linguistic diversity in south Asia: studies in regional and functional variation. [RCAFL-P 13; *International Journal of American Linguistics* 26 (3), pt. III].

Fock, Niels, 1965, Cultural aspects of the "oho" institution among the Waiwai. *Proceedings of the International Congress of Americanists*, pp. 136–40.

Gumperz, John J., 1962, Types of linguistic communities. *Anthropological Linguistics* 4, 1:28–40.

Hymes, Dell, 1964, Introduction: toward ethnographies of communication. In John J. Gumperz and Dell Hymes (eds.), The ethnography of communication. *American Anthropologist* 66, 6, pt. II:1–34.

Hymes, Dell, 1969, Linguistic aspects of comparative political research. In Robert T. Holt and John Turner (eds.), *Methodology of comparative research*. New York: Free Press.

McCawley, James, 1968, The role of semantics in grammar. In Emmon Bach and Robert Harms (eds.), *Universals in linguistic theory*, pp. 125–70. New York: Holt, Rinehart and Winston, Inc.

Malinowski, Bronislaw, 1935, *Coral gardens and their magic*, vol. II. London: Allen and Unwin.

Miller, G. A., 1956, The magical number seven, plus or minus two: some limits on our capacity for processing information. *The Psychological Review* 63:81–97.

Pike, Kenneth L., 1967, *Language in relation to the unified theory of the structure of human behavior.* (2nd rev. ed.). The Hague: Mouton.

Revill, P. M., 1966, Preliminary report on paralinguistics in Mbembe (Eastern Nigeria). Tagmemic and matrix linguistics applied to selected African languages, by K. L. Pike, 245–54, appendix VIII. Final report, contract no. OE-5-14-065. Washington, DC, US Department of Health, Education and Welfare, Office of Education, Bureau of Research.

Sapir, Edward, 1949, Speech as a personality trait. In David Mandelbaum (ed.), *Selected writings of Edward Sapir*, pp. 533–43. Berkeley: University of California Press. (Reprinted from *American Journal of Sociology* 32 (1927):892–905.)

Snyder, Gary, 1969, *Earth household: technical notes and queries to fellow Dharma revolutionaries.* New York: New Directions.

Watson, O. Michael, and T. D. Graves, 1966, Quantitative research in proxemic behavior. *American Anthropologist* 68:971–85.

Weinreich, Uriel, 1953, Languages in contact. Linguistic Circle of New York.

2

Ethnography of Speaking: Toward a Linguistics of the Praxis

Alessandro Duranti

2.0 Introduction

The ethnography of speaking (henceforth ES) studies language use as displayed in the daily life of particular speech communities. Its method is ethnography, supplemented by techniques developed in other areas of study such as developmental pragmatics, conversation analysis, poetics, and history.[1] Its theoretical contributions are centered around the study of *situated discourse*, that is, linguistic performance as the locus of the relationship between language and the socio–cultural order.[2]

From the point of view of the *content* of daily verbal interaction, ES is interested in the relationship between language use and local systems of knowledge and social conduct. ES views discourse as one of the main loci for the (re)creation and transmission of cultural patterns of knowledge and social action. More specifically, ES studies what is accomplished through speaking and how speech is related to and is constructed by particular aspects of social organization and speakers' assumptions, values, and beliefs about the world. The meaning of speech for particular speakers in specific social activities is thus a central concern for ES. Some typical questions asked by ethnographers of speaking in analyzing a particular strip of verbal interaction are: what is the goal of speech in this case? Which attributes of the linguistic code warrant its use in this context? What is the relation of this interaction to other, similar acts performed by the same actors or to other events observed in the same community?

With respect to the *form* of daily language use, ES has been focussing on patterns of variation across socio–cultural contexts, both within and across societies, with particular emphasis on the interrelation of the emergent and the culturally predictable structure of verbal performance in the conduct of social life.

Alessandro Duranti, "Ethography of speaking: Toward a linguistics of the praxis" from *Linguistics: The Cambridge Survey. Volume IV – Language: The Socio-cultural context*, edited by Frederick J. Newmeyer (Cambridge: Cambridge University Press, 1989), pp. 210–28. © by Cambridge University Press, reproduced with permission of the author and publisher.

The question often arises, whether explicitly or not, as to the relationship between ES and the supposedly wider area of sociolinguistics.

If we understand sociolinguistics as the systematic study of language use in social life, there should then be no doubts that ES should be considered a subfield of sociolinguistics. Such an inclusion of ES within the larger spectrum of sociolinguistic research could only benefit ES, which has often been criticized for its limited typology of actually analyzed linguistic phenomena (e.g. too much emphasis on ritualized speech or formal events) (Bloch 1976) and for its lack of concern for more explicit indications about its relevance for other branches of linguistics and anthropology (Leach 1976).

There are, however, peculiarities both in the methods and in the very object of inquiry of ES that make it related to, but distinct from, much of sociolinguistic research. Such differences, both at the methodological and at the theoretical level, accompanied by an abundance of new and stimulating research in some of the areas comprised by Hymes's notion of *communicative competence* (see below), have made more and more apparent the need to keep expanding the range of data and theoretical discussion within the ES approach before merging it with other fields of inquiry.

2.1   Language use

Like sociolinguists in general, ethnographers of speaking are interested in language *use*. A distinction must be drawn, however, between the commonly accepted sense of this term within linguistics at large and that meant by ES. Formal grammarians, historians of linguistics, and even sociolinguists at times interpret 'language use' in a narrow sense, namely as the actual employment of particular utterances, words, or sound by particular speakers at a given time and place, as linguistic 'tokens,' in other words, as opposed to 'types' (Lyons 1972). *Use* is thus often identified with *parole* as opposed to *langue* (cf. Saussure 1916). The sociolinguist's goal is thus to infer patterns of variation on the basis of the systematic sampling of more or less controlled 'uses' (or *actes de parole*). This notion of language use is strictly related to the view of sociolinguistics as merely a different *methodology*, a different way of obtaining data from that usually practiced by formal grammarians (Labov 1972: 259). In this view, the sociolinguist is depicted as someone who refuses to accept or test linguistic intuitions and prefers to them a tape-recorder with which to gather data from actual speech. Although formal grammarians have accepted the *social* significance of socio-linguistic research, many of them are still unable to see its significance from the point of view of *grammatical theory* (Chomsky 1977: 55).[3] What is missing here is both the realization by the formal grammarians, and the ability to convince by the sociolinguists, that mere structural descriptions of linguistic forms are useful and interesting but consistently lacking some essential feature of what makes language so precious to the human species, namely, its ability to function *in context* as an instrument of both reflection and action upon the world. So-called 'cognitive models' rely on the assumption that it is possible – and in fact mandatory in order to have a *theory* – to account for human behavior by means of context-independent rules. But we know now that decontextualized features pick out objects and provide analyses that are qualitatively different from those handled by social actors (Bourdieu 1977; Dreyfus 1983; Dreyfus & Dreyfus 1986). The use of 'intuitions' in linguistic as well as in metalinguistic behavior can be seen as an individual ability to rely upon or reconstruct (intrapsychologically) contextual information.

Thus, for ethnographers of speaking, as well as for many other researchers in the social sciences, *language use* must be interpreted as *the use of the linguistic code(s) in the conduct of social life*. ES accepts Wittgenstein's (1958) claim that the unity of '(a) language' is an illusion and one should rather look at specific contexts of use (or 'language games') in order to explain how linguistic signs can do the work they do. The interaction between speech and social action is so important that the methodologies and notations developed to study the referential (or denotational) uses of speech may be inadequate to study its *social* uses (Silverstein 1977, 1979). The term *speaking* was introduced by Hymes to stress the active, praxis-oriented aspect of the linguistic code, as opposed to the more contemplative, static notion of 'language' as seen and described by structural (synchronic) linguistics. Speaking must thus be thought of as a form of *human labor*, the phylogenetically and ontogenetically most powerful form of cooperative behavior (Vygotsky 1978; Leontyev 1981; Rossi-Landi 1983).

The concern with language use is thus not only a methodological commitment toward getting what speakers *really* say in a variety of contexts but also a consequence of the interest in what speakers *do* with language, whether willingly or unwillingly, consciously or unconsciously, directly or obliquely. In particular, ethnographers of speaking have been concerned with the work done by and through language in (1) establishing, challenging, and recreating social identities and social relationships, (2) explaining to others as well as to ourselves why the world is the way it is and what could or should be done to change it; (3) providing frames for events at the societal as well as individual level; (4) breaking, or more often sustaining, physical, political, and cultural barriers. Some of these areas of inquiry have also been studied within *pragmatics* (Gazdar 1979; Levinson 1983). What usually distinguishes the ethnographic approach from pragmatic analysis is a stronger concern for the socio-cultural context of the use of language, with the specific relationship between language and local systems of knowledge and social order, and a lesser commitment to the relevance of logical notation to the strategic use of speech in social interaction.

2.2   Communicative competence

The ethnographic study of language use aims at describing the knowledge that participants in verbal interaction need and display in order to communicate successfully with one another. *Communicative competence* is the term Hymes (1972b) used for this kind of complex expertise, which includes but goes beyond Chomsky's (1965) *competence* (Hymes 1982b).

> We have . . . to account for the fact that a normal child acquires knowledge of sentences, not only as grammatical, but also as appropriate. He or she acquires competence as to when to speak, when not, and as to what to talk about with whom, when, where, in what manner. In short, a child becomes able to accomplish a repertoire of speech acts, to take part in speech events, and to evaluate their accomplishment by others. This competence, moreover, is integral with attitudes, values, and motivations concerning language, its features and uses, and integral with competence for, and attitudes toward, the interrelation of language, with the other codes of communicative conduct. (Hymes 1972b: 277–8)

Within ES and sociolinguistics, the discussion of communicative competence versus linguistic (or grammatical) competence usually centers around two issues: (1) the need to accompany grammatical description with conditions of appropriateness; (2) the complementarity of the grammatical (or linguistic) code with other aspects of cooccurring rule-governed behavior (e.g. gestures, eye-gaze) (Hymes 1982b).

In fact, a crucial difference between Chomsky's notion of *competence* and Hymes's notion is that the former relies on the assumption that knowledge can be studied separately from performance, meant as the implementation of that knowledge in language use, whereas for Hymes, participation, performance, and intersubjective knowledge are all essential features of the ability to 'know a language.' Furthermore, Chomsky presents the hypothesis of autonomous grammar as a prerequisite to maintaining 'order' in the object of study (see note 3). The very possibility of 'doing science' on linguistic phenomena is tied to the researchers' ability to construct hypotheses about linguistic forms without having to make reference to nonlinguistic factors such as beliefs and attitudes (Chomsky 1977).

But the assumption that grammar of an idealized language is necessarily *orderly*, whereas patterns of actual verbal communication are *chaotic*, can hardly be supported by empirical investigation. Anyone who has ever engaged in grammatical analysis of the 'idealized' sort knows that disagreement among speakers on sentence acceptability is common; and anyone who has ever read any study on linguistic variation and linguistic performance knows that there are a lot of people out there finding 'order' in the apparent 'chaos' of language use. Although these are not sufficient reasons either for rejecting the use of introspection and idealization or for claiming full understanding of linguistic performance, they are arguments in favor of wanting to keep under a common roof – the notion of *communicative competence*, that is – the variety of phenomena that speakers must be able to handle in order to be considered 'competent.'

We all know that a large part of the work done by Chomsky and his students is based on their ability to find (i.e. imagine) appropriate contexts for the uttering of certain utterance-types. Despite the theoretical assumption of the innateness of certain aspects of grammar as pure cognitive/biological endowment, the actual definition of such aspects rests on the possibility of matching sentences with possible worlds, which are, in turn, constructed on the basis of the experience linguists have of the world in which they live. Criticism of such a methodology by ES and other approaches is not a rejection of abstraction or idealization, but rather a fundamental skepticism about the uncritical use of what phenomenological sociology calls 'preunderstanding' of the world (Bleicher 1982). In the case of linguistic research, it is the preunderstanding of the relationship between linguistic and nonlinguistic behavior that is usually ignored by formal grammarians. The same criticism drawn by Husserl toward objectivism in psychology applies here:

> The psychologists simply fail to see that they too [like physicists] study neither themselves nor the scientists who are doing the investigating nor their own vital environing world [*Umwelt*]. They do not see that from the very beginning they necessarily presuppose themselves as a group of men belonging to their own environing world and historical period. (Husserl 1965: 186–7)

Within ES, the explicit discussion of the relationship between the researchers' expectations and norms and the system they try to describe has become a major concern for the study of language acquisition and socialization. Ochs & Schieffelin (1984) have taken 'the descriptions of caregiving in the psychological literature as ethnographic descriptions' (1984: 283) and compared them with other accounts provided by members of other societies on how children acquire language and develop into competent members of their society. What is taken for granted by linguists and psychologists describing language development to other members of their own society is thus unveiled by a process of estrangement:

> using an ethnographic perspective, we will recast selected behaviors of white middle-class caregivers and young children as pieces of one 'developmental story.' The white middle-class developmental story . . . will be compared with two other developmental stories from societies that are strikingly different: Kaluli (Papua New Guinea) and Western Samoan. (Ochs & Schieffelin 1984: 285)

The result is a new discussion of the relationship between the process of acquiring language and the process of becoming a competent member of a society. An understanding of the ways in which the two processes are interwoven provides the necessary perspective for assessing the relevance of local theories of self and of knowledge for members' linguistic behavior on the one hand and our description of it on the other.

Ultimately, any attempt at relating linguistic forms to their *content* depends on the ability that both members and researchers have to utilize the *context* of speech as a resource for achieving understanding and getting things done.

2.3   Context

In formal linguistic analysis, context is usually brought in when difficulties or doubts arise with respect to the interpretation or acceptability of certain linguistic expressions. Although context is in fact crucial for imagining possible alternative interpretations of structurally ambiguous sentences, its use and role are not officially recognized in formal models of linguistic competence. The ethnographer's job, on the other hand, crucially relies on the ability skilfully and explicitly to relate patterns of behavior, speech included, to their immediate as well as broader sociocultural context. It is not by accident then that it was Malinowski, the father of modern ethnography, who first stressed the need to interpret speech in its *context of situation*, 'an expression which indicates on the one hand that the conception of *context* has to be broadened and on the other that the *situation* in which words are uttered can never be passed over as irrelevant to the linguistic expression' (1923: 306).

Although Malinowski originally thought that the need to keep speech and context tied to one another was restricted to the study of 'primitive people,' for whom language 'is a mode of action and not an instrument of reflection' (1923: 312), he later reformulated his views to include the importance of context in the interpretation of all languages, across all kinds of uses, literacy included (Malinowski 1935, vol. 2: part IV):[4]

> Our definition of meaning forces us to a new, a richer and wider type of observation. In order to show the meaning of words we must not merely give sound of utterance and equivalence of significance. We must above all give the pragmatic context in which they

are uttered, the correlation of sound to context, to action and to technical apparatus; and incidentally, in a full linguistic description, it would be necessary also to show the types of drills or conditioning or education by which words acquire meaning. (1935, vol. 2: 60)

Behavioristic tones aside, this passage expresses concerns and assumptions that were, thirty years later, at the heart of Hymes's call for an *ethnography of speaking* (Hymes 1964a, b).

In the last twenty years or so the term *context* has been broken down and variedly redefined to include the range of actual or potential speakers, the spatio-temporal dimensions of the interaction, the participants' goals. Three notions have been adopted and discussed within ES and related approaches: *speech community*, *speech event*, *speech act*.

2.3.1 Speech community

The widest context of verbal interaction for ES as well as for sociolinguistic research is usually taken to be the *speech community*, defined as a group of people who share the rules for interpreting and using at least one language (Gumperz 1972: 16) or linguistic variety (Hymes 1972a: 54). One of the reasons for taking the speech community as the starting point for linguistic research was to avoid the assumption that the sharing of the same 'language' implies shared understanding of its use and meaning in various contexts (Hymes 1972a, b).

It has been shown that the notion of speech community should not be simply equated with linguistic homogeneity of a well-defined set of features (Hudson 1980; Hymes 1982b). In the Norwegian community studied by Blom and Gumperz (1972), for instance, individual speakers who were born and raised in the community exhibited fundamental differences in terms of the uses of code-switching, of its interpretation and its value. One way of accounting for such diversity is to claim that it is characteristic of the very use of linguistic communication in social life:

> When studied in sufficient detail, with field methods designed to elicit speech in significant contexts, all speech communities are linguistically diverse and it can be shown that this diversity serves important communicative functions in signaling interspeaker attitudes and in providing information about speakers' social identities. (Gumperz 1972: 13)

Another way to deal with the kind of diversity documented by Gumperz and others is to propose that in fact speech communities do not exist except as 'prototypes' in people's minds (Hudson 1980: 30). To test such a hypothesis, it would be necessary to show that there is a psychological reality of some prototypical or 'ideal' core features of language use within a certain group of people. Some of Labov's (1972) findings on the uniformity of overt types of evaluative behavior could be used in such an argument. At the same time, his detailed work on *patterns* of variation in phonological and lexical domains points to a different, if not opposite, hypothesis, namely, the idea that the 'types' or regularities to be found are not in anyone's head but rather somewhere *out there*, in the (real) world of performance.

Any notion of speech community (and this would be also true for defining 'dialect' or 'vernacular') will thus depend on two sets of phenomena: (1) patterns of variation in a group of speakers also definable on grounds other than linguistic homogeneity (e.g.

speakers of this town tend to drop post-vocalic /r/ in the following contexts) and (2) emergent and cooperatively achieved aspects of human behavior as strategies for establishing comembership in the conduct of social life. The ability to explain (1) ultimately relies on our success in understanding (2).

2.3.2 Speech event

In contrast to sociolinguists, researchers in ES tend to start their analyses of speech behavior from the loci of use of speech rather than from the surveying of a particular set of norms for a particular range of social actors. The notion of *speech event* is the analytical tool for such a research program. The basic assumption of a speech-event analysis of language use is that an understanding of the form and content of everyday talk in its various manifestations implies an understanding of the social activities in which speaking takes place (Hymes 1964a, 1972a; Levinson 1979; Duranti 1985). Such activities, however, are not simply 'accompanied' by verbal interaction, they are also *shaped* by it: there are many ways, that is, in which speech has a role in the constitution of a social event. The most obvious cases are perhaps gossip sessions and telephone conversations, neither of which could take place if talk were not exchanged. But even the most physically oriented activities such as sport events or hunting expeditions rely heavily on verbal communication for the participants' successful coordination around some common task.

How is one to face the formidable task of isolating and describing event-units? Hymes (1964a) proposed a preliminary list of features or components of communicative events. The idea was to provide 'a useful guide in terms of which relevant features can be discerned – a provisional phonetics, as it were, not an *a priori* phonemics, of the communicative event' (Hymes 1964a: 13). The first list was later extended to include 16 components, grouped under 8 main entries, to be remembered with the acronym SPEAKING (Hymes 1972a): S (situation: setting and scene); P (participants: speaker/sender, addressor, hearer/receiver/audience, addressee); E (ends: outcomes, goals); A (act sequence: message form and message content); K (key); I (instrumentalities: channel, forms of speech); N (norms: norms of interaction and interpretation); G (genres). (See also Saville-Troike 1982; Duranti 1985).

In the last ten years or so, the speech-event unit has become a useful tool for the analysis of language use within and across societies. Many of the most recent contributions to the understanding of the constitutive role of speaking in political arenas, child-rearing practices, literacy activities, and counseling, have made use, whether explicitly or not, of the notion of speech event (Duranti 1981; Scollon & Scollon 1981; Heath 1983; Philips 1983; Anderson & Stokes 1984; Brenneis & Myers 1984; Schieffelin & Ochs 1986; Watson-Gegeo & White 1990). For many researchers, the speech event still represents a level of analysis that has the advantage of preserving information about the social system as a whole while at the same time allowing the researcher to get into the details of personal acts (Duranti 1990).

The Speaking model also represents a basic difference between ES and other branches of linguistics: the grid, in its various versions, has always maintained an *etic* status and was never accompanied by a (general) theory of the possible relationships among the various components. Such a theoretical discussion, in Hymes's program, seemed to be possible only at the *local* level (i.e. with respect to particular communities) and not within a more global, comparative framework. This entails that, within ES, there has never been an attempt at formulating a *general phonemics* of communicative events. The relationships among the components of the model are each time shown to be meaningful within a particular society – as an *emic* description, that is, – but do not necessarily exemplify any universal principle of the relation between speech and context in *societies in general*. The few attempts to draw general principles, such as Irvine 1979, are in fact discussions of how one should *not* infer universal features from what a given group chooses to do in a particular type of speech event; that is, what is 'formal' in one context need not be formal in another. (The only exceptions here are some attempts at elucidating general *areal* patterns where there are enough local studies to allow for it, e.g. Roberts & Forman 1972; Abrahams 1983.)

Is this tendency simply a reflection of the cultural relativism that ES shares with most of modern anthropology? It might well be the case. But most importantly, I think, the care for specific *emic* accounts and the reluctance to posit universal principles (with the exception of Brown & Levinson 1978) is strongly related to the fundamental anti-Universalism that characterizes ES as originally defined by Hymes. If some kind of universal claim is ever accepted by ES, it will be similar to what Merleau-Ponty (1964) called *lateral universal*, that is, the universality of the intersubjective enterprise rather than of the structures. To understand this, we must reflect again on the goals of ES. Differently from other approaches within linguistics, ES is concerned with language use as a link to and as an instrument of social life. This means that ethnographers of speaking, through a number of subjective, objective, and intersubjective methods (e.g. intuitions, audio-recording, transcription, interviews, participation in the life of the 'subjects'), get involved in studying an 'object' which is more complex and multiform than that typically studied in other branches of linguistics. One of the goals of ES is to maintain the complexity of *language as praxis* rather than reduce it to abstract, independent principles. In other words, the kind of universality ES is interested in cannot be the abstract kind of generative grammar or of conversational maxims. In the latter cases (i.e. for Chomsky and Grice), many aspects of the context must be removed in order to 'see' the principles at work. The researcher must create a vacuum wherein to show that certain structures or constraints are operating 'under' or 'above' what is going on. Once this is achieved, the researcher's work is over: the pieces are left on the ground. The whole is not put together again. Ethnographers, on the other hand – like the people they study – struggle to both capture and maintain the whole of the interaction at hand. The elements of one level (e.g. phonological register, lexical choice, discourse strategies) must be related to the elements of another level (e.g. social identities, values) – which, in turn, is further defined and constituted by those elements. In this process, ethnographers act as the linking elements between different levels and systems of communication. In so doing, they act in a similar fashion to those psychologists who study learning and cognitive development by consciously creating functional environments where behavior can be observed without destroying elements of the 'whole task' (Luria 1979; Griffin, Cole & Newman 1982; LCHC 1984).

A possible criticism of speech-event analysis is that it tends to select strips of interaction that are labeled by a culture, but it may overlook those interactions which are not recognized as units of some sort by the members. It should be mentioned here that, although the presence of a lexical term for a given activity or 'strip of interaction' is only one level of local organization of experience – perhaps the most obviously ideological – the lack of a term for any given such 'strip' is an interesting clue for fieldworkers.[5]

There is nothing, however, in the Speaking model or in the very idea of speech event that invites research on one kind of activity over another. Although ethnographers take native taxonomies seriously (Abrahams & Bauman 1971; Gossen 1972), what they end up studying is a by-product of what members of the culture describe as relevant or important and what they are expected to document as practitioners of a particular research tradition.

2.3.3   Speech act

The notion of speech *act* stresses the pragmatic force of speech, its ability not only to describe the world but to change it by relying on public, shared conventions (Austin 1975). Historically, the importance of Austin's work was to provide a philosophically sophisticated discussion of meaning in language that did not solely rely on the notion of truth (Levinson 1983). In order to explain the *illocutionary* force of an utterance one must be able to relate the *locution* – i.e. the words used – with its context. Thus, the sentence *I don't like to watch tv* can be used to do different things according to when it is used, by whom, etc. The different *uses* of such an utterance may all share the same linguistic *form* – actually, some abstraction of it – but they will serve different *functions* – e.g. to justify the absence of a tv set in my house, to object to an evening at home, to explain why I can't follow a conversation about tv programs. The same utterance can thus be used to different ends, by relying on different shared understanding of the social event in which speech occurs. The analyst's task is to explain the relationship between the speaker's subjective reality, the linguistic form chosen, and the audience response: 'The level of speech acts mediates immediately between the usual levels of grammar and the rest of a speech event or situation in that it implicates both linguistic form and social norms' (Hymes 1972a: 57).

The acceptance of the notion of speech act does not necessarily imply the acceptance of the epistemological foundations or underlying ideology (Pratt 1981) of speech-act theory. In particular, such a theory has been said to give too much prominence to the speaker's intentions for the definition of the utterance meaning. A number of researchers have lately shown that the role assigned to the speaker's intentions in the interpretation of speech actually varies across cultures and contexts (Streeck 1980; Ochs 1982; Rosaldo 1982; Kochman 1983; Duranti 1984). In the cases of verbal dueling among Blacks discussed by Kochman (1983), for instance, a speech act cannot be defined as insult until the receiver has chosen to interpret it as such. In the Samoan *fono* – a traditional politico-judiciary arena – the speaker's original intentions and understanding of certain events at the time of the speech act seem at times irrelevant for those who interpret his words and assess his responsibility (Duranti 1984). As demonstrated by analysts of conversation, however, even within American white middle class society, the emergent model of verbal interaction is much more dialogical than is usually recognized by the dominant ideology (Streeck 1980; Goodwin 1981; Schegloff 1982).

More generally, ES is interested in the relationship between the Austinian notion of speech act and various aspects of the local theories of communication and interpretation, including (1) the relationship between modes of production and modes of interpretation, as for instance found in the local organization of task accomplishment (Duranti & Ochs 1986); (2) the notion of self and the speaker's ability to control the interpretation of his or her own words (Rosaldo 1982; Shore 1982; Holquist 1983); (3) the local ontology of interpretation (e.g. whether it involves the ability to be in someone else's place or mind) (Ochs 1984); (4) the relevance of 'sincerity' for the performance of any speech act (Rosaldo 1982).

2.4   Other approaches: conversation analysis

By no means do the three kinds of context discussed above exhaust the possible or the existing levels of study of talk in social interaction (see for instance the papers in van Dijk 1985; Schiffrin 1984). Let me mention here another approach that shares with ES some important concerns and goals. The approach I have in mind is conversation analysis (CA). The relationship between CA and ES over the last ten or fifteen years has been a complex one, with moments of great unity (see Gumperz & Hymes 1972) and moments of separation and misunderstanding. Some recent developments in terms of both theoretical pronouncements and participation in conferences and symposia seem to indicate the possibility of a fruitful osmosis between the two schools. Although their methodologies are quite distinct, ES and CA do share some important assumptions and concerns (see the relevant papers and their introductions in Gumperz & Hymes 1972). In particular, both ES and CA tend to stress the role of speech in *creating* context, the need to take the participants' perspective in the analysis of their interaction, the cooperative nature of verbal communication – the latest feature being related, but not identical, to the claim of the emergent nature of (some aspects of) the social order.

There are at least two sources of apparent disagreement between CA and ES: (1) a different notion of what constitutes 'context'; (2) the issue of the universality of the turn-taking system and its correlates. A brief discussion of these issues should help clarify some possible misunderstandings.

2.4.1   Context

CA looks at talk-in-interaction, claiming the independence of the turn-taking system from various aspects of the socio-cultural context of speech such as the socioeconomic status or ethnic identity of the speakers (e.g. American white middle class, American working class, Thai peasants); the speech acts that are being performed (e.g. threats, promises, apologies); or the particular social occasion that has brought the participants together (e.g. a birthday party, waiting for the bus, calling the police). According to CA, the relevance of these contextual features should be used by the analyst only when the participants themselves explicitly evoke such features (Schegloff & Sacks 1973; Schegloff 1986a). On the other hand, certain principles such as 'one speaker at a time' and notions like 'prior speaker,' 'current speaker,' and 'recipient' are instead said to be always relevant, regardless of the specific occasion on which conversation takes place (Sacks, Schegloff & Jefferson 1974; Moerman 1977; Schegloff, Jefferson & Sacks 1977; Schegloff 1986a, 1986b). CA has thus defined an area of study in which the 'problems' and the 'solutions' speakers encounter in conversation can be described without referring to aspects of what ES researchers would define as crucial elements of the socio–cultural context. In so doing, CA shares something with the 'autonomous' trends within contemporary formal linguistics. Both CA and generative grammar, for instance, claim to be dealing with a level of structural relationships and dependencies among speech forms which can be studied separately from the occasion in which they are produced (unless we consider 'conversation' a kind of occasion). CA, however, makes no claim as to the innate nature of the turn-taking mechanisms and, more importantly, shares with ES (and ethnomethodology) the concern for the participants' point of view (or 'orientation'). The methods for arriving at defining the participants' perspective, however, may differ. For CA, what is found in the interaction (on a transcript, for instance) is the only legitimate source of knowledge for inferring the participants' concern. For ES, on the other hand, certain aspects of the social identity of the speakers as well as their past history are important. Furthermore, ethnographers routinely rely on members' accounts and explanation of what they (or others) were doing and meaning in a given verbal interaction. Those accounts, however, cannot by themselves constitute the only evidence of certain notions or practices. The researcher must search for both direct and indirect evidence of certain patterns of behavior. Let me give an example from my own work. In Samoan society, members can often articulate their expectations about particular social actors' duties and rights *vis à vis* different contexts. When I analyzed the speech of chiefs and orators participating in village council meetings (*fono*), those expectations seemed important for both me and the Samoan research assistants in interpreting the interaction. Despite the fact that participants' verbal behavior during the meetings was clearly part of the *stuff* that members of the society use to define certain people as 'chiefs' and others as 'orators,' native competent speakers were continuously trying to match the recorded performance with some ideal notion of what was appropriate for a given actor in a particular situation. Given the importance of the interplay between projected and actual behaviors in the interpretation of talk, it would seem to be a logical error to accept certain role notions only in their emergent versions, and not as part of people's guidelines for explaining how social order could or should be achieved in particular contexts.

2.4.2   Universality

Although, as far as I know, CA has never officially claimed the universality of the English turn-taking system and its corollaries across societies and languages, such a claim has been taken to be implicit in their practice.[6] A few studies, some of which are in the ES tradition, have challenged the universality of certain aspects of the turn-taking mechanisms (Philips 1976; Godard 1977; Philips 1983; Wolfson 1983). As discussed by Schegloff (1986b), however, the issue is not really resolved by simply concentrating on variation and differences. We would not gain very much insight into the phenomena being described by simply lining up – *à la* Popper – a set of apparent counterexamples to what is claimed by CA for English. The issue is at least twofold: (1) what is in common beyond (or despite) the differences (Schegloff 1986b); and (2) how are those differences related to *other differences* – a point recently recognized by Schegloff in discussing cross-linguistic work on repair mechanisms. In fact, even if the universal nature of the phenomena described by CA were to be further corroborated by a wide range of cross-cultural data, the 'autonomous' level of the discoveries about conversational interaction would still leave open the question of the *meaning* of those 'problems' and 'solutions' for different cultures. Silence is a typical example of a phenomenon that, differently distributed across cultures, can acquire different meanings (Basso 1970; Reisman 1974; Bauman 1983). More generally, what appears identical on a transcript (e.g. a sequence, a set of words or interruptions, a pause) might be quite different in people's lives or in their minds. For this reason, I believe that both CA and ES are needed to help clarify the mechanisms and meaning of daily verbal interaction.

2.5   Conclusions

Speaking or its absence seem significant in most, if not all, human interactions. The very moment we start looking at a sequence of talk, we realize that the accompanying interaction could have not been the same without it. Even in its most phatic or seemingly redundant uses, talk is always *constitutive of* some portion of reality: it either makes something already existing *present* to (or for) the participants or creates something anew.

ES's fundamental theoretical contribution, beyond description of communicative patterns within and across societies, is the discussion of the role of speaking in the shaping of people's lives. It is thus the true *semantics* of human language. Without necessarily rejecting formal or structural accounts of language use, ES remains an important element in establishing a linguistics of human praxis, a field of study in which the analysts do not lose track of the sociohistorical context of speech, while trying to bridge the gap between linguistic form and linguistic content. In its attempts to describe what other subfields of linguistics leave out or take for granted, ES stays within the tradition of what Luria (1978) called 'romantic science.' Its goal is not to strive for simplicity measures or one-dimensional patterns, but rather to capture, through ethnography and linguistic analysis, the inherent 'heteroglossia' of any (one) language (Bakhtin 1981), the complexity of the human experience as defined and revealed in everyday discourse.

Notes

Several friends and colleagues provided comments on earlier drafts of this chapter. In particular, I would like to thank for their helpful criticism Richard Bauman, Donald Brenneis, Charles Goodwin, Frederick J. Newmeyer, Bambi Schieffelin, and Joel Sherzer. During the writing of this chapter, I also benefited from conversations with Emanuel Schegloff on the notion of context and its relevance to the analysis of talk.

1   See, for instance, Bauman 1977; Schenkein 1978; Ochs & Schieffelin 1979; Hymes 1981; Bauman 1983; Heath 1983.

2   For a general discussion and overview of the ethnographic approach to the study of language use, see Hymes 1974; Bauman & Sherzer 1975; Coulthard 1977: Chapter 3; Sherzer 1977; Hymes 1982b; Saville-Troike 1982; Sherzer 1983: 11–20; Duranti 1985.

3   For Chomsky, to 'incorporate nonlinguistic factors into grammar: beliefs, attitudes, etc.' would amount 'to a rejection of the initial idealization of language, as an object of study'; it would mean that 'language is a chaos that is not worth studying' (Chomsky 1977: 152–3). This attitude has produced a culturally extremely impoverished object of inquiry ('core grammar'). To think that such an 'object'

bears some relationship to 'language' is an interesting and provoking hypothesis, but to give it the theoretical status of a phylogenetically defined organ and claim that it is the only object worth of study still seems, to many of us, at least unwarranted by the data.

4   Here is the official statement that sanctions Malinowski's 'turn': 'in one of my previous writings, I opposed civilised and scientific to primitive speech, and argued as if the theoretical uses of words in modern philosophic and scientific writing were completely detached from their pragmatic sources. This was an error, and a serious error at that. Between the savage use of words and the most abstract and theoretical one there is only a difference of degree. Ultimately all the meaning of all words is derived from bodily (sic!) experience' (Malinowski 1935, vol. 2: 58).

5   The lack of native labeling for certain kinds of often unbounded activities may however be a problem for the necessary coordination between participants and observer. Those who are being observed might feel that they need to be 'doing something' in order for someone to be observing them. When Elinor Ochs, Martha Platt and I were collecting data on language use and language acquisition in a western Samoan village, for instance, we recorded and studied different kinds of events. While I mostly concentrated on conversations among adults and formal meetings of the village council, Ochs and Platt documented household interaction between young children and their caretakers (older siblings, parents, or grandparents). Whereas participants almost immediately accepted the intrusion of my tape-recorder during conversations and important meetings without any major or lasting shift in the nature of their interaction, the people who were home with their younger children kept trying, during the first weeks, to frame their interaction with each other and with the researchers as 'doing school' (*fai le aaoga*). It was only after the startling realization that the researcher had nothing to teach and in fact wanted to learn something from them that people stopped performing school routines and body postures and accepted the intrusion of the researcher with the tape-recorder. The asymmetry between these contexts – the conversations and meeting on the one hand and the household interaction on the other – interestingly correlates with the presence versus absence of native labels for the activity at hand: whereas there are local labels for 'conversation' (*talanoaga*) and 'meeting' (*fono*), there is no native category for staying home with the kids. It would seem then that by reframing the interaction as 'doing school,' participants tried to create a context that could be reportable and perhaps valuable, within the local range of known and admissible activities.

6   Again, perhaps paradoxically, CA finds itself aligned with traditional generative grammarians, who claim that the in-depth study of one language, viz. English, might be sufficient for making interesting hypotheses about Universal Grammar.

References

Abrahams, R. D. 1983. *The man-of-words in the West Indies: performance and the emergence of creole culture*. Baltimore: Johns Hopkins University Press.

Abrahams, R. D. & Bauman, R. 1971. Sense and nonsense in St. Vincent: speech behavior decorum in a Caribbean community. *American Anthropologist* 73: 262–72.

Anderson, A. B. & Stokes, S. J. 1984. *Social and institutional influences on the development and practice of literacy*. In H. Goelman, A. Oberg & F. Smith (eds.) *Awakening to literacy*. London: Heinemann.

Austin, J. L. 1975. *How to do things with words*, 2nd edn., ed. J. O. Urmson & M. Sbisa. Cambridge, MA: Harvard University Press.

Bakhtin, M. M. 1981. *The dialogic imagination*. Ed. M. Holquist, trans. by C. Emerson & M. Holquist. Austin: University of Texas Press.

Basso, K. 1970. 'To give up on words': silence in western Apache culture. *Southwestern Journal of Anthropology* 26: 213–30.

Bauman, R. 1977. *Verbal art as performance*. Rowley: Newbury House.

Bauman, R. 1983. *Let your words be few: symbolism of speaking and silence among seventeenth-century Quakers*. Cambridge: Cambridge University Press.

Bauman, R. & Sherzer, J. 1975. The ethnography of speaking. *Annual Review of Anthropology* 4: 95–119.

Bleicher, J. 1982. *The hermeneutic imagination: outline of a positive critique of scientism and sociology*. London: Routledge & Kegan Paul.

Bloch, M. 1976. Review of R. Bauman & J. Sherzer (eds.) *Explorations in the ethnography of speaking*. *Language in Society* 5: 229–34.

Blom, J.-P. & Gumperz, J. J. 1972. Social meaning in linguistic structures: code-switching in Norway. In Gumperz & Hymes 1972.

Bourdieu, P. 1977. *Outline of a theory of practice*. Cambridge: Cambridge University Press.

Brenneis, D. & Myers, F. (eds.) 1984. *Dangerous words: language and politics in the Pacific*. New York: New York University Press.

Brown, P. & Levinson, S. 1978. Universals in language usage: politeness phenomena. In E. Goody (ed.) *Questions and politeness: strategies in social interaction*. Cambridge: Cambridge University Press.

Chomsky, N. 1965. *Aspects of the theory of syntax*. Cambridge, MA: MIT Press.

Chomsky, N. 1977. *Language and responsibility. Based on conversation with Mitsou Ronat*. Trans. by J. Viertel. New York: Pantheon.

Coulthard, M. 1977. *An introduction to discourse analysis*. London: Longman.

Dijk, T. A. van (ed.) 1985. *Handbook of discourse analysis*, 4 vols. New York: Academic Press.

Dreyfus, H. 1983. Why current studies of human capacities can never be scientific. Berkeley: Berkeley Cognitive Science Report No. 11.

Dreyfus, H. & Dreyfus, S. 1986. *Mind over machine: the power of human intuition and expertise in the era of the computer*. London: Macmillan/The Free Press.

Duranti, A. 1981. *The Samoan fono: a sociolinguistic study*. Pacific Linguistics B80. Canberra: The Australian National University.

Duranti, A. 1984. Intentions, self, and local theories of meaning: words and social action in a Samoan context. Technical Report No. 122. San Diego: University of California Center for Human Information Processing.

Duranti, A. 1985. Sociocultural dimensions of discourse. In van Dijk 1985. Vol. 1: *Disciplines of Discourse*.

Duranti, A. 1990. Doing things with words: conflict, understanding, and change in a Samoan *fono*. In Watson-Gegeo & White 1990.

Duranti, A. & Ochs, E. 1986. Literacy instruction in a Samoan village. In B. B. Schieffelin & P. Gilmore (eds.) *Acquisition of literacy: ethnographic perspectives*. Norwood: Ablex.

Gazdar, G. 1979. *Pragmatics: implicature, presupposition, and logical form*. London: Academic Press.

Godard, D. 1977. Same setting, different norms: phone call beginnings in France and the United States. *Language in Society* 6: 209–19.

Goodwin, C. 1981. *Conversation organization: interaction between speakers and hearers*. New York: Academic Press.

Gossen, G. 1972. Chamula genres of verbal behavior. In A. Paredes & R. Bauman (eds.) *Toward new perspectives in folklore*. Austin: University of Texas Press.

Griffin, P., Cole, M. & Newman, D. 1982. Locating tasks in psychology and education. *Discourse Processes* 5: 111–25.

Gumperz, J. J. 1972. Introduction. In Gumperz & Hymes 1972.

Gumperz, J. J. & Hymes, D. (eds.) 1972. *Directions in sociolinguistics: the ethnography of communication*. New York: Holt.

Heath, S. 1983. *Ways with words: language, life, and work in communities and classrooms*. Cambridge: Cambridge University Press.

Holquist, M. 1983. The politics of representation. *The Quarterly Newsletter of the Laboratory of Comparative Human Cognition* 5: 2–9.

Hudson, R. 1980. *Sociolinguistics*. Cambridge: Cambridge University Press.

Husserl, E. 1965. Philosophy and the crisis of European man. In *Phenomenology and the crisis of philosophy*, trans. with an introduction by Q. Lauer. New York: Harper & Row.

Hymes, D. 1964a. Introduction: toward ethnographics of communication. In *American Anthropologist* 66, *Special publication*: J. J. Gumperz & D. Hymes (eds.) *The ethnography of communication*.

Hymes, D. (ed.) 1964b. *Language in culture and society: a reader in linguistics and anthropology*. New York: Harper & Row.

Hymes, D. 1972a. Models for the interaction of language and social life. In Gumperz & Hymes 1972.

Hymes, D. 1972b. On communicative competence. In J. B. Pride & J. Holmes (eds.) *Sociolinguistics*. Harmondsworth: Penguin.

Hymes, D. 1974. *Foundations in sociolinguistics*. Philadelphia: University of Pennsylvania Press.

Hymes, D. 1981. '*In vain I tried to tell you*'. *Essays in native American ethnopoetics*. Philadelphia: University of Pennsylvania Press.

Hymes, D. 1982a. *Vers la compétence de communication*. Trans. by F. Mugler. Paris: Hatier-Crédif.

Hymes, D. 1982b. Postface. In Hymes 1982a.

Irvine, J. T. 1979. Formality and informality in communicative events. *American Anthropologist* 81: 773–90.

Kochman, T. 1983. The boundary between play and nonplay in Black verbal dueling. *Language in Society* 12: 329–37.

LCHC. 1984. Re-mediation, diagnosis and remediation. San Diego: University of California, Laboratory of Comparative Human Cognition.

Labov, W. 1972. *Sociolinguistic patterns*. Philadelphia: University of Pennsylvania Press.

Leach, E. 1976. Social geography and linguistic performance. *Semiotica* 16: 87–97.

Leontyev, A. N. 1981. *Problems of the development of mind*. Moscow: Progress Publishers.

Levinson, S. 1979. Activity types and language. *Linguistics* 17: 365–99.

Levinson, S. 1983. *Pragmatics*. Cambridge: Cambridge University Press.

Luria, A. R. 1979. *The making of mind: a personal account of Soviet psychology*, ed. M. Cole & S. Cole. Cambridge, MA: Harvard University Press.

Lyons, J. 1972. Human language. In R. A. Hinde (ed.) *Non-verbal communication*. Cambridge: Cambridge University Press.

Malinowski, B. 1923. The problem of meaning in primitive languages. In C. K. Ogden & I. A. Richards (eds.) *The meaning of meaning*. New York: Harcourt, Brace & World.

Malinowski, B. 1935. *Coral gardens and their magic*, 2 vols. New York: American Book Company. (Republished 1961 by Dover Publications, New York.)

Merleau-Ponty, M. 1964. *Signs*. Trans. with an introduction by R. C. McCleary. Evanston: Northwestern University Press.

Moerman, M. 1977. The preference for self-correction in a Tai conversational corpus. *Language* 53: 872–82.

Ochs, E. 1982. Talking to children in Western Samoa. *Language in Society* 11: 77–104.

Ochs, E. 1984. Clarification and culture. In D. Schiffrin (ed.) *Georgetown University Round Table on Languages and Linguistics 1984*. Washington: Georgetown University Press.

Ochs, E. & Schieffelin, B. (eds.) 1979. *Developmental pragmatics*. New York: Cambridge University Press.

Ochs, E. & Schieffelin, B. 1984. Language acquisition and socialization: three developmental stories. In R. Schweder & R. Levine (eds.) *Culture theory*. Cambridge: Cambridge University Press.

Philips, S. U. 1976. Some sources of cultural variability in the regulation of talk. *Language in Society* 5: 81–95.

Philips, S. U. 1983. *The invisible culture: communication in classroom and community on the Warm Spring Indian Reservation*. New York: Longman.

Pratt, M. L. 1981. The ideology of speech-act theory. *Centrum* New Series 1: 5–18.

Reisman, K. 1974. Contrapuntal conversations in an Antiguan village. In R. Bauman & J. Sherzer (eds.) *Explorations in the ethnography of speaking*. Cambridge: Cambridge University Press.

Roberts, J. & Forman, M. 1972. Riddles: expressive models of interrogation. In Gumperz & Hymes 1972.

Rosaldo, S. 1982. The things we do with words: Ilongot speech acts and speech act theory in philosophy. *Language in Society* 11: 203–37.

Rossi-Landi, F. 1983. *The language of work and trade: a semiotic homology for linguistics and economics*. Trans. by M. Adams & others. South Hadley: Bergin & Garvey.

Sacks, H., Schegloff, E. & Jefferson, G. 1974. A simplest systematics for the organization of turn-taking for conversation. *Language* 50: 696–735.

Saussure, F. de 1916. *Cours de linguistique générale*. Lausanne: Payot.

Saville-Troike, M. 1982. *The ethnography of communication: an introduction*. Oxford: Blackwell.

Schegloff, E. 1982. Discourse as an interactional achievement: Some uses of 'uh huh' and other things that come between sentences. In D. Tannen (ed.) *Georgetown University Round-table on Languages and Linguistics 1981*. Washington: Georgetown University Press.

Schegloff, E. 1986a. Between macro and micro: contexts and other connections. In J. Alexander, B. Giesen, R. Munch & N. Smelser (eds.) *The micro–macro link*. Berkeley and Los Angeles: University of California Press.

Schegloff, E. 1986b. The routine as achievement. *Human Studies* 9: 111–51.

Schegloff, E., Jefferson, G. & Sacks, H. 1977. The preference for self-correction in the organization of repair in conversation. *Language* 53: 361–82.

Schegloff, E. & Sacks, H. 1973. Opening up closings. *Semiotica* 8: 289–327.

Schenkein, J. 1978. *Studies in the organization of conversational interaction*. New York: Academic Press.

Schieffelin, B. & Ochs, E. (eds.) 1986. *Language socialization across cultures*. Cambridge: Cambridge University Press.

Schiffrin, D. (ed.) 1984. *Georgetown University Round Table on Languages and Linguistics 1984: Meaning, form, and use in context: linguistic application*. Washington: Georgetown University Press.

Scollon, R. & Scollon, S. K. 1981. *Narrative, literacy, and face in interethnic communication*. Norwood: Ablex.

Sherzer, J. 1977. The ethnography of speaking: a critical appraisal. In M. Saville-Troike (ed.) *Georgetown University Round Table on Languages and Linguistics 1977*. Washington: Georgetown University Press.

Sherzer, J. 1983. *Kuna ways of speaking*. Austin: Texas University Press.

Shore, B. 1982. *Sala'ilua: a Samoan mystery*. Columbia University Press.

Silverstein, M. 1977. Cultural prerequisites to grammatical analysis. In M. Saville-Troike (ed.) *Linguistics and anthropology*. Washington: Georgetown University Press.

Silverstein, M. 1979. Language structure and linguistic ideology. In P. R. Clyne, W. F. Hanks & C. L. Hofbauer (eds.) *The elements: a parasession on linguistic units and levels*. Chicago: Chicago Linguistic Society.

Streeck, J. 1980. Speech acts in interaction: critique of Searle. *Discourse Processes* 3: 133–54.

Vygotsky, L. S. 1978. *Mind in society*. Cambridge, MA: Harvard University Press.

Watson-Gegeo, K. & White, G. (eds.) 1990. *Disentangling: conflict discourse in Pacific societies*.

Wittgenstein, L. 1958. *Philosophical investigations*, 3rd edn. trans. by G. E. M. Abscombe. New York: Macmillan.

Wolfson, N. 1983. Rules of speaking. In J. C. Richards & R. W. Schmidt (eds.) *Language and communication*. New York: Longman.

3

Interethnic Communication

John J. Gumperz

Chapters 6 and 7 [the chapters preceding this one in the original publication] outline a perspective to conversation that focuses on conversational inference and on participants' use of prosodic and phonetic perceptions as well as on interpretive preferences learned through previous communicative experience to negotiate frames of interpretation. Using this perspective we can account for both shared grammatical knowledge and for differences in communicative style that characterize our modern culturally diverse societies.

This approach to speaking has both theoretical and practical significance. On the theoretical level it suggests a way of carrying out Garfinkel's program for studying naturally organized activities through language without relying on a priori and generally untestable assumptions about what is or is not culturally appropriate. Although it might seem at first glance that contextualization cues are surface phenomena, their systematic analysis can lay the foundation for research strategies to gain insights into otherwise inaccessible symbolic processes of interpretation.

On the practical level, the study of conversational inference may lead to an explanation for the endemic and increasingly serious communication problems that affect private and public affairs in our society. We can begin to see why individuals who speak English well and have no difficulty in producing grammatical English sentences may nevertheless differ significantly in what they perceive as meaningful discourse cues. Accordingly, their assumptions about what information is to be conveyed, how it is to be ordered and put into words and their ability to fill in the unverbalized information they need to make sense of what transpires may also vary. This may lead to misunderstandings that go unnoticed in the course of an interaction, but can be revealed and studied empirically through conversational analysis.

The main purpose of earlier chapters was to illustrate the nature of the cues and the inferential mechanisms involved. To that end, the discussion largely relied on examples

John J. Gumperz, "Interethnic communication," chapter 8 of Gumperz's *Discourse Strategies* (Cambridge: Cambridge University Press, 1982), pp. 172–86 plus associated references. © by Cambridge University Press, reproduced with permission of the author and publisher.

of brief encounters. Miscommunications occurring in such brief encounters are annoying and their communicative effect may be serious. But the social import of the phenomena in question and their bases in participants' cultural background is most clearly revealed through case studies of longer events. The following two chapters present in depth analyses of two such events. To begin with, let me give one more brief example to illustrate the scope of the analysis and the subconscious nature of the interpretive processes involved.

In a staff cafeteria at a major British airport, newly hired Indian and Pakistani women were perceived as surly and uncooperative by their supervisor as well as by the cargo handlers whom they served. Observation revealed that while relatively few words were exchanged, the intonation and manner in which these words were pronounced were interpreted negatively. For example, when a cargo handler who had chosen meat was asked whether he wanted gravy, a British assistant would say "Gravy?" using rising intonation. The Indian assistants, on the other hand, would say the word using falling intonation: "Gravy." We taped relevant sequences, including interchanges like these, and asked the employees to paraphrase what was meant in each case. At first the Indian workers saw no difference. However, the English teacher and the cafeteria supervisor could point out that "Gravy," said with a falling intonation, is likely to be interpreted as 'This is gravy,' i.e. not interpreted as an offer but rather as a statement, which in the context seems redundant and consequently rude. When the Indian women heard this, they began to understand the reactions they had been getting all along which had until then seemed incomprehensible. They then spontaneously recalled intonation patterns which had seemed strange to them when spoken by native English speakers. At the same time, supervisors learned that the Indian women's falling intonation was their normal way of asking questions in that situation, and that no rudeness or indifference was intended.

After several discussion/teaching sessions of this sort, both the teacher and the cafeteria supervisor reported a distinct improvement in the attitude of the Indian workers both to their work and to their customers. It seemed that the Indian workers had long sensed they had been misunderstood but, having no way of talking about this in objective terms, they had felt they were being discriminated against. We had not taught the cafeteria workers to speak appropriate English; rather, by discussing the results of our analysis in mixed sessions and focusing on context bound interpretive preferences rather than on attitudes and stereotypes, we have suggested a strategy for self-diagnosis of communication difficulties. In short, they regained confidence in their own innate ability to learn.

The first of the longer case studies examines excerpts from an interview–counselling session recorded in an industrial suburb in London. The participants are both educated speakers of English; one is a Pakistani teacher of mathematics, who although born in South Asia went to secondary school and university in England. The other is a staff member of a center funded by the Department of Employment to deal with interethnic communication problems in British industry. The teacher has been unable to secure permanent employment and having been told that he lacks communication skills for high school teaching, he has been referred to the center. While both participants agree on the general definition of the event as an interview–counselling session, their expectations of what is to be accomplished, and especially about what needs to be said, differ radically.

Such differences in expectation are of course not unusual even where conversational-ists have similar cultural backgrounds. Conversations often begin with an introductory phase where common themes are negotiated and differences in expectation adjusted. What is unusual about this situation is that participants, in spite of repeated attempts at adjustment over a period of more than an hour, utterly fail to achieve such negotia-tion. Our analysis concentrates on the reasons for this failure and shows how it is based on differences in linguistic and socio-cultural knowledge.

Methods used for the discovery of contextualization cues have been described in chapter 6 [of the original publication]. They rely partly on comparative analysis of a wide variety of ethnically homogeneous in-group and ethnically mixed encounters. Indirect elicitation procedures are used along with experiments in which participants in a conversation or others of similar background listen to tape recorded passages and are questioned to discover the perceptual cues they use in arriving at their interpretation.

Case study 1
A: Indian male speaker
B: British female speaker
The recording begins almost immediately after the initial greetings. B has just asked A for permission to record the interview, and A's first utterance is in reply to her request.

1. A: exactly the same way as you, as you would like
2.   ⌈to put on
3. B: ⌊Oh no, no
4. A: there will be some of ⌈the things you would like to
5. B: ⌊yes
6. A: write it down
7. B: that's right, that's right (laughs)
8. A: but, uh . . . anyway it's up to you
      (pause, about 1 second)
9. B: um, (high pitch) . . . well . . . ⌈I I Miss C.
10. A: ⌊first of all
11. B: hasn't said anything to me you see
      (pause, about 2 seconds)
12. A: I am very sorry if ⌈she hasn't spoken anything
13. B: (softly)   ⌊doesn't matter
14. A: on the telephone at least,
15. B: doesn't matter
16. A: but ah . . . it was very important uh thing for me
17. B: ye:s. Tell, tell me what it ⌈is you want
18. A: ⌊umm
19.   Um, may I first of all request for the introduction please
20. B: Oh yes sorry ⌈
21. A: ⌊I am sorry
      (pause, about 1 second)
22. B: I am E.

23.   A: Oh yes ⎡(breathy) I see . . . oh yes . . . very nice
24.   B: ⎢and I am a teacher here in the Center
25.   A: very nice⎢
26.   B: ⎣and we run ⎡
27.   A: ⎣pleased to meet you (laughs) ⎡
28.   B: ⎣different
29.   courses (A laughs) yes, and you are Mr. A?
30.   A: N.A.
31.   B: N.A. yes, yes, I see (laughs). Okay, that's the
32.   introduction (laughs)
33.   A: Would it be enough introduction?

Note that apart from a few seemingly odd phrases the passage shows no readily apparent differences in linguistic code, yet the oddness of A's question, (33) "Would it be enough introduction?" coming as it does after B's (31) "Okay, that's the introduction," clearly suggests that something is going wrong. Normally one might explain this sort of utterance and the awkward exchanges that precede it in psychological terms as odd behavior, reflecting participants' personal motives. But a closer examination of the interactive synchrony of the entire passage, as revealed in the coordination of speakers' messages with backchannel cues such as "um," "yes" or "no no," suggests that the problem is more complex than that.

Studies of interactive synchrony (Erickson & Schultz 1982), focusing primarily on nonverbal signs, have shown that in conversation of all kinds, speakers' moves and listeners' responses are synchronized in such a way as to conform to a regular and measurable rhythmic beat. Most longer encounters alternate between synchronous or smooth phases exhibiting a high degree of coordination and phases of asynchrony which Erickson calls "uncomfortable moments." Experiments carried on at Berkeley (Bennett, Erickson & Gumperz 1976, Bennett 1981) with ethnically mixed student groups reveal that the relationship of back-channel signals to speakers' utterances is closely related to interactional synchrony at the nonverbal level. In synchronous phases back-channel signals stand in regular relationship to points of maximum information content in the speaker's message, as marked by stress and intonation contour. Asynchronous phases lack such coordination. It has furthermore been noted that when participants are asked to monitor video- or audiotapes of their own encounters, they have little difficulty in agreeing on the boundaries between synchronous and asynchronous phases. But when they are asked to interpret what was going on in these phases, their interpretations tend to differ. Conversational synchrony thus yields empirical measures of conversational cooperation which reflect automatic behavior, independent of prior semantic assumptions about the content or function of what was said. Analysis of conversational synchrony can form a useful starting point for comparative analysis of interpretive processes.

In interactions among individuals who share socio-cultural background, which are not marked by other overt signs of disagreement, asynchronous movements tend to reflect the initial negotiation transitions in verbal activity or routines, or unexpected moves by one or another participant, and are relatively brief. In our passage here, however, lack of coordination is evident throughout.

Note, for example, the placement of B's "oh no" (3). In a coordinated exchange this should appear shortly after A's verb phrase "write it down" (6). Here it occurs after the auxiliary "like." Similarly B's "yes" (5) overlaps with A's "the" (4). The same is true of B's "doesn't matter" (13) and A's "umm" (18). Similar asynchronous overlaps are found throughout the tape. In line 9 B shifts to a high pitched "um, well," and as she is about to go into her message, A simultaneously begins with "first of all." In addition there are premature starts, i.e. starts which lack the usual rhythmic interval, in lines 21, 23 and 25; in lines 8, 11 and 21, we find arhythmic pauses of one, two, and one seconds respectively.

Lack of coordination seems to increase rather than decrease with the progress of the interaction, culminating in several bursts of nervous laughter (27, 29, 31, 32) which suggest that both participants are becoming increasingly ill at ease. Given what we know about conversational rhythm and synchrony there is strong evidence for systematic differences in contextualization and interpretive strategies in this interaction.

To find out what these differences are, we must turn to content. The passage divides into roughly three sequentially ordered subepisodes. These are distinct in manifest topic. But beyond that, they also have semantic import in terms of the role relations and expected outcomes they imply, and can thus be seen as reflecting distinct activity types.

The first subepisode begins with A's response to B's request for permission to tape record. This gives A the option either to agree or to refuse, and further to explain or justify his decision. His words here indirectly suggest that he is agreeing and is taking advantage of his option, in order to comment on the importance of his problem. B, however, does not seem to understand what he's trying to do. Her "no, no" (3) suggests she is defensive about her request to record, and her "that's right" (7) seems intended to cut short the preliminaries. In line 9, B attempts to lead into the interview proper. Her rise in pitch is of the type English speakers use elsewhere in our comparative tapes to mark shifts in focus to introduce important new information. A's interruption here suggests that he either does not recognize or disagrees with her change in focus.

Subepisode 2, lines 9–17, consists of B's indirect attempts to get A to state his problem. These are temporarily sidetracked by his responses. In subepisode 3 B once more tries to get started with the interview proper, whereupon A responds with an asynchronous "umm" and counters by asking for an introduction. The remainder of the passage then focuses on that introduction.

Looking in more detail at the process of speaker–listener coordination, we note that in line 11, B simply ignores A's interruption. Her message is followed by a long pause of two seconds. A's statement following that pause is marked by what, when compared to his preceding and following statements, is unusually slow rhythm and highly contoured intonation. "Very sorry" (12) and "very important" (16) are stressed. Many Indian English speakers readily identify the prosody here as signalling that the speaker is seriously concerned and wants the listener to understand the gravity of his situation before he goes on to give more detail. Similar contouring occurs in a number of other interethnic encounters as well as elsewhere in the present interview. Listeners of English background tend not to be attuned to the signalling value of such cues; those who notice this shift in prosody tend to dismiss it as a rather minor and somewhat misplaced indication of affect. What we seem to be faced with is an ethnically specific signalling system where contoured prosody and slowed rhythm contrast with flattened contours and normal rhythm to suggest personal concern.

In this episode, B is either unaware of this signalling convention or has decided to ignore it, since she fails to respond. In Western English conventions her statement "Miss C. hasn't said anything to me" counts as an indirect request for more detail as to what the problem is. She seems to want to go on with the interview and when A does not respond as expected she twice interrupts with "doesn't matter" (13, 15). Both her interruptions are asynchronous with A's talk. She seems to be interpreting A's statement as a somewhat irrelevant formulaic excuse, rather than as a preamble, or an attempt to prepare the ground for what is to come. As A continues, "it was very important," she responds with a "yes" spoken with normal intonation, and without raising her pitch at all she attempts once more to begin the interview proper. When A then asks for the introduction, she counters with "oh yes sorry," whereupon A immediately, i.e. without the normal rhythmic interval, says: "I am sorry." Now B seems thrown off balance. She takes a full second to formulate her reply, and it is easy to see why. Her own "sorry" indicates that she interprets A's preceding remark as implying she has been remiss, but when he himself then replies with "I am sorry" he seems to be suggesting it is his own fault.

When B then gives her name in line 22, A replies with a very breathy and contoured "very nice." Indian English speakers who listen to the tape will readily identify this last as a formulaic utterance. It is the Indian English equivalent of Urdu *bahut accha* which is used as a back-channel sign of interest similar to our "O.K. go on." The breathy enunciation and contoured intonation are signs of polite emphasis. For Western English speakers, however, the meaning is quite different. "Very nice" is used to respond to children who behave properly. In this situation moreover, it might be interpreted as having sexual overtones. In any case, B ignores the remark and in line 26 attempts to shift the focus away from herself to talk about the center where she works. A does not follow her shift in focus however. His "pleased to meet you" focuses once more on her as a person. This is either intentional or it could be the result of his slowness in following her shift in focus. In any case his laughing now suggests lack of ease or nervousness.

B continues as if he hadn't spoken and then when A laughs again asks "and you are Mr. A?" When A then gives his name she repeats it. Her subsequent laugh and her concluding statement, "Okay, that's the introduction," indicate that she has interpreted A's original suggestion that they introduce each other as simply a request to exchange names, which given her frame of reference she regards as somewhat superfluous in this situation.

A's subsequent "would it be enough introduction?" in line 33, however, shows that he has quite different expectations of what the introduction was to accomplish. We can begin to see what these expectations are by examining the following exchange which takes place much later in the interview.

Case study 2

1. A: then I had decided because I felt all the
2.   way that whatever happened that was totally
3.   wrong that was not, there was no trace of
4.   truth in it. I needed teaching. I wanted

```
 5.        teaching, ⌈I want teaching
 6.  B:            ⌊hu
 7.  A: I want to um um to waive ⌈that
 8.  B:                           ⌊hu
 9.  A: ⌈condition so that by doing
10.  B: ⌊hu
11.  A: some sort of training ⌈language training
12.  B:                       ⌊hu
13.  A: I can fulfill the condition and then I can
14.     come back
15.  B: hu
16.  A: and reinstate in ⌈teaching condition
17.  B:                  ⌊hu
18.  A: this is what I had the view to write to
19.     the Department of ⌈Education and Science and
20.  B:                   ⌊yes I see
21.  A: with the same view I approached
22.  B: Twickenham
23.  A: Twickenham as well as Uxbridge ⌈University
24.  B:                                ⌊yes
25.  A: as well as Ealing Technical College
26.  B: college
27.  A: and at the end they had directed me to
28.     ⌈give the ⌈best possible advice
29.  B: ⌊yes     ⌊yes
30.  A: by doing some sort of language course in
31.     which I could best help, so I can be reinstated
32.     and I can do something productive rather
33.     than wasting my time ⌈and the provincial and
34.  B:                      ⌊yes I see, yes I understand
35.  A: the money and time
36.  B: Okay now the thing is Mr A. there is no course here
37.     which is suitable for you at the moment
38.  A: this I had seen the ⌈pro . . . prospectus ⌈this
39.  B:                     ⌊yes                  ⌊yes
40.  A: teachers' training ⌈(        )
41.  B:                    ⌊yes that's teachers' training
42.     is for teachers who are employed doing language
43.     training in factories
44.  A:        per . . . perhaps perhaps there will be
45.     some way out for you for to for to to
46.     ⌈to help me
47.  B: ⌊to help there might be but I can't tell you now
48.     because I shall have to, you see at the moment there
49.     is no course sui . . . suitable for you ⌈the
50.  A:                                          ⌊um
```

51.   B: Teachers' training course is run one day here, one
52.   day there, two days here, two days there and these are
53.   connected with a specific project
54.   A: I don't mind doing any sort of ⌈pro . . . project but
55.   B: ⌊no but th . . .
56.   th . . . that's not suitable, I can tell you honestly
57.   you won't find it suitable for you, ⌈it won't
58.   A: ⌊but
59.   B: is is ⌈nothing to do what you want
60.   A: ⌊but no it is not what actually I want I want
61.   only to waive the condition, waive the condition
62.   which I have been ⌈restricted from the admission
63.   B: ⌊but you see it it
64.   would only be may five days a year, it's only
65.   conferences, we don't have a teachers' training
66.   course here
67.   A: nothing (looks at program)
68.   B: Yes, oh that's the RSA course
69.   A: Yes
70.   B: that's at Ealing Technical College, that isn't here
71.   A: But it's it's given here
72.   B: Yes that's ⌈right it's at Ealing Technical College
73.   A: ⌊it's it's

A has here completed his story of the experiences that led to his present predicament, and begins to explain what he wants. The phrase "I want to waive that condition" (7, 9) and his repeated use of the word "condition" (13, 16) are his references to the fact that he has been told that he needs additional communication skills. He then proceeds to ask to be admitted to a training course. When, in line 36, B tells him that there is no course which is suitable for him, he disputes this by mentioning the center's prospectus. Then in response to B's remarks in lines 51–3, he says "I don't mind doing any sort of project." When B then insists that this would not be suitable, and is not what he wants, he says once more, repeating the same phrase twice, that all he wants to do is to "waive the condition." In other words he wants another certificate, not more training.

From this, from our analysis of similar situations, and from our interviews with Asians in British industry, we can see that A, along with many others of similar background, views these counselling situations in terms which are similar to the way many Indians view contacts between government functionaries and members of the lay public in general. Following a type of cultural logic which is perhaps best illustrated in Dumont (1970), these situations are seen as basically hierarchical situations in which the counselee acts as a petitioner requesting the counselor to facilitate or grant access to a position. It is the petitioner's role in such situations to plead or present arguments based on personal need or hardship (as in A's expressions of concern in case study 1, lines 12ff.), which the functionary then either grants or refuses.

In the present case, having been told he lacks communication skills, A interprets this to mean that he needs to get another certificate to qualify for a new teaching post. What he wants to ask of B is that she help him get such a certificate. Before he can make his request, however, he needs to find out what her position in the organization is so that he can judge the extent to which she is able to help him. This is what he wants to accomplish with his request for introductions. His awkward sounding comments are simply attempts at using indirect verbal strategies to get the information he needs.

Seen from this perspective B's response is clearly insufficient. We know, for example, that although B is a trained teacher and does occasionally teach, her main function is that of assistant director of the center in charge of curriculum planning. In identifying herself as a teacher she follows the common English practice of slightly understating her actual rank. Most of us would do likewise in similar situations. If someone were to ask me to introduce myself, I might say that I teach anthropology at Berkeley, but I would certainly not identify myself directly as a full professor, and list my administrative responsibilities. Anyone who needs this type of information would have to elicit it from me. To do so requires command of indirect strategies which could induce me to volunteer the required information, strategies which are dependent on socio-culturally specific background knowledge. A's probes in case study 1, lines 23, 25, 27 and 33 fail because he has neither the socio-cultural knowledge to know what to expect, nor the contextualization strategies needed to elicit information not freely offered.

What B's expectations are emerges from the following passage which in the actual interview follows immediately after case study 1.

Case study 3
1. B: well tell me what you have been studying . . .
2. A: um . . .
3. B: up till now
4. A: um, I have done my MSc from N. University
5. B: huh
6. A: I have done my graduate certificate in Education from L. Uni-
7. versity. I had been teaching after getting that teachers' training in
8. H., in H.
9. B: Oh, so you have *done* some teaching
10. A: Some ⌈I have done I have done some ⌈teaching
11. B: ⌊in H.   ⌊I see
12. A: Um . . . I completed two terms . . . uh, unfortunately I had to
13. leave from that place because ⌈uh I was appointed only
14. B: ⌊oh
15. A: for two terms
16. B: Oh so you didn't get to finish your probation, I suppose
17. A: (sighs) so that is uh ⌈my start was alright but later
18. B: ⌊oh
19. A: on what happened it is a mi – a great chaos, I don't know
20. where I stand or what I can do . . . um, ⌈after
21. B: ⌊and now you find
22. you can't get a job
23. A: no this is not actually the situation, ⌈I have not
24. B: ⌊oh

25. A: completely explained ⌈my position
26. B: ⌊yes yes
27. A: After um completing two um um terms of my probation ⌈teaching
28. B: ⌊huh huh
29. A: I had to apply somewhere else. I, there was a job in the borough,
30.   London borough of H., I applied and there that was first applica-
31.   tion which I made and I got the job, but since the beginning the
32.   teach–teaching situation was not suitable for a probationary
33.   teacher.

The initial question here calls for information about the subjects A has studied. Yet A responds first with an asynchronous "um" and then, following the amplification, "up till now," he gives a list of his degrees starting with his first degree. B's "so you have done some teaching" (10) focuses on "done" and is thus an indirect probe for more details on A's actual work experience. A's response to this probe is rhythmically premature and simply copies the last phrase of her remark. It almost sounds as if he were mimicking her, rather than responding to the question.

When interpreted in the light of what transpired later, A's next remarks (12–15) are intended to lead into a longer narrative. He starts by mentioning the first of several teaching posts he has held, a temporary appointment which lasted for two terms. However his contextualization practices create problems. Following the initial stressed sentence "I completed two terms," his voice drops and the tempo speeds up. Thus the key bit of information about the limited nature of this first appointment is appended to what to English ears must sound like a qualifying remark, which moreover starts with the word "unfortunately." The strategy recalls that of the Indian speaker in chapter 6 [of the original publication] (example (11)) who tends to lower his pitch before making the main point of his argument, and who thus finds himself continually interrupted by American participants.

In the present case B clearly does not respond to what is intended. Being familiar with personnel policies in British education, she knows that new graduates usually begin probationary appointments which last for three terms. Her asynchronous "oh" (14) and the subsequent response in (16) show that she assumes that A is talking about such a post and that something may have happened to cause his premature dismissal. Given A's prosody and his use of "unfortunately," her conclusion seems justified. When A continues with, "so that is uh my start was alright" (17), she interjects another surprised "oh." Viewed purely in terms of its propositional content, A's remark could count as a repair or a correction. What he is saying is that the teaching experience he has just referred to was satisfactory. But his choice of words and prosody again go counter to English speakers' expectations. Repairs and corrections imply that new or non-shared information is being introduced. Ordinarily this is conventionally marked by accent or rise in pitch and by lexicalized transitions such as "no" or "I mean." In the Western English system his initial "so that is . . ." implies that he thinks that what he is saying follows from his previous remarks. He seems to be inconsistent and more-over he is not responding to B's reply. This explains her second interjection.

In line 19 A continues once more with unmarked prosody, but after the initial phrase ending with "chaos" there is a short pause. This is followed by "I don't know where I stand or what I can do" spoken with contoured intonation similar to that found in case study 1 (lines 12–16). As was pointed out before, Indian English speakers interpret this type of contouring as a signal that what is to come is of great concern to the speaker. In other words A would seem to be saying: "now listen to what I have to say next, it's important." But when he is about to go on to his next point and starts with "after," B interrupts to continue her own line of reasoning with "and now you find you can't get a job."

Notice that the "can't" here can refer either to the addressee's qualifications or to outside circumstances which prevent the desired condition from coming about. A, having been interrupted and recognizing that he is not being listened to, seems to adopt the first interpretation. His reply "no this is not the actual situation" has the prosodic characteristics of his earlier phrase "Would it be enough introduction?" (case study 1, line 33) and suggests annoyance. He then goes on to insist on explaining his case in minute detail.

Line 29 marks the beginning of his narrative which lasts for more than half an hour. Throughout this period B makes regular attempts to get him to concentrate on what she thinks is the point of the interview: talk about the skills he has acquired, about his classroom experiences and about the kind of training he might still need to improve his skills. But the interaction is punctuated by long asides, misunderstandings of fact and misreadings of intent. A, on the other hand, finds he is not being listened to and not given a chance to explain his problem. Neither participant can control the interview. More importantly the fundamental differences in conceptions of what the interview is about that emerge from our discussion of case study 2 are never confronted.

The immediate consequences of this type of miscommunication are perhaps not too different from those in chapters 6 and 7 [of the original publication]. Moreover, even when participants have the same background, it is by no means uncommon for counselling interviews to end in mutual frustration. What is important about this case is not the misunderstanding as such but the fact that, in spite of repeated attempts, both speakers utterly fail in their efforts to negotiate a common frame in terms of which to decide on what is being focused on and where the argument is going at any one time. As one Indian English speaker put it in connection with a similar case study, "they're on parallel tracks which don't meet" (Gumperz & Roberts 1980).

The fact that two speakers whose sentences are quite grammatical can differ radically in their interpretation of each other's verbal strategies indicates that conversational management does rest on linguistic knowledge. But to find out what that knowledge is we must abandon the existing views of communication which draw a basic distinction between cultural or social knowledge on the one hand and linguistic signalling processes on the other. We cannot regard meaning as the output of nonlinear processing in which sounds are mapped into morphemes, clauses and sentences by application of the grammatical and semantic rules of sentence-level linguistic analysis, and look at social norms as extralinguistic forces which merely determine how and under what conditions such meaning units are used. Socio-cultural conventions affect all levels of speech production and interpretation from the abstract cultural logic that underlies all interpretation to the division of speech into episodes; from their categorization in terms of semantically relevant activities and interpretive frames, to the mapping of prosodic contours into syntactic strings and to selection among lexical and grammatical options. The failure to recognize this is another consequence of the fact that linguistic analysis has been sentence-based and influenced by the culture of literacy.

This view of social knowledge is implicit in modern theories of discourse. But work in this tradition has been limited by an unnecessarily diffuse view of extralinguistic knowledge as 'knowledge of the world,' and by its failure to account for the interactive nature of interpretive processes and the role of linguistic contextualization processes in retrieving information and in processing of verbal messages. We can avoid some of the ambiguities inherent in linguists' notions of meaning and intent by concentrating on what participants have to know in order to enter into a conversation and on the inferences they must make to maintain thematic progression. This is essentially what sociologists concerned with conversational analysis have begun to do. But in dealing with these problems we cannot assume that interpretive processes are shared. Only by looking at the whole range of linguistic phenomena that enter into conversational management can we understand what goes on in an interaction.

References

Bennett, A. F., Erickson, F. & Gumperz, J. J. 1976. Coordination of verbal and non-verbal cues in conversation. MS. (Report on Workshop at the University of California, Berkeley, January 1976.)

Bennett, A. 1981. Everybody's got rhythm. In *Aspects of Non-Verbal Communication*, ed. W. von Raffler-Engel & B. Hoffer. San Antonio, Texas: Trinity University Press.

Dumont, L. 1970. *Homo Hierarchicus*. London: Weidenfeld and Nicolson.

Erickson, F. & Schultz, J. J. (eds.) 1982. *The Counselor as Gatekeeper: social and cultural organization of communication in counselling interviews*. New York: Academic Press.

Gumperz, J. J. 1982. *Discourse Strategies*. Cambridge: Cambridge University Press.

Gumperz, J. J. & Roberts, C. 1980. Developing awareness skills for interethnic communication. In *Occasional Papers*, no. 12. Seameo Regional Language Center, Singapore.

4

Communication in a Multilingual Society: Some Missed Opportunities

Rajendra Singh, Jayant Lele, and Gita Martohardjono

You know as well as we know that what is just is arrived at in human arguments only when the necessity on both sides is equal, and that the powerful exact what they can, while the weak yield what they must. (Thucydides, Book V)

The multiplicity of cultures and ethnicities found in industrialized pluralist democracies creates what Singh (1983) refers to as "laboratory conditions" for studying abstract notions such as *the cultural specificity of language, the linguistic specificity of culture* (Sapir 1921; Winch 1958), and *the ideal speech situation* (Habermas 1979). The flowering of what Hymes (1962) calls the ethnography of speaking is, in other words, not an accident. This flowering, however, is accompanied by what Fishman (1977) refers to as the ethnic revolution in industrialized societies and has made the planning of multiethnicity an immediate and urgent issue, giving rise, as Mannheim (1956:119) would have predicted, to a body similar to the priests, the contemporary interethnic interactional sociolinguists.

This article critically examines contemporary interactional studies of the cultural specificity of human language conducted in modern, multiethnic, industrialized societies (e.g., Clyne 1979; Gumperz 1982a, 1982b; Valdés & Pino 1981). Although they provide empirical ways for studying the cultural specificity of language, they often [. . .] fail to see that their necessary detours through cultural contingencies provide what is probably the best window on undistorted communication (Habermas 1979). Their examination of distorted communication in the laboratory conditions of contact begins and ends with description of differences in what they refer to as discourse strategies (Gumperz 1982a, 1982b). Although these differences are presented within the context of a superficially charitable relativism, the explorations themselves are generally unidirectional (e.g., Gumperz 1982a, 1982b; Morris 1981). And those that attempt bidirectionality, such as Mishra (1982), Young (1982), Olshtain (1983), and Scarcella (1983), fail to reconcile the hypotheses they propose and the evidence they unearth.

Rajendra Singh, Jayant Lele, and Gita Martohardjono, extract from "Communication in a multilingual society: Some missed opportunities" in *Language in Society* 17:1 (March 1988), pp. 43–59. © by Cambridge University Press, reproduced with permission of the authors and publisher.

What is often presented as the "linguistic evidence" for miscommunication in multi-ethnic, industrialized societies is, even within the relativist framework, the locus of the violations of the cooperative principles of discourse (Grice 1975)[1] and human interaction, such as the Principle of Charity (Davidson 1974)[2] and the Principle of Humanity (Grandy 1973).[3] This evidence is very often vitiated by the fact, for which considerable empirical evidence exists, that the native speaker's repairability threshold depends crucially on nonlinguistic variables (Hackman 1977). Only a cross-cultural analysis of how or whether these misconstruals entail analogous consequences, regardless of who is being misunderstood by whom, can produce the sort of evidence these studies claim to uncover.

Although we do not wish to deny that discourse strategies can and do vary from one language to another, we shall argue that miscommunications and misconstruals of the sort documented in the studies in question result in no small measure from institutionally encouraged suspension of the universal principles of discourse that *can*, if allowed to, override the culturally imposed contingencies of interpretation. As these principles are practiced at liberating moments and suspended at hegemonic ones, their status at a given time and a given place is, as Hymes (personal communication) puts it, "an especially revealing way to understand communication within any community as well as between communities." Their status in a society at a given time is, in other words, not only a key to understanding its ways of speaking but also its modes of being.

Most of these studies overtly accept the claims of the dominant ideas – ideology of the ruling classes – as true (subject to minor modifications at best) in their desire to "help" the ethnics to cope with situations of dominance and even to help them become capable in sharing that dominance by becoming successful. The real crux of the problem and also a potentially fruitful line of inquiry is the resistance that the ethnics offer against such attempts and associated threats and rewards for assimilation. Gumperz, for example, speaks in favour of "flexibility," but he does not realize that those with flexibility have a cultural identity, the crucial ingredients of which are ego-focality and domination, that is historically developed and distinct. It is these ingredients that allow the speakers of South African English, for example, to expect Zulu-English speakers to use *powerless* language and to label them as "unreliable" or "fickle" when they don't (Chick 1985:314). It is very different from the identity of those who resist assimilation. Even the most ardent modernization theorists know that. Resistance by ethnics, in the face of such dire consequences as being thrown out of jobs, has to be understood in light of the human sense for the joyfulness of speech. Their resistance to the demands of joyless formalisms of bureaucratic societies expresses itself even in a language such as English.

For most interactional sociolinguists, the notion of new ethnicity is heavily loaded with the prejudices of modern day instrumentalism. These are to be seen in the normal, day-to-day behaviour of the elites of the so-called pluralist democracies (Lele 1981b). For them ethnicity is meaningful only when it manifests itself as "interest-group" activity. Thus, for Gumperz, "new ethnicity" is a strategy of getting things done. The mode of thinking involved here is "modern" – that is, unidimensional in the sense of Marcuse.

Interethnic interactional sociolinguistics of the type adovcated by, amongst others, Graham (1980), Gumperz (1982a, 1982b), Gumperz and Tannen (1979), Scarcella (1983), and Scollon and Scollon (1980), moves in the Parsonian world of dichotomous decisionisms: of pattern variables of tradition and modernity (Lele 1981a, 1984). It fails to see that industrial bureaucratic societies, having transcended the old contradictions, are now mired in some new ones and that out of those transcendence can come not by preaching flexibility to the ethnics, but perhaps only out of their resistance to hegemony, the all-encompassing hegemony of capital. It also misunderstands the neo-Marxian insight that, in contemporary capitalism, knowledge is as much a property relation as is the traditional control of the material means of production. A critical sociological sense for that relationship requires, minimally, a full understanding of the Habermasian (1968) claim that science and technology are the modern day ideology of industrial capitalism. Without it, interethnic sociolinguistics is in danger of merely using the new significance of communication to peddle its handbooks for flexible adaptation to the demands of new capital.

The contemporary interethnic interactionists examine stretches of discourse between bi- or multilingual speakers in an attempt to isolate those features of conversational inference which, according to them, make "for cultural, subcultural and situational specificity of interpretation" (Gumperz 1982a:3). Insight into such culturally specific inferences should, they suggest, help us understand the nature of misunderstanding in human society, particularly in advanced, industrialized societies. The issue being investigated by them is how ethnicity and different cultural background determine speakers' linguistic and discourse strategies and how these differences account for communicational asynchrony.[4]

If we are to judge the application of contemporary interactionist theory by the way it handles specific cases of interethnic miscommunications, it looks very gloomy indeed for the unprivileged. Given the interactionists' premises, it is not surprising to find, for example, that Gumperz's answers to the well-known problem of interracial urban living avoid such fundamental questions as institutional racism and the effect it has on individual behaviour and perception. Consider, for example, his treatment of the case dealing with the "problem" of a group of Indian and Pakistani cafeteria workers in Britain. Although it is immediately clear to the reader that the problem at hand is not one of communication on the part of workers but rather one of perception on the part of the supervisors and clients, Gumperz sidesteps the question of prejudice. He suggests that the victims of misperception should, like he has taught the cafeteria workers to do, acquire "a strategy for self-diagnosis of communication difficulties" (1982a:147). This "strategy," besides bestowing upon those who master it the "confidence in their own innate abilities to learn" (ibid.), seems to have the added advantage of saving the energies of those whose tacit task it is to assimilate.

It is quite evident that rhetorical differences do exist across languages and that they can further be analyzed to be of a certain nature (e.g., syntactic, prosodic, or structuro-thematic), but it is not evident that these differences are the cause of misunderstanding and the resulting friction among ethnic groups as most interactionists would have us believe. Nor is it clear that they constitute the locus of misunderstanding, although they, of course, constitute the locus of the linguistic evidence available for that misunderstanding. In order to establish such a causal relationship, it is simply not sufficient to investigate how certain types of English are prone to misperception. What is needed, even under the terms of liberal relativism, is a cross-cultural study of contextualization conventions of various languages.

Only a cross-cultural analysis of (mis)interpretations by native hearers of nonnative speakers and nonnative hearers of native speakers, and, most importantly, of how or whether these misperceptions entail the same sort of consequences, regardless of who is being misunderstood by whom, can help us understand what is involved. It is obvious that all differences do not cross the native speaker's threshold of repairability and that the Principles of Charity and of Humanity are applied or suspended according to the nonlinguistic parameters of power, hegemony, and domination. It is difficult to believe that the sociolinguists under consideration are not aware of the parameters that enter into the intelligibility of, say, Quebec French, Faroese, or Hindi and Urdu (Singh 1985c). All of their interethnic data focus on minority speakers "misunderstood" by majority hearers, and, typically, they do not mention this imbalance.

Contradictions abound in contemporary interethnic interactional sociolinguistics. [. . .] Consider, for example, what Gumperz and Cook-Gumperz (1982) refer to as the "linguistic analysis" of a West Indian social worker's request for increased funding or Mishra's (1982), Young's (1982), and Scarcella's (1983) attempts to save the Erikson–Graham–Gumperz hypothesis. Had it not been for the intervention of the other committee members, the Gumperzes suggest, the West Indian social worker would have failed for not using standard English discourse strategies. They submit the conversational data to two sets of judges, of West Indian and British background respectively, and conclude that the different interpretations hinge upon ethnic style. On the other hand, they point to the speech of two other committee members, also typically West Indian, but easily "interpretable for the funding officer." "The explanation," they are forced to admit, "must be a more complicated one than the clash of two different styles in rhetoric" (Gumperz & Cook-Gumperz 1982:149). This, however, does not stop them from implying that the fault lies with the social worker himself, who, unlike his more agile compatriots, does not master the efficient rhetoric of "committee talk," of primordial importance to anyone who wants to be understood in committee meetings.

Through such "analysis" the authors end up qualifying the West Indian speaker's style of self-correction as "odd and rude" sounding (ibid.: 159). The officer's speech, on the other hand, shows how in the "English system" "self-corrections carry a fall rise and . . . are . . . lower in pitch and less loud" (ibid.). In fact, the fallacy here is twofold: (1) in informal English speech (which is after all, the most common), self-correction *can* feature rise as well as high pitch. Consider, for example, the emphatic highlighting in a sentence such as

I had only 3, ⌐Í méan 2́ drinks.

(2) The rather contrived style of the funding officer can hardly be said to be representative of the "English system," unless we are to believe that all or most native speakers of English sound like members of a committee perennially in full session.

Finally, the fact that another native speaker of English on the committee had no trouble interpreting the intentions of the West Indian speaker, and even states that "he has made [himself] very clear" leads one to conclude that either (1) the funding officer lacks, either as an individual or as a member of a power structure, cognitive faculties, available to other native speakers of English, or (2) the analysis of the interaction based exclusively on linguistic and paralinguistic factors is wrong, and other factors caused the officer to doubt the urgency of the social worker's request.

Mishra's (1982) study of the differences between the discourse style of a South Asian speaker of English and that of a standard British English speaker contrasts the former's use of prosody against the latter's use of syntactic signals to indicate a referent. Following the hypothesis proposed by Gumperz (1982a), Mishra suggests that a careful study of such differences will lead to a better understanding of interethnic communication problems. In the case at hand, the speaker of South Asian English had lost his job on three different occasions, and by implying that by correcting his faulty use of prosody he can prevent such unfortunate incidents, Mishra undermines her own assumption that, a priori, "there are no compelling criteria to accept or reject [the South Asian speaker's] account as incoherent" (60), as well as the fact that if not amongst speakers of different languages, surely amongst speakers of different varieties of the same language there exists the potential of mutual charitable interpretation.

In a discussion of the differences underlying Chinese and English discourse (topic-comment vs. subject-predicate) Young (1982:83) also acknowledges this potential. To the fact that Chinese speakers of English are sometimes characterized by their English interlocutors as "imprecise, unwieldy, and downright inept," she points out that this is but the "callous" interpretation, and that the "charitable" one would see the Chinese style as emphasizing "cooperation, prudence, and clearheaded caution" (81). She even comes close to the bidirectionality so sorely lacking in these studies when she cites a Chinese speaker's impression of the "American style" of speech:

> I don't find the American Style, where the topic sentence appears first, to be effective. It's not necessarily more persuasive nor convincing than the Chinese Style, where the speaker, at the same time as he is speaking, is reasoning with the listener to see whether what he says makes sense or not. This Chinese speech style is more open-minded, less biased, not constrictive as is the American style, where it immediately sets you up to a particular frame of mind. You see, with the American style, you can react immediately to what the speaker says without listening to the rest of his explanation. (82)

In the final analysis, however, she does not do her own hypothesis of mutual charitability justice, for she fails to ask why, although two interpretations exist, one seems to be more prevalent. Instead, she offers us the standard sociolinguist's phrase that the tension in intercultural contact is "not only just [sic] a product of resource competition and power relations; it can also stem from failures in the communicative process" (83).

Scarcella's (1983) study investigates two hypotheses. The first, proposed by Erikson, Graham, Gumperz, and Tannen, postulates that interethnic conversations are fraught with more difficulties than are conversations between speakers sharing the same ethnic background. This is further hypothesized to be so due to differential usage of conversational features. Her results show, however, that such conversational difficulties were not found throughout interethnic conversations. "Rather, they only seemed to appear in situations in which participants lacked shared background knowledge" (310). The hypothesis that most abrupt topic shifts (which are taken as signalling communication difficulties) are specific to interethnic communication is not completely borne out either. She found that more generally, abrupt topic shifts were characteristic of conversations between people who had little in common, whether of differing backgrounds or not. She did, of course, find differences in the number of interruptions during interethnic conversations and English-only conversations.

The second hypothesis she tests is that even proficient second language speakers of English have what she calls a "discourse accent," that is, they use conversational features such as topic introduction, backchannel cues (*uhuh*, *right*, etc.), and pause fillers in the way they are used in the speaker's native language rather than in the target language. The weak statistical support she is able to come up with in favour of her hypothesis regarding the use of backchannel cues and pause fillers is more than undermined by the fact that she finds that for topic selection the ethnic speakers in her experiments avoided topics that – although expected to come up in their own conversations (family, etc.) – are considered too intimate in English conversations. Finally, in a list of "disclaimers," Scarcella herself raises several points well worth noting: (1) use of conversational features may not vary with one's ethnicity, but with one's personality, (2) her own sociocultural background may have tinged her interpretation and she suggests that Chicano researchers should undertake the same type of studies in order to counterbalance any possible biases, and (3) situational variables such as sex, status, and familiarity should be investigated. While we admire the integrity that informs the academic honesty of these disclaimers, we find her decision to stop there unfortunate. It does, however, reveal precisely what some of the paradoxes and contradictions of the enterprise under scrutiny are.

What is needed, minimally, is serious bidirectional investigation of each such case. Such bidirectional studies help expose the ignorance through which such miscontruals arise by underlining the unity that allows one to transcend that ignorance. Consider, for example, Singh's (1985a, 1985b) analysis of denials in Hindi and English. He notes that the major difference between Hindi and English is that whereas in Hindi the burden of denial is assumed by a statement about the world, in English it is assumed by what appears to be a statement of personal responsibility. The obligatory nature of the statement about the world or about the self, however, requires that it not be subjected to validation or assigned truth–value precisely because it is a structurally required step in these networks. The contrast can be seen in the examples below (from Singh 1985a: 84–5).

(1) English   A: Could you stay for lunch?
               B: I'd love to but I can't.
(2) Hindi   A: *Kya men apki saIkII le lun*
                   Q I   your bicycle take
                   Could I borrow your bicycle?
               B: *De to deta   par mujhe bazar jana hei*
                   give of course but I   market go   have
                   I would have of course given it to you but I
                   have to go to the market.

It is important to note that B in (2) did not, in fact, have to go to the market any more than B in (1) loved the invitation. The latter had a date that he had been looking forward to for weeks and the former was planning to enjoy a game of bridge.

Initially, Singh argues, one could say something like the following: Hindi speakers feel that responsibility-assuming statements are neither appropriate nor enough and insist on something like what they provide because it supplies what they believe to be an objective reason or what Olshtain calls an explanation. The catch, to put it in relativistic terms, is that within the culture one is not allowed to subject these reasons or accounts to truth verification and just about anything would do.

An inability to see the obligatory Hindi step as a predictable part of conventionalized verbal routines may lead speakers of a language like English to accuse Hindi speakers of lying when the world is not the way the relevant assertion says it is. The absence of a statement about the world in the English denial may lead Hindi speakers to think that English speakers are not only morally irresponsible but also blunt. In the final analysis, however, both must be seen as the same thing: "I'd love to" is, after all, only short-hand for "I am ready to, if the world were somewhat different."

It is quite easy to see that these differences in verbal strategies provide convenient pegs on which to hang prejudicial hats. Such misinterpretations can themselves be institutionalized and we submit that any unidirectional study is a step in the direction of the legitimization of such an institutionalization. Consider the case of the verbal expression of gratitude in South Asian languages and in English (Apte 1974). The constraints on verbalization of gratitude in the former are perhaps motivated by the assumption that "verbalizing one's gratitude is a cheap way of getting out of obligations" (82). English, on the other hand, uses expressions like *thank you* rather profusely. This difference leads to comments such as "I have never understood why Indians don't ever bother to thank any one" from native speakers of English and "They don't mean anything when they say 'thank you'. It's like their saying 'it's interesting'" from native speakers of South Asian languages (Singh 1983). The accusation of impoliteness ignores the nonverbal ways in which Hindi speakers habitually express their gratitude. By focusing on the absence of what they ritually indulge in, English speakers forget that even their own language acknowledges the virtue of silence, the counterpoint of speech.

If contemporary interethnic interactionists want to be taken as interactional sociolinguists and not as apologists for the system, they must look at power structure as an independent variable. They cannot, in other words, legitimately ignore the ways in which their immediate contexts are embedded in more inclusive social and institutional contexts (cf. Chick 1985; Dore & McDermott 1982). The fact that the construals of the dominated minority are almost entirely left out of their accounts suggests quite strongly that they are not only tolerant of the expectations of the powerful but also willing to oblige them by justifying them with what they call linguistic evidence. If, for example, the non-Westerners Gumperz et al. get their data from for the "analyses" presented in Gumperz (1982b) do in fact speak an independent variety of English, as Gumperz maintains, the problem is not misunderstanding but misperception that arises from an institutional suspension of general conventions of communicative cooperation. If they don't, the observations contained in the book derive from the rather trivial fact that these people originally learnt the language in a different social context.[5]

We are not suggesting that there is a conspiracy, but simply that the relevant institutional framework discourages the use of universally available principles of human decency, including decency in communication which requires, even on the relativist interpretation, that we attribute the same rationality to our interlocutor that we would attribute to ourselves. The problem with the literature we have reviewed is not that the dominant speakers don't apply the Principle of Charity and the Principle of Humanity – given this time and this place, we almost expect them not to – but that the interactionists don't apply them in analyzing their data.

Consider, for example, the case study reported in Varonis and Gass (1985). In analyzing a misoriented conversation between an English-speaking TV repair service person

(NS = Native Speaker) and a nonnative speaker of English (NNS) who had called the former to inquire about the price of a new TV, they give the native all the credit she deserves and none to the nonnative caller. The conversation begins in the following way:

NS: Hello
NNS: Hello. Could you tell me the price and size of Sylvania color TV?
NS: Pardon?
NNS: Could you tell me the price and size of Sylvania TV. . . . Color?
NS: What did you want? A service call?

The problem is that the NNS has called a repair shop in order to inquire about the price of a new Sylvania TV. The NS begins working her way through the discourse with the assumption that what is involved is either an estimate or a service call. Roughly halfway through the conversation, the NNS reasserts his goal and makes it absolutely clear that he "wan' buy one please." The NS misinterprets his response. Slightly modifying her initial assumption, she now believes, according to Varonis and Gass, that the NNS is trying to sell a TV to her store! When the NNS wants to know its size, she does not revise her mistaken hypothesis but comes out with what the investigators themselves describe as a "put off." The conversation continues for another few lines and terminates with a rather unexpected announcement from the NS that she has "a seventeen inch new RCA" for sale and an equally unexpected "opt out" from the NNS: "OK. Thank you. Bye."

The analysis Varonis and Gass provide of the episode reported above is, despite its apparent charitability, clearly biased in favour of the NS. That their sympathies are with the NS is borne out by the fact that whereas they compliment her for her "extreme cooperation," they have very little to say about the fact that the three transparent statements by the NNS regarding his goal are uncharitably lost in the presuppositions of the NS. What they do say regarding his statement "Yeah, I wan' buy one please" is instructive: "However, she misinterprets his response. Again, accepting what Carlos [the NNS] said would involve a major change of beliefs and resulting change in goals" (339). And this on behalf of the NS who has been liberally complimented for having undergone the ordeal of changing her discourse goals five times (340)!

As far as the NNS's mistake of calling a TV repair shop is concerned, it is useful to remind the reader that the repair shop did in fact have a new RCA for sale! Varonis and Gass seem to reprimand the NNS for choosing to opt out by offering a closing "just when they could actually proceed to the fulfilment of his first and only goal" (as opposed to just one out of five goals the poor NS has had to abandon en route). There is no reason not to interpret the NNS's "closing" as a "put off," albeit an extremely polite one compared to the one used earlier by the NS: "Well I'd – you know the only thing I can tell you to do is you'd have to come to the shop, I'm on the extension at home. The shop's closed" (339). One of the things she could have told our NNS at at least three distinct points in the discourse was that it would perhaps be better for him to call the TV section of a department store! The cooperation, civility, and politeness with which the NNS not only terminates the discourse but with which he carries it forward before he does is so transparent that the reasons for which it escapes our investigators must be very deeply imbedded in one of the "variety of social and linguistic factors" they speak of (341).[6] Our intention in pointing this out is to highlight why the less than efficient comprehension abilities of our NS escape attention and not to gloss over the fact that our NNS's language skills are, as our investigators put it, "deficient" (338).

Our interactional sociolinguists ought to know that in cross-cultural studies "the student must feel he or she is answerable to and in uncoercive contact with the culture or people being studied" (Said 1981:155), that their data must be as distortion-free as possible – free both of observer's influence and, generally, of the "distorting effects of power" (Lukes 1982:305) – and that they must be maximally aware of their inter-pretive situation without supposing that they can escape it (Weber 1930:47ff.).

There is no cognitive interaction in this interactional sociolinguistics; there is only the opportunity for the ethnics to correct themselves. There is virtually no linguistics in interactional sociolinguistics that is of any importance to the grammarian, though it contains some data that must someday be accounted for in a theory of discourse. Interactional sociolinguistics' sociology is anecdotal and superficial, since it makes no serious effort to see through what Berger (1963:31) calls "the facades of social struc-tures," and its politics are alarmingly close to the politics of complete integration. We wonder if our interactionists are too willing to accept that misunderstanding is caused by the misunderstood, poverty by the poor, misery by the miserable, and social handi-cap by the socially handicapped.

If interethnic interactional sociolinguistics wants to explicate the nature of commun-ication in the industrialized world, it must not ignore the distortions introduced by power. It must, in other words, systematically and empirically identify the linguistic and the political, and that cannot be achieved by merely glossing over the latter.[7] It must, we submit, learn to locate the sources of misunderstanding not only in the occasional lapses of the foreigner but also in the systematic distortions introduced by the institutionally encouraged, if not constrained, interpretive schema of the native. It is not enough to pay lip service in a footnote, as Jupp, Roberts, and Cook-Gumperz (1982) do, to the training of the dominant group. The innate human ability to learn that Gumperz appeals to belongs not only to the ethnic but also to the nonethnic. He assumes that the dominant have nothing to learn, only something to teach. The kind of integration and assimilation he advocates is, as Adorno (1981) points out, disintegration (see also Yalden [1981] for a defense of diversity).

Our claim that the contemporary interethnic interactional enterprise is merely the standard theory of transfer at the discourse level in an interactionist garb is further borne out by the fact that the patterns that our interactionists take as their *point de départ* do not, as they should after their excursus, stand out as strange, remarkable, and demanding of explanation (see Horton 1982; Lévi-Strauss 1955). The relevant litera-ture, unfortunately, shows precisely how uncritical those who do not make the return journey to re-examine the place they left can be. It conveys the shock and the pride of ethnocentrism but not the joy and the excitement which are supposed to accompany such explorations (see Berger 1963:23).

In an age where most social scientists are trying to cope with what Douglas (1973) calls "our cognitive precariousness," the research in question provides a confirmation of Nietzsche's (1873) insight of more than a hundred years ago that ethnocentrism is typically rationalized and made the basis of detrimental programmes of action. It is almost a prime example of bureaucratic discpline, which, according to Weber (1968:1149), is nothing but the consistently rationalized, methodically prepared, and exact execution of the received order, in which all personal criticism is unconditionally suspended.

Although we have suggested that to understand the nature of what is involved, we need, minimally, to undertake bidirectional studies of cross-cultural communication, we must also point out that while bidirectional studies will perhaps open the eyes of those who consider only their way of doing things appropriate, and thus find only one way studies to be useful for coping with the ethnicity "problem," they will not necessarily produce the kind of self-reflection about the very instrumentality of all of our socio-linguists' chosen situations of discourse. The notion of "discourse strategies" is itself fraught with an instrumental understanding (unidimensional) of speech acts. American business people, whose repairability threshold can be shown to increase in proportion to the wealth of the Arab sheiks they deal with, will, no doubt, be described as clever, flexible, and even "modern." Resistant ethnics, on the other hand, have already been condemned, indirectly, as stupid for not knowing what is good for them.

To be meaningful, interactional studies must be guided by a theory that understands communication not as understanding, in a static way, but as a creation of new understanding (meaning) that transcends and hence potentially/actually involves immediate and perhaps intuitive self-reflection on the speaker's cultural context, out of which the process of communication was first initiated. Involved here, in the final analysis, is neither the Principle of Charity nor that of Humanity (they may serve as good first approximations), as given by Davidson (1974) and Grandy (1973). Both of them are expressions of self-righteous monadism (treat the other as a person like you; that way you will never find out how awful you are even though he or she may in fact be an angel) and are not therefore capable of self-reflection.

A true interactional sociolinguistics cannot afford to ignore these considerations, and in order to provide a reasonable account of them, it must ask and attempt to answer questions of the following sort:

(1) What unites the native speakers of a language across the boundaries of internal social differentiation, for example, caste, religion, class, and history or education (both actually and potentially or, in other words, hegemonically and in freedom)?

(2) What divides the native speakers of one language from those of others in spite of the actual and potential bonds of class and other commonalities?

[...]

Notes

An earlier version of this paper was presented at the Seventh World Congress of Applied Linguistics, Brussels, August 6–10, 1984. Work on it was supported by a research grant to Singh from the Multiculturalism Program of the Government of Canada. The Minister of State of Multiculturalism and the Multiculturalism Directorate disclaim any responsibility – in whole as in part – for the views and opinions expressed and for the completeness or accuracy of information included in this paper.

We are grateful to Chi Hang Chung and Michael Leong for assistance beyond the call of duty. We are also grateful to M. Ahmad, J. Connolley, J. Reighard, S. R. Sharma, and U. N. Tiwari for asking some very pertinent questions. We have also benefited from the comments, made in another context, of an anonymous reviewer for *Language in Society* and to Nessa Wolfson for some very insightful comments and for drawing our attention to some important work that had escaped our attention. Last, but not least, we are grateful to Dell Hymes for his willingness to listen when there was, perhaps, reason to suspect. This paper is related to Singh and Martohardjono (1985a, 1985b).

1   Although Gricean principles of communicative cooperation perhaps err in the direction of, as Hymes (personal communication) puts it, imputing to other languages and cultures values and beliefs that may not be their own, they can be easily relativized, should such relativization be needed, to particular ways of speaking and of life. The extent to which predicates like "relevant" characterize dimensions to which speaking is oriented in ways in keeping with specific ways of life, the generality of these principles can be saved from the danger of ethnocentricity. Part of the problem here is almost terminological: "relevant" after all is an English predicate. It would perhaps be better to use mnemonic, metalinguistic terms, such as RELEV, and have them realized as local terms for whatever dimensions turn out to be consonant with specific ways of life. The point here, however, is that these principles cannot be dismissed in the cavalier fashion in which some interactionists attempt to dismiss them (cf. n. 6).

2   Davidson formulates it thus: "the basic strategy must be to assume that by and large a speaker we do not yet understand is consistent and correct in his beliefs – according to our own standards, of course" (238). It advises people to count other people right in most matters (cf. Lukes 1982:264).

3   Grandy's Principle of Humanity is "the condition that the imprinted pattern of relations among beliefs, desires and the world be as similar to our own as possible" (1973:445). It prescribes "the minimizing of unintelligibility [and] counsels 'Count them, intelligible or perhaps count them right, unless we can't explain their being right or can better explain their being wrong'" (Lukes 1982:264).

4   It is interesting to note that all such studies deal with speakers that come from "low prestige" backgrounds. Although the linguistic backgrounds investigated range from Apache (Bartelt 1983) to Zulu (Chick 1985), they all have "low prestige." We wonder why intercultural encounters involving, for instance, Swedish or German speakers of English have not been studied. That these speakers are not seen as contributing to the "ethnicity problem" may be a good reason for excluding them from studies devoted to that problem but not from excluding them from studies allegedly designed to investigate the influence of linguistic background on communicational asynchrony. Such studies will, we believe, allow us to separate the linguistic from the nonlinguistic factors that throw discourse harmony out of gear. We shall, however, content ourselves with what is available in the relevant literature.

5   See Gadamer (1975:347): "The hermeneutic problem is not therefore a problem of the correct mastery of a language . . . Such mastery . . . is a precondition for understanding in dialogue." The fact that native speakers of standard Western English see the communicative innovations to meet the needs of a different social context as fossilization of imperfect learning is a reflection on their institutionally encouraged inability to hear. They exhibit, predictably, the same insensitivity towards nonstandard varieties of natively spoken English. The center, in other words, is quite adept at keeping what it sees as the periphery at a respectable distance. Despite its "liberal" overtures to South-Asian and other instituionalized nonnative varieties in their native contexts, it predictably says *No* to them in their transplanted contexts.

6   It is these factors that allow Varonis and Gass to cast doubts on Grice's principles of cooperation. Their rider regarding Grice must be understood as the powerful insisting that the powerless cooperate on the terms of the former. Should they decide to treat the latter as what Chick calls "doormats," the latter's linguistic behaviour must satisfy their expectations. This can hardly be referred to as cooperation in the Gricean sense. The distortion does, however, provide an indication of what it would be were it not for power-induced pathologies. Grice justifiably presupposes what McCarthy (1978:325) refers to as "an effective equality of chances to assume dialogue roles."

7   Such glosses abound in the literature. Consider, for example, the sole concession Gumperz (1982a) makes to the nonlinguistic aspects of miscommunication: "not all problems of inter-ethnic contact are communicative in nature. Economic factors, differences in goals and aspirations as well as other historical and cultural factors may be at issue" (210). Or, what we consider to be a gloss par

excellence: "Native and non-native speakers of English in conversations with one another may be pre-disposed to breakdowns in communication" (Varonis & Gass 1985:341). The conditions that lead to such a predisposition are, we submit, very much at issue (pace Gumperz).

References

Adorno, T. W. (1981). *Prisms*. Cambridge, Mass.: MIT Press.

Apte, M. (1974). "Thank you" and South Asian languages: A comparative sociolinguistic study. *International Journal of the Sociology of Language* 3:67–89.

Bartelt, H. G. (1983). Transfer and variability of rhetorical redundancy in Apachean English interlanguage. In Gass & Selinker (1983):297–305.

Berger, P. L. (1963). *Invitation to sociology*. New York: Anchor.

Chick, J. K. (1985). The interactional accomplishment of discrimination in South Africa. *Language in Society* 14: 299–326.

Clyne, M. G. (1979). Communicative competence in contact. *Review of Applied Linguistics* 41:17–38.

Davidson, D. ([1974] 1982). Psychology as philosophy. Reprinted in D. Davidson, *Essays on actions and events*. Oxford: Clarendon.

Dore, J., & McDermott, R. P. (1982). Linguistic indeterminacy and social context in utterance interpretation. *Language* 58:374–98.

Douglas, M. (ed.) (1973). *Rules and meaning: The anthropology of everyday knowledge*. Harmondsworth, Middlesex: Penguin.

Duncan, G., & Lukes, S. (1963). The new democracy. *Political Studies* 11(2):156–77.

Erikson, E. H. (1963). *Childhood and society*. New York: Norton.

Fishman, J. (1977). Language and ethnicity. In H. Giles et al. (eds.), *Language, ethnicity, and intergroup relations*. New York: Academic.

Gadamer, H. G. (1975). *Truth and method*. New York: Crossroad.

Gass, S. M., & Selinker, L. (eds.) (1983). *Language transfer in language learning*. Rowley, Mass.: Newbury House.

Graham, J. (1980). Cross-cultural negotiation. PhD dissertation, University of California, Berkeley.

Grandy, R. (1973). Reference, meaning, and belief. *Journal of Philosophy* 70:439–52.

Grice, H. P. (1975). Logic and conversation. In P. Cole & J. L. Morgan (eds.), *Syntax and semantics, vol. 3: Speech acts*. New York: Academic. 41–58.

Gumperz, J. (1982a). *Discourse strategies*. Cambridge: Cambridge University Press.

Gumperz, J. (1982b). *Language and social identity*. Cambridge: Cambridge University Press.

Gumperz, J., & Cook-Gumperz, J. (1982). Interethnic communication in committee negotiations. In Gumperz (1982b). 145–62.

Gumperz, J., & Tannen, D. (1979). Individual and social differences in language use. In C. Fillmore, D. Kemplar, & W. S. Wand (eds.), *Individual differences in language ability and language behavior*. New York: Academic.

Habermas, J. (1968). *Toward a rational society*. Boston: Beacon Press.

Habermas, J. (1979). *Communication and the evolution of society*. Trans. by T. McCarthy. Boston: Beacon Press.

Hackman, D. J. (1977). Patterns in purported speech acts. *Journal of Pragmatics* 1:143–54.

Hollis, M., & Lukes, S. (eds.) (1982). *Rationality and relativism*. Cambridge, Mass.: MIT Press.

Horton, R. (1982). Tradition and modernity revisited. In Hollis & Lukes (1982). 201–60.

Hymes, D. (1962). The ethnography of speaking. In T. Gladwin & W. C. Sturtevant (eds.), *Anthropology and human behavior*. Washington, DC: Anthropological Society of Washington. 15–53.

Joshi, L. (1981). Anandamimansa. In *Lekhasangraha*, vol. I. Pune: Srividya Prakashan. 437–69.

Jupp, T. C., Roberts, C., & Cook-Gumperz, J. (1982). Language and disadvantage: The hidden process. In Gumperz (1982b). 232–56.

Lele, J. K. (1981a). *Tradition and modernity in Bhakti movements*. Leiden: Brill.

Lele, J. K. (1981b). *Elite pluralism and class rule*. Toronto: Toronto University Press.

Lele, J. K. (1984). Dnyaneshwar and Tukaram: An exercise in hermeneutics. Paper presented at the First International Conference on Maharashtra: Culture and Society. Toronto, March 18–20.

Lele, J. K., & Singh, R. (1987). The politics of nutrition and food symbolism. A plea for the discourse of the unprivileged. In *Language and society: Steps towards on integrated theory*. Leiden: E. J. Brill.

Lévi-Strauss, C. (1955). *Tristes tropiques*. Paris: Plon.

Lukes, S. (1982). Relativism in its place. In Hollis & Lukes (1982). 261–305.

Mannheim, K. (1956). *Essay on the sociology of culture*. London: Routledge & Kegan Paul.

McCarthy, T. (1978). *The critical theory of Jurgen Habermas*. Cambridge, Mass.: MIT Press.

Mishra, A. (1982). Discovering connections. In Gumperz (1982b). 57–71.

Morris, M. (1981). *Saying and meaning in Puerto Rico*. New York: Pergamon.

Nietzsche, F. (1873). On truth and lie in an extra-moral sense. In W. Kaufman (ed.), *The portable Nietzsche*. New York: Viking. 42–7.

Olshtain, E. (1983). Sociocultural competence and language transfer: The case of apology. In Gass & Selinker (1983). 232–49.

Said, E. W. (1981). *Covering Islam: How the media and the experts determine how we see the rest of the world*. London: Routledge & Kegan Paul.

Sapir, E. (1921). *Language*. New York: Harcourt Brace.

Scarcella, R. C. (1983). Discourse accent in second language performance. In Gass & Selinker (1983). 306–26.

Scollon, R., & Scollon, S. (1980). *Linguistic convergence: An ethnography of speaking at Fort Chipewyan, Alberta*. New York: Academic.

Singh, R. (1983). Explorations in the ethnography of discourse. In S. Pendakur (ed.), *The proceedings of the 1983 CASA conference*. Vancouver: University of British Columbia. 35–41.

Singh, R. (1985a). On denying a reasonable request in Hindi. *Review of Applied Linguistics* 66:79–89.

Singh, R. (1985b). Andaze bayan. *Hindi Samvad* 3(1):14–15.

Singh, R. (1985c). Modern Hindustani and formal and social aspects of language contact. *Review of Applied Linguistics* 70.

Singh, R., & Martohardjono, G. (1985a). Review of Gumperz, *Discourse strategies*. *Journal of Multicultural and Multilingual Development* 6(2):193–9.

Singh, R., & Martohardjono, G. (1985b). Review of Gumperz, *Language and social identity*. *The Canadian Journal of Linguistics* Spring: 218–25.

Valdés, G., & Pino, C. (1981). *Muy a tus órdenes*: Compliment responses among Mexican-American bilinguals. *Language in Society* 10:53–72.

Varonis, E. M., & Gass, S. (1985). Miscommunication in native/nonnative conversation. *Language in Society* 14:327–43.

Weber, M. (1930). *The Protestant ethic and the spirit of capitalism*. Trans. by T. Parsons. London: Allen and Unwin.

Weber, M. (1968). *Economy and society*. Ed. by G. Roth & C. Wittich. New York: Bedminster.

Winch, P. (1958). *The idea of a social science and its relation to philosophy*. London: Routledge & Kegan Paul.

Yalden, M. (1981). The bilingual experience in Canada. In M. Ridge (ed.), *The new bilingualism*. Los Angeles: University of Southern California Press. 71–87.

Young, L. W. L. (1982). Inscrutability revisited. In Gumperz (1982b). 72–84.

5

Linguistic Etiquette

Gabriele Kasper

The label *linguistic etiquette* refers to the practice in any speech community of organizing linguistic action so that it is seen as appropriate to the current communicative event. The scope of phenomena assembled under this label is thus much broader than what is suggested by the dictionary definition of *etiquette,* which restricts the term to denote "the formal rules of proper behaviour" (*Longman Dictionary of Contemporary English,* 1978: 373). Etiquette manuals from Erasmus of Rotterdam's *De civilitate morum puerilium* (1530) to the latest edition of *The Amy Vanderbilt Complete Book of Etiquette* (Vanderbilt and Baldridge, 1978) do not cover verbal routines such as the "rules for ritual insult" enacted among inner city African-American adolescents (Labov, 1972), yet they fall under the proposed definition. A related and more widely used term, *(linguistic) politeness,* is equally problematic because of its connotation of "deference" and "refined" behavior (e.g., Green, 1992a). For lack of preferable alternatives, both terms will be used interchangeably.

5.1 The "Phenomenon"

The somewhat nebulous definition proposed initially is indicative of much disagreement about the theoretical status and scope of linguistic etiquette. For most authors, politeness is a feature of language *use* (cf. the subtitle of Brown and Levinson's *Politeness: Some universals in language usage*). The action-theoretical view of politeness shared by Brown and Levinson (1978, 1987) and Leech (1983) firmly places linguistic etiquette in the arena of language use. Yet the same authors classify decontextualized speech acts as inherently polite or impolite. Fraser (1990: 233), commenting that the politeness of linguistic acts is determined by their occurrence in communicative contexts rather than by inherent properties, pushes the issue even further by noting that being "polite" is attributable only to speakers, not to language. But since social judgments are made on the basis of speakers' conduct, it is the conduct itself, whether in form of language use

Gabriele Kasper, "Linguistic etiquette" from *The Handbook of Sociolinguistics,* edited by Florian Coulmas (Oxford: Blackwell, 1997), pp. 374–85 plus associated references. Reprinted by permission of Blackwell Publishing Ltd.

or other behaviors, that is routinely assessed as more or less polite relative to community values and norms. From a cross-linguistic perspective, Coulmas argues that language systems may be described as differentially polite, depending on the number of means specialized for politeness marking (1992: 321) and the level of delicacy encoded in polite forms. Watts, Ide, and Ehlich (1992) suggest that politeness operates at all three levels of analysis – in language systems, usage, and use, as implied by the title of their volume *Politeness in Language.*

A useful and fairly uncontroversial first distinction is between first-order and second-order politeness (Watts, Ide, and Ehlich, 1992: 3). *First-order politeness* refers to politeness as a folk notion: How do members of a community perceive and classify action in terms of politeness? Such assessments and classifications manifest themselves in etiquette manuals, the do's and dont's in socializing interaction, metapragmatic comments on what is and is not polite behavior, and so forth – what Fraser (1990) refers to as the "social norm view" of politeness. *Second-order politeness* is a theoretical construct, located within a theory of social behavior and language use. The distinction is thus methodological, because it specifies the relationship between statements about linguistic etiquette at different levels of analysis. The relationship is one of data to theory, as noted by Hobart from a social-anthropological perspective ("indigenous classifications in use are part of the empirical evidence," 1987: 36). First-order politeness phenomena, be they observable behavior or action-guiding cognitions crystallized as "core cultural concepts" (Wierzbicka, 1991), are the material on which researchers base their theorizing. In their unanalyzed form, core cultural concepts are like folk beliefs: They have no explanatory value in themselves, but need to be explained through second-order politeness theory – just as linguistic productions or grammaticality judgments need explanation through linguistic theory. Once analyzed in their historical and sociocultural context, such core concepts provide frameworks to explain practices of linguistic action in the community. Thus Mao (1994) demonstrated how Chinese interlocutors orient themselves towards the *face* notions *lian* and *mianzi* in giving and receiving invitations and offers (for further analysis of *mianzi* in conversational interaction, see Chen, 1990/91; in speech-act realization, Kasper, 1995). Observationally and descriptively adequate accounts of first-order politeness are needed in order for politeness theory to be firmly anchored in the communicative practices and conceptualizations of speech communities.

First-order politeness data come from a wide variety of sources, most of them observational or experimental studies of the current practices in communities or groups within larger communities (see below), carried out within the theoretical and methodological traditions of several disciplines: linguistic pragmatics, sociolinguistics, the social psychology of language, psycholinguistics, developmental psychology, communications, and anthropology. Studies adopting a historical perspective on linguistic etiquette in particular communities and in literature are likewise gaining ground; e.g., politeness in the Ancient Orient, Greece, Rome, the Middle Ages, and the German Early Modern period (see Ehlich, 1992; also Beetz, 1990, for the latter period, and Elias, 1977, for a social history of manners in Europe); in the Nibelungenlied (Rings, 1987); Chaucer (Eun, 1987; Sell, 1985a, b); Shakespeare's four major tragedies (Brown and Gilman, 1989) and Henry VIII (Magnusson, 1992); in the works of Lessing (Claus, 1983); Rabelais (Morrison, 1988); Stendhal (Crouzet, 1980); Hemingway (Hardy, 1991); seventeenth-century England and France (Klein, 1990) and the eighteenth-century philosophers, Berkeley and Shaftesbury

(Klein, 1986); Islamic culture (Ostrup, 1929); in languages such as Chinese (Yuan, Kuiper, and Shaogu, 1990; Song-Cen, 1991); French (Kremos, 1955; Krings, 1961; Held, 1988); Old Greek (Zilliacus, 1949); Japanese (Wenger, 1983); Korean (Soh, 1985); Old Polish (Wojtak, 1989); Russian (Popov, 1985); and classical Sanskrit (Van De Walle, 1991).

5.2   Politeness and the Cooperative Principle

A matter of controversy is the relationship of politeness to the Gricean *Cooperative Principle* (CP) (Grice, 1975). Views reach from entirely subsuming politeness under the CP to affording the CP and politeness equal status. According to Green (1992a, b), politeness, defined as "considerateness," is one of many maxims representing "instantiations in a context of the Cooperative Principle" (1992a: 6), on the same epistemological footing with the maxims of quality, quantity, relevance, and manner. Consequently, violating the politeness maxim gives rise to conversational inference, just as in the case of any other maxim – a point also made by Matsumoto (1989) with respect to inappropriate use of honorifics in Japanese.

In the best articulated politeness theory to date, Brown and Levinson postulate the Cooperative Principle and its four maxims as a "presumptive framework" assumed by conversationalists about the nature of talk (1987: 4). Quite unlike Green (1992b), they do not view politeness as yet another conversational maxim but rather as a motivating force for maxim violation. The reason for language users not to follow the most efficient course of action, as they would do by observing the Gricean maxims, is their concern for face (see below). While observance of the CP and concern for face are both under-pinned by actors' rational orientations, these orientations are of quite different status. The CP represents participants' orientation to get on with the business of talk, or any other kind of linguistic (inter)action, in an optimally economical and efficient manner. Face, in its most general sense, encapsulates participants' mutual recognition as social members. Attending to face may be at odds with the CP, such as when a speaker violates the maxim of quantity or manner by being indirect. It is important that Brown and Levinson's view of politeness is *not* coextensive with attending to face concerns but considerably more narrow: Politeness operates only when face interests are at risk, and actors are therefore required to make strategic choices about how to handle imminent face threat. It is only these strategic options of handling face-threat that are called "politeness" in Brown and Levinson's theory. Their proposal is consequently referred to by Fraser (1990) as the "face-saving view" of politeness.

While politeness thus has a secondary status vis-à-vis the CP in Green's (1992a, b) and Brown and Levinson's (1987) theories, Lakoff (1973) and, in a much elaborated version, Leech (1983) see politeness as a coordinate construct to the CP. For Lakoff, pragmatic competence is constituted by two major "rules": "1. Be clear. 2. Be polite," where clarity amounts to a condensed version of the Gricean maxims, while politeness serves to avoid conflict between participants. In Leech's proposal of an "interpersonal rhetoric," the CP is complemented by a politeness principle (PP): "Minimize the expression of impolite beliefs" (1983: 79). Both CP and PP are "first-order principles," each elaborated by a set of "contributory maxims": the Gricean maxims in the case of the CP, and six maxims of politeness – the maxims of tact, generosity, approbation, modesty, agreement, and sympathy – in the case of the PP (pp. 131 ff.). The "conversational maxim view" (Fraser, 1990) of politeness thus comes in different versions, depending on how the relationship between the CP and politeness is conceptualized.

Yet another, perhaps the broadest view of politeness has been proposed by Fraser (1990) with his notion of the *conversational contract* (CC). On this view, politeness is seen neither as complementing the CP, nor as motivating deviation from it, but as the default setting in conversational encounters: "being polite constitutes operating within the then-current terms and conditions of the CC" (1990: 233). But since the same is true for the CP, *mutatis mutandis* ("being cooperative involves abiding by the CC," p. 233), and the difference between being cooperative and being polite is never explained, the conversational contract view appears to be predicated on an equation of "being cooperative = being polite = abiding by the CC," which does little to clarify, let alone present in empirically testable format, the interaction of communicative efficiency and relational concerns in linguistic exchange.

5.3   Universality and Relativity in Politeness Theory

The range of politeness theories – what are the phenomena they serve to explain, intra- and interculturally – has been yet another issue of contention among students of linguistic etiquette. Brown and Levinson (1987) and Leech (1983) explicitly assert universal status for their proposed theories. Reviewing their approaches and offering his own, Fraser (1990) provides no discussion of the purported universality and thus implicitly affirms the universality claim. By contrast, Green (1992a, b) argues cogently for the universal applicability of the CP. Since, on her view, the conversational maxims are instantiations of the CP, demonstrated nonapplicability of some maxim or other in a particular cultural setting would not invalidate the CP itself. While thus conceding that conversational maxims may be culturally specialized, Green holds that cultural variation in maxim applicability is more likely to be an effect of different cultural values on the specific shape of a maxim than a question of whether a particular maxim is observed at all.

5.4   Politeness and the Notion of Face

Views opposing the universal availability of the proposed politeness constructs have mostly taken issue with the cornerstone of Brown and Levinson's theory, their notions of negative and positive face. *Negative face* is defined as "the basic claim to territories, personal preserves, rights to non-distraction – i.e. freedom of action and freedom from imposition." *Positive face* refers to "the positive consistent self-image or 'personality' (crucially including the desire that this self-image be appreciated and approved of) claimed by interactants" (1987: 61). The two complementary sides of face have been referred to by other authors as "distance vs. involvement" (Tannen, 1986), "deference vs. solidarity" (R. and S. B. K. Scollon, 1983), "autonomy vs. connection" (Green, 1992b), "self-determination vs. acceptance," or "personal vs. interpersonal face" (Janney and Arndt, 1992). Politeness is activity serving to enhance, maintain, or protect face: Addressing negative face results in *negative politeness* ("deference politeness," R. and S. B. K. Scollon, 1983), manifest in indirectness, formality, emphasis of social distance, and respect for the interlocutor's entitlements and resources. Positive face gives rise to *positive politeness* ("solidarity politeness," R. and S. B. K. Scollon, 1983), displayed in directness, informal language use, emphasis of common ground, appreciation of the interlocutor, her actions, possessions, etc. Positive or negative politeness *strategies* are redressive action, used to mitigate the *face-threat* which a linguistic act might pose for the interlocutor. In Brown and Levinson's theory, *face-threatening acts* are speech acts which clearly involve an interpersonal dimension – directives, commissives, and expressives, in Searle's (1976) classification. According to Green (1992a), all linguistic action involves face-threat of some kind; therefore politeness strategies are ubiquitously called for.

Different kinds of complaint have been voiced against the role of face in Brown and Levinson's theory. The common denominator of these objections is that the intended universality of the theory is untenable.

The first type of objection accepts the derivative role of politeness from face, but argues against the notion of face as "the public *self*-image that every member wants to claim for himself" (Brown and Levinson, 1987: 61, my emphasis). This social-psychological notion with its emphasis on individuals' self-generated projection of their favored persona has been contrasted, first, with the earlier formulation proposed by Goffman (1967). Goffman's (sociological) construct describes face as a *public* rather than personal property, "on loan" from society rather than an unalienable possession, and a negotiable outcome of social interaction (cf. Aston, 1988; Mao, 1994). The interpersonal orientation of Goffman's face concept is deemed more compatible with "nonwestern" face constructs (see Hu, 1944; Ho, 1975; Gu, 1990; Mao, 1994, for Chinese; Ervin-Tripp, Nakamura, and Guo, 1995, for a comparison of face concepts in English, French, Chinese, Japanese, Korean). Acknowledging the different premium placed on individuals' desires and social recognition by Anglo-American societies and Chinese and Japanese communities, Mao proposes a *relative face orientation*:

> an underlying direction of face that emulates, though never completely attaining, one of two interactional ideals that may be salient in a given speech community: the *ideal social identity*, or the *ideal individual autonomy*. The specific content of face in a given speech community is determined by one of these two interactional ideals sanctioned by the members of the community. (1994: 472, my emphasis)

Whereas Mao's face constructs thus embrace the relative placement of individuals in social hierarchies, other authors view the notions of face and *place* as mutually exclusive. Both Matsumoto (1988, 1989) and Ide (1989) complain that Brown and Levinson's face constructs do not capture the principles of Japanese interaction because they do not include the acknowledgement of social relationships ("social relativism," "proper place occupancy," Lebra, 1976). Whereas Matsumoto rejects the notion of negative face as being inapplicable to Japanese culture (a position also supported by Ervin-Tripp et al., 1995), Ide accepts the validity of positive and negative face, but suggests that this model be complemented by a component called discernment (*wakimae*), signalling social relationships. Politeness in any society comprises a "volitional" component (strategic politeness attending to face concerns) and discernment, or social marking. These two components of politeness are regarded as universals; communities differ in the emphasis they put on each. Thus for Japanese interlocutors, "place" purportedly takes precedence before "face" (Ide, 1989).

Neither the strong place instead of face position (Matsumoto) nor the weak place before face variety (Ide) have yet received empirical support. While the comprehensive literature on honorifics in Japanese (Coulmas, 1992; Matsumoto, 1993; see also references in Yoshinaga, Maeshiba, and Takahashi, 1992) attests the importance of social marking, it does not speak to the issue of (negative) face. At the same time, the literature on speech act realization in Japanese documents differential strategy use depending on context factors (e.g., Barnlund and Yoshioka, 1990, on apologies; Ikoma and Shimura, 1993, on refusals; Ikoma, 1993, on expressions of gratitude; Kitao, 1990; Takahashi, 1992, on requests; Takahashi and Beebe, 1993, on corrections). Since a great number of the identified strategies are recognizably negative politeness strategies (e.g., *oisogashii tokoro* "you must be busy," *moshiwake arimasenga* "excuse me" to preface a request; apologetic expressions such as *sumimasen (deshita), gomeiwaku o okake si mashita* for conveying gratitude), the claim that negative face wants are absent in Japanese interaction is difficult to maintain. The assumption that social indexing may be more prevalent in some languages than others is well supported by the fact that in Asian languages such as Japanese, Korean, Thai, Javanese, and others, relationship marking is grammaticized in highly complex morphological systems, whereas such specialization is only rudimentary in European languages. A more problematic issue than the cross-linguistic comparison of obligatory social indexing is Ide's (1989) conjecture that Japanese linguistic etiquette emphasizes "discernment" more than strategic politeness. To date, no studies have been carried out to support this position, and indeed no measure has been proposed to test Ide's hypothesis. Furthermore, data-based studies on the use of honorifics reveal that, rather than being used invariably to index a specific social relationship, honorific use can alter in the same encounter, depending on the particular attitude the speaker wishes to convey (Cook, 1993, 1994). Empirical observation thus contradicts the claim that speakers "submit passively to the requirements of the system" (Hill et al., 1986: 348) once a particular status relationship has been identified. Rather than being entirely predetermined, social indexing remains a sociolinguistic choice, even when there is a strong statistical preference for particular usage. The forms actually chosen depend on the current state of the "conversational contract" (Fraser, 1990) and appear thus as more dynamic and "volitional" than static views of honorific language use suggest. From this perspective, unmarked use of honorifics simply reflects speakers' adherence to accepted politeness norms (cf. Green, 1992b).

Yet another line of criticism denies the role of face in politeness altogether. Watts (1989) asserts that, rather than being motivated by face concerns, politeness is located in the wider context of *politic* behavior, understood as (linguistic) activity serving to establish and maintain interpersonal relationships. With special reference to Chinese politeness, Gu (1990) argues that politeness is more appropriately seen as adherence to social norms than attending to individuals' face wants. While these authors' proposals are thus at variance with Brown and Levinson's individualistic notion of face, they are quite compatible with the relative face concept proposed by Mao (1994).

5.5   Face and Self

Writers who recognize a role for face in linguistic etiquette have recently pointed out that face can be correctly understood only in the context of notions of self, emphasizing that such notions are necessarily informed by culturally varying perceptions of personhood and relationships between an individual and society. While a comprehensive review of studies on self concepts in different communities points to a consistent opposition between *interdependent* and *independent* notions of self (Markus and Kitayama, 1991), an alternative view questions the adequacy of categorizing cross-culturally varying self-orientations according to these categories, or even as ordered on a continuum between these. Thus Rosenberger (1989) argues against the popular belief of a consistent sociocentric self concept in the Japanese community, and for a dialectic model which captures the switches of the Japanese self (*jibun*) between opposing orientations: "group productivity, personal accomplishment, harmony or affection, and pure impulse or gratification" (1989: 89f.). Switching between these modes is brought about through the flow of a person's vital energy (*ki*) and actualization according to a social, spatial, and temporal context (see also Lebra, 1993). The key difference between "Western" and Japanese notions of self thus rests not so much in "independent"/"egocentric" vs. "interdependent"/"sociocentric" orientations but in the diverging beliefs about the *unity* of self: The "Western" ideal of a consistent self that transcends conflicting contextual demands, and the Japanese ideal of an accommodative self that optimally responds to varying contexts and purposes. The ideological character of the "Western" construction of a consistent self has been illustrated in a lucid analysis of team sport in the US (Green, 1992b), demonstrating how athletes are required to switch from the individualistic orientation prevalent in the society at large to a strongly group-oriented, hierarchical subculture. The facility by which these adjustments are performed suggests that "Western" selves are more contextually sensitive than presumed by folk beliefs as well as some scientific models of self, e.g., in Freudian or Jungian psychodynamic theory. It is therefore important for research on linguistic etiquette to explore practices of social marking and strategic politeness in different groups and speech events within larger cultural communities in order to establish *intra*culturally varying orientations of self and face. Such research is not only indispensable for descriptively adequate accounts of politeness within and across cultures but also a necessary safeguard against unhelpful stereotyping along the received lines of "Eastern" and "Western" ways of perceiving personhood and social relations.

5.6   Variables in Linguistic Etiquette

Any theory of politeness has built into it the sociolinguistic axiom that politeness invest-ment varies according to contextual factors. The two most elaborated theories, Brown and Levinson (1987) and Leech (1983), concur in this regard. First, they identify the same factors as independent variables in politeness marking: social distance (Brown and Levinson, Leech), social power (Brown and Levinson) or authority (Leech), and the degree of imposition associated with a given face-threatening act (Brown and Levinson) or the costs and benefits of an act (Leech). Second, both theories posit a linear relationship between these factors and politeness investment. Third, they both assume a positive correlation between politeness and indirectness.

Data-based studies lend strong support to the identified context variables, whereas the correlational issues are problematic. Each of the proposed factors represents a composite construct which is culturally and contextually elaborated and weighted. *Social power* includes factors such as:

- interlocutors' relative positions in social hierarchies (Becker, 1982; Becker and Smenner, 1986; Becker, Kimmel, and Bevill, 1989; Beebe and Takahashi, 1989a, b; Bryan and Gallois, 1992; Ervin-Tripp, O'Connor, and Rosenberg, 1984; Hill et al., 1986; Lampi, 1993; McMullen and Krahn, 1985; Morand, 1991; Pearson, 1988; Takahashi and Beebe, 1993);
- age; e.g., in communication by and with the elderly (Coupland, Coupland, and Giles, 1991; James, 1978; Milan, 1976) and children (Axia, McGurk, and Martin, 1987; Baroni and Axia, 1989; Bates, 1976; Bates and Silvern, 1977; Becker, 1990; Blum-Kulka, 1990; Clancy, 1986; Cook, 1990; Edelsky, 1977; Eisenberg, 1982; Ervin-Tripp and Gordon, 1986; Ervin-Tripp, Guo, and Lampert, 1990; Ervin-Tripp, O'Connor, and Rosenberg, 1984; Gleason, 1980; Gleason, Perlmann, and Greif, 1984; Nippold, Leonard, and Anastopoulos, 1982; Ochs, 1988; Perlmann, 1984; Schieffelin, 1990; Schieffelin and Eisenberg, 1984; Smith-Hefner, 1988; Snow et al., 1990; Waller and Schoeler, 1985; Waller and Valtin, 1992; Wilhite, 1983; Zammuner, 1991);
- gender (Becker and Smenner, 1986; Bell, 1985; Bresnahan, 1993; Brouwer, 1982; Brouwer, Gerritsen, and De Haan, 1979; P. Brown, 1980; Burstein, 1989; Crosby and Nyquist, 1977; Dubois and Crouch, 1975; Eliasoph, 1986; Harris, 1992; Herbert, 1990; Hoar, 1987; Holmes, 1984, 1989, 1990, 1993; Ide, 1982, 1983, 1992; Ide et al., 1986; Keenan, 1974; Lakoff, 1975; Loveday, 1981; Milan, 1976; Morgan, 1991; Preisler, 1986; Reynolds, 1985, 1989a, b, 1990; Shibamoto, 1987; Smith-Hefner, 1981, 1988; Takahara, 1991; Watts, 1992; Yabar, 1975; Yamashita, 1983; Zimin, 1981);
- language impairment (Abbeduto, 1984; Bates and Wilson, 1981; Bliss, 1992; Rimac, 1986; Stemmer, 1994; Stemmer, Giroux, and Joanette, 1994).

Social distance (Boxer, 1993; Delisle, 1986; Garcia, 1992; J. H. and K. C. Hill, 1978; McMullen and Krahn, 1985; Miller, 1991; Morosawa, 1990) has been demonstrated to affect politeness in a more complex way than theoretically predicted. Reviewing a number of studies on speech act realization, Wolfson (e.g., 1989) concludes that rather than correlating in a linear fashion, social distance and politeness are related in a reverse bell-shaped curve ("bulge"): Most politeness appears to be expended in negotiable relationships with familiars but nonintimates, such as coworkers and friends. In more fixed relationships at opposite ends of the social distance continuum, intimates and strangers, politeness is found to decrease. More recent evidence for the bulge hypothesis comes from studies on complaining (Olshtain and Weinbach, 1993) and expressions of gratitude (Eisenstein and Bodman, 1993).

While there is a comprehensive literature on the impact of social variables on politeness implementation, much less research exists on the influence of psychological factors. To some extent, this may simply reflect the fact that demographic variables are easy to identify whereas (social-)psychological factors are not. Ciliberti (1993) argues that inter-actional style is as much a product of participants' cultural background as of personality, and an analogous argument can be made for demographic profiles and personal variables. Slugoski (1985) demonstrates that familiarity (= social distance) has to be distinguished from affect (= psychological distance), a hypothesis supported by historical evidence from a study of politeness in Shakespearian tragedies (Brown and Gilman, 1989; on the impact of affect see also Boxer, 1993; Camras, Pristo, and Brown, 1985; Haviland, 1989; Sussman and Rosenfeld, 1982).

In addition to these participant variables, features of linguistic acts themselves – the "*imposition*," or costs and benefits accruing from them – shape politeness enactment. For several speech acts, the elements of the composite construct "imposition" have been identified, for instance, in:

- requesting: urgency (Morosawa, 1990), legitimacy (Hoppe-Graff et al., 1985; House, 1989; Blum-Kulka and House, 1989; Hirokawa, Mickey, and Miura, 1991), the likelihood of the hearer's compliance and the speaker's psychological difficulty in carrying out the request (Blum-Kulka and House, 1989);
- apologizing: perceived severity of the offence, subsuming obligation to apologize and likelihood of apology being accepted (House, 1989; Olshtain, 1989; Vollmer and Olshtain, 1989; Bergman and Kasper, 1993);
- thanking: indebtedness, comprising the degree of received benefit and trouble undergone by the benefactor (Ikoma, 1993);
- complaining: magnitude of social obligation violated by the offender (Olshtain and Weinbach, 1993).

Participant factors and properties of contextualized linguistic action interact in complex ways and vary cross-culturally in their impact on linguistic politeness. For instance, in request performance, Israeli speakers varied their strategy selection according to requestive goal, age, and power (Blum-Kulka, Danet, and Gerson, 1985); Japanese and German speakers modified their requests according to legitimacy and the likelihood of the hearer's compliance, but the German not the Japanese speakers made their strategy selection also contingent on urgency (Hermann, 1982; Morosawa, 1990); Israelis, Germans, and Argentinians differed in their perceptions of interlocutors' rights and obligations, the likelihood of the hearer's compliance, and the speaker's difficulty in performing the request (Blum-Kulka and House, 1989); requestees' obligation to comply was perceived as higher by American than by Japanese raters (Shimamura, 1993).

Just as the relationship between context variables and politeness varies intra- and interculturally, so does the relationship between patterns of linguistic action and their politeness value. Negative politeness strategies were perceived as more polite by Japanese residing in the US than by Japanese in Japan (Kitao, 1990). Japanese and Americans also gave different appropriateness judgments of requests with and without supportive moves (Shimamura, 1993). A particularly intriguing issue is the relationship between indirectness and politeness. Contrary to theory-derived predictions, it was conventional indirectness (e.g., preparatory strategies such as "can/could you") rather than nonconventional indirectness (hinting) that was rated most polite by Israeli, American (Blum-Kulka, 1987), and German (House, 1986) judges. The preference for conventional indirectness appears to be motivated by the balance struck between clarity and consideration, and low processing costs to the hearer. Consistent with this finding, Weizman (1985, 1989, 1993) has suggested that nonconventional indirectness is not motivated by politeness at all but by the "deniability potential" inherent in ambiguous language use.

5.7 Discourse Context

Rather than isolating specific context variables and examining their impact on politeness, a large body of literature explores the linguistic etiquette of different discourse contexts. Such contexts include:

- institutional discourse, e.g., courtrooms (Adelsward, 1989; Berk-Seligson, 1988; Cashion, 1985; Lakoff, 1989; Parkinson, 1981; Wright, 1987), medical discourse (Aronsson and Rundstroem, 1989; Aronsson and Saetterlund-Larsson, 1987; Robins and Wolf, 1988), psychotherapy (Batten, 1990; Lakoff, 1989), academic advising (Bardovi-Harlig and Hartford, 1990, 1993), counselling (Erickson and Shultz, 1982; Fiksdal, 1988, 1991), supervisory conferences (Roberts, 1992), special education conferences (DuFon, 1992, 1993), classroom discourse (Cazden, 1979; Chick, 1989; Ellis, 1992; Heath, 1983; Lörscher and Schulze, 1988; Sadow and Maxwell, 1983), consumer service agencies (Johnson and Fawcett, 1987), sermons (Dzameshie, 1992); citizen–bureaucracy interaction (Hero, 1986), opinion poll interviews (Johnstone, 1991; Johnstone, Ferrara, and Bean, 1992), church business meetings (Pearson, 1988);
- workplace communication (Bryan and Gallois, 1992; Chick, 1986, 1989; Clyne, Bell, and Neil, 1991; Holmqvist and Andersen, 1987; Myers, 1991; Nunes, 1981) and other professional interaction, e.g., aviation discourse (Linde, 1988a, b), business negotiations (Yamada, 1990), sales negotiations (Lampi, 1993), organizational interaction (Morand, 1991), sports teams (Green, 1992a, b; Jones, 1992);
- interpersonal discourse, e.g., family dinners (Blum-Kulka, 1990; Blum-Kulka and Sheffer, 1993; Perlmann, 1984; Wilhite, 1983); dinner entertainment (Befu, 1986), phatic communion (Coupland, Coupland, and Robinson, 1992), intimate conversation (Frank, 1988), interpersonal decision-making (Scheerhorn, 1991);
- discourse in different media, e.g., telephone conversations (Clark and French, 1981; Plascencia, 1992; Schegloff, 1979; Sifianou, 1989), computer games (Covato, 1991), computer messages (Hama, 1991), translated discourse (DuFon, 1993; Knapp-Potthoff, 1992; Knapp-Potthoff and Knapp, 1987);
- written discourse, e.g., letters of request (Cherry, 1988; Pickett, 1989), business letters (Hagge, 1984; Hagge and Kostelnick, 1989; Larson, 1988; Limaye and Cherry, 1987; Marier, 1992), narratives (R. and S. B. K. Scollon, 1981), argumentative writing (Zammuner, 1991), scientific writing (Kreml, 1992; Myers, 1989), peer reviews (Johnson, 1992; Johnson and Yang, 1990).

The common message from these different studies is that linguistic etiquette is both a highly context-sensitive aspect of human communication and one that shapes context and participants' relationships. Politeness is thus not only determined by the current state of the conversational contract but a context-creating and modifying force in its own right.

References

Abbeduto, L. (1984) Situational influences on mentally retarded and nonretarded children's production of directives. *Applied Psycholinguistics*, 5, 147–66.

Adelsward, V. (1989) Defendants' interpretations of encouragements in court: The construction of meaning in an institutionalized context. *Journal of Pragmatics*, 13, 741–9.

Aronsson, K. and Rundstroem, B. (1989) Cats, dogs, and sweets in the clinical negotiation of reality: On politeness and coherence in pediatric discourse. *Language in Society*, 18, 483–501.

Aronsson, K. and Saetterlund-Larsson, U. (1987) Politeness strategies and doctor–patient communication. On the social choreography of collaborative thinking. *Journal of Language and Social Psychology*, 6, 1–27.

Aston, G. (1988) *Learning Community: An approach to the description and pedagogy of interactional speech.* Bologna: Cooperativa Libraria Universitaria Editrice Bologna.

Axia, G., McGurk, H., and Martin, G. (1987) The development of social pragmatics: A cross-national study of the case of linguistic politeness. Paper presented at the Annual Conference of the Developmental Section, British Psychological Society, York, England (ERIC Document Reproduction Service no. ED287595).

Bardovi-Harlig, K. and Hartford, B. (1990) Congruence in native and nonnative conversations: Status balance in the academic advising session. *Language Learning*, 40, 467–501.

—— (1993) Learning the rules of academic talk: A longitudinal study of pragmatic development. *Studies in Second Language Acquisition*, 15, 279–304.

Barnlund, D. C. and Yoshioka, M. (1990) Apologies: Japanese and American styles. *International Journal of Intercultural Relations*, 14, 193–206.

Baroni, M. R. and Axia, G. (1989) Children's meta-pragmatic abilities and the identification of polite and impolite requests. *First Language*, 9, 285–97.

Bates, E. (1976) Acquisition of polite forms: Experimental evidence. In E. Bates (ed.), *Language and Context: The acquisition of pragmatics*, 255–94. New York: Academic Press.

Bates, E. and Silvern, L. (1977) Social adjustment and politeness in preschoolers. *Journal of Communication*, 27, 104–11.

Bates, M. and Wilson, K. (1981) *Interactive Language Instruction Assistance for the Deaf.* Final report No. 4771. Cambridge, MA: Bolt, Beranek and Newman.

Batten, C. (1990) Dilemmas of "crosscultural psychotherapy supervision." *British Journal of Psychotherapy*, 7, 129–40.

Becker, J. A. (1982) Children's strategic use of requests to mark and manipulate social status. In S. Kuczaj (ed.), *Language Development: Language, thought and culture*, 1–35. Hillsdale, NJ: Erlbaum.

—— (1990) Processes in the acquisition of pragmatic competence. In G. Conti-Ramsden and C. E. Snow (eds.), *Children's Language*, 7–24. Hillsdale, NJ: Erlbaum.

Becker, J. A. and Smenner, P. C. (1986) The spontaneous use of *thank you* by preschoolers as a function of sex, socioeconomic status, and listener status. *Language in Society*, 15, 537–46.

Becker, J. A., Kimmel, H. D., and Bevill, M. J. (1989) The interactive effects of request form and speaker status on judgments of requests. *Journal of Psycholinguistic Research*, 18, 521–31.

Beebe, L. M. and Takahashi, T. (1989a) Do you have a bag?: Social status and patterned variation in second language acquisition. In S. Gass, C. Madden, D. Preston, and L. Selinker (eds.), *Variation in Second Language Acquisition: Discourse and pragmatics*, 103–25. Clevedon and Philadelphia: Multilingual Matters.

—— (1989b) Sociolinguistic variation in face threatening speech acts. In M. Eisenstein (ed.), *The Dynamic Interlanguage*, 199–218. New York: Plenum.

Beetz, M. (1990) *Frühmoderne Höflichkeit. Komplimentierkunst und Gesellschaftsrituale im altdeutschen Sprachraum* [Early modern politeness. The art of complimenting and social rituals in the old German area]. Stuttgart: Metzler.

Befu, H. (1986) An ethnography of dinner entertainment in Japan. In T. S. Lebra and W. P. Lebra (eds.), *Japanese Culture and Behavior*, 108–20. Honolulu, HI: University of Hawaii Press.

Bell, K. M. (1985) The relationship of gender and sex role identity to politeness in speech behavior. *Dissertation Abstracts International*, 45, 2678-B.

Bergman, M. L. and Kasper, G. (1993) Perception and performance in native and nonnative apology. In G. Kasper and S. Blum-Kulka (eds.), *Interlanguage Pragmatics*, 82–107. New York: Oxford University Press.

Berk-Seligson, S. (1988) The impact of politeness in witness testimony: The influence of the court interpreter. *Multilingua*, 7, 411–39.

Bliss, L. S. (1992) A comparison of tactful messages by children with and without language impairment: *Language, Speech, and Hearing Services in Schools*, 23, 343–7.

Blum-Kulka, S. (1987) Indirectness and politeness in requests: same or different? *Journal of Pragmatics*, 11, 131–46.

—— (1990) You don't touch lettuce with your fingers: parental politeness in family discourse. *Journal of Pragmatics*, 14, 259–88.

Blum-Kulka, S. Danet, B., and Gerson, R. (1985) The language of requesting in Israeli society. In J. Forgas (ed.), *Language and Social Situation*. New York: Springer.

Blum-Kulka, S. and House, J. (1989) Cross-cultural and situational variation in requesting behavior. In S. Blum-Kulka, J. House, and G. Kasper (eds.), *Cross-cultural Pragmatics: Requests and Apologies*, 123–54. Norwood, NJ: Ablex.

Blum-Kulka, S. and Sheffer, H. (1993) The metapragmatic discourse of American-Israeli families at dinner. In G. Kasper and S. Blum-Kulka (eds.), *Interlanguage Pragmatics*, 196–223. New York: Oxford University Press.

Boxer, D. (1993) Social distance and speech behavior: the case of indirect complaints. *Journal of Pragmatics*, 19, 103–25.

Bresnahan, M. I. (1993) Gender difference in initiating requests for help. *Text*, 13, 7.

Brouwer, D. (1982) The influence of the addressee's sex on politeness in language use. *Linguistics*, 20, 697–711.

Brouwer, D., Gerritsen, M., and De Haan, D. (1979) Speech differences between women and men: on the wrong track? *Language in Society*, 8, 33–50.

Brown, P. (1980) How and why are women more polite: some evidence from a Mayan community. In S. McConnell-Ginet, R. Borker, and N. Furman (eds.), *Women and Language in Literature and Society*, 111–36. New York: Praeger.

Brown, P. and Levinson, S. D. (1978) Politeness: some universals in language usage. In E. N. Goody (ed.), *Questions and Politeness: Strategies in social interaction*, 56–289. Cambridge: Cambridge University Press.

—— (1987) *Politeness: Some universals in language usage*. Cambridge: Cambridge University Press.

Brown, R. and Gilman, A. (1989) Politeness theory and Shakespeare's four major tragedies. *Language in Society*, 18, 159–212.

Bryan, A. and Gallois, C. (1992) Rules about assertion in the workplace: effect of status and message type. *Australian Journal of Psychology*, 44, 51–9.

Burstein, J. (1989) Politeness strategies and gender expectations. *CUNY Forum: Papers in Linguistics*, 14, 31–7.

Camras, L. A., Pristo, T. M., and Brown, M. J. K. (1985) Directive choice by children and adults: affect, situation, and linguistic politeness. *Merrill-Palmer Quarterly*, 31, 19–31.

Cashion, J. L. (1985) Politeness in courtroom language. Paper presented at the Annual Meeting of the Western Speech Communication Association. Fresno, CA (ERIC Document Reproduction Service No. ED254882).

Cazden, C. B. (1979) Language in education: variation in the teacher-talk register. In J. E. Alatis and G. R. Tucker (eds.), *Georgetown University Round Table on Languages and Linguistics 1979: Language in public life*, 144–60. Washington, DC: Georgetown University.

Chen, V. (1990/91) *Mien tze* at the Chinese dinner table: a study of the interactional accomplishment of face. *Research on Language and Social Interaction*, 24, 109–40.

Cherry, R. D. (1988) Politeness in written persuasion. *Journal of Pragmatics*, 12, 63–81.

Chick, K. (1986) Interactional perspectives on the linguistic needs of Zulu work seekers. *Journal of Multilingual and Multicultural Development*, 7, 479–91.

—— (1989) Intercultural miscommunication as a source of friction in the workplace and in educational settings in South Africa. In O. García and R. Otheguy (eds.), *English across Cultures, Cultures across English: A reader in cross-cultural communication*, 139–60. Berlin: Mouton de Gruyter.

Ciliberti, A. (1993) The personal and the cultural in interactive styles. *Journal of Pragmatics*, 20, 1–25.

Clancy, P. M. (1986) The acquisition of communicative style in Japanese. In B. B. Schieffelin and E. Ochs (eds.), *Language Socialization across Cultures*, 213–49. New York: Cambridge University Press.

Clark, H. and French, J. W. (1981) Telephone goodbyes. *Language in Society*, 10, 1–19.

Claus, M. (1983) *Lessing und die Franzosen: Hoeflichkeit – Laster – Witz* [Lessing and the French: Politeness – vice – joke]. Rheinfelden: Schauble.

Clyne, M., Ball, M., and Neil, D. (1991) Intercultural communication at work in Australia: complaints and apologies in turns. *Multilingua*, 10, 251–73.

Cook, H. M. (1990) The role of the Japanese sentence-final particle *no* in the socialization of children. *Multilingua*, 9, 377–95.

—— (1993) Social meanings of Japanese humble verb forms as used by government officials. Paper presented at the Fourth International Pragmatics Conference, Kobe, July.

—— (1994) The use of addressee honorifics in Japanese elementary school classrooms. Paper presented at the 17th L.A.U.D. Symposium on Language and Space, Duisburg, March.

Coulmas, F. (1992) Linguistic etiquette in Japanese society. In R. J. Watts, S. Ide, and K. Ehlich (eds.), *Politeness in Language: Studies in its history, theory and practice*, 299–323. Berlin and New York: Mouton de Gruyter.

Coupland, J., Coupland, N., and Robinson, J. D. (1992) "How are you?": Negotiating phatic communion. *Language in Society*, 21, 207–30.

Coupland, N., Coupland, J., and Giles, H. (1991) *Language, Society and the Elderly*. Oxford: Blackwell.

Covato, L. G. (1991) The design of an adventure game authoring tool for exploring polite requests in an English as Second Language context. *Dissertation Abstracts International*, 53, 430-A.

Crosby, F. and Nyquist, L. (1977) The female register: an empirical study of Lakoff's hypotheses. *Language in Society*, 6, 313–22.

Crouzet, M. (1980) Polémique et politesse ou Stendhal pamphletaire [Polemic and politeness, or Stendhal as pamphleteer]. *Stendhal Club: Revue Internationale d'Etudes Stendhaliennes*, 23 (89), 53–65.

Delisle, H. H. (1986) Intimacy, solidarity and distance: the pronouns of address in German. *Die Unterrichtspraxis*, 19, 4–15.

Dubois, B. I. and Crouch, I. (1975) The question of tag questions in women's speech: They don't really use more of them, do they? *Language in Society*, 4, 289–324.

DuFon, M. A. (1992) Politeness in interpreted and non-interpreted IEP (Individualized Education Program) conferences with Hispanic Americans. *Master's Abstracts International*, 30, 25. (University Microfilms No. 1345950), Master's thesis, University of Hawaii, 1991.

—— (1993) Referential and relational meaning in interpreted discourse. *Journal of Pragmatics*, 20, 533–58.

Dzameshie, A. K. (1992) Motivations for the use of politeness strategies in Christian sermonic discourse. *Dissertation Abstracts International*, 53, 1143-A.

Edelsky, C. (1977) Acquisition of an aspect of communicative competence: learning what it means to talk like a lady. In S. Ervin-Tripp and C. Mitchell-Kernan (eds.), *Child Discourse*, 225–43. New York: Academic Press.

Ehlich, K. (1992) On the historicity of politeness. In R. J. Watts, S. Ide, and K. Ehlich (eds.), *Politeness in Language: Studies in its history, theory and practice*, 71–107. Berlin: Mouton de Gruyter.

Eisenberg, A. R. (1982) Understanding components of a spontaneous use of politeness routines by Mexicano 2-year-olds. Papers and reports on Child Language Development, Stanford University Department of Linguistics, 21, 46–54.

Eisenstein, M. and Bodman, J. (1993) Expressing gratitude in American English. In G. Kasper and S. Blum-Kulka (eds.), *Interlanguage Pragmatics*, 64–81. New York: Oxford University Press.

Elias, N. (1977) *Über den Prozess der Zivilisation.* Vol. 1. Frankfurt a.M.: Suhrkamp. [English translation: The History of Manners, Vol. 1: The civilizing process. New York: Random House, 1978].

Eliasoph, N. (1986) Politeness, power and women's language: rethinking study in language and gender. *Berkeley Journal of Sociology,* 32, 79–103.

Ellis, R. (1992) Learning to communicate in the classroom. *Studies in Second Language Acquisition,* 14, 1–23.

Erickson, F. and Shultz, J. (1982) *The Counsellor as Gatekeeper.* London: Academic Press.

Ervin-Tripp, S. and Gordon, D. P. (1986) The development of children's requests. In R. E. Schiefelbusch (ed.), *Communicative Competence: Assessment and intervention,* 61–96. San Diego, CA: College Hill Press.

Ervin-Tripp, S., Guo, J., and Lampert, M. (1990) Politeness and persuasion in children's control acts. *Journal of Pragmatics,* 14, 307–31.

Ervin-Tripp, S., Nakamura, K., and Guo, J. (1995) Shifting face from Asia to Europe. In M. Shibatani and S. Thompson (eds.), *Essays in Semantics and Pragmatics.*

Ervin-Tripp, S., O'Connor, M., and Rosenberg, J. (1984) Language and power in the family. In C. Kramarae, M. Schultz, and W. M. O'Barr (eds.), *Language and Power,* 116–35. Belmont, CA: Sage Press.

Eun, H. L. (1987) Polite speech: a sociolinguistic analysis of Chaucer and the Gawain poet. *Dissertation Abstracts International,* 49, 493-A.

Fiksdal, S. (1988) Verbal and non-verbal strategies of rapport in cross-cultural interviews. *Linguistics and Education,* 1, 3–17.

—— (1991) *The Right Time and Pace: A microanalysis of cross-cultural gatekeeping interviews.* Norwood, NJ: Ablex.

Frank, J. (1988) A comparison of intimate conversations: pragmatic theory applied to examples of invented and actual dialog. *SECOL Review,* 12, 186–208.

Fraser, B. (1990) Perspectives on politeness. *Journal of Pragmatics,* 14, 219–36.

Gleason, J. B. (1980) The acquisition of social speech routines and politeness formulas. In H. Giles, W. P. Robinson, and P. M. Smith (eds.). *Language: Social Psychological Perspectives,* 21–7. Oxford: Pergamon Press.

Gleason, J. B., Perlmann, R. Y., and Greif, E. B. (1984) What's the magic word: learning language through politeness routines. *Discourse Processes,* 7, 493–502.

Goffman, E. (1967) *Interaction Ritual: Essays on face-to-face behavior.* New York: Anchor Books.

Green, G. (1992a) *Implicature, Rationality, and the Nature of Politeness.* Unpublished manuscript, University of Illinois.

—— (1992b) *The Universality of Gricean Accounts of Politeness; You gotta have wa.* Unpublished manuscript, University of Illinois.

Grice, H. P. (1975) Logic and conversation. In P. Cole and J. L. Morgan (eds.), *Syntax and Semantics,* Vol. 3: *Speech Acts,* 41–58. New York: Academic Press.

Gu, Y. (1990) Politeness phenomena in modern Chinese. *Journal of Pragmatics,* 14, 237–57.

Hagge, J. (1984) Strategies for verbal interaction in business writing. Paper presented at the 35th Annual Meeting of the Conference on College Composition and Communication. New York City, NY (ERIC Document Reproduction Service No. ED246473).

Hagge, J. and Kostelnick, C. (1989) Linguistic politeness in professional prose: a discourse analysis of auditors' suggestion letters with implications for business communication pedagogy. *Written Communication,* 6, 312–39.

Hama, Y. (1991) The effects of impolite computer messages on workers. *Japanese Journal of Psychology,* 61, 40–6.

Hardy, D. E. (1991) Strategic politeness in Hemingway's "The short happy life of Francis Macomber." *Poetics,* 20, 343–62.

Harris, M. B. (1992) When courtesy fails: gender roles and polite behaviors. *Journal of Applied Social Psychology,* 22, 1399–416.

Haviland, J. B. (1989) "Sure, sure": Evidence and affect. *Text,* 9, 27–68.

Heath, S. B. (1983) *Ways with Words: Language, life, work in communities and classrooms.* Cambridge: Cambridge University Press.

Held, G. (1988) Danken – semantische, pragmatische und soziokulturelle Aspekte eines höflichen Sprechakts (gezeigt am Beispiel des Französischen) [Thanking – semantic, pragmatic, and socio-cultural aspects of a polite speech act (demonstrated by reference to French)]. *Klagenfurter Beiträge zur Sprachwissenschaft*, 13–14, 203–27.

Herbert, R. K. (1990) Sex-based differences in compliment behavior. *Language in Society*, 19, 201–24.

Hero, R. (1986) Citizen contacting and bureaucratic treatment-response in urban government: some further evidence. *Social Science Journal*, 23, 181–7.

Herrmann, T. (1982) Language and situation: the "pars pro toto" principle. In C. Fraser and K. R. Scherer (eds.), *Advances in the Social Psychology of Language*, 123–58. Cambridge: Cambridge University Press.

Hill, B., Ide, S., Ikuta, S., Kawasaki, A., and Ogino, T. (1986) Universals of linguistic politeness. Quantitative evidence from Japanese and American English. *Journal of Pragmatics*, 10, 347–71.

Hill, J. H. and Hill, K. C. (1978) Honorific usage in modern Nahuatl: the expression of social distance and respect in the Nahuatl of the Malinche Volcano area. *Language*, 54, 123–55.

Hirokawa, R. Y., Mickey, J., and Miura, S. (1991) Effects of request legitimacy on the compliance-gaining tactics of male and female managers. *Communication Monographs*, 58, 421–36.

Ho, D. Y. (1975) On the concept of face. *American Journal of Sociology*, 81, 867–84.

Hoar, N. (1987) Genderlect, powerlect, and politeness. In C. A. Valentine and N. Hoar (eds.), *Women and Communicative Power: Theory, research, and practice* (ERIC Document Reproduction Service No. ED294263).

Hobart, M. (1987) Summer's days and salad days: the coming of age of anthropology? In L. Holy (ed.), *Comparative Anthropology*, 22–51. Oxford: Blackwell.

Holmes, J. (1984) Women's language: a functional approach. *General Linguistics*, 24, 149–78.

—— (1989) Sex differences and apologies: One aspect of communicative competence. *Applied Linguistics*, 10, 194–213.

—— (1990) Politeness strategies in New Zealand women's speech. In A. Bell and J. Holmes (eds.), *New Zealand ways of speaking English*, 252–76. Clevedon: Multilingual Matters.

—— (1993) New Zealand women are good to talk to: an analysis of politeness strategies in interaction. *Journal of Pragmatics*, 20, 91–116.

Holmqvist, B. and Boegh Andersen, P. (1987) Work language and information technology. *Journal of Pragmatics*, 11, 327–58.

Hoppe-Graff, S., Hermann, T., Winterhoff-Spurk, P., and Mangold, R. (1985) Speech and situation: a general model for the process of speech production. In J. P. Forgas (ed.), *Language and Social Situation*, 81–97. New York: Springer.

House, J. (1986) Cross-cultural pragmatics and foreign language teaching. In K. R. Bausch, F. G. Koenigs, and R. Kogelheide (eds.), *Probleme und Perspektiven der Sprachlehrforschung*, 281–95. Frankfurt: Scriptor.

—— (1989) Politeness in English and German: the functions of "please" and "bitte." In S. Blum-Kulka, J. House, and G. Kasper (eds.), *Cross-cultural Pragmatics*, 96–119. Norwood, NJ: Ablex.

Hu, H. C. (1944) The Chinese concept of "face." *American Anthropologist*, 46, 45–64.

Ide, S. (1982) Japanese sociolinguistics: politeness and women's language. *Lingua*, 57, 357–85.

—— (1983) Two functional aspects of politeness in women's language. In S. Hattori, K. Inoue, T. Shimomiya, and Y. Nagashima (eds.), *Proceedings of the XIIIth International Congress of Linguists*, 805–8. Tokyo: Tokyo Press.

—— (1989) Formal forms and discernment: two neglected aspects of linguistic politeness. *Multilingua*, 8, 223–48.

—— (1992) Gender and function of language use: quantitative and qualitative evidence from Japanese. In L. F. Bouton and Y. Kachru (eds.), *Pragmatics and Language Learning*, Vol. 3. Urbana: Division of English as an International Language, University of Illinois at Urbana-Champaign.

Ide, S., Hori, M., Kawasaki, A., Ikuta, S., and Haga, H. (1986) Sex differences and politeness in Japanese. *International Journal of the Sociology of Language*, 58, 25–36.

Ikoma, T. (1993) "Sorry for giving me a ride": the use of apologetic expressions to show gratitude in Japanese. Unpublished master's thesis, University of Hawaii at Manoa, Honolulu.

Ikoma, T. and Shimura, A. (1993) Eigo kara nihongo e no puragumatikku toransufaa: "Kotowari" toiu hatsuwa kooi ni tsuite [Pragmatic transfer from English to Japanese: the speech act of refusal]. *Nihongo Kyoiku* [Journal of Japanese Language Teaching], 79.

Janney, R. W. and Arndt, H. (1992) Intracultural tact versus intercultural tact. In R. J. Watts, S. Ide, and K. Ehlich (eds.), *Politeness in Language: Studies in its history, theory and practice*, 21–41. Berlin: Mouton de Gruyter.

Johnson, D. M. (1992) Compliments and politeness in peer-review texts. *Applied Linguistics*, 13, 51–71.

Johnson, D. M. and Yang, A. W. (1990) Politeness strategies in peer review texts. In L. F. Bouton and Y. Kachru (eds.), *Pragmatics and Language Learning*, 99–114. Urbana-Champaign: Division of English as an International Language, University of Illinois at Urbana-Champaign.

Johnson, M. D. and Fawcett, S. B. (1987) Consumer-defined standards for courteous treatment by service agencies. *Journal of Rehabilitation*, 53, 23–6.

Johnstone, B. (1991) Individual style in an American public opinion survey: personal performance and the ideology of referentiality. *Language in Society*, 20, 557–76.

Johnstone, B., Ferrara, K., and Bean, J. M. (1992) Gender, politeness, and discourse management in same-sex and cross-sex opinion-poll interviews. *Journal of Pragmatics*, 18, 405–30.

Jones, K. (1992) A question of context: directive use at a Morris team meeting. *Language in Society*, 21, 427–45.

Kasper, G. (ed.) (1995) *Pragmatics of Chinese as Native and Target Language* (Technical Report #5). Honolulu: University of Hawaii, Second Language Teaching & Curriculum Center.

Keenan, E. (1974) Norm-makers, norm-breakers: uses of speech by men and women in a Malagasy community. In R. Bauman and J. Sherzer (eds.), *Explorations in the Ethnography of Speaking*. Cambridge: Cambridge University Press.

Kitao, K. (1990) A study of Japanese and American perceptions of politeness in requests. *Doshisha Studies in English*, 50, 178–210.

Klein, L. E. (1986) Berkeley, Shaftesbury, and the meaning of politeness. *Studies in Eighteenth-Century Culture*, 16, 57–68.

—— (1990) Politeness in seventeenth-century England and France. *Cahiers du Dix-septième*, 4, 91–106.

Knapp-Potthoff, A. (1992) Secondhand politeness. In R. J. Watts, S. Ide, and K. Ehlich (eds.), *Politeness in Language: Studies in its history, theory and practice*, 203–18. Berlin: Mouton de Gruyter.

Knapp-Potthoff, A. and Knapp, K. (1987) The man (or woman) in the middle: discoursal aspects of non-professional interpreting. In K. Knapp, W. Enninger, and A. Knapp-Potthoff (eds.), *Analyzing Intercultural Communication*, 181–211. New York: Mouton de Gruyter.

Kreml, N. M. P. (1992) Relevance, textual unity, and politeness in writing about science. *Dissertation Abstracts International*, 53, 2794-A.

Kremos, H. (1955) *Höflichkeitsformeln in der französischen Sprache. Aufforderungs- und Bittformeln. Dankesbezeugungen.* (Mit historischem Rückblick bis ins 16. Jahrhundert.) [Politeness formulae in the French language: Request and petition formulae. Expressions of gratitude. (With a historical review from the 16th century.)]. Unpublished doctoral dissertation, University of Zurich, Switzerland.

Krings, H. (1961) *Die Geschichte des Wortschatzes der Höflichkeit im Französischen* [The History of the Vocabulary of Politeness in French]. Unpublished doctoral dissertation, University of Bonn.

Labov, W. (1972) Rules for ritual insults. In D. Sudnow (eds.), *Studies in Social Interaction*. New York: Free Press.

Lakoff, R. (1975) *Language and Women's Place*. New York: Harper and Row.

Lakoff, R. T. (1973) The logic of politeness, or, minding your p's and q's. In C. Corum, T. C. Smith-Stark, and A. Weiser (eds.), *Papers from the Ninth Regional Meeting of the Chicago Linguistic Society*, 292–305. Chicago: Chicago Linguistic Society.

—— (1989) The limits of politeness: therapeutic and courtroom discourse. *Multilingua*, 8, 101–30.

Lampi, M. (1993) Discourse organization and power: Towards a pragmatics of sales negotiations. In L. F. Bouton and Y. Kachru (eds.), *Pragmatics and Language Learning*, Vol. 4, 195–208. Urbana: Division of English as an International Language, University of Illinois at Urbana-Champaign.

Larson, B. E. (1988) An investigation of grammatical differences in writing as found in Japanese and American professional letters. *Dissertation Abstracts International*, 48 (10), 2616-A.

Lebra, T. S. (1976) *Japanese Patterns of Behavior*. Honolulu: University of Hawaii Press.

—— (1993) Culture, self, and communication in Japan and the United States. In W. B. Gudykunst (ed.), *Communication in Japan and the United States*, 57–87. Albany: State University of New York Press.

Leech, G. (1983) *Principles of Pragmatics*. London: Longman.

Limaye, M. and Cherry, R. (1987) Pragmatics, "situated" language, and business communication. *Iowa State Journal of Business and Technical Communication*, 1, 68–88.

Linde, C. (1988a) The quantitative study of communicative success: politeness and accidents in aviation discourse. *Language in Society*, 17, 375–99.

—— (1988b) Who's in charge here? Cooperative work and authority negotiation in police helicopter missions. Paper presented at the 2nd Annual ACM Conference on Computer Supported Collaborative Work (ERIC Document Reproduction Service No. ED301038).

Lörscher, W. and Schulze, R. (1988) On polite speaking and foreign language classroom discourse. *International Review of Applied Linguistics in Language Teaching*, 26, 183–99.

Loveday, L. (1981) Pitch, politeness and sexual role: an exploratory investigation into the pitch correlates of English and Japanese politeness formulae. *Language and Speech*, 24, 71–89.

McMullen, L. M. and Krahn, E. E. (1985) Effects of status and solidarity on familiarity in written communication. *Language and Speech*, 28, 391–401.

Magnusson, A. L. (1992) The rhetoric of politeness and Henry VIII. *Shakespeare Quarterly*, 43, 319–409.

Mao, L. R. (1994) Beyond politeness theory: "Face" revisited and renewed. *Journal of Pragmatics*, 21, 451–86.

Marier, P. (1992) Politeness strategies in business letters by native and non-native English speakers. *English for Specific Purposes*, 11, 189–205.

Markus, H. R. and Kitayama, S. (1991) Culture and the self: implications for cognition, emotion, and motivation. *Psychological Review*, 98, 224–53.

Matsumoto, Y. (1988) Reexamination of the universality of face: politeness phenomena in Japanese. *Journal of Pragmatics*, 12, 403–26.

—— (1989) Politeness and conversational universals – observations from Japanese. *Multilingua*, 8, 207–22.

—— (1993) The pragmatic functions of object honorification in Japanese. Paper presented at the Fourth International Pragmatics Conference, Kobe, July.

Milan, W. G. (1976) The influence of the sex and age factors in the selection of politeness expressions: a sample from Puerto Rican Spanish. *Bilingual Review*, 3, 99–121.

Miller, R. S. (1991) On decorum in close relationships: why aren't we polite to those who we love? *Contemporary Social Psychology*, 15, 63–5.

Morand, D. A. (1991) Power and politeness: a sociolinguistic analysis of dominance, deference, and egalitarianism in organizational interaction. *Dissertation Abstracts International*, 52, 2207-A.

Morgan, M. H. (1991) Indirectness and interpretation in African-American women's discourse. *Pragmatics*, 1, 421–51.

Morosawa, A. (1990) Intimacy and urgency in request forms of Japanese: a psycholinguistic study. *Sophia Linguistica*, 28, 129–43.

Morrison, I. R. (1988) Remarques sur les pronoms allucutifs chez Rabelais [Remarks on the allocative pronouns in Rabelais]. *Zeitschrift für Romanische Philologie*, 104, 1–11.

Myers, G. (1989) The pragmatics of politeness in scientific articles. *Applied Linguistics*, 10, 1–35.

—— (1991) Politeness and certainty: the language of collaboration in an AI project. *Social Studies of Science*, 21, 37–73.

Nippold, M. A., Leonard, L. B., and Anastopoulos, A. (1982) Development in the use and understanding of polite forms in children. *Journal of Speech and Hearing Research*, 25, 193–202.

Nunes, S. A. (1981) Ordering and serving: an analysis of the social interactions of bartenders and waiters at a Waikiki drink call station. Unpublished master's thesis, University of Hawaii at Manoa, Honolulu.

Ochs, E. (1988) *Culture and Language Development: Language acquisition and language socialization in a Samoan village.* Cambridge: Cambridge University Press.

Olshtain, E. (1989) Apologies across languages. In S. Blum-Kulka, J. House, and G. Kasper (eds.), *Cross-cultural Pragmatics*, 155–73. Norwood, NJ: Ablex.

Olshtain, E. and Weinbach, L. (1993) Interlanguage features of the speech act of complaining. In G. Kasper and S. Blum-Kulka (eds.), *Interlanguage Pragmatics*, 108–22. New York: Oxford University Press.

Ostrup, J. (1929) *Orientalische Hoeflichkeit. Formen und Formeln im Islam. Eine kulturgeschichtliche Studie* [Oriental politeness. Forms and formulas in Islam. A study in cultural history]. Leipzig: Harrassowitz.

Parkinson, M. G. (1981) Verbal behavior and courtroom success. *Communication Education*, 30, 22–32.

Pearson, B. (1988) Power and politeness in conversation: encoding of face-threatening acts at church business meetings. *Anthropological Linguistics*, 30, 68–93.

Perlmann, R. (1984) Variations in socialization styles: family talk at the dinner table. *Journal of Child Language*, 12, 271–96.

Pickett, A. M. (1989) ESL business letters of request: a discourse analysis of written text. Unpublished master's thesis, University of Hawaii at Manoa, Honolulu.

Plascencia, M. (1992) Politeness in mediated telephone conversations in Ecuadorian Spanish and British English. *Language Learning Journal*, 6, 80–2.

Popov, P. (1985) On the origin of Russian "vy" as a form of polite address. *Slavic and East European Journal*, 29, 330–7.

Preisler, B. (1986) *Linguistic Sex Roles in Conversation: Social variation in the expression of tentativeness in English.* Berlin: Mouton de Gruyter.

Reynolds, K. A. (1985) Female speakers of Japanese. *Feminist Issues*, Fall, 13–46.

—— (1989a) Gengo to sei yakuwari [Language and sex roles]. In N. W. E. Center (eds.), *Joseigaku koza* [Women's Studies Lectures], 61–5. Tokyo: Daiichi Hoki.

—— (1989b) Josei zasshi no kotoba [Language in women's magazines]. In T. Inoue (ed.), *Josei zasshi wo kaidoku-suru* [Decoding women's magazines], 209–27. Tokyo: Kakiuchi Shuppan.

—— (1990) Female speakers of Japanese in transition. In S. Ide and N. McGloin (eds.), *Aspects of Japanese Women's Language*, 1–17. Tokyo: Kuroshio Shuppan.

Rimac, R. T. (1986) Comprehension and production of indirect requests by language disordered and normal children: an examination of politeness and pragmatic development. *Dissertation Abstracts International*, 46, 3811-B.

Rings, L. (1987) Kriemhilt's face work: a sociolinguistic analysis of social behavior in the Nibelungenlied. *Semiotica*, 65, 317–25.

Roberts, J. (1992) Face-threatening acts and politeness theory: contrasting speeches from supervisory conferences. *Journal of Curriculum and Supervision*, 7, 287–301.

Robins, L. S. and Wolf, F. M. (1988) Confrontation and politeness strategies in physician–patient interactions. *Social Science and Medicine*, 27, 217–21.

Rosenberger, N. R. (1989) Dialectic balance in the polar model of self: the Japan case. *Ethos*, 17, 88–113.

Sadow, S. A. and Maxwell, M. A. (1983) The foreign teaching assistant and the culture of the American university class. Paper presented at the 16th Annual TESOL Convention, Honolulu, HI (ERIC Document Reproduction Service No. ED228897).

Scheerhorn, D. R. (1991) Politeness in decision-making. *Research on Language and Social Interaction*, 25, 253.

Schegloff, E. (1979) Identification and recognition in telephone conversation openings. In G. Psathas (ed.), *Everyday Language. Studies in ethnomethodology*, 23–78. New York: Irvington.

Schieffelin, B. B. (1990) *The Give and Take of Everyday Life: Language socialization of Kaluli children.* Cambridge: Cambridge University Press.

Schieffelin, B. B. and Eisenberg, A. R. (1984) Cultural variation in children's conversations. In R. L. Schiefelbusch and J. Pickar (eds.), *The Acquisition of Communicative Competence*, 377–420. Baltimore, MD: University Park Press.

Scollon, R. and Scollon, S. (1981) *Narrative, Literacy and Face in Interethnic Communication*. Norwood, NJ: Ablex.

Scollon, R. and Scollon, S. B. K. (1983) Face in interethnic communication. In J. C. Richards and R. W. Schmidt (eds.), *Language and Communication*. London: Longman.

Searle, J. R. (1976) A classification of illocutionary acts. *Language in Society*, 5, 1–23.

Sell, R. D. (1985a) Tellability and politeness in the Miller's tale: first steps in literary pragmatics. *English Studies*, 66, 496–512.

—— (1985b) Politeness in Chaucer: suggestions towards a methodology for pragmatic stylistics. *Studia Neophilologica*, 57, 175–85.

Shibamoto, J. S. (1987) The womanly woman: manipulation of stereotypical and nonstereotypical features of Japanese female speech. In S. U. Philips, S. Steel, and C. Tanz (eds.), *Language, Gender, and Sex in Comparative Perspective*, 26–49. Cambridge: Cambridge University Press.

Shimamura, K. (1993) Judgement of request strategies and contextual factors by Americans and Japanese EFL learners. Unpublished master's thesis, University of Hawaii at Manoa.

Sifianou, M. (1989) On the telephone again! Differences in telephone behaviour: England versus Greece. *Language in Society*, 18, 527–44.

Slugoski, B. R. (1985) *Grice's Theory of Conversation as a Social Psychological Model*. PhD dissertation, Oxford.

Smith-Hefner, N. J. (1981) To level or not to level: Codes of politeness and prestige in rural Java. In C. S. Masek, R. A. Hendrick, and M. F. Miller (eds.), *Papers from the Parasession on Language and Behavior: Chicago Linguistic Society*, 211–17. Chicago: Chicago Linguistic Society.

—— (1988) Women and politeness: the Javanese example. *Language in Society*, 17, 535–54.

Snow, C. E., Perlmann, R. Y., Gleason, J. B., and Hooshyar, N. (1990) Developmental perspectives on politeness: sources of children's knowledge. *Journal of Pragmatics*, 14, 289–305.

Soh, J.-C. (1985) Social changes and their impact on speech level in Korean. In J. D. Woods and R. R. K. Hartmann (eds.), *Language Standards and their Codification: Process and application*, 29–41. Exeter: University of Exeter Press.

Song-Cen, C. (1991) Social distribution and development of greeting expressions in China. *International Journal of the Sociology of Language*, 92, 55–60.

Stemmer, B. (1994) A pragmatic approach to neurolinguistics: requests (re)considered. *Brain and Language*, 46, 565–91.

Stemmer, B., Giroux, F., and Joanette, Y. (1994) Production and evaluation of requests by right hemisphere brain-damaged individuals. *Brain and Language*, 47, 1–31.

Sussman, N. M., and Rosenfeld, H. M. (1982) Influence of culture, language, and sex on conversational distance. *Journal of Personality and Social Psychology*, 42, 66–74.

Takahara, K. (1991) Female speech patterns in Japanese. *International Journal of the Sociology of Language*, 92, 61–85.

Takahashi, S. (1992) *Transferability of indirect request strategies*. University of Hawaii Working Papers in ESL, 11, 69–124.

Takahashi, T. and Beebe, L. M. (1993) Cross-linguistic influence in the speech act of correction. In G. Kasper and S. Blum-Kulka (eds.), *Interlanguage Pragmatics*, 138–57. New York: Oxford University Press.

Tannen, D. (1986) *That's not what I meant*. New York: Ballantine Books.

Van De Walle, L. C. (1991) Pragmatics and classical Sanskrit: a pilot study in linguistic politeness. *Dissertation Abstracts International*, 53, 1503-A.

Vollmer, H. and Olshtain, E. (1989) The language of apologies in German. In S. Blum-Kulka, J. House, and G. Kasper (eds.), *Cross-cultural Pragmatics*, 197–218. Norwood, NJ: Ablex.

Waller, M. and Schoeler, J. (1985) Die Entwicklung des Verständnisses der situativen Variationsbreite unterschiedlich höflicher Fragen [The development of the comprehension of the situational variety of differentially polite questions]. *Zeitschrift für Entwicklungspsychologie und Pädagogische Psychologie*, 17, 27–40.

Waller, S. and Valtin, R. (1992) Children's understanding of white lies. In R. J. Watts, S. Ide, and K. Ehlich (eds.), *Politeness in Language: Studies in its history, theory and practice*, 231–51. Berlin: Mouton de Gruyter.

Watts, R. J. (1989) Relevance and relational work: linguistic politeness as politic behavior. *Multilingua*, 8, 131–66.

—— (1992) Linguistic politeness and politic verbal behaviour: reconsidering claims for universality. In R. J. Watts, S. Ide, and K. Ehlich (eds.), *Politeness in Language: Studies in its history, theory and practice*, 43–69. Berlin: Mouton de Gruyter.

Watts, R. J., Ide, S., and Ehlich, K. (1992) Introduction. In R. J. Watts, S. Ide, and K. Ehlich (eds.), *Politeness in Language: Studies in its history, theory and practice*, 1–17. Berlin: Mouton de Gruyter.

Weizman, E. (1985) Towards analysis of opaque utterances: hints as a request strategy. *Theoretical Linguistics*, 12, 153–63.

—— (1989) Requestive hints. In S. Blum-Kulka, J. House, and G. Kasper (eds.), *Cross-cultural Pragmatics*, 71–96. Norwood, NJ: Ablex.

—— (1993) Interlanguage requestive hints. In G. Kasper and S. Blum-Kulka (eds.), *Interlanguage Pragmatics*, 123–37. New York: Oxford University Press.

Wenger, J. R. (1983) Variation and change in Japanese honorific forms. *Papers in Linguistics*, 16, 267–301.

Wierzbicka, A. (1991) Japanese key words and core cultural values. *Language in Society*, 20, 333–85.

Wilhite, M. (1983) Children's acquisition of language routines: the end-of-meal routine in Cakohiquel language. *Language in Society*, 12, 47–61.

Wojtak, M. (1989) Grzecznosc postaropolsku w swietle pamietnikow Jana Chryzostoma Paska [Politeness in old Polish in the light of the diaries of Jan Chryzostom]. *Poradnik Jezykowy*, 8, 528–33.

Wolfson, N. (1989) *Perspectives: Sociolinguistics and TESOL*. Cambridge, MA: Newbury House.

Wright, J. D. (1987) The effects of hedges and hesitations on impression formation in a simulated court-room context. *Western Journal of Speech Communication*, 51, 173–88.

Yabar, P. (1975) Sobre la particula japonesa *wa* en el habla femenina [The Japanese particle *wa* in women's speech]. *Lenguaje y Ciencias*, 15, 89–96.

Yamada, H. (1990) Topic management and turn distribution in business meetings: American versus Japanese strategies. *Text*, 10, 271–95.

Yamashita, M. Y. (1983) An empirical study of variation in the use of honorific forms in Japanese: an analysis of forms produced by a group of women in an urban setting. *Dissertation Abstracts International*, 44, 1780A.

Yoshinaga, N., Maeshiba, N., and Takahashi, S. (1992) Bibliography on Japanese pragmatics. In G. Kasper (ed.), *Pragmatics of Japanese as Native and Target Language* (Technical report #3), 1–26. Honolulu: University of Hawaii, Second Language Teaching & Curriculum Center.

Yuan, J. F., Kuiper, K., and Shaogu, S. (1990) Language and revolution: formulae of the cultural revolution. *Language in Society*, 19, 61–79.

Zammuner, V. L. (1991) Children's writing of argumentative texts: effects of indirect instruction. *European Journal of Psychology of Education*, 6, 243–56.

Zilliacus, H. (1949) *Untersuchungen zu den abstrakten Anredeformen und Höflichkeitstiteln im Griechischen* [Investigation of abstract terms of address and politeness titles in Greek]. Helsingfors: Centraltrykkeriet.

Zimin, S. (1981) Sex and politeness: factors in first- and second-language use. *International Journal of the Sociology of Language*, 27, 35–58.

6

Constructing Social Identity: A Language Socialization Perspective

Elinor Ochs

6.1 Introduction

The New York Times (Rimer, 1992) recently printed a journal essay on immigrant parents who react to their children learning English with a sense of pride mingled with a sense of loss. Their sense of loss concerns children's shifting social identities, including shifts in their relationship to their parents as well as transformations of family values that often accompany children's adoption of another language. Rather than children being dependent on parents, parents find themselves dependent on children, who become mediators for their parents as they interact with the local environment. In some families, generational ties are tested as children and parents increasingly struggle to find common ground.

The thrust of *The New York Times* piece is old news to those linguists who for several decades have charted the linguistic and sociocultural journeys of language acquirers, who by choice or necessity operate in complex multicode and multicultural universes. In this article, I provide a theoretical perspective on this and other circumstances in which language acquisition is closely tied to social identity. For purposes of this discussion, I consider "social identity" as a cover term for a range of social personae, including social statuses, roles, positions, relationships, and institutional and other relevant community identities one may attempt to claim or assign in the course of social life.

Linguistic constructions at all levels of grammar and discourse are crucial indicators of social identity for members as they regularly interact with one another; complementarily, social identity is a crucial dimension of the social meaning of particular linguistic constructions. But no matter how crucial language is for understanding social identity and social identity for understanding the social meaning of language, social identity is rarely grammaticized or otherwise explicitly encoded across the world's languages.[1] In other words, the relation between language and social identity is predominantly a sociolinguistically *distant* one.

Elinor Ochs, "Constructing social identity: A language socialization perspective" from *Research on Language and Social Interaction* 26:3 (1993), pp. 287–306. Reprinted by permission of Lawrence Erlbaum Associates, Inc.

In this article, I suggest ways in which researchers of language socialization and language development might understand this distant and complex relation between language and social identity. Specifically, I argue that speakers attempt to establish the social identities of themselves and others through verbally performing certain social *acts* and verbally displaying certain *stances*. In this article, "social act" means any socially recognized, goal-directed behavior, such as making a request, contradicting another person, or interrupting someone (Ochs, 1990). "Stance" means a display of a socially recognized point of view or attitude (Biber & Finegan, 1989; Ochs & Schieffelin, 1989). Stance includes displays of *epistemic* attitudes, such as how certain or uncertain a speaker is about some proposition (Chafe & Nichols, 1986), and displays of *affective* attitudes, such as intensity of emotion or kind of emotion about some referent or proposition (Besnier, 1990; Ochs & Schieffelin, 1989).

6.2   Linguistic Resources for Constructing Social Identity

My discussion explores how competent native speakers build identities such as woman, man, mother, father, child, scientist, and foreigner by performing particular kinds of acts and displaying particular kinds of epistemic and affective stances. Speakers may use a verbal act or stance in an attempt to construct not only their own identities but the social identities of other interlocutors. Thus, for example, I may attempt to build my identity as a professional academic by performing a range of professional acts, such as hypothesizing, claiming, instructing, and assessing, and displaying stances, such as objectivity, knowledgeability, and intellectual flexibility. On the other hand, *other* people in my environment are also trying to construct my identity. Thus, I may run into someone who, in the course of the same encounter, directs a number of compliments toward me. I may infer, on the basis of recognizing those conventional acts of flattery, that my interlocutor is perhaps attempting to foreground my gender identity as a woman or perhaps trying to forge an intimate social relationship with me or to establish me in an exalted position and/or make me indebted to him or her for so establishing me in this position.

In all of these cases, the relation of language to social identity is not direct but rather *mediated* by the interlocutors' understandings of conventions for doing particular social acts and stances and the interlocutors' understandings of how acts and stances are resources for structuring particular social identities (Brown & Levinson, 1979; Ochs, 1988, 1993). Membership in a social group, whether it be a distinct language community or a distinct social group within a language community, depends on members' knowledge of local conventions for building social identities through act and stance displays. Somewhat like the valences that chemical elements have that bind them together in particular ways to form chemical compounds, particular acts and particular stances have local conventional links that bind them together to form particular social identities. Social identity is a complex social meaning that can be distilled into the act and stance meanings that bring it into being. From this point of view, social identity is not usually explicitly encoded by language but rather is a social meaning that one usually *infers* on the basis of one's sense of the act and stance meanings encoded by linguistic constructions. Of course, although some acts and stances are closely associated with particular social identities, other acts and stances are resources for constructing a wide range of social identities. Hence, some identities are more readily inferrable from acts and stances (e.g., the identity of teacher inferrable from asking a test question in the US or the identity of low-ranking person inferrable from a stance of attentiveness and accommodation in traditional Samoan communities) than others.

A chemical analogy (i.e., valences) is appealing to characterize cultural conventions for linking acts and stances to social identity. The analogy stops here, however, because social identities are not automatic reactions or stable outcomes of particular act and stance displays. As is discussed in Section 5, acts and stances are related in complex ways to social identities. There is not necessarily a rigid or obligatory mapping of certain acts and stances onto certain identities. Rather members of communities may use different kinds of acts and stances to construct themselves variably within some particular social status or social relationship. Further, whether or not a particular social identity does indeed take hold in a social interaction depends minimally on (a) whether the speaker and other interlocutors share cultural and linguistic conventions for constructing particular acts and stances; (b) whether the speaker and other interlocutors share economic, political, or other social histories and conventions that associate those acts and stances with the particular social identity a speaker is trying to project; and (c) whether other interlocutors are able and willing or are otherwise constrained to ratify the speaker's claim to that identity.

6.3   Levels of Competence in Constructing Social Identity

In this sense, assignment of social identity is a complex inferential and social process. And if we want to understand as researchers and acquirers of language and culture why an acquirer's claim to a social identity failed at some particular moment, we need to sort out the level that accounts for the failure.

Did the acquirer produce the verbal action or stance in a conventional manner? For example, did the acquirer compliment, ask a question, make a hypothesis, or display a stance of certainty or intimacy in a conventional manner? If not, the failure may be due to the acquirer's lack of knowledge concerning local conventions for act or stance production. Is the acquirer displaying acts and stances that are consonant with local understandings of particular statuses, relationships, ranks, and group identities? For example, is the way a first or second language acquirer is complimenting, asking a question, formulating a hypothesis, or displaying certainty or intimacy consonant with local understandings and expectations concerning what it is to be a child, a student, a woman, a man, or a foreigner? If not, failure to establish social identity may not be due to the acquirer's lack of understanding of how to perform particular acts and stances linguistically but to a lack of understanding as to how in that particular community those acts and stances are conventionally related to particular social identities.

And, even if all of these understandings are in place, a projected social identity may not take hold if an acquirer does not know the conventions for linguistically *ratifying* a speaker's claim to social identity. An acquirer may not know how to show alignment with a speaker concerning the social identity of one or other interlocutor or some nonpresent referent. These questions need to be probed to discern how human beings construct social identity in social interactions the world over. Such questions also begin to illuminate breakdowns in the communication of social identity in everyday life.

6.4   Constructing Social Identity in Childhood

It makes good sense to understand social identity as a social construct that is both inferred and interactionally achieved through displays and ratifications of acts and stances, from the point of view of an infant or small child coming to understand social order. Even before birth, fetuses are aware of the movement and tone of voice of their mothers (Grimwade, Walker, Bartlett, Gordon, & Wood, 1970; Salk, 1973). These sensations are the perceptual building blocks of infants' rudimentary understandings of another person (Cole & Cole, 1989). And from birth on, infants come to know objects in the world, including themselves and others, through their own sensorimotor actions and interactions with those objects (Piaget & Inhelder, 1969).

Actions such as touching, reaching, sucking, manipulating, and transforming are not only ways of knowing objects, but they are also fundamental conceptual dimensions of children's representations of objects. For example, actions are fundamental to children's concepts of objects as agents and patients (Piaget, 1952; Bruner, Jolly, & Sylva, 1976; Bruner, 1986). Objects can be touchers and touchables, reachers and reachables, suckers and suckables, manipulators and manipulatables, transformers and transformables, and, in the case of human objects, interactors and interactables. These sensorimotor identities are some of the first identities that a child constructs in life, and they are derivative of actions in the world.

Stances are also building blocks of children's concepts of objects both animate and inanimate. In the course of their first year of life, infants come to recognize and use conventional facial and prosodic markers of affect (Halliday, 1975; Campos & Stenberg, 1981; Cruttenden, 1986). Further, they come to associate particular kinds of affect with particular objects in the world. Studies of the development of social cognition indicate, for example, that infants confronted with a new person or thing will attend to the affective displays of their co-present mothers before deciding on whether or not or how to approach that person or thing. This behavior, called *social referencing*, suggests that infants' understandings of novel persons or things is mediated by the affective stances of mothers (Campos & Stenberg, 1981; Sroufe, Schork, Motti, Larowski, & LaFreniere, 1984). Or, to put it another way, when mothers display a particular affective stance toward a person or thing, they are attempting to construct a social relationship between their child and that person or thing. When children react to novel objects (e.g., by approaching or avoiding) in ways compatible with their mother's affective displays, they ratify their mother's construction of how the child ought to relate to some object. In this way, mother and child *jointly* construct the relationship between the child and some person or thing in the world (Vygotsky, 1978). These joint constructions produced in the course of moment-to-moment interaction socialize infants into how they should think about people around them and provide them with models of how they themselves might use affective displays to create, transform, or destroy relationships and other social identities.

As infants develop their capacity to conceptualize and remember, they come to associate certain actions and stances with the structuring of their own and other's identities. Certain recurrent act and stance displays by certain persons that are routinely ratified by others become part of the child's experiential knowledge of such fundamental social identities as mother, father, daughter, son, younger sibling, older sibling, or what it means to be a family (Ainsworth, 1982; Dunn, 1984, 1986). One example of how social identity is jointly constituted and socialized through the display and ratification of particular actions comes from research on language socialization in traditional Western Samoan communities (Ochs, 1988). As in many communities, Western Samoans are keenly interested in their child's first word. And, again as in many communities, Western Samoans have expectations about what that first word will be. When asked about the first word of some child in the family, each Samoan caregiver provided the very same word. The first word is *tae*, a fragment of an expression that literally means "eat shit!" That is, in this community, children's earliest meaningful sounds were interpreted and ratified as a particular social act, namely a conventional curse. As infants recurrently are interpreted in this fashion, they become ratified and eventually take on the expected social identity of cursers. One mother articulated the role of others in constituting the young child as curser as follows:

Mother: . . . you know, when the Samoan kids ⌈say something⌉
Elinor: ⌊u h   h u h⌋
Mother: then the Samoan ((pause)) WOMAN you know
Elinor: hmm.
Mother: or Samoan people ⌈said 'Oh! she said "Tae" ((laughs)) *Tae!*
Elinor: ⌊hmm. yeah
Mother: So maybe that's the FIRST word they know
         ((pause))
Elinor: hmm.
Mother: *Tae.* And so the people ((empathic particle)), we- we as adults. . . .
         ((laughs))
         ((pause))
         then we know- then we know
Elinor: Hmm.
Mother: ((soft)) oh my- my- my child is starting to first say the
         word *tae* ⌈or ((pause)) stupid
Elinor: ⌊Yeah ((pause)) swearing a lot ((laughs))
Mother: stupid. That's a first word but ((pause)) to a kid,
Elinor: Hmm. ((pause)) Hmm.
Mother: to a kid it is ((pause)) he doesn't REALLY mean *tae*
Elinor: Hmm.
Mother: He doesn't. We are translating ⌈into that word *tae*
Elinor: ⌊Hmm.
Mother: because we- we mean he says *tae.*
Elinor: Hmm.
Mother: But to a kid. NO!
         ⋮

Mother: There's a time when they grow up and they know the ((pause)) *tae* is a BAD
        word
Elinor: Hmm!
Mother: And they hear their parent. They (are) then to say *tae* when they-when you
        get mad ⌈you know
Elinor: ⌊Hmm!
Mother: And so the kid learns!
Elinor: Hmm!
Mother: When you get mad, you say *tae*. That's why ((pause))
Elinor: Hmm. mmm.
Mother: uhh- when they call out, they know the word.

There is a sociocultural concept of the Samoan child as wild and cheeky by nature that underlies this interpretation of the child's first word as a curse. But the point of import here is that this concept of the child as curser is jointly constructed, maintained, and socialized through on-the-ground social interactions. As this Samoan mother put it, the child makes a sound, others "translate it" into the act of cursing, and eventually the child becomes the curser she or he is expected "by nature" to be.

Another example of how children come to understand social identity through recurrently displayed actions comes from a language socialization study of American families with young children at dinner time (Ochs, Taylor, Rudolph, & Smith, 1992; Ochs & Taylor, 1992a, 1992b; Ochs, 1993). A characteristic activity of these family dinners is collaborative or jointly produced storytelling and reporting of the day's events. Those participating in the dinner meal do not merely nod their heads nonchalantly in acknowledgment of an unfolding narrative. Rather, they actively supply and elicit crucial narrative material such as settings, inciting events, psychological states, and actions and consequences among other narrative parts. They also introduce narratives about other family members present, problematize the way protagonists attempted to resolve a narrative problem, and challenge one another's and other people's versions of the narrative events, such that over the course of the dinner, narratives become co-authored by those present. Such intense co-authoring of narratives is, in our eyes, constitutive of the family itself. Those people participating in the dinner meal constitute themselves as a family not only through the activity of eating together but also through the activity of co-narration. The acts that construct a narrative are also acts that construct a family. Many scholars have noted the socializing power of narrative for children who hear them, but they have primarily focused on the socializing messages carried in the *content* of narratives. The point of the family dinner narrative study is, however, that, beyond content, it is the narrative interaction itself – the joining together of narrative acts from different persons to form a narrative – night after night that socializes co-present children into an understanding of the family. It is of course true that families are legally defined institutions independent of co-authoring stories. But from a child's point of view, a family is what a family *does*. For some children, a family is those persons who recurrently eat dinner together and participate in co-authoring narrative events that they usually have not themselves experienced firsthand. For other children, these activities are not necessarily constitutive of their families. Or, for the same children, these activities may diminish over historical time, thereby transforming their representation of the family. In some cases, the transformation may be gradual; or, as in cases of economic or marital woes or therapeutic interventions, the transformation may be radical. In every case, the identity of the family is an outcome of jointly constructed actions.

6.5   Correlational Studies of Language and Social Identity

This view of social identity as an inferential *outcome* of linguistically encoded acts and stances goes dead against sociolinguistic analyses that assume social identities as a priori givens, including all correlational studies of language and social identity, where taken-for-granted social identities are posited as independent variables. In the social constructive approach to identity advocated here, the researcher (and, I might add, the interlocutor as well) asks "What kind of social identity is a person attempting to construct in performing this kind of verbal act or in verbally expressing this kind of stance?" (see Gumperz, 1982). In the social-identity-as-a priori-social-fact approach, the researcher asks "How does a person having this social identity speak?" In correlational studies of urban sociolinguistic variation, the question usually is "How do members of particular socioeconomic, ethnic, or generational groups speak across these situations?" In the case of gender studies the questions are "How do women speak?" and "How do men speak?" In other studies, the question might be "How do caregivers and children or foreigns and locals speak?" We recognize that social identities have a sociohistorical reality independent of language behavior, but, in any given actual situation, at any given actual moment, people in those situations are actively constructing their social identities rather than passively living out some cultural prescription for social identity. Interlocutors are actively constructing themselves as members of a community or professional organization, as persons of a particular social rank, as husbands and wives, as teachers, as foreigners, and even, I dare say, as language learners. In *all* situations, even the most institutionalized and ritualized, people are *agents* in the production of their own and others' social selves. When researchers ask "What does such and such a social identity do?," they *assume* interlocutors are identifying themselves through language as specified by the researcher, but this may not necessarily be the case. All situations allow room for play in the social identities that any one person may take on (Duranti, 1981).

In addition to these misgivings, the social-identity-as-a priori-social-fact approach at best *under*represents the social meanings that speakers and other interlocutors are accomplishing and at worst *mis*represents those meanings altogether. When researchers treat social identity as an independent variable, they treat that social variable as an *explanation* for language variation. The social identity is the stimulus, and the language behavior is the response. But this is hardly an explanation in that few accounts explain why these *particular* linguistic structures are selected to signal these *particular* social identities. The choice of linguistic structures themselves is treated as *arbitrary* – that is, social identity is often considered to be signaled through arbitrary phonological, morphosyntactic, lexical, or discursive structures. When researchers focus exclusively on social identity in this way, they do not see *other* social meanings, *other* social contexts – such as social acts and stance – that those same linguistic structures encode, and they do not see that, far from arbitrary, these linguistic structures are linked to social identities *rationally*, because of systematic cultural expectations linking certain acts and stances encoded by these linguistic structures to certain identities. Thus, from a social constructivist perspective, it is not arbitrary that a speaker might use a linguistic structure, such as a tag question in English, to project the gender identity of "woman," *if* tag questions are linguistic resources for constructing the act of requesting confirmation and the stance of uncertainty and if that act and that stance are conventionally linked to local socio-political realizations for being a woman (Ochs, 1992).

It has been demonstrated over and over that the fit between social identity and language behavior is not a tight one and that linguistic structures cannot be neatly assigned to the purview of one or another social identity (see Irvine, 1974, and Brown & Levinson, 1979, for extended discussion). Correlational studies of language and social identity rely on average frequencies or probabilities of usage and often cannot account for why some of those recorded use a linguistic structure *often*, yet others of supposedly the same social identity hardly use the same structures *at all*, and why others of supposedly a *different* social identity may also use those structures.

In an approach that is social constructivist in nature, we can begin to understand some of this variation. We look first at the kinds of acts and stances the linguistic features in question are helping to construct and ask if the variation in frequency of the particular linguistic structures is because the speakers are attempting to construct different kinds of social acts and stances. Only then might we ask why some particular speaker constructs these particular social acts and stances more often than or in a different fashion from some other speaker. Is it because local sociocultural entitlements or obligations to construct those acts or those stances favor certain persons over others? Is it because society allows for the possibility of act and stance variation within the same gross social identity, such that people may vary their act and stance displays to construct themselves and others to be, for example, different kinds of children, different kinds of parents, different kinds of students, or different kinds of foreigners? Or can parties use acts and stance displays to construct, for example, different kinds of families, classrooms, or, more globally, different kinds of communities? Or is it that some speakers more than others are struggling to *change* social expectations concerning particular social identities through systematically altering their social acts and stances? Or do we find linguistic variation because the same speakers do not necessarily sustain a constant social identity throughout the course of a single interaction with the same interlocutors? The same speakers may shift their acts and stances many times and, in so doing, reconfigure the social identities of themselves and others over a brief period of time. Social identities evolve in the course of social interaction, transformed in response to the acts and stances of other interlocutors as well as to fluctuations in how a speaker decides to participate in the activity at hand.

The social constructivist approach to social identity captures the ebbs and tides of identity construction over interactional time, over historical time, and even over developmental time. It provides a nonarbitrary account of how language can relate to social identity without grammaticizing it. By rooting social identity in the interactional production of acts and stances, the social constructive approach allows us to further understand some of the existential conditions of life in society. Without appearing too glib, we can understand "identity crises" as anxieties over one's inability or failure to achieve some identity through failure to act and feel in some expected or desired way or through the failure of others to ratify those displayed acts and feelings. Within the social constructivist approach, we can examine how different displays of and different reactions to acts and stances give rise to different familial and professional identities. These displays and reactions can be examined for what they reveal about the interactional generation and social orderliness of distressed and dysfunctional relationships. A social constructivist perspective also holds some promise as a means of illuminating how people construct satisfactory lives and a coherent sense of self out of manifold, shifting, momentary identities. A social constructivist approach allows us to examine the building of multiple, yet perfectly compatible identities – identities that are subtle and perhaps have no label, blended identities, even blurred identities. It is just this sort of construction that every language and culture acquirer must learn to accomplish, because there are no simple social or linguistic formulae that spit out how to compose suitable identities for the occasion.

6.6   Cultural Universals and Differences in the Linguistic Construction of Social Identity

Finally, the social constructivist approach illuminates cross-cultural similarities and differences in the production and interpretation of social identity (Gumperz, 1982). Cross-cultural comparisons can be made in terms of conventions for performing and reacting to particular acts and expressing stances, especially linguistic conventions for doing so, and in terms of conventions that tie particular act and stance displays to the construction of particular social identities (Irvine, 1974; Brown & Levinson, 1978).

We could in theory find vast differences in the construction of social identities across communities because communities differ radically in the linguistic conventions for indexing what act or stance is in play at the moment. In practice, however, it appears that there are many cross-cultural similarities in the linguistic construction of social acts and affective and epistemic stances.

Candidate universals in the linguistic structuring of social acts include the use of interrogative pronouns and syntax and rising intonation to construct requests for information and requests for goods and services (Searle, 1970; Clark & Lucy, 1975; Gordon & Lakoff, 1975; Blum-Kulka & Olshtain, 1984; Ervin-Tripp & Gordon, 1984; Goodwin, 1990), the use of tag questions and particles to construct requests for confirmation (Lakoff, 1973; Dubois & Crouch, 1975), and the use of imperatives and address terms to constitute summons and order (Schegloff, 1972; Platt, 1986). Further, probably all societies have affirmative and negative particles to construct the acts of agreement and disagreement and acceptance, rejection, and refusal. In addition, there are commonalities across languages and communities in the linguistic shape of other acts such as greeting, announcing, thanking, assessing, complimenting, claiming, suggesting, granting permission, complaining, and threatening among others.

Universals or near universals also appear in the linguistic marking of epistemic and affective stances, including the marking of relative certainty and uncertainty (Levinson, 1983; Givon, 1989), and direct and indirect sources of knowledge (Chafe & Nichols, 1986), surprise, anger, fear, worry, alignment, and pleasure among others (Ochs & Schieffelin, 1989; Besnier, 1990; Irvine, 1990). For example, the stance of certainty is widely marked through factive predicates, determiners, cleft constructions, and other presupposing structures (Levinson, 1983; Givon, 1989), whereas uncertainty is widely marked through modals, rising intonation, and interrogative constructions (Lakoff, 1972). Possible universals in the marking of affective intensity include the use of vowel lengthening, modulation of volume and pace of delivery, use of a morphologically marked form (e.g., use of plural marking for a single referent, use of demonstrative pronoun to refer to a person rather than a thing), and code switching (Stankiewicz, 1964; Duranti, 1984; Ochs & Schieffelin, 1989).

Such commonalities in the representation of social acts and stances indicate that human beings share elements of a universal culture. That is, children the world over are being socialized into and acquiring certain common ways of linguistically structuring the world. These commonalities constitute a corpus of basic cultural resources for constituting social identities, and anyone who travels across the borders of their own communities to cultural *terra incognita* brings with them this common repertoire. It is this common human culture that allows us to make some sense of fellow members of our species in intercultural encounters.

Cross-cultural differences in the interactional construction of social identity, I suggest, lie predominantly in the links, or valences as I have referred to them earlier, that obtain between acts and stances on the one hand and social identity on the other. And, it is at this level that intercultural communication often flounders (Gumperz, 1982). Communities often differ in which acts and stances are preferred and prevalent cultural resources for building particular identities. In one community, a stance or act may be widely used to construct some social identity, whereas in another that stance or act is rarely drawn on to construct that identity. For example, Schieffelin and I (Ochs & Schieffelin, 1984; Schieffelin & Ochs, 1986) found that the identities of caregivers and children are constructed differently across societies. In some societies, such as middle class America, the identities of caregivers and infants are constructed through acts and stances that display a great deal of cognitive accommodation by the caregiver to the child, including especially the use of a simplified register in the presence of the infant. In other societies, such as the Kaluli of Papua New Guinea and the Samoan society, the identities of caregivers and infants are constructed by the inverse orientation, namely through acts and stances that display cognitive accommodation by the child to the caregiver (Ochs, 1988; Schieffelin, 1990). Whereas accommodation by the caregiver is a valued characteristic of middle class American caregivers, in societies such as Western Samoa a caregiver who accommodates in this fashion would not be viewed as a very competent one. Samoan caregivers place heavy emphasis on socializing the infant to attend and accommodate to others as early as possible and try not to engage themselves in communicative activities that would necessitate their linguistic and cognitive accommodation to the infant.

It is important to note that linguistic acts and stances of cognitive accommodation are by no means absent from the Samoan behavioral repertoire – there is a simplified register, for example – but although known to members, these acts and stances are not the preferred resources for constructing the particular identity of caregiver. In part because Samoans see accommodation as a form of respect, accommodating acts and stances, including the use of a simplified register, are resources for constructing the identities of relatively low- and high-ranking persons interacting with one another. Hence, one might use a simplified register to high-ranking foreigns such as missionaries, government workers, teachers, or even anthropologists. But infants and small children do not warrant this demeanor and are, rather, constructed as lower-ranking interlocutors who must notice what others are doing, saying, and needing, and they must adjust their own speech to be intelligible to caregivers and other high-ranking persons in their presence. In other words, by not accommodating, Samoan caregivers elicit from infants and small children the very acts and demeanors that construct them as lower in rank. Such complex social and linguistic interactions form the experiential core of language acquisition and socialization. The interactions are the means through which social identities are constructed and socialized. At the same time, act and stance displays and responses are objects of knowledge in themselves that need to be acquired by all those desiring membership in a local community. This experiential core is also what members draw on, for better or for worse, when they cross cultural boundaries.

6.7   Taking up the Social Constructivist Challenge

But what does take place linguistically when culture travelers step over cultural lines to launch novel identities? Do they draw on new linguistic structures to display familiar acts and stances and to construct old familiar social identities? That is, do they map second language onto first culture?

Are first language structures for indexing acts and stances used creatively to construct culturally new and unfamiliar identities? Can we speak of intercultures just as we speak of interlanguages, and what are the interactional and dialectical processes through which old and new constructs give rise to culturally blended social identities? To return to the immigrant families described in *The New York Times* article (Rimer, 1992), how are old, new, or blends of old and new identities interactionally established from one interactional moment to the next in these families? When children of immigrants are recurrently obliged to translate for parents, how does this act impact the construction of parental and child identities, their relationship to one another, and their relationship to the rest of the world? I offer these questions to the scholars of language acquisition and socialization to pursue. The constructivist approach to social identity is represented in sociology (e.g., conversation analysis, ethnomethodology, and practice theory), anthropology (e.g., linguistic and interpretive anthropology), psychology (e.g., Vygotskian paradigms such as activity theory and the newly formed cultural psychology), and in the history and philosophy of science. Just about the only social science that has not developed a social constructivist paradigm is linguistics. It is, then, high time, indeed an opportune time, for developmental psycholinguists and developmental sociolinguists, with their interdisciplinary profile and commitment to understanding and promoting the achievement of linguistic competence by all of humankind, to *carpe diem*, and to take up the social constructivist challenge.

Notes

This article draws on research projects generously supported by the Spencer Foundation (1990–3), the National Institute of Child Health and Development (1986–90), The National Science Foundation (1978–80, 1986–90), and the John Simon Guggenheim Foundation (1984–5). A preliminary version of this article was presented as a plenary address at the American Association for Applied Linguistics Annual Meetings, March 1992, Seattle.

1 Pronominal systems would seem an exception to this claim in that pronouns *directly* mark interlocutory identities such as speaker, hearer, other, speaker and hearer, speaker and other, and speaker and hearer and other. In some languages, pronominal systems can also directly encode gender and, more rarely, kinship identities (see Mühlhaüsler & Harré, 1990, for an extended treatment of these systems). In other cases, however, pronouns *indirectly* mark social identity because they index particular stances associated with those identities. For example, plural or third person forms may be used to refer to an addressee of high rank because they index distance between interlocutors.

References

Ainsworth, M. D. S. (1982). Attachment: Retrospect and prospect. In C. M. Parkes & J. Stevenson-Hinde (eds.), *The place of attachment in human behavior*. New York: Basic Books.

Besnier, N. (1990). Language and affect. *Annual Review of Anthropology*, 19, 419–51.

Biber, D., & Finegan, E. (1989). Styles of stance in English: Lexical and grammatical marking of evidentiality and affect. *Text*, 9(1), 93–124.

Blum-Kulka, S., & Olshtain, E. (1984). Requests and apologies: A cross-cultural study of speech act realization patterns. *Applied Linguistics*, 5(3), 196–212.

Brown, P., & Levinson, S. C. (1978). Universals of language usage: Politeness phenomena. In E. N. Goody (ed.), *Questions and politeness strategies in social interaction* (pp. 56–311). Cambridge, England: Cambridge University Press.

Brown, P., & Levinson, S. (1979). Social structure, groups, and interaction. In K. Scherer & H. Giles (eds.), *Social markers in speech* (pp. 291–341). Cambridge, England: Cambridge University Press.

Bruner, J. S. (1986). *Actual minds, possible worlds*. Cambridge, MA: Harvard University Press.

Bruner, J. S., Jolly, A., & Sylva, K. (1976). *Play – Its role in development and evolution*. New York: Basic Books.

Campos, J., & Stenberg, C. (1981). Perception, appraisal, and emotion: The onset of social referencing. In M. E. Lamb & L. R. Sherrod (eds.), *Infant social cognition*. Hillsdale, NJ: Lawrence Erlbaum Associates, Inc.

Chafe, W., & Nichols, J. (1986). *Evidentiality: The linguistic coding of epistemology*. Norwood, NJ: Ablex.

Clark, H. H., & Lucy, P. (1975). Understanding what is said from what is meant: A study in conversationally conveyed requests. *Journal of Verbal Learning and Verbal Behavior*, 14, 56–72.

Cole, M., & Cole, S. (1989). *The development of children*. New York: Scientific American Books.

Cruttenden, A. (1986). *Intonation*. Cambridge, England: Cambridge University Press.

Dubois, B. L., & Crouch, I. (1975). The question of tag questions in women's speech: They don't really use more of them, do they? *Language in Society*, 4(3), 289–94.

Dunn, J. (1984). *Sisters and brothers*. Cambridge, MA: Harvard University Press.

Dunn, J. (1986). Growing up in a family world: Issues in the study of social development in young children. In M. Richards & P. Light (eds.), *Children of social worlds: Development in a social context* (pp. 98–115). Cambridge, MA: Harvard University Press.

Duranti, A. (1981). *The Samoan fono: A sociolinguistic study* (Pacific Linguistics Monographs, Series B, vol. 80). Canberra: Australian National University, Department of Linguistics.

Duranti, A. (1984). The social meaning of subject pronouns in Italian conversation. *Text*, 4(4), 277–311.

Ervin-Tripp, S., & Gordon, D. (1984). The development of requests. In R. Scheifelbusch (ed.), *Communicative competence: Assessment and intervention*. Baltimore: University Park Press.

Givon, T. (1989). *Mind, code, and context: Essays in pragmatics*. Hillsdale, NJ: Lawrence Erlbaum Associates, Inc.

Goodwin, M. H. (1990). *He-said-she-said: Talk as social organization among Black children*. Bloomington: Indiana University Press.

Gordon, D., & Lakoff, G. (1975). Conversational postulates. In P. Cole & J. Morgan (eds.), *Syntax and semantics* (vol. 3, pp. 83–106). New York: Academic.

Grimwade, J. C., Walker, D. W., Bartlett, M., Gordon, S., & Wood, C. (1970). Human fetal heart-rate change and movement-response to sound and vibration. *American Journal of Obstetrics and Gynaecology*, 109, 86–90.

Gumperz, J. J. (1982). *Discourse strategies*. Cambridge, England: Cambridge University Press.

Halliday, M. A. K. (1975). *Learning how to mean*. London: Arnold.

Irvine, J. T. (1974). Strategies of status manipulation in Wolof greeting. In R. Bauman & J. Sherzer (eds.), *Explorations in the ethnography of speaking* (pp. 167–91). Cambridge, England: Cambridge University Press.

Irvine, J. T. (1990). Registering affect: Heteroglossia in the linguistic expression of emotion. In C. Lutz & L. Abu-Lughod (eds.), *Language and the politics of emotion* (pp. 126–85). New York: Cambridge University Press.

Lakoff, G. (1972). Hedges: A study in meaning criteria and the logic of fuzzy concepts. *Papers from the Eighth Regional Meeting of the Chicago Linguistics Society* (pp. 271–91). Chicago: University of Chicago.

Lakoff, R. T. (1973). The logic of politeness, or minding your P's and Q's. *Papers from the Ninth Regional Meeting of the Chicago Linguistic Society* (pp. 292–305). Chicago: University of Chicago.

Levinson, S. C. (1983). *Pragmatics*. Cambridge, England: Cambridge University Press.

Mühlhäusler, P., & Harré, R. (1990). *Pronouns & people: The linguistic construction of social and personal identity*. Oxford: Basil Blackwell.

Ochs, E. (1988). *Culture and language development: Language acquisition and language socialization in a Samoan village*. Cambridge, England: Cambridge University Press.

Ochs, E. (1990). Indexicality and socialization. In J. W. Stigler, R. Shweder, & G. Herdt (eds.), *Cultural psychology: Essays on comparative human development* (pp. 287–308). Cambridge, England: Cambridge University Press.

Ochs, E. (1992). Indexing gender. In A. Duranti & C. Goodwin (eds.), *Rethinking context* (pp. 335–58). Cambridge, England: Cambridge University Press.

Ochs, E. (1993). Stories that step into the future. In D. Biber & E. Finegan (eds.), *Perspectives on register: Situating language variation in sociolinguistics*. Oxford: Oxford University Press.

Ochs, E., & Schieffelin, B. B. (1984). Language acquisition and socialization: Three developmental stories and their implications. In R. Shweder & R. LeVine (eds.), *Culture theory: Essays on mind, self and emotion* (pp. 276–320). New York: Cambridge University Press.

Ochs, E., & Schieffelin, B. (1989). Language has a heart. *Text*, 9, 7–25.

Ochs, E., & Taylor, C. (1992a). Mothers' role in the everyday reconstruction of "Father Knows Best." In K. Hall (ed.), *Locating power: Proceedings of the 1992 Berkeley Women and Language Conference* (pp. 447–62). Berkeley, CA: University of California, Berkeley.

Ochs, E., & Taylor, C. (1992b). Science at dinner. In C. Kramsch (ed.), *Text and context: Cross-disciplinary perspectives on language study* (pp. 29–45). Lexington, MA: Heath.

Ochs, E., Taylor, C., Rudolph, D., & Smith, R. (1992). Story-telling as a theory-building activity. *Discourse Processes*, 15(1), 37–72.

Piaget, J. (1952). *The origins of intelligence in children*. New York: International Universities Press.

Piaget, J., & Inhelder, B. (1969). *The psychology of the child*. London: Routledge & Kegan Paul.

Platt, M. (1986). Social norms and lexical acquisition: A study of deictic verbs in Samoan child language. In B. B. Schieffelin & E. Ochs (eds.), *Language socialization across cultures* (pp. 127–51). Cambridge, England: Cambridge University Press.

Rimer, S. (1992). Racing to learn to speak English: Parents worry their children will leave them behind. *The New York Times*, January 17, B1.

Salk, L. (1973). The role of the heartbeat in the relationship between mother and infant. *Scientific American*, 228, 24–9.

Schegloff, E. A. (1972). Sequencing in conversational openings. In J. J. Gumperz & D. Hymes (eds.), *Directions in sociolinguistics: The ethnography of communication* (pp. 346–380). New York: Holt, Rinehart & Winston.

Schieffelin, B. B. (1990). *The give and take of everyday life: Language socialization of Kaluli children.* Cambridge, England: Cambridge University Press.

Schieffelin, B. B., & Ochs, E. (1986). *Language socialization across cultures.* Cambridge, England: Cambridge University Press.

Searle, J. R. (1970). *Speech acts: An essay in the philosophy of language.* Cambridge, England: Cambridge University Press.

Sroufe, L., Schork, E., Motti, F., Larowski, N., & LaFreniere, P. (1984). The role of affect in social competence. In C. Izard, J. Kagan, & R. Zajonc (eds.), *Emotions, cognition, and behavior.* Cambridge, England: Cambridge University Press.

Stankiewicz, E. (1964). Problems in emotive language. In T. A. Sebeok, A. S. Hayes, & M. G. Bateson (eds.), *Approaches to semiotics* (pp. 239–64). The Hague: Mouton.

Vygotsky, L. S. (1978). *Mind in society: The development of higher psychological processes.* Cambridge, MA: Harvard University Press.

7

Norms of Sociocultural Meaning in Language: Indexicality, Stance, and Cultural Models

Scott F. Kiesling

In this chapter I will focus on how speaker norms have been conceptualized in recent studies of language and culture and attempt to arrive at a synthesis which suggests how a speaker's knowledge about language and context contributes to the patterning of language by social factors such as ethnicity, culture, social class, and gender. This discussion provides a synthesized discussion of the ways that three important concepts are used in studies of linguistic differences across cultures: *indexicality*, *stance*, and *cultural model*.[1] I will focus on what we can "objectively" describe about a society, as well as how speakers "subjectively" conceive of society, and then how these conceptions might have consequences for language use. In addition, I explore the connection between social meanings in particular interactions and wider societal ideologies.

7.1 What are Norms?

7.1.1 Norms and sociolinguistic meaning

A norm in the statistical sense is simply a way of describing some majority of the data, usually an average or mean, or a certain distribution of data. It can thus be thought of as something like the majority behavior in a population. Outside of these ways of *describing* human behavior, there are behaviors that are *expected* of people. The former are usually referred to as *descriptive norms*, the latter *evaluative norms*.

A third kind of norm is a *linguistic norm*, which we usually refer to as simply meaning. In this kind of norm, there is an association between a linguistic form ("tree") and some concept (a thing with a woody trunk, branches, roots, and leaves or needles). Linguists distinguish between three kinds of association for linguistic norms: symbolic, indexical, and iconic. *Iconic* associations hold when a word sounds like the concept it is associated with.

Scott Fabius Kiesling, "Norms of sociocultural meaning in language: Indexicality, stance, and cultural models." This is an adapted version of his essay "Prestige, cultural models, and other ways of talking about underlying norms and gender" which appeared in *The Handbook of Language and Gender*, edited by Janet Holmes and Miriam Meyerhoff (Oxford: Blackwell, 2003), pp. 509–27. Reprinted by permission of Blackwell Publishing Ltd.

So "buzz" is partly iconic because the sound it describes is part of the word itself. *Symbolic* associations are what we normally think of when we think of word meaning: the word is conventionally associated with a concept, and there is no inherent connection between the word and the sound. The "tree" example above is an example of symbolic meaning.

Indexical meanings are less straightforward than either of these other two, but are the most important for this chapter. Indexical meanings are associations between the linguistic form and the context. *Context* is defined as anything that isn't part of the denotation of the utterance; context is thus made up largely of "socio-cultural things." Indeed, one way to think about indexicality is as "socio-cultural meaning." Some examples of the kinds of things included in context are:

Is the speaker being friendly or rude?
Is the speaker masculine or feminine, upper-class or lower-class?
Does the speaker think the situation is a formal one or an informal one?

All that has to happen for an index to work is for the linguistic form to have a shared association with some context. For example, most English speakers share an understanding that the form "walkin'," by virtue of the way the end of the word is pronounced, is used in a more casual context than "walking." These indexicalities are a kind of norm as well, because they are based on the fact that most speakers share the association between the form and the context, or that they expect the association, or both.

7.1.2   The division of indexical norms

While the concept of indexicality is fairly straightforward, the ways in which these kinds of norms and social meanings are organized can be quite complex. The first important distinction that needs to be made is between norms for the social identity of a speaker (*social group norms*) and norms for the social meaning of a linguistic item (*social action norms*). For example, we might propose that a low-pitched voice is indicative of (means) masculinity. But we can show that the same kind of voice has connotations of authority, even for women. We are thus more accurate in describing the relationship between masculinity and voice pitch by saying there is an (arbitrary) social action norm that connects authority and pitch, and a further social group norm that connects masculinity and authority. Ochs (1992) has characterized the connection between linguistic forms and social identity as *indirect* indexicality, because there are one or more social actions (a stance – defined below, speech act, or speech activity) that come between a linguistic feature and the group that uses it the most, rather than a *direct indexicality* between the group and the linguistic feature.

The connection between each type of norm is functionally bidirectional, and in fact a linguistic form can be used to indirectly index a stance (a person's expression of their relationship to their talk and/or their interlocutors) by first indexing a social group. For example, a White American speaker might use a feature of African American English (AAE) to index a stance stereotypically associated with African Americans. For example, I found an Asian American using AAE phonology and an AAE phrase to help create a boasting stance when talking about his basketball abilities. The language form helps him create the stance because similar stances are associated with African American men, particularly because of their high profile in professional basketball, and the frequency with which the boasting speech act is performed by professional players. This bidirectional, web-like view of these norms is illustrated more fully below.

In interactional discourse studies, such as are summarized in Tannen (1993b) and discussed by Gumperz (this volume, chapter 3), the distinction between social group norms and social action norms is central: Different linguistic features carry different social meanings for different groups. Thus, Tannen (this volume, chapter 9) shows that overlapping speech can have different interpretations for New York Jews and Californians. For the New Yorkers, overlap shows involvement in the talk, building solidarity. For the Californians, overlap shows inconsiderateness and does not show respect for their wish to finish their utterance. In this example, the social action norms of the two groups are different.

7.1.3   The role of prescriptive norms

Another more common way of describing norms is as *descriptive* or *prescriptive*. As noted above, descriptive norms are those that simply describe a group, usually through some statistic like the average, such as "the average height of men." Prescriptive norms are those values that people are expected to adhere to (or at least strive for), such as "Men should be tall." Both kinds of norms have played a part in sociolinguistic research; often, they are difficult to tease apart, as prescriptive norms frequently affect descriptive ones. Moreover, both social group norms and indexical norms can also be either prescriptive or descriptive. In general, sociolinguistic studies try to find out what the descriptive norm is, and then use prescriptive norms to help explain the existence of the descriptive norms, although in practice the two often become confused. Indeed, prescriptive norms, such as "Women should be more polite" (see Lakoff 1975), often turn out to be descriptively accurate: It has been found (Holmes 1995) that women do tend to be more positively polite. The interaction between the two, however, is bidirectional, with each kind of norm influencing the other. For example, men are, on average, taller than women in most societies, but this has led to a prescriptive gender dichotomy whereby *all* men are expected to be taller than *all* women. This prescriptive norm makes life difficult for short men and tall women, and one rarely sees couples in the US in which the man is shorter than the woman. A descriptively average difference has been turned into a prescriptively categorical difference, such that men and women are understood to inhabit non-overlapping categories which differ completely on many traits. The prescriptive height norm does affect men's and women's partner choice, so that we find a much more categorical pattern in couple's relative heights in the US than would appear by chance.

I summarize this section by listing the types of norms discussed above:

- descriptive norm: statistical norms that describe a sociocultural group, usually probabilistic;
- prescriptive norm: norms of behavior expected by a sociocultural group, usually categorical;
- social action norm: the direct indexical connection between a linguistic form and social context, such as low pitch and authority;
- social group norm: the direct indexical connection between two parts of social context, such as masculinity and authority.

7.1.4   Levels of indexicality

Further complicating matters, at least three interacting levels of context need to be distinguished when connecting context with language: (1) the wider society consisting of large census group categories; (2) institutions such as corporations, clubs, families, universities, etc.; and (3) specific speech events (e.g., a lecture, a casual conversation, a business meeting, a visit to a doctor's office) with their individual speakers. At each level there are norms of each type discussed above. On the societal level we have patterns such that speakers of the same kind of identity use a linguistic form more or less, on average, than another, and they are often expected to exhibit this distinction as well. An example of such a norm is the fact that working-class speakers will use *ain't* more than upper-class people. At the institutional level, like how to behave in a particular workplace or company, we have more specific patterns and expectations which may be idiosyncratic to a particular community or a certain role in an institution. Finally, each speech event, such as a business meeting, a party, or a religious service, will develop both prescriptive and descriptive norms as the event unfolds. As a type of speech event recurs, prescriptive norms for those events will develop. Speakers have knowledge of all of these levels of norms, and of course each individual has a way of approaching these norms (among these approaches are resistance, compliance, and active promotion).

How might this knowledge be characterized, and how do different "levels" of norms interact? In order to explore this question further, I will rely on an extended example, based on my own research with fraternity men. I will examine how norms have been used in language and gender through this example, and then explore how they might be combined to arrive at an understanding of the relationships among the various underlying norms that speakers use when making choices about how to say something, and making meaning out of the choices of other speakers.

7.1.5   The fraternity study: background and data

For more than a year, I spent time with a fraternity at a University in Northern Virginia, USA. A fraternity of this kind is an all-male social group. It is essentially an institutionalized friendship network which also does volunteer work to help the university and the surrounding community. I examined *style shifting* by individual men: How did they speak differently in varying situations? I focused on how they used the (ING) variable, i.e., whether they pronounced words like *walking* as *walkin'* or *walking*. I compared which variant they used in three types of situations: (1) while socializing; (2) in interviews with me; and (3) in fraternity meetings (see Kiesling 1998 for a more detailed account of methods used). I found that, while most men used a high percentage of the *-in* pronunciation in socializing situations, in the meeting and interview situations there were some men who continued to use the high rate of *-in*, while most of the men used a lower rate of *-in* (see figure 7.1). I also explored what discourse features and strategies the men used to create authority – power and hierarchy – and what *kind* of power and authority the men displayed based on their position in the fraternity and the speech event (Kiesling 1997, 2001b). For all of the patterns found, I relied on explanations based on a number of underlying norms the men have about gender and society, usually as described in their own words.

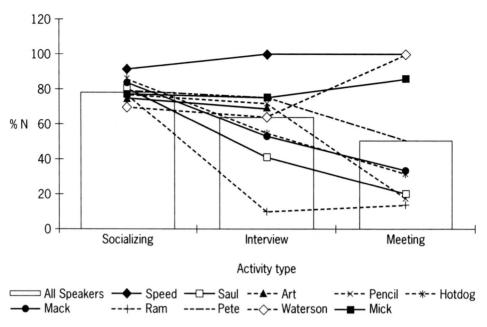

Figure 7.1   Cross-tabulation of speaker and activity type for progressive verb forms only. N = *in*. (From Kiesling 1998: 84.)

7.2   Norms and Identity: Toward a Synthesis

All linguistic patterns of use arise from decisions people make in interaction, when they are talking to a real person and thinking about "who they are" with respect to that person or people. So in explaining these patterns, we must ask what kinds of (sub)conscious knowledge speakers draw on to achieve these stances. Here I propose a way of characterizing the knowledge people rely on during this process. Following Ochs, I propose that people's primary way of organizing interaction (including language) is through *stances*. A stance is a person's expression of their relationship to their talk (e.g., certain about what they are saying) and to their interlocutors (e.g., friendly or dominating). This focus on the immediate interaction does not mean that local knowledge relating to larger "census" categories does not come into play, just that this knowledge is invoked in the service of creating stances situated in particular speech events.

Another way of thinking about stance is in terms of personal style (Eckert 2000), where a single linguistic feature is part of a wider personal style of a speaker, or even category of speakers. In this view, a linguistic feature does not, in speakers' real-time processing, do the work of creating an identity. Rather, particular linguistic features are simply an indication of personal style (but not definitive of a single style); a linguistic feature in this view has slightly different *specific* indexicalities from person to person, but may share a more general indexicality when viewed across individuals and situations. For example, *dude* is an address term that in general indexes solidarity combined with casualness, especially among younger male speakers in North America. In student cultures, it may be used by a person with a "stoner" identity (one identified with smoking marijuana and the culture surrounding this drug), as well as a student who is not a "stoner" but is popular and has many friends. When the "stoner" uses *dude*, it combines with other aspects of his or her identity to reinforce the "stoner" identity and emphasize casualness, but for the popular student it will emphasize the solidarity aspect. So the address term has a different *specific* indexicality in each personal style (casualness vs. solidarity), but it has a general, overall indexicality that both speakers can and do use to perform their identities. As the California Style Collective (1993) explains, each personal style is unique, made up of a bricolage of linguistic (and other) behaviors that index various sociological and cultural meanings. Stances are local instantiations of a personal style, performed in a particular speech event.

7.2.1   (ING) and the web of norms in the fraternity

In order to make this discussion more concrete, let us return to the fraternity. Given the explanation above, *-in* should indicate (but not necessarily fully index) a certain general personal style, which can be discerned through an examination of the specific personal styles of those who use it. We should be able to show that it helps create specific stances in interaction. In this regard, the three men who use high amounts of *-in* in the meeting are worth focusing on; by examining the behavior of the non-normative group, we further an understanding of the norm. We should thus be able to analyze the stances and styles of these three men and identify how they are specifically different in this regard. This analysis will yield a better understanding of the kinds of specific indexicality being used when these men use *-in* and the others use *-ing*.

I focus on a speech given by Brian Waterson (a pseudonym), a first-year member of the fraternity. In this speech he is running for the office of vice-president. It is unusual for someone in his position in the fraternity (a new member) to run for such an office (and even more unusual to succeed, which he does not). In fact, this is the only time in my corpus when he speaks in a meeting.

Waterson's Speech[2]

1	Hotdog:	Could we have Brian Waterson
2		((Long pause as Waterson walks in, goes to the front of the room))
3	Waterson:	Um . . . I'm not gonna f:- um put a load of shit in you guys whatever.
4		Um . . . You guys know I'm a **fuckin'** hard worker.
5		I work my ass off for everything.
6		I don't miss anything,
7		I'm always I'm always there,
8		I'll do anything for you guy:s,
9		and if you nominate me for this position,
10		I'll put a hundred percent ef- effort towards it,
11		I mean I have **nothin'** else to do 'cept **fuckin'** school work.
12		and the fraternity.
13		and uh and uh like uh like you guys said um this:
14		we need a change because we're **goin'** down?
15		A:nd I know I don't have a lot of experience?
16		In like position-wise?

17	But when this fraternity first started . . .
18	back in uh April of of nineteen eighty-nine,
19	um the guys that were elected for positions then didn't have too much . . . uh: experience in positions either.
20	So just keep that in mind when you vote.
21	Thank you boys.
22	Remember I'm the I'm the ice ma:n.[3] ((final two words said in an emphasized whisper as he walks out of the room))

Since Waterson would not be able to perform an "electable identity" based on his experience in the fraternity, or on past offices he has held, he must construct some other kind of electable identity suitable for the authority of this office. He does this by presenting a "hard-working" stance, where hard-working means giving time to the fraternity to perform often mundane and tedious chores requiring stamina and consistency. His use of -*in* helps create this stance, through its social significance indexing of the working class, which in turn indexes stances (through social group norms) of tough physicality and endurance.

7.2.2 Linguistic norms, linguistic ideology, metapragmatics: standard vs. nonstandard

We might say that Waterson is simply a non-standard speaker and leave it at that. But the non-standard is sometimes equated with a covertly prestigious form, a term which suggests that a speaker will gain something in their use of it.[4] So we should ask what specifically Waterson gains by using -*in* – how it builds his status. The answer is that it helps build his *ability*-oriented authority rather than a *structurally* oriented authority. Speakers who use more -*ing* tend to identify themselves with the established age hierarchy of the fraternity (based on how long a member has been in the fraternity), which Waterson is trying to circumvent since he is low down on that hierarchy. He is relying on his audience's linguistic ideology to help create his stance: -*ing* is indexed to an *ascribed* establishment (structural, natural) hierarchy, while -*in* is indexed to an *achieved* establishment (ability, effort-based) hierarchy. In fact, the other men who use a high rate of -*in* create similar stances through similar indexings. So here we find that the linguistic feature (-*in*) actually indexes an entire ideology, but crucially, it is still used in interaction as a resource to create a stance. This is the kind of indexing referred to by Silverstein (1993, 1996; see also Morford 1997) as a second-order indexical, because it relies on speakers' knowledge of the social distribution and evaluation of linguistic forms.

Thus, both direct and indirect indexicality are at work here, but the stance of the speaker is still central. In this case, the speaker is relying on a social significance association between a social group (working class) and a linguistic feature (-*in*), and then using that value to help create a stance (hard-working) through a social group norm (working-class people are hard-working, stated most simply; below I propose an elaboration of this norm).

7.2.3 Cultural models

Another way of making the concept of prestige more specific is to explore the kinds of cultural models that Waterson may index, in a similar way as he indexes a linguistic ideology (see Holland and Quinn 1987; D'Andrade and Strauss 1992, Holland et al. 1998 for discussions of cultural models). Here I want to suggest that he is doing more than indexing a shared social hierarchy. Rather he is indexing a shared narrative or *cultural model*. An example of such a model is Holland and Skinner's study of how college women talk about gender types, particularly their use of derogatory terms: "Without knowledge of the [cultural model] scenarios, we would have been at a loss to explain why respondents thought some terms for gender types could be used as insults whereas others could not" (Holland and Skinner 1987:104).

We can apply this "scenario" approach to the fraternity case, by appealing to cultural models of masculinity in the US. We can identify one cultural model for American men that follows a trajectory of technical, intellectual, and eventually structural attainment and expertise. We might call this model the corporate lawyer or CEO model, because such people are structurally powerful, have established hierarchies and ideologies in their interest, and as a prototype are assumed to come from families that already have societal structural power. Opposing this model is the "Rocky" model, after the movie character who wins a world boxing title through hard work, physical power, determination, and stamina, and who comes from a working-class background. Waterson's -*in* use helps bring such an underdog scenario to mind and helps him create a potentially electable identity of the underdog who works hard and in the end does a good job. However, the fraternity members valued experience more than hard work for this position: In the discussion that followed the speeches, many speakers stated that they valued Waterson's hard work and dedication to the fraternity, but thought that experience was necessary for the vice-president position, and Waterson lost the election.

Eckert (2000), while not using the cultural model concept in her discussion, seems to make a similar point. She explores the local, subjective, meanings associated with different ways of pronouncing vowels in Detroit. In her analysis of a suburban high school, she shows that the different pronunciations have meanings such as "urban" vs. "suburban," and are understood in terms of "rich," detailed cultural models of the social landscape. These cultural models help Eckert explain with precision the kinds of social forces and meanings at work in the linguistic patterns in the school. Other studies that use a cultural model or similar perspective are Bucholtz 1999, Gal 1978, Kendall 1999, Mendoza-Denton 1997, Meyerhoff 1999, Morford 1997.

Cultural models thus give the researcher an important explanatory tool which does not exclude traditional explanatory terms such as prestige, power, and solidarity, but rather renders these terms more specific to the speakers being investigated. They inform an analysis based on local ideologies: Why is something prestigious? What kind of power is valued? How do people value solidarity? Moreover, if interlocutors in an interaction do not share cultural models – as people from different cultures are likely not to do – they will come to different understandings of the same interaction and misunderstand each other.

7.2.4   Institutional norms

At the institutional level, we find yet more specific realizations of cultural models, so that norms in the institution to some extent mirror those of society as a whole. This "fractal recursivity" (Irvine and Gal 2000, p. 38) can be found in the hierarchies the men construct within the fraternity. These can be seen as institutional cultural models, in that they construct normative paths and categories of members through their stories. They are similar to the institutional categories identified by Eckert in her study of the school in two ways. First, they reproduce with local meaning "objective" categories found by social scientists looking at the larger society, such as socioeconomic class and race/ ethnicity. A similar view was found in a Pittsburgh middle school, where students are "objectively" stratified by social class, when measured by source of income, level of education, and locality of residence. But the students themselves are only attentive to these factors as they are related to their relevant cultural models, which are indicated locally by membership in sports teams, labels displayed on clothes, and what school buses each student rides. These cultural models are detailed pictures of prototypical *personae*, governing not just one trait, but a whole constellation of behavior and practices, for example the fact that a popular boy is a star football player, but also that he may be weak academically, ride a bus from a certain area of the city known for its athletes, and appear to be sexually active, all of which may be indexed when he talks like a "jock." It is these local models that are more relevant in particular institutions like schools, fraternities, and corporations, but they mirror to a large extent society-wide models. These models thus help us connect the wider, global indexings to the narrower, local, social indexings, and account for institutional variants of major patterns of cultural behavior.

7.2.5   Speech activity norms and indexing

Speech activities also have norms: norms for the kind of language expected, the kind of stances expected, and generic structure. These norms have been called frames in the discourse analysis literature (see Tannen 1993a). In general, speakers use such norms to help them make sense of meaning in a speech activity, and many misunderstandings have been shown to be based on a mismatch of frames (see Watanabe, this volume, chapter 15). However, the norms can be "broken," or, to view it another way, more *marked* linguistic forms (forms that are unexpected; that is, non-normative for that speech activity) are used, and the marked form in fact may index another speech activity. For example, note that in the style-shifting picture for the fraternity presented in figure 7.1, the Socializing speech activity (which is broadly conceived, from hanging out in dorm rooms to conversations in bars) has a high -*in* use by all speakers.[5] So in the Socializing speech activity, the use of -*in* is unmarked – the norm – in the sense that its use is the "rule" for the speech activity. We might suggest that a similar rule holds for the Meeting speech activity, although in this case the -*ing* variant is unmarked. The high -*in* users in the meeting are therefore using a marked form in the meeting to index the Socializing speech activity *within* the Meeting speech activity (i.e., momentarily reframing the speech activity from meeting to socializing).

   This reframing helps the men create a stance similar to that typically created in the Socializing activity. What is it from the Socializing activity that these men would want to bring into the Meeting activity? We can see this in Waterson's speech, more so in the second half, when he begins to try to take a stance of *casual* hard work (line 11): *I mean I have nothin' else to do 'cept fuckin' school work.* He is also relying on his less formal (less hierarchical) relationship with the men, as evidenced by his reminder of his fraternity nickname (*I'm the Iceman*) and by addressing the men with the term *boys*.

In this case, indexing a speech activity in which stances of casual confidence and non-hierarchical relationships are the norm helps to create such a stance. This approach is not always approved of by the audience. In a discussion following the speeches for the vice-president office, Pete, the vice-president at that time, broke frame and began boasting in a way more typical of Socializing situations. The other members shouted him down until he focused his topic on the issue at hand (see Kiesling 2001b).

This indexing of one speech event within a different speech event is related to other interactional patterns in a somewhat subtle, but important, way. We are likely to find a different style-shifting pattern for different groups in similar situations in terms of overall percentages. We will be able to explain this difference among groups by relying on cultural models. So in a relatively formal setting like the meeting, we would likely find that working-class African Americans are style-shifting from African American Vernacular English (AAVE) to a variety closer to White middle-class English. But we would also likely find that the working-class speakers shift to speech that is not as close to the White middle-class "target" as their middle-class African American counterparts. We could explain this fact by focusing on the fact that the cultural models valued by the working-class group (perhaps focusing on resistance to established hierarchies), and available to them as African Americans, may be very different from those valued by the middle-class African Americans (who may be more likely to value establishment models). What's important to notice is the centrality of stance and its relation to interactional performance: an activity type has an unmarked stance which can be created in another activity type by using a linguistic feature associated with the "embedded" speech activity. Again, we find a parallel in these frames to the more global cultural models discussed above.

7.2.6   The interaction of different cultural models: the web of indexicality

None of these kinds of norms is necessarily primary in indexicality; rather, they create a web of imbricated norms.[6] One level may come to the fore depending on other aspects of context, such as the topic. A speaker's stance does emerge as the central construct, however, since it is mostly on the level of speech event that speakers experience language and interaction, especially when we are dealing with probabilistic features such as (ING). That is, even if speakers evaluate -in and -ing differently when asked, they don't consciously keep track of their and others' percentages. Rather, they take a stance to their interlocutors, and it is in the service of this stance taking that other levels of social organization and indexicality come into play. I am not claiming that stance is the "prime indexicality," but I do claim that *speakers' experience of social meaning is primarily stance-focused*. Stances are thus central to understanding sociocultural linguistic norms. By focusing on stances and different kinds of schemata (cultural models and speech events), we have a way of accounting for the way speakers subjectively feel interaction to happen, while being able to relate it to the "objective" patterns we find in speech communities. In other words, we can generalize and explain without being lost in a mire of individual relativity.

Where do norms come from and how are they reproduced, especially if they are not conscious? This is also accomplished through interactions, and by repeated use of the kinds of indexings explored above. Thus, a performance of indexicality reinforces that indexical relationship, much the way the use of a particular neural pathway in the brain strengthens the connection between neurons. Sidnell (2003) illustrates other interactional processes in which social norms, especially the rules for speech events, can be reinforced and even created through interaction. However, to make sense of these indexicalities, interlocutors must share a particular cultural model or schema for these social meanings to be successfully created. It is through this sense making that indexicality occurs, and thus the reinforcement of these underlying norms.

7.3   Conclusion

In this chapter, I have synthesized a number of views on how norms are used by speakers to create social meaning, and how hearers use these norms to interpret the meanings (in the broadest sense) of utterances. I have tried to address the relationship between the "objective" norms described by linguists, anthropologists, and psychologists and the "subjective" experience of speakers. In that vein, I have argued that stance is the speaker's primary concern, and that linguistic features index social meanings in the service of the speaker creating or performing a certain stance. This discussion has focused primarily on the role of the speaker in indexing a stance and performing an identity, and has assumed that hearers share norms and cultural models with the speaker.

This assumption is not valid in the study of intercultural discourse, where actors are likely to have different norms. Studying intercultural encounters and comparing similar interactional situations across cultures inform our understanding of the way norms work in language, and explain why interpretations differ. We see studies in which there is a different social group norm (Bailey's chapter addressing different ideologies of race and ethnicity for Dominican Americans) and studies which show a different social action norm (Tannen's chapter about the differing interpretation of overlap as rude or friendly). This chapter thus provides a theoretical discussion of basic concepts through which to analyze the cultural meanings in discourse.

Notes

1   This chapter is adapted from a chapter in *The Handbook of Language and Gender* (Holmes and Meyerhoff 2003). The original focuses primarily on gender and its relation to norms of interaction, rather than all "kinds" of social identity.

2   Text in double parentheses is comments; a dash represents an incomplete morpheme; a colon indicates lengthening of the preceding sound. The four coded ING tokens are in bold; *anything* and *everything* are not bold because a secondary stress on the ING morpheme in trisyllabic words makes them categorically *-ing*, similar to monomorphemic *thing*; see Houston 1985.

3   "Iceman" is Waterson's nickname in the fraternity.

4   Prestige is often assumed to be associated with upper-class or standard speech. Labov 1966 and Trudgill 1972 introduced the term *covert prestige* to explain the fact that some speakers seem to want to use more non-standard language than others, which would be a puzzle, since everyone should want to use the most prestigious (standard) form. Trudgill studied speech in Norwich, England, collecting speech samples from inhabitants and asking them what kind of language they tended to use. Trudgill found that men in particular were likely to tell him that they use more

non-standard language than they actually used. This difference between reported and actual use led him to conjecture that the men attached a covert prestige to non-standard language.

5   Waterson actually has the lowest *-in* use in Socializing, but the individual differences here are not statistically significant.

6   These webs of indexicality are also another way of thinking about the ideological Discourse as discussed by Foucault (1980, 1982) and used by Critical Discourse Analysts in their work (Fairclough 1989, 1992).

References

Bucholtz, Mary (1999). You da man: narrating the racial other in the production of white masculinity. *Journal of Sociolinguistics* 3, 443–60.

California Style Collective (Jennifer Arnold, Renee Blake, Penelope Eckert, Catherine Hicks, Melissa Iwai, Norma Mendoza-Denton, Julie Solomon, and Tom Veatch) (1993). Variation and personal/group style. Paper presented at NWAVE-XXII, University of Ottawa, Canada.

D'Andrade, Roy G. and Strauss, Claudia (1992). *Human Motives and Cultural Models*. Cambridge: Cambridge University Press.

Eckert, Penelope (1989). The whole woman: sex and gender differences in variation. *Language Variation and Change* 1, 245–67.

Eckert, Penelope (2000). *Linguistic Variation as Social Practice*. Oxford: Blackwell.

Fairclough, Norman (1989). *Language and Power*. London: Longman.

Fairclough, Norman (1992). *Discourse and Social Change*. Cambridge: Polity Press.

Foucault, Michel (1980). *Power/knowledge: Selected interviews and other writings 1972–1977*. New York: Pantheon.

Foucault, Michel (1982). The subject and power. *Critical Inquiry* 8, 777–95.

Gal, Susan (1978). Peasant men can't get wives: language change and sex roles in a bilingual community. *Language in Society* 7, 1–16.

Holland, Dorothy and Quinn, Naomi (1987). *Cultural Models in Language and Thought*. Cambridge: Cambridge University Press.

Holland, Dorothy and Skinner, Debra (1987). Prestige and intimacy: the cultural models behind Americans' talk about gender types. In Dorothy Holland and Naomi Quinn (eds.), *Cultural Models in Language and Thought*, pp. 78–111. Cambridge: Cambridge University Press.

Holland, Dorothy, Lachicotte, William, Skinner, Debra, and Cain, Carole (1998). *Identity and Agency in Cultural Worlds*. Cambridge, MA: Harvard University Press.

Holmes, Janet (1995). *Women, Men, and Politeness*. Harlow, Essex: Longman.

Holmes, Janet and Meyerhoff, Miriam (2003). *The Handbook of Language and Gender*. Malden, MA: Blackwell Publishers.

Houston, Ann (1985). Continuity and change in English morphology: The variable (ING). PhD dissertation. Philadelphia: University of Pennsylvania Department of Linguistics.

Irvine, Judith and Gal, Susan (2000). Language ideology and linguistic differentiation. In Paul Kroskrity (ed.), *Regimes of Language*, pp. 35–83. Santa Fe, NM: School of American Research Press.

Kendall, Shari (1999). The interpenetration of (gendered) spheres: an interactional sociolinguistic analysis of a mother at work and at home. PhD dissertation. Washington, DC: Georgetown University.

Kiesling, Scott F. (1997). Power and the language of men. In U. H. Meinhof and S. Johnson (eds.), *Language and Masculinity*, pp. 65–85. Oxford: Blackwell.

Kiesling, Scott F. (1998). Variation and men's identity in a fraternity. *Journal of Sociolinguistics* 2, 69–100.

Kiesling, Scott F. (2001a). Stances of whiteness and hegemony in fraternity men's discourse. *Journal of Linguistic Anthropology* 11(1), 101–15.

Kiesling, Scott F. (2001b). "Now I gotta watch what I say": shifting constructions of masculinity in discourse. *Journal of Linguistic Anthropology* 11(2), 250–73.

Labov, William (1966). *The Social Stratification of English in New York City*. Washington, DC: Center for Applied Linguistics.

Lakoff, Robin (1975). *Language and Women's Place*. New York: Harper and Row.

Mendoza-Denton, Norma (1997). Chicana / Mexicana identity and linguistic variation: an ethnographic and sociolinguistic study of gang affiliation in an urban high school. PhD dissertation. Stanford, CA: Stanford University.

Meyerhoff, Miriam (1999). *Sorry* in the Pacific: defining communities, defining practices. *Language in Society* 28, 225–38.

Morford, Janet (1997). Social indexicality in French pronominal address. *Journal of Linguistic Anthropology* 7, 3–37.

Ochs, Elinor (1992). Indexing gender. In A. Duranti and C. Goodwin (eds.), *Rethinking Context: Language as an Interactive Phenomenon*, pp. 335–58. Cambridge: Cambridge University Press.

Sidnell, Jack (2003). Constructing and managing male exclusivity in talk-in-interaction. In Janet Holmes and Miriam Meyerhoff (eds.), *The Handbook of Language and Gender*, pp. 327–52. New Malden, MA: Blackwell.

Silverstein, Michael (1993). Metapragmatic discourse and metapragmatic function. In John A. Lucy (ed.), *Reflexive Language: Reported Speech and Metapragmatics*, pp. 33–58. Cambridge: Cambridge University Press.

Silverstein, Michael (1996). Indexical order and the dialectics of sociolinguistic life. In Risako Ide, Rebecca Parker, and Yukako Sunaoshi (eds.), *SALSA III: Proceedings of the Third Annual Symposium about Language and Society – Austin*, pp. 266–95. Austin, TX: University of Texas Department of Linguistics.

Tannen, Deborah (ed.) (1993a). *Framing in Discourse*. New York: Oxford University Press.

Tannen, Deborah (1993b). The relativity of linguistic strategies: Rethinking power and solidarity in gender and dominance. In Deborah Tannen (ed.), *Gender and Conversational Interaction*. New York: Oxford University Press.

Trudgill, Peter (1972). Sex, covert prestige and linguistic change in the urban British English of Norwich. *Language in Society* 1, 179–95.

Discussion Questions

1. Choose a speech event that you engage in frequently, such as a meeting or doctor visit. Write a short ethnography of speaking for it using the SPEAKING template outlined by Hymes. Does the resulting description capture what you need to know to competently engage in that speech event? What parts of the template are unclear? If possible, compare your description to one from a different culture. Does the template make it easier to compare?

2. Do you agree with Singh et al.'s criticisms of Gumperz's approach to intercultural communication? Why or why not? What would you say the key concept is? How might the interactional sociolinguistic approach be updated to take into account Singh et al.'s concerns? (See also chapter 20 by Eades for a specific example.)

3. Are the approaches described here compatible or incompatible? That is, could they all be combined into a single view of intercultural discourse? If so, how? If not, why not?

4. What is the difference between an index and a contextualization cue? Think of an example of each and suggest whether or not that example fits the definition of both terms. Is the difference between the two important or can the terms be used interchangeably? Why or why not?

Part II

Intercultural Communication:
Case Studies

Introduction

In this part, the eight case studies seek to explore some of the basic constructs and conceptualizations in comparing different cultural groups in contact as discussed in part I, "Approaches to Intercultural Discourse." By different cultural groups we mean groups and subgroups who have differing sociocultural rules for behavior, including speaking (see the discussion of Keesing 1974 in Paulston, this volume, chapter 18), and who can range from groups at the national level like linguistic minorities (recent immigrants, the Quechua in Peru), to ethnic and racial minorities (Jewish, African American) as well as groups we rarely think of as having different rules for speaking like gender and social class. These sociocultural rules take different forms in different national contexts, but all groups have rules for speaking. These case studies attempt to describe those rules and demonstrate how the groups vary from each other, often with consternation and misinterpretation. Each hearer tends to interpret the interaction using her or his own linguistic and pragmatic rules, which may differ from the speaker's. We have not specifically focused on such miscommunication but it is of course one rationale for studying intercultural discourse and communication.

Janet Holmes in "Why tell stories?" (chapter 8) contrasts the rhetorical organization of natural narratives told by Maori (autochthonous group) and Pakeha (Anglos) in New Zealand. She explores possible differences in the social meaning of these stories, and the contribution such stories make to constructing a particular ethnic, social, and gender identity.

Deborah Tannen in an amusing and well-known account of a Thanksgiving dinner suggests that "the stereotype of the pushy New York Jew" may be the result of discourse conventions practiced by some native New Yorkers of East European Jewish background. Any visitor to New York may be forgiven for wondering if those discourse conventions have by now spread to the entire city. Tannen explores in a scholarly fashion, based on Gumperz's notions, how such a stereotype can come into being.

Difference often leads to discrimination, whether difference of looks or religion or sexual orientation or any kind of difference which takes on salient aspects. Sweden which for hundred of years has been, in perception at least, a very homogeneous country now counts one million immigrants and refugees among its seven million Swedes. They are very noticeable in fair-haired Sweden, and the government is concerned about the difficulty of fitting them into a Swedish environment. Åke Daun's chapter "Swedishness as an obstacle in cross-cultural interaction" was written as part of a larger research project on Swedish mentality for a governmental committee investigating discrimination against immigrants in Sweden. It will readily be seen that its ethnographic perspective is at a much more general level than Tannen's more minute linguistic analysis, but both use cross-cultural analysis for the same purpose, the purpose of describing and explaining stereotyping and discrimination which can result from ethnic groups in contact when their interactional rules differ.

Penelope Harvey is, like Daun, an ethnographer (of the British social anthropology school) and here examines "The Presence and Absence of Speech in the Communication of Gender," i.e. the function of silence in a bilingual (Quechua and Spanish), autochthonous community in a small Andean town. She explores "how Quechua monolingualism is associated with subordination, suppression, and ignorance and that this is an image associated with race and colonial domination and is one with which both male and female monolinguals identify." But bilingualism carries different possibilities for men and women, and women become "at best the silent partners of men, at worst the object of male ridicule." This chapter is representative of much of the work on language and gender as well as the later American work by linguistic anthropologists on language and ideology.

H. Samy Alim, himself African American, has based his account of Black Language, "Hearing what's not said and missing what is: Black language in White public space," on a three-year ethnographic study of an African American community in California. Like Harvey, Alim sees racial tension as carrying strong interpretative power for understanding local language functions. Alim's chapter introduces a complete reconceptualization of language in the Black speech community where he considers Black Language similar to a creole continuum where African American Vernacular English represents the basilect and Standard English the acrolect, terms he does not use nor approve of. In his words, Black Language includes all the speech styles used by (American) Blacks from street talk to White Mainstream English, his term for standard English. While the linguistic justice of Alim's thesis is clear, there still remains the problem of how Black children in segregated inner-city communities will have access to standard English acquisition if the schools do not teach it. Christina Bratt Paulston's chapter "Pronouns of address in Swedish: social class semantics and a changing system" is also based on an ethnographic study – in Stockholm, Sweden. The results were totally unanticipated; although a native speaker of Swedish, Paulston had no idea that the rules for address were social-class-linked. Communication between speakers of the same language in the same nation but from different social classes remains virtually unstudied from an intercultural perspective. We need many more such studies from many more cultures, and on broader topics than just the address system.

Maria Sifianou's chapter on polite requesting, "Off-record indirectness and the notion of imposition" (Greek-English), demonstrates the use of speech acts as the unit of research in comparative intercultural communication. Speech acts can be and are variously defined (see the discussion of speech acts in the various texts discussed in the

Preface and in the Hymes chapter, 1), but they are basically "doing things with words": requesting, promising, apologizing, insulting, etc. When such acts have different rules for interpretation and use, their illocutionary force, i.e. the speaker's intent, can easily be misinterpreted by the hearer. In a fictitious example from the philosophy literature to illustrate felicity conditions of promising, John Searle points out that a husband who promises his wife that he will be faithful all of next week is likely to cause more unhappiness than reassurance. The husband is also stupid because, as a speaker of English, he should know that, but the fact remains that even speakers of the same language frequently misunderstand the illocutionary force of speech acts, and so speech acts are the darling of intercultural discourse research.

Finally, Watanabe's chapter "Cultural differences in framing: American and Japanese group discussions" uses the notion of framing: "The term 'frame' is used to refer to messages defining intentions of communication in the sense that a picture frame delimits the picture within it." We have never seen a study comparing the degree of miscommunication between differing rules of speech acts and differing rules of framing, but it is easy to speculate that illocutionary force is more difficult to interpret and that different rules of framing come across as just odd ways of doing things rather than being misunderstood. It would make a nice study.

8

Why Tell Stories? Contrasting Themes and Identities in the Narratives of Maori and Pakeha Women and Men

Janet Holmes

8.1 Introduction

Stories can provide a window on cultural and social consciousness. The stories told by particular groups tend to reflect the preoccupations, the values, beliefs and attitudes of group members. Analysing narratives can thus provide interesting insights into the cultural and social preoccupations of society members at a particular point in time. Stories also serve a variety of functions: they may entertain, educate, socialise, and inform; they may express individual preoccupations, perspectives and feelings, and contribute to building a particular identity for an individual; they may be used to establish social connections, express social solidarity and mark social boundaries. Often one narrative will realise several of these functions simultaneously. Narrative analysis is thus a rich source of insight into the current cultural and social concerns of a society.

8.1.1   Ethnic groups

In New Zealand/Aotearoa the two major ethnic groups, Maori and Pakeha, differ along many cultural and social dimensions.[1] Maori are the indigenous people currently constituting about 14.5% of the population. "Pakeha" is a Maori term widely used to refer to those New Zealanders of European (mainly British) origin who colonised Aotearoa in the 19th century, and who now make up the majority of the population. English is the dominant language of New Zealand in most domains for both Maori and Pakeha people, and the Maori language is in very real danger of disappearing (Benton, 1991). Recent estimates suggest that, despite efforts to revive it, the number of really fluent adult speakers of Maori has dropped to as low as 22,000 (National Maori Language Survey 1995), or about 5% of the Maori population, with perhaps 10–20% moderately fluent speakers.

Janet Holmes, abridged version of "Why tell stories? Contrasting themes and identities in the narratives of Maori and Pakeha women and men" from *Journal of Asian Pacific Communication* 8:1 (1998), pp. 1–7, 9–20, 22–9. Reprinted with kind permission by John Benjamins Publishing Company, Amsterdam/Philadelphia, www.benjamins.com.

Though Maori and Pakeha interact freely in New Zealand, there are many aspects of Maori and Pakeha culture which differ, and some of them are very subtle (see Metge, 1995). Pakeha culture, a culture derived from Europe, and from Britain in particular, is the dominant culture. Maori culture is much less prominent, and it is neither understood nor appreciated by the majority of Pakeha New Zealanders. So it is Maori who are of necessity bicultural; most Pakehas "are far from knowledgeable about any culture but their own" (Metge, 1976: 322).

Metge and Kinloch (1978) discuss a variety of differences in Maori and Pakeha ways of communicating, pointing out that unrecognised differences are often the source of misunderstandings, and of people "talking past each other" (1978: 8–9). Maori people, for instance, emphasise non-verbal signals more, and verbalisation less, than Pakeha; indeed many Pakeha tend to define communication in terms of verbal expression. As a result, Pakeha often consider Maori unresponsive and difficult to talk to, while from a Maori perspective, Pakeha often miss the intended message because "they are listening with their ears instead of their eyes" (1978: 10).[2] Compared to Pakeha, Maori people place a very high value on social relationships and especially on kinship and the mutual obligations of members of the extended family. They value connections between people, and put a great deal of emphasis on the affective functions of discourse, and on involvement in interaction (Howard, 1974; Ito, 1985; Besnier, 1989; Edwards & Sienkewitz, 1990). Maori people tend to emphasise example and modelling as ways of teaching and learning, whereas Pakeha put more stress on explicitness and verbal rather than non-verbal teaching strategies. While Pakeha parents generally let their children know when they are pleased with their behaviour or achievements, it is considered inappropriate in Maori culture for parents to explicitly and directly praise their children – this is left to grandparents or other family members (Metge, 1995).

Clearly, Maori and Pakeha ways of doing things with words differ in a variety of areas. The analysis in this paper is a preliminary exploration of another particular speech function, namely telling stories, where there appear to be differences in the ways in which Maori and Pakeha communicate. The analysis is exploratory, rather than definitive, focusing on possible differences in the functions of narratives for Maori and Pakeha in a relaxed informal social context. In particular, the analysis suggests ways in which stories may be used to construct distinctive ethnic and social identities, and explores some of the particular preoccupations of Maori and Pakeha women and men reflected in their stories.

8.1.2   Gender and New Zealand culture

Though cultural differences are the main focus of this paper, it was not possible to ignore another contrastive social dimension of relevance in analysing the functions of story-telling, namely gender. Gender has been identified by feminist sociologists as a major preoccupation of New Zealand culture. Because of the pervasive influence of symbols of the pioneer origins of New Zealand Pakeha society such as "Man Alone" and "Dependent Woman", it has been suggested that Pakeha women and men are more effectively trapped in gender roles still in New Zealand than in European societies such as Britain. It is certainly the case that gender has proved an important and relevant dimension of analysis in many areas of sociolinguistic and pragmatic analysis in New Zealand (e.g., Holmes, 1995a, 1997; Holmes & Stubbe, 1997).

It is equally clear that gender is a salient dimension in New Zealand Maori culture. Many aspects of Maori culture are gender-differentiated with clearly demarcated female and male social roles. Female–male relationships are very traditional, with males dominating most overtly authoritative and statusful positions and formal speech events, while females generally take a less prominent role. Metge describes these roles as functionally complementary, and argues that female influence, though relatively covert, is nonetheless pervasive and highly valued in Maoridom (1995: 91–8). Nevertheless, the overall picture of gender relations, both Pakeha and Maori, in Aotearoa/New Zealand is one in which traditional gender roles are emphasised and reinforced, and many areas of public discourse represent women in what Weedon (1987: 3) describes as their "primary role – that of wife and mother." Hence, it is not surprising that gender differences as well as ethnic differences emerged as important social dimensions of this exploratory analysis of New Zealand narratives.

8.1.3   Social constructionist framework

Stories are remarkably flexible discourse units which can serve many different purposes. One important function, which has increasingly been a focus of research, is the ways in which, from a psychological perspective, people use narratives in the presentation of self (Bruner, 1987, 1990; Linde, 1993) or, from a more socio-cultural point of view, people use narrative to construct a particular identity (e.g., Bruner, 1990; Chafe, 1994). Deborah Schiffrin succinctly summarises:

> The form of our stories (their textual structure), the content of our stories (what we tell about), and our story-telling behaviour (how we tell our stories) are all sensitive indices not just of our personal selves, but also of our social and cultural identities. (1996: 170)

Schiffrin's very detailed and illuminating analysis of the content, linguistic structures, and pragmatic meanings expressed in two stories told to her by women in an interview, demonstrates how these particular stories "display their teller's sense of who they are" (1996: 191).

A social constructionist framework provides a useful means of exploring the ways in which narrators may use stories to emphasise different aspects of their identity in different contexts (see Holmes, 1997). Stories can provide a means of expressing and exploring issues relating to ethnic identity (Michaels, 1981; Heath, 1982; Gee, 1991; Blum-Kulka, 1993), though, as I will show, it seems that it is predominantly minority group members who use narrative in this way. Stories also provide one way in which women and men construct their gender identity in a range of social settings (e.g., Johnstone, 1990; Riessman, 1990; Attanucci, 1993; Schiffrin, 1996; Holmes, 1997a, b). Within a social constructionist framework, language is viewed as "a set of strategies for negotiating the social landscape" (Crawford, 1995: 17). Language is the site of the cultural production of gender identity: subjectivity is discursively constituted (see also Weedon, 1987; Butler, 1990). In other words, each person's subjectivity is constructed, ethnicised and gendered within the social, economic and political discourse to which they are exposed (Weedon, 1987: 21). Using this approach people operate within subject positions, positions created and sustained by the use of language (Fairclough, 1989, 1995); speakers are regarded as constantly "doing ethnicity" or "doing gender," and the different ways in which people behave are accounted for by the socio-cultural contexts in which they operate.

In their stories, Maori and Pakeha women and men actively construct their ethnic and gender identities, reproducing and reinforcing society's cultural and gender divisions, and sometimes challenging and changing traditional patterns. On the basis of an exploratory analysis of a sample of New Zealand narratives, I will suggest that Maori women and men, in particular, may differ in the types of socio-cultural identities they construct through their narratives.

8.2   Approaching the Analysis

8.2.1   The data base

The stories used in this analysis occurred spontaneously in the course of 30 excerpts from conversations between friends which were collected for the one million word Wellington Corpus of Spoken New Zealand English (WCSNZE).[3] Participants were volunteers located using a typical social network process ("friend of a friend"), who agreed to contribute to the WCSNZE. This sample set was selected from a total of 185 excerpts to provide precise contrasts in gender and ethnicity, where social class (measured by occupation and education) and age were matched as closely as possible. 24 of the conversationalists were Maori and 36 were Pakeha; half were women and half men. Each conversation was a relaxed chat between two friends of the same age, gender, social class and ethnicity: i.e. 60 contributors in all. Two age groups were involved: "young" participants were between 18 and 30 years old, "middle-aged" between 40 and 55 years. The conversationalists were predominantly middle class, well-educated New Zealanders. Most of the conversations were collected in the home of one of the participants; in a few cases recordings were made at work in a coffee or lunch break. In all cases, only the participants were present and they recorded themselves. The contributers were simply asked to record between 30–60 minutes of a typical conversation between them: i.e. they were not asked to tell stories; hence all the stories in the data occurred spontaneously. Using Labov's (1972) definition of a narrative as a sequence of temporally ordered clauses used to recapitulate past experience, this conversational data base yielded 96 narratives.[4]

While the Maori in our sample told relatively more stories than the Pakeha, the difference was not great: the Maori people produced 45 stories in the twelve conversational excerpts analysed, compared to 51 stories in the eighteen Pakeha excerpts. Given the problems of deciding where to draw boundaries between stories, the greatly differing lengths of stories, and the fact that the excerpts in the WCSNZE were generally taken from longer conversations, no particular weight should be put on this difference. Moreover, not all conversations are equally conducive to story-telling. Conversational topics and "moods" differ greatly, though in fact all but two of the recorded conversations included at least one story. In both the story-less interactions the conversations developed into task-oriented discussions of the merits and demerits of a proposed course of action – one concerning plans to buy a piece of land, the other about plans to build a ramp. The remaining conversations include a range from one to nine stories. There are examples of very short and very long stories in both the Maori and the Pakeha conversations. Indeed, in relation to story length, age was a more relevant factor than gender: older contributors tended to produce longer stories than younger ones.

8.2.2   A Pakeha perspective

As mentioned above, the stories people tell can serve many purposes, and in this sample there were stories told by Maori and Pakeha, and by women and men which were told to amuse, to amaze, to instruct, to express solidarity with others, to explore power relations, to express individuals' feelings, and so on. There are naturally many areas of overlapping interest and concern between any human beings who share a common geographical environment and a common political structure.

Consequently, there were many similarities among the stories analysed. [. . .] In this chapter I focus on the concerns evident in Maori narratives in the corpus.

I have discussed my analysis with a number of Maori women and men, but it is unavoidably an analysis undertaken from a female Pakeha perspective. An analysis from a Maori perspective might well identify rather different themes. However, since Pakeha dominate New Zealand society, it could be argued that this is not entirely a disadvantage. Pakeha dominance means that Pakeha attitudes, values, and ways of doing things are inevitably treated by both ethnic groups as the norm in many social contexts in which Maori and Pakeha interact. A Pakeha perspective to this extent may more closely represent the area of overlap or of shared perspective between the groups. It may therefore be useful in distinguishing background and foreground characteristics for the benefit of those interested in cross-cultural differences.

For similar reasons, it is possible that some of the concerns which distinguish Maori from Pakeha narratives may be particularly apparent to a Pakeha analyst. Maori people are much more often bicultural than Pakeha, and may not always be as aware of features which distinguish the stories of each group, since both "modes" are equally available to them, with each adopted in an appropriate context. Clearly, it is correspondingly more important that Pakeha become aware of the concerns reflected in Maori narrative.

In what follows, therefore, the analysis is exploratory and tentative, and quintessentially qualitative rather than quantitative. I focus on what *distinguishes* the stories of Maori and Pakeha women and men in New Zealand, the ways in which the functions of their narratives and the concerns expressed in their stories differ.[5] Because at a political and economic level, New Zealand Maori and Pakeha belong to one society, there are many areas of overlap, but in this chapter it is areas of contrast which are highlighted. The contrasting features identified are thus by no means characteristic of all Maori or all Pakeha narratives. They are of interest, however, because they may provide insights into potential areas of inter-ethnic miscommunication, and a possible way forward in exploring social and cultural issues of demonstrable concern to different social and ethnic groups. My aim is thus to identify potential areas for further exploration; this is a preliminary analysis and the interpretations offered are speculative, and hopefully stimulating.

8.2.3   Constructing ethnic identity through narrative

One of the most obvious features which distinguished the Maori and Pakeha conversations in our Corpus was the extent to which "being Maori" seemed always a relevant factor in the Maori interactions. Ethnicity, it appears, is omnipresent for Maori conversationalists: it is sometimes foregrounded, the explicit focus of attention, but even when other issues are the ostensible focus of discussion, Maori identity is almost always a relevant background factor contributing to a thorough understanding and in-depth interpretation of what is being expressed.[6] By contrast, the Pakeha narratives do not indicate any awareness of ethnicity as an issue; it does not appear to be an ever-present part of the Pakeha narrators' consciousness, as it is for the Maori contributors. Being Pakeha is simply experienced as "normal" and unmarked.[7]

There is evidence of this consciousness of ethnic identity in almost every conversation involving Maori participants. In some cases, aspects of being Maori are the explicit focus of narratives, and Maori identity is foregrounded. In the following story, for example, Keti explains why her sister had not learned Maori from their mother as Keti herself had.

Example 1: Adopting out my sisters[8]

Context: two middle-aged Maori women in a casual conversation

Keti: oh yes my sister 'cause she was brought up um [tut]
when my dad went to war um my mother was working
she was milking cows on our on our farm
and um she er m-sort of adopted out um two two (in the) family my older sister Rahera and
er my younger one er
until you know my dad was supposed to come back from the war
well she was working at the farm
and so there were only two of us with her
and she used to take us to the cowshed every day
I suppose it was a bit much taking four kids [laughs] to the cowshed every day and doing

Tia: wow that's morning and night

Keti: morning and night
so um one auntie had one girl
and another auntie who they were Pakeha people er took Rahera
well when it came time and my dad was killed
um she went back you know (to-) to get these two back
but they were you know
those two aunties said no they couldn't part with them

Tia: wouldn't give them oh oh

Keti: so she let them have them and
they'd just come and have holidays with us

Tia: mm

Keti: it was really quite sad in a way no no

The story captures many aspects of Maori life in Aotearoa/New Zealand in the 1940s and 1950s. Most Maori lived in the country and worked on farms. Child-sharing or atawhai adoption along the lines described in this story was common, as Joan Metge describes in detail in her book about Maori extended families, *New Growth from Old*: "children belong, not to their parents exclusively, but to each of the whanau to which they have access through their parents" (1995: 140).

Informal "adoption" of children by aunties and grandparents, though very unfamiliar and little understood in Pakeha society, is generally recognised in Maori society and still practiced in some Maori communities.[9] The parents are typically regarded as being generous rather than as shirking their responsibilities (Metge, 1995: 212–13). Indeed Metge describes in just these terms the situation recounted in this story, where an auntie cannot bear to give up the children, and the mother generously leaves them with her. An understanding of normal Maori family relationships is thus an important background component in this story, though its main function is to account for why Rahera does not know Maori, an important aspect of Maori identity for many Maori of her age, as Keti indicates. Keti's final comment that it was "really quite sad in a way" perhaps reflects current changes in attitudes to such child-rearing practices among educated Maori (see Metge, 1995: 254ff).

In another conversation, one of the stories focuses quite specifically on the importance of the relationship between familiarity with the Maori language and a strong Maori identity. The narrator recounts a struggle with a young boy, Mark, who initially resisted using Maori in school but finally became very fluent in Maori and proud of his Maori identity. Other stories describe the importance of doing things in a Maori way, the difficulties some Maori have in conforming to the Pakeha system, differences between a Maori and Pakeha sense of humour, and so on. The Pakeha stories, however, do not focus explicitly on components of Pakeha identity; nor do they discuss ways of doing things which are specifically Pakeha, or contrast them with ways characteristic of other groups. Being Pakeha and doing things in a Pakeha way appears to be a taken-for-granted fact of life. It is rarely a relevant factor in understanding the significance of a narrative, at least from the perspective of a Pakeha analyst.

[. . .]

8.3   Identity Construction in Maori and Pakeha Women's Narratives

The previous section has suggested that Maori and Pakeha narratives contrast along a major dimension, namely their relative consciousness of ethnic identity. On the basis of the stories in this sample, one important function of narrative for Maori but not for Pakeha people appears to be the expression, construction and exploration of a distinct cultural identity within New Zealand society. [. . .] This theme was even more evident in the stories told by some of the Maori women, and it became particularly apparent when their stories were contrasted with the Pakeha women's stories.

8.3.1   Personal vs powerful identities

The Pakeha women's stories often presented rather conservative women who conformed to society's norms, who often lacked confidence in themselves, and who were constructed as helpless victims of accidental circumstances or institutional exploitation. Their stories typically reflected preoccupation with personal rather than social issues; they tended to focus on relationships with friends and family, and with everyday successes and failures, including such topics as family illnesses, visits to the dentist, hairdresser, etc., shopping for clothes and gifts, and so on.

A number of stories constructed the identity of the protagonist (who was usually the narrator) as a good mother, or wife or daughter, in other words, rather conservative identities with women defining themselves in terms of their role in the family; and there were many stories where the point was typically a personal concern, problem or small achievement. So, for example, one long story described a woman's trip to the swimming pool with her young daughters, a trip which she combined with a visit to her father. The story presents the narrator as a thoughtful mother and daughter, and a skilful manager of her family's needs and personalities [. . .]. Example 4 is a very brief story recounting how a young woman gave blood, an exemplary public-spirited action which is presented in a low key way as just an unexciting personal experience.

Example 4: Giving blood

Context: Young Pakeha woman talking to a friend in her flat.

Pam: I gave blood today

Rose: did you whereabouts

Pam: Oh the-you know up at work this place just past work
and sometimes they have on the notice board that you can go up there and give blood
so I thought [tut] now's as good a day as e-ever
so I-I went up and they took my blood

Another Pakeha woman told a story about a disaster associated with having her hair coloured at the hairdressers. She was treated very badly and the story explores her personal feelings of frustration and distress, and constructs her identity as a helpless victim of unpleasant circumstances. The account also pays considerable attention to her relationship with the hairdresser and her associates, but this is analysed in personal terms rather than along any social or institutional power dimension. Another woman who makes what her friends consider an over-hasty marriage is constructed in equally individualistic terms, as a woman over-anxious to secure a husband in order to provide a family context for her child.

Example 5: A hasty marriage

Context: Young Pakeha woman talking to a friend in her flat.

Viv: OH and um did I tell you Jude's got married

Meg: JUDE

Viv: yeah

Meg: when did that happen

Viv: last week
she- she met a guy at church camp which was um two months ago
they got engaged the week before last and they got married last week

Meg: OH MY GOODNESS what's he like

Viv: oh I've only met him once I don't know him

Meg: mm

Viv: at all but-

Meg: THAT'S AMAZING
'cause last time she was up here wa- she wasn't going out with anybody
was she when I- when I spoke to her

Viv: no no no
and like it's sort of- it's really sad
because I think she's made a really big mistake
um because th- like they don't know each other
they've only- they only met two months ago
they don't know each other AT ALL hardly

Meg: [tut] far out ( )

Viv: and I think she's getting married because she wants Ursula back

Meg: yeah

Viv: and sh- and she said

Meg: oh

Viv: she'd been saying for a while
I want- that she wants her back before Christmas

Meg: oh

Viv: and I suspect that the only way she'd be able to get her back through the courts is by being in a stable family

Meg: [tut] yeah

Viv: so I d- I mean I don't know but I just

Meg: mm
[tut] oh it's awful but I mean at least it's a Christian guy

Viv: yeah

Meg: and she's been out with lots of ( )

Viv: yeah

Again the focus is on the personal relationships involved, rather than the social and institutional issues. I have selected this example as the one which most closely resembles the Maori women's stories (discussed below). It is an interesting story because it offers plenty of potential for constructing an identity for Jude as a victim of unfair societal forces, a woman pressured into an over-hasty marriage by institutional demands to belong to a "stable family" in order to claim her daughter. Jude is constructed as a woman to feel sorry for, but the focus of the story is on Jude as a victim of circumstances, an individual who has made "a really big mistake". She is presented as a woman willing to conform to societal demands that a woman should be in a stable relationship if she is to be considered fit to be a mother. We are given no hint that Jude challenges this societal edict.

Does the narrator think that Jude should challenge the system? There is no hint of this in the story which focuses firmly on the averred "inadequate" basis for the relationship she has contracted with the "guy" from the "church camp". The narrator questions whether a satisfactory marriage can result from such a brief period of acquaintance, again a rather traditional position. In a variety of ways, then, the identities presented and the attitudes and values expressed in this story are socially conservative, reflecting conformist views, a concern with personal relationships, and a focus on individual rather than social concerns.

Other stories also present their protagonists as the helpless victims of circumstances: a young Pakeha women recounts how she failed her driving test; another tells how her friend passed a horse trial but ended up with sprained wrists; yet another describes how she was duped by a young pupil. These young women appear to construct themselves as victims of accidental unfortunate circumstances, rather than as participants in a complex social and political system which constrains their options and choices. The stories are vehicles for the expression of their personal feelings, often focus on personal relationships, and present their protagonists as women with conservative interests, beliefs, and behaviour patterns.

By contrast, the predominant identity constructed by Maori women in their stories was a strong, self-secure, confident person, capable of handling difficult and challenging situations. Indeed, the young Maori women often constructed a rather "feisty" and somewhat socially subversive identity for themselves, telling stories of women who challenge social norms and female stereotypes. Moreover, many of the Maori women's narratives reflected a strong interest in social issues – issues such as the way power is asserted and distributed in society, issues of legitimate authority, and strategies for effective management. The problems presented in their stories were often constructed as social or cultural problems rather than as individual, personal problems.

The Maori women's stories often portray women in influential social positions such as teacher, lawyer, and manager. One story, for example, describes the role played by a young Maori lawyer, Kathryn, in protecting her family's rights. The story constructs Kathryn as an intellectually sharp, effective young lawyer and emphasises her success in preventing the Maori family from being exploited by the Pakeha system and duped by Pakeha business interests. Another story presents a young female Maori teacher struggling with recalcitrant teenage boys and succeeding in asserting her authority to first discipline, and then socialise, one particularly difficult customer.[10] The story presents her as a capable and thoughtful teacher, aware of the complexities of handling adolescent males, and also of the wider social implications that the particular case raises.

Another long story describes a confrontation between a group with institutional authority to deal with the case and a woman who had physically abused her children.

The story is introduced to exemplify Maori ways of doing things, and specifically as an illustration of the Maori concept of *aroha* (usually glossed as "love" but having a much more complex meaning in this context involving features such as "compassion", "respect" and "dutiful caring"). The narrator focuses on the fact that although the woman's behaviour was rejected because she had violated significant and widely accepted social norms, she was treated caringly, with respect and cultural sensitivity by the group of Maori women who confronted her. Example 6 is an abbreviated excerpt from this long narrative.

Example 6: Confronting an offender

Context: Maori woman talking to a friend in a relaxed context.

> **Kiwa:** we did it with aroha and her mana ['self-respect'] was intact and to me that's one of the most important things you have to learn you know ....
> she walked away with her mana intact
> and we walked away with ours intact ....
> if she had left without her mana intact
> we would've been just as bad as she was
>
> **Roi:** mm
>
> **Kiwa:** I mean she would
> there's no way that she would've improved and gotten over a- these bad things because she's got nothing there to s- to build on....she'd also have no reason to 'cause she'd look at us and think oh you're just as bad as me
>
> **Roi:** mm
>
> **Kiwa:** and her she'd still be harbouring feelings bad ones about us and have no reason to want to change

The narrator, Kiwa, constructs an identity for herself as a member of a compassionate, but firm and authoritative group concerned with maintaining the group's cultural and social values. She also makes very explicit the rationale for the group's behaviour. The frame within which the narrative is presented is consistently social – the focus is firmly on the social consequences of the protagonists' behaviours. Maintaining the woman's *mana* or self-respect is important not only for her sake but because the way she is treated reflects also on the group, and those they represent. They must ensure they do not abuse their position of authority or they would be no better than the woman they are confronting. The woman is presented as deserving respect as a human being, despite her reprehensible behaviour, a group member who has deviated from group norms. The narrator presents herself as a confident, strong and powerful woman, part of a group exercising proper institutional authority in an exemplary fashion.

There are a number of further examples where the protagonist presents herself as assertive and strong, sometimes effectively resisting in-group pressure. Example 7 illustrates the narrator Rachel's claim that her relatives are trying to marry her off, and that "over the last couple of years everyone seems to have a perfect cousin or friend or mate or friend's friend".

Example 7: Resisting a set-up

Context: Young Maori woman talking to a friend in a relaxed context.

Rachel: talking about set-ups
oh I'm getting sick of it man
um Sam said to me after land [lecture] today
oh so Rachel who're you going to the ball with
and I said um why [laughs]
she said because I've got someone for you to go with
I said I'm going with Jonathan Davis [laughs]
she said oh I've got this really gorgeous nephew
and I want him to meet you [laughs]

Hera: [laughs]

Rachel: I said well bring him along anyway [laughs]

Hera: yeah bring him along 'cause we got to sell the the tickets

While at one level the story expresses Rachel's resentment at being treated as a commodity, someone who needs to be paired off, it also illustrates her refusal to accept this role, and her assertive pro-active response. She deals with the offender with humour, but also with firmness and self-confidence.

[. . .]

Overall, then, a surprising number of the stories in this sample focus on Maori women in their social contexts, and often in statusful institutional roles, presenting them as confident, assertive individuals. Moreover, the young women, in particular, tend to construct for themselves an authoritative and powerful identity in a range of different contexts, often challenging conservative norms or subverting Pakeha institutionally based authority.

Another point that emerged in comparing the middle-aged Pakeha and Maori women's stories, was the different ways in which each presented their approach to resolving problems or achieving their goals. Interestingly, both groups indicated that they recognised the need to "manage" situations in order to achieve a satisfactory outcome. However, the ways of managing situations adopted by the Maori women were often rather different from those adopted by the Pakeha. This point is best illustrated by a couple of examples.

The first is an excerpt from a much longer story ("The pool story") [. . .]. A middle-aged Pakeha woman, Helen, has a difficult teenage daughter, Annie. In the course of her long story about her attempts to take her children swimming, Helen describes to her friend Joan how Annie repeatedly complains that she doesn't want to do what is currently being proposed. For example:

so then we get 'I don't want to go to' – Annie didn't want to go to Freyburg........

and later, in response to Helen's proposal that they visit the children's grandfather, Jason,

Annie was saying 'I don't want to go in will you drop me home'

Helen resolves this situation by a direct and successful appeal to Annie to make her grand-father's lunch.

Example 9: Excerpt from "The pool story"

Context: Two Pakeha women friends talking in the kitchen of one of them.

Hel: and I said why don't you stay with Jason and make him some lunch

Joan: mm

Hel: so we went in and visited him
and I said Annie'll stay with you and make you some lunch
and she gets on quite-
and she chats away with Jason
and they have quite a nice (relationship)

The problem is resolved through Helen's intimate knowledge of both personalities and how they "tick"; she is confident that a suggestion that appeals to Annie's pride and "competence" as a capable young cook will succeed. So Helen presents herself in this story as using a personal appeal to Annie to skilfully persuade her daughter to look after her grandfather's needs (socialising her incidentally into a very conservative subservient "female" role!). The focus in the story is on the personal family relationships, and in the process of recounting the story Helen constructs her own identity as a caring mother and daughter, and as an effective manager of her family, while constructing Annie as a "manageable" and pleasant daughter (thus contradicting evidence from earlier in the narrative).

Maori women's ways of "managing" people, as represented in their narratives, often involved a slower, less directive approach. The enormous patience and astonishing faith that the end result would eventually be achieved are the outstanding features of this approach as viewed through Pakeha eyes. One example is a story told by a middle-aged Maori woman about the way she managed to achieve a smoke-free marae (a tradi-tional Maori meeting place, including a meeting house). The story provides a graphic account of how the goal was achieved through patient management of a wide variety of complicated and difficult characters. The story is long and involved; I present here an excerpted version.

Example 10: Achieving a smoke-free marae

Context: Two Maori women friends talking in the kitchen of one of them.

La: because we've just we managed [to make our marae] smoke-free with the help of the health collective o- on the campus

An: mm

La: though they're a bit preachy and they started going on
and I said to them no no no leave it to us
WE'LL um [tut] make it smoke-free but we'll do it our way
and we kept talking about it we kept mentioning it every week

and saying we understood people's addictions
and then of course we had a marae taurima ['mother'] who was chain smoker

An: mm

La: Rhonda who seemed to be under constant stress
she kept breaking all the rules
and the kids kept saying to me oh I thought you said we're gonna make the ma- the marae
  the dining room and that all smoke free
I said yeah
and then Rhonda left she- to move back to Rotorua you know
because Kiri's got so sick....

An: oh yeah I know

La: (right): the week she left I put up a smoke-free notice ....
yes so we put up huge notices all round the walls ....
because of that our cook walked out
and Hepa didn't turn the zips on
and when we came to have afternoon tea there was no hot (water) ....
so we said to her when she came back that her job had gone ....

An: mm

La: but we got you know [tut] this is a smoke-free marae

An: well b- y- y-

La: it's been really hard for the s- for the students who smoke........
and we helped them talk it through
and what we've provided for them out the back is um big tins with sand in them and a few
  chairs....

An: mm

La: and if they smoke they go home to their flat
and most- um [tut] find it + you know quite acceptable
and there's- they go on about how nice the marae smells

In this story Lara provides an account of the ways she and her co-workers patiently worked towards a smoke-free marae, taking opportunities as they arose, in one case waiting for someone to leave, in another pushing an offending person out, creating an environment in which smoking was still possible out of doors, but clearly signalling that it was not approved behaviour. In the process of telling this story, Lara constructs her identity as a successful manager, one who is patient or pro-active as appropriate.

The mix of patience and assertion, of support and disapproval, described in this story nicely expresses the complexity of the management process, and typifies other accounts in the sample of how Maori women achieved challenging goals through their skilful management of people and situations. The story provides a graphic illustration of a culturally based belief that while direct appeals to authority are often technically possible, the most satisfactory outcome will often be achieved by patience and good example.

Hence, in the stories in our sample, the identities constructed and the concerns expressed by the Pakeha and Maori women were often rather different in scope and focus. The

Maori women's stories tended to construct Maori women as powerful protagonists, rather than stereotypical passive, quiescent females.[11] They tell stories which recount ways in which Maori women have successfully exercised authority, often challenging the system, and in some cases making skilful use of institutionally based authority in order to achieve a satisfactory outcome. The Maori women were also more often concerned with broader political, social and cultural issues, such as the uses and abuses of power and authority, and the most effective ways of operating in complex or challenging situations. The Pakeha women, by contrast, tended to construct rather conservative social identities, as actual or potential mothers, daughters, wives, and generally good citizens. Their stories focused more often on individual problems, and on personal relationships, and they tended to describe events as individual experiences, often presenting themselves as helpless victims rather than exploring the social implications of their stories.

8.4   Identity Construction in Maori and Pakeha Men's Narratives

The men's stories also provided some interesting ethnic contrasts. The Pakeha men's stories, like those of the Pakeha women, tend to relate individual experiences rather than placing protagonists in an institutional context, but they tend to focus on the protagonist, rather than on his relationships with others. While the women's stories describe personal experiences involving family and friends, the men's more often focus on work and leisure activities, including topics such as playing soccer, painting the house, and dealing with work problems. One of the distinguishing features of these stories, compared to those of other groups, is the extent to which the Pakeha men in describing an event or an experience revealed their assumptions that they will be able or should be able to control situations. The main identity constructed by the Pakeha men is that of the knowledgeable, competent hero who solves problems, overcomes adversities, and demonstrates control in a range of situations (and when things go wrong, this persona is presented as sophisticated, self-aware and reflective). [. . .]

One long story recounts a middle-aged Pakeha man's success in operating his video equipment. Tom's story, describing a relatively minor achievement, is presented as a triumph of man over machine.

Example 11: Excerpt from "I drove our video last night"

Context: Two Pakeha male friends in a relaxed context.

> I pushed the appropriate buttons
> and it ALL worked ....
> th- the whole point about this is
> I solved the technology problem
> I had programmed the video

In this story, Tom constructs himself a competent, intelligent identity by describing in detail his achievement in mastering the programming of the video. The story builds up the task as a complex challenge which Tom meets (although he also admits to some problems introduced by external forces beyond his control!). Tom presents himself as a man who has successfully mastered the workings of a complicated piece of machinery. The story is one of personal triumph, a mock-heroic tale, presented perhaps a little tongue-in-cheek.

[. . .]

Other male narratives similarly recount personal experiences where "man triumphs over adversity" is the underlying theme: there is a story of how the narrator overcame the problems involved in painting and repainting a particular room in which the paint kept cracking, a story of a tramping trip where all went smoothly, a story of a confrontation with the boss over job conditions where the narrator presents himself as getting the better of the boss, and so on. So the Pakeha men's stories often involve a problem solved or a challenge overcome. They are the heroes of their stories. They describe how, using personal skill and initiative, they solved the problem or mastered the challenge; or alternatively, how the forces against them were simply insuperable. The narrators consistently imply that they expect to control situations.

The Maori men's stories deal with similar topics, but they often treat them rather differently. If Pakeha men present an identity as hero, the identity constructed by Maori men is anti-heroic. The focus is often on how laughable, incompetent, naive and unheroic they were. And while both Maori and Pakeha males discuss work and leisure activities, especially sport, the Maori stories include many reminiscences about earlier shared experiences compared to the Pakeha stories, which tend to focus on individual experiences and achievements. The following example presents an interesting case of shared reminiscences which are jointly reconstructed by both participants. It also illustrates the theme of young Maori male as anti-hero which recurs in many of these Maori men's stories. The story begins with an account of how the two young men were hooked on playing video games and tried to get downtown as often as possible to play in a video parlour. One night they tried to "wire up" the game with a spoon.

Example 13: A trip to the video games parlour

Context: Two Maori male friends in a relaxed context.

Wiri: and we tried to take spoons remember [laughs]

Pou: [laughs]

Wiri: trying to wire up the game eh [laughs]

Pou: [laughs] yeah with a spoon
it's just you actually think about it eh

Pou: [laughs]

Wiri: [laughs] we're the spoons trying to fucking
we were the spoons [laughs] all right
oh what eggs man

Pou: I- I felt like crying one time when we lost
you know we [laughs] died
fuck we got to walk all the fucking way home [laughs]

Wiri: [laughs] yeah I'll say we had to walk all the way home

Pou: fucking hell we only got down with eighty cents
and that was about bloody four or five games worth

Unlike many of the Pakeha men discussed above, these two young Maori men construct themselves on one level as "dumb", as well as rather wild and crazy, a very anti-heroic caricature of their younger selves. In the process, of course, since this story is firmly placed in the past, they imply that they are now much more sophisticated. A number of other Maori stories recount childhood experiences in rural areas where the anti-heroic protagonists are presented as "hick", unsophisticated – and amusing!

Indeed humour is one of the most distinctive characteristics of the Maori men's stories. (Humour in Maori and Pakeha conversation is analysed in Holmes and Hay 1997). [. . .] Another story told by a middle-aged Maori man describes an amusing incident, presented in equally unheroic terms, where he and his brother used a horse to pull a cow out of a swamp. In this story the brothers are clearly characterised as country bumpkins scrambling about in the mud, rather than as heroes whose presence of mind saved the cow. Example 14 provides a similar briefer example. The two men are discussing their grandmother.

Example 14: The uses of an encyclopedia

Context: Two Maori brothers in the home of one of them.

Tama: she had pets

Hemi: all those yeah she had me as a pet
and gave me all those encyclopedias

Tama: mm

Hemi: which we er which we er we tried to keep
but but I mean we had no bloody toilet paper at (placename)

Tama: [laughs]

Hemi: and the last bloody page left out of ten encyclopedias
was the the golden eagle or something like that [sniffs]

Tama: [laughs]

The story illustrates the poverty these brothers experienced in childhood, but the incident selected to make the point is designed to amuse. To some extent the narrator is also "sending up" those naive young boys with their unarguable priorities.

The identity constructed for the characters in such narratives is certainly not heroic. It is also worth noting that in both examples 13 and 14 the narrators are recalling shared experiences, rather than individual adventures, a feature of a number of Maori stories. Other stories present the narrator as one of a group, rather than an individual (see example 6 above), a pattern also more common in Maori than in Pakeha stories.

In constructing an unheroic identity, Maori men's stories also often reflect their awareness of Pakeha norms. As mentioned above, this suggests that Maori are constantly aware of the differences between Maori and Pakeha ways of doing things in a way that Pakeha are not. So, for example their narratives often implicitly, and sometimes explicitly, compare rural Maori ways of doing things with ways that they associate with sophisticated urban, mainly Pakeha, lifestyles. The stories are sometimes complex, with levels of irony leaving a great deal understated; they often ridicule "proper" behaviour, while recognising that their own performance in such contexts betrays them as naive. One story, for instance, makes fun of the ways in which Pakeha business meetings are run, and debunks the jargon used in big organisations. At the same time the narrator constructs an identity for himself as the country bumpkin come to town, who is out of his depth in a sophisticated commercial context.

[. . .]

Stories such as these reflect important differences in the background experiences of Maori and Pakeha. They occur especially often in the Maori men's narratives, where they often form the basis for amusing, anti-heroic tales about the past. And the fact that such differences are more often the focus of attention in the Maori than the Pakeha narratives returns us to the point made in the opening section. Maori, and Maori men, in particular, are very aware of the differences between Maori and Pakeha norms and values. If these stories are an accurate indication of the concerns of the contributors, ethnic identity seems to be a much more salient, relevant and ever-present dimension for Maori than for Pakeha.

8.5   Discussion

While there were many similarities in the New Zealand narratives in the sample, as well as similarities between stories told by those of the same gender, regardless of ethnicity [. . .], there were also some interesting differences between the Maori and Pakeha stories, particularly in the way they constructed the identity of their protagonists, and in the scope of the themes explored by each group.

The stories told by Maori in this corpus were distinctive because of the emphasis they placed on Maori identity. The Maoriness of the participants was a relevant factor in understanding and interpreting almost every Maori story. In some stories it was the explicit focus of the story, the story served to emphasise the ethnic boundary between Maori and Pakeha; in others it was an important background assumption, contributing an additional layer of meaning to the narrative. This preoccupation with ethnic identity in the Maori stories is understandable, as I have suggested, in the light of the social position of Maori in New Zealand. Where Pakeha values, beliefs, attitudes and behaviours are treated by the wider society as the norm, Maori are, not surprisingly, very aware of the ways in which these norms do not reflect Maori ways of thinking and Maori ways of doing things.

In general, the Pakeha stories tended to be concerned with individual experience, whereas the Maori stories often focused on the experiences of families and groups, and on relationships between family members. These preoccupations, too, reflect well-documented cultural differences between Maori and Pakeha (see, for example, King, 1985; Metge, 1995). As mentioned above, Maori tend to value kinship and extended family relations particularly highly, and this is evident in a number of the Maori narratives.

The Maori and Pakeha stories also contrasted in the ways in which people framed problems and constructed their versions of the deeper issue of culturally appropriate ways of achieving goals. For example, where stories explicitly presented a problem, different groups tended to focus on different aspects of the problem. Pakeha men presented heroic tales, emphasising how they use their skills and expertise to solve the problem, while Maori men constructed rather unheroic identities, making fun of themselves with humorous tales of disaster or incompetence. For Pakeha women, problems were often framed in emotional terms. Pakeha female protagonists were often constructed as victims of circumstances, with the story exploring the emotional, moral and evaluative aspects of a difficult experience.[12] Maori women, on the other hand, tended to confront problems with bravado and panache, or solve them through patient persistence. Indeed in the stories they told in this sample, the Maori women were often preoccupied by issues with significant social implications – issues such as the way power is asserted and distributed in society, issues of legitimate authority, and strategies for effective management.

Why should Maori men construct such "unheroic" male identities in many of their narratives? The answer is no doubt very complex and will benefit from further research, but one possibility is that the Maori anti-hero serves a number of functions. He is undoubtedly a source of amusement: indeed, the unheroic character represented in some of the Maori men's narratives is very reminiscent of the stereotype of a hick, "dumb", Maori male so skilfully created by the late Maori comedian, Billy T. James. The use of an exaggerated stereotype as a source of entertainment is a well-attested feature of minority group humour (Ziv, 1988; Davies, 1982, 1990).

The anti-hero also, represents, perhaps, one response to the threat of Pakeha dominance. On the one hand, he does not compete, he gives the game away without a fight. On the other, he ridicules and sends up the rules. Indeed, by his very existence this unheroic, non-conformist, and unsophisticated character subverts the underlying rationale on which the game is based. By paying it so little mind, he suggests the values it represents are not important. This is certainly one effective way of responding to an imposed and uncomfortable set of norms.

A third point worth noting about the "unheroic" identity constructed in Maori male stories is that it skilfully satisfies the cultural requirement for modesty, while also suggesting that the story-teller is no longer the same person as the character he presents. Maori culture has a strong prohibition on "skiting", boasting, arrogance or self-promotion, a concept captured by the Maori word *whakahiihii*.[13] Individuals are expected to act in a self-abnegating way, and to avoid seeking personal glory, recognising that their contributions should always be seen in the context of the group (Metge, 1995: 166; Holmes, 1998). Metge comments that Maori disapprove of "pride which focuses on the self separate from the group" (1995: 103). Those who boast "are quickly cut down to size by other whanau [extended family] members, for they threaten whanau harmony and reflect badly on the group" (1995: 103). The anti-hero featuring in so many Maori stories satisfies these cultural requirements perfectly. By constructing an unheroic identity, Maori men protect themselves against the charge of *whakahiihii*.

On the other hand, the men telling the stories indicate their awareness of the extent to which the identity they are constructing betrays ignorance, social gaucheness, lack of education and urban sophistication, and so on. The story is told from the perspective of an older and wiser identity. So in some respects these stories encapsulate the cognitive dissonance of the ambitious, well-educated modern Maori male. They satisfy Maori cultural imperatives while indicating their awareness of the extent to which these imperatives do not fit with the demands and expectations of modern Pakeha-dominated society. They perhaps reflect the concern and anxiety of some Maori men that the requirements of traditional Maori culture are not compatible with the economic and political imperatives of life in modern urban New Zealand.

It is also interesting to consider why some of the Maori women's narratives should focus so obviously on issues of power, and why (especially in contrast to the anti-heroes constructed by Maori men) Maori women so consistently constructed identities as women in charge or in control, strong, self-secure, confident people, asserting themselves effectively in a range of contexts, successfully managing situations, with the young women often challenging norms and female stereotypes. Here, too, further research is needed.

Overall, as mentioned above, relationships between the sexes in both ethnic groups in Aotearoa/New Zealand are still relatively traditional. Conservative gender roles tend to be emphasised: in the media and in much public discourse women are overwhelmingly represented as (potential) wives and mothers, and women are implicitly, and sometimes explicitly, treated as socially subordinate to men. Most of the Pakeha women's stories are consistent with this to the extent that they tend to construct rather conservative gender identities for their protagonists (Holmes, 1997a, b). Maori are a numerical minority, and as a group Maori people have relatively little access to power. As Metge (1986: 139) says,

All the main institutions of public life in New Zealand are grounded in Pakeha culture and dominated by Pakeha in positions of power. By law, Maori must participate in these institutions whether they want to or not, and their participation is judged by standards and values of Pakeha origin.

In this context, Maori women could be regarded as the bottom of the social pecking order, and might therefore be expected to be the most conformist and least radical group in their behaviour.

In fact, however, it seems that some Maori women, especially those who combine strong traditional roots with a good education, form a strong, assertive and increasingly articulate group who are beginning to challenge traditional patterns of authority in a range of areas. Fitzgerald (1979, 1993) notes that Maori women are often culturally less conservative than Maori men. Analysing female and male roles within the context of his socio-psychological model, he claims that Maori men typically derive more status from affiliation with Maori culture: they have greater access to traditional knowledge. By contrast, Maori women, excluded from such areas, seem readier to adapt to the wider New Zealand society:

Women – often forbidden to participate in traditional Maori religious and political activities – as a result, were more receptive to European-inspired roles as New Zealand society became increasingly integrated. On several indices, Maori women were revealed to be more progressive, more open to cultural changes, and less traditional in attitudes and behaviour than their male counterparts. (Fitzgerald, 1993: 128)

It is interesting, in the light of these comments, to note that the Maori women often presented themselves in their narratives as strong and assertive characters, as women with authority, and as effective managers. The stories suggest that educated Maori women are adapting and adopting (though not without reflection) Pakeha ways of doing things where they see advantages, and that these women feel increasingly confident in taking on positions of authority and using the associated power to good effect.[14]

Another relevant factor worth considering is the availability to young Maori women of many powerful and effective Maori female role models whose behaviour challenges the traditional conservative models in often dramatic ways.[15] These role models stretch from mythical figures such as Mahuika, Murirangawhenua, and Hine-nui-te-Po from Maori legends, through powerful historical figures such as Te Puea and Wairaka, to enormously influential contemporary women such as the late and much-loved Whina Cooper, Te Ata-i-Rangikaahu, the much respected Maori Queen, and current activists such as Tuaiwa (Eva) Rickard, and Annette Sykes. Such factors no doubt contribute to the sense of self-esteem and confidence apparent in many of the Maori women's stories.

Finally, in considering the reasons for the focus on power and the confident identities projected by a number of the Maori women in their stories, it is worth reflecting on the parallels with ethnicity. I noted above that the stories told by Maori contributors often reflected a preoccupation with ethnicity, whereas for Pakeha, the majority dominant group, ethnicity was not a focus of narratives. It seems possible that, for the same reason (namely relative perceptual salience because of their social position) some Maori women's stories reflect their concern with issues of authority and institutional power.

In discussing the themes which emerged in the spontaneous stories of our Corpus contributors, a number of questions have been raised which clearly require further research. Moreover, this exploratory analysis has generated a number of possible explanations for the patterns observed, all of which need further examination using a larger and more varied data base. In the light of the suggestions in this paper, it would be useful to explicitly elicit stories on particular topics from Maori and Pakeha, matched on other social criteria. It would also seem fruitful to interview a range of selected informants to validate the proposed interpretations and explanations, and to establish the extent to which the themes identified are recognised as characteristic by members of the relevant ethnic and social groups.

8.6   Conclusion

Stories serve many functions, sometimes simultaneously. Stories may entertain and amuse, an important function for many of those in the New Zealand sample which was especially evident in the stories told by both Pakeha and Maori men. They may explore social issues such as the uses and abuses of power, and ways of managing people, a function particularly apparent in the Maori women's stories in this sample. They may express personal feelings and moral dilemmas, or simply express an individual's daily concerns and worries, a function most obvious in the Pakeha women's narratives.

Stories may also serve to bolster the narrator's ego, allowing the construction of a heroic identity, as was apparent in some of the Pakeha male stories. But they also permit self-exploration and may reflect an individual's awareness of growth and complexity. The skilful treatment (often satirical but always humane) of the very unheroic characters who feature in the Maori men's stories, indicates their narrators' awareness of the distance they have moved into a sophisticated, Pakeha-dominated urban world. But these narratives also perhaps reflect concern about the incompatible aspects of Maori and Pakeha culture which inevitably clash in that world, and which are generally resolved by repression and loss of aspects of Maori culture.

Stories can socialise, acculturate and educate listeners. The identity which was overwhelmingly evident in Pakeha women's stories was a relatively conservative, traditional identity as good wife, mother, daughter, friend, citizen, and so on. The Pakeha women's stories tended to reconstruct these identities over and over again, apparently signalling to their listeners their willingness to accept such roles. The Maori women's stories by contrast tended to construct powerful, capable identities for women, and some presented less conformist women who acted authoritatively and challenged conservative norms. Maori women, it seems, are developing confidence in their ability to resist the dominant norms and assert their own values.

This analysis has thus identified some interesting differences in the kinds of social identities constructed and the range of social concerns expressed in stories told by Maori and Pakeha women and men in a sample of New Zealand English. The description, discussion and suggested interpretations of these patterns should be treated as speculative and exploratory at this stage. There is no implication that the patterns described will necessarily generalise to other samples, but I hope they may stimulate further research. Similarly, in suggesting that the features identified may reflect the cultural and social values of those telling the stories, I hope to encourage others to explore, test and challenge what has been proposed. As Betsy Rymes says: "social roles, social identity and moral agency are reconstituted collaboratively through narrative and in turn construct narrative" (1995: 497).

Exploring areas of contrast between Maori and Pakeha narratives may be a source of insight into the current cultural and social issues for different ethnic and social groups in New Zealand society. In other words, narrative analysis can be a valuable resource for studying the contrasting styles, the very different social identities, and the potentially conflicting socio-cultural concerns of Maori and Pakeha in Aotearoa.

Transcription Conventions

All names are pseudonyms.

ALL Capitals indicate emphatic stress
[laughs] Paralinguistic features in square brackets
[tut] A dental click
+ Pause of up to one second
(hello) Transcriber's best guess at an unclear word or utterance
(........) Unintelligible word
? Rising or question intonation
- Incomplete or cut-off utterance
.... something omitted

Notes

This research was made possible by a grant from the New Zealand Foundation for Research, Science and Technology. I would like to express appreciation to Mary Boyce, Harima Fraser, Maria Stubbe and two further readers who preferred to remain anonymous. Their comments and perceptions were of great value in revising this paper.

1   Aotearoa is the Maori name for New Zealand.
2   See also Holmes and Stubbe (1997).
3   The composition of the WCSNZE is described in Holmes (1995b) and the method of collecting the Corpus in Holmes (1996). See also Holmes, Vine and Johnson (1998).
4   More formally, a narrative is "one method of recapitulating past experience by matching a verbal sequence of clauses to the sequence of events which (it is inferred) actually occurred" (Labov, 1972: 359–60). This definition is appropriate since it was developed to account for oral narratives of personal experience. The issues of "what counts as a story" and features of the structure of different narratives are addressed in Holmes (1997b) and (1998).
5   Moreover, the analysis focuses on the content of the narratives; structural and pragmatic features which distinguish the ethnic groups are dealt with elsewhere. See Holmes (1998), Holmes and Stubbe (1997).
6   The discussion in Metge (1995) supports this viewpoint, and it has been confirmed by the Maori people whom I have consulted.
7   It is possible that this perception simply reflects my Pakeha perspective (discussed above). However, Maori readers and people with whom I have discussed the material endorse the interpretation offered here. See also King (1985), especially the early chapters.
8   See appendix for transcription conventions. For ease of reading, examples have been edited in relation to features such as overlapping speech which are irrelevant to the discussion in this paper. Names have been changed to protect people's identity.
9   The Maori term "whaangai" meaning "nurture, feed, bring up", captures the concept better than the term "adoption".
10   Interestingly, this story raises the issue of the appropriate way to socialise young Maori boys, an issue which is the focus of an advert discussed in Holmes (1997a).
11   Parallels with the proactive role of powerful female protagonists in many Maori myths and legends are obvious, but there is not space to explore them here.
12   See also Johnstone, 1990; Riessman, 1990, 1993; Coates, 1995; Schiffrin, 1996, for example, for similar findings.
13   In this context Harima Fraser, one of the Maori women consulted, quotes the Maori proverb "waiho maa te tangata mihi", which translates "Let someone else sing your praises".
14   Note too that Maori female radical action is also apparent in relation to the revival of Maori language and culture. In the last fifteen years women have played a pivotal role in attempts to revive the Maori language. The kohanga reo movement (Maori language immersion pre-schools), for example, has been successful largely due to the extraordinary efforts of committed Maori women. This is a good example of radical action aimed at conserving or re-establishing an important traditional cultural treasure, the Maori language.
15   I owe this point to Maria Stubbe.

References

Attanucci, J. (1993). Time characterization of mother–daughter and family–school relations: Narrative understandings of adolescence. *Journal of Narrative and Life History* 3, 99–116.
Benton, R. A. (1991). The Maori language: Dying or reviving. *East-West Centre Association Working Paper* No. 28. Honolulu: East-West Centre Association.

Besnier, N. (1989). Information withholding as a manipulative and collusive strategy in Nukulaelae gossip. *Language in Society* 18, 315–41.

Blum-Kulka, S. (1993). "You gotta know how to tell a story": Telling, tales, and tellers in American and Israeli narrative events at dinner. *Language in Society* 22, 361–402.

Bruner, J. (1987). Life as narrative. *Social Research* 54, 11–32.

Bruner, J. (1990). Autobiography as self. In J. Bruner (ed.), *Acts of meaning* (pp. 33–66). Cambridge, MA: Harvard University Press.

Butler, J. (1990). *Gender trouble.* New York: Routledge.

Chafe, W. (1994). *Discourse, consciousness, and time.* Chicago: University of Chicago Press.

Coates, J. (1995). *Women talk.* Oxford: Blackwell.

Crawford, M. (1995). *Talking difference: On gender and language.* London: Sage.

Davies, C. (1982). Ethnic jokes, moral values and social boundaries. *British Journal of Sociology* 33(3), 383–403.

Davies, C. (1990). *Ethnic humor around the world.* Bloomington: Indiana University Press.

Edwards, V. & Sienkewicz, T. J. (1990). *Oral cultures past and present: Rappin' and Homer.* Oxford: Blackwell.

Fairclough, N. (1989). *Language and power.* London: Longman.

Fairclough, N. (1995). *Critical discourse analysis.* London: Longman.

Fitzgerald, T. K. (1979). Male and female identity among New Zealanders. In A. McElroy and C. Matthiasson (eds.), *Sex roles in changing societies.* SUNY Occasional Papers in Anthropology Series.

Fitzgerald, T. K. (1993). *Metaphors of identity: A culture–communication dialogue.* New York: State University of New York Press.

Gee, J. (1991). A linguistic approach to narrative. *Journal of Narrative and Life History* 1, 15–39.

Heath, S. B. (1982). What no bedtime story means? *Language in Society* 11, 49–76.

Holmes, J. (1995a). *Women, men and politeness.* London: Longman.

Holmes, J. (1995b). The Wellington corpus of spoken New Zealand English: A progress report. *New Zealand English Newsletter* 9, 5–8.

Holmes, J. (1996). Collecting the Wellington corpus of spoken New Zealand English: Some methodological challenges. *New Zealand English Journal* 10, 10–15.

Holmes, J. (1997a). Women, language and identity. *Journal of Sociolinguistics* 2(1), 195–223.

Holmes, J. (1997b). Story-telling in New Zealand women's and men's talk. In R. Wodak (ed.), *Gender and discourse.* London: Sage.

Holmes, J. (1998). Narrative structure: Some contrasts between Maori and Pakeha story-telling. *Multilingua* 17(1), 25–57.

Holmes, J. & Hay, J. (1997). Humour as an ethnic boundary marker in New Zealand interaction. *Journal of Intercultural Studies* 18(2), 127–51.

Holmes, J. & Stubbe, M. (1997). Good listeners: Gender differences in New Zealand conversation. *Women and Language* 20(2), 7–14.

Holmes, J., Vine, B. & Johnson, G. (1998). Manual accompanying the Wellington Corpus of spoken New Zealand English. Wellington: Victoria University of Wellington.

Howard, A. (1974). *Ain't no big thing: Coping strategies in a Hawaiian American community.* Honolulu: University Press of Hawaii.

Ito, K. L. (1985). Affective bonds: Hawaiian interrelationships of self. In G. M. White & J. Kirkpatrick (eds.), *Person, self and experience: Exploring Pacific ethnopsychologies* (pp. 301–27). Berkeley: University of California Press.

Johnstone, B. (1990). *Stories, community, and place.* Bloomington: Indiana University Press.

King, M. (1985). *Being Pakeha.* Auckland: Hodder and Stoughton.

Labov, W. (1972). The transformation of experience in narrative syntax. *Language in the inner city* (pp. 354–96). Philadelphia: University of Pennsylvania.

Linde, C. (1993). *Life stories: The creation of coherence.* Oxford: Oxford University Press.

Metge, J. (1976). 2nd edn. *The Maoris of New Zealand.* London: Routledge and Kegan Paul.

Metge, J. (1986). *In and out of touch: Whakamaa in cross-cultural context.* Wellington: Victoria University Press.

Metge, J. (1995). *New growth from old: The Whaanau in the modern world*. Wellington: Victoria University Press.

Metge, J. & Kinloch, P. (1978). *Talking past each other: Problems of cross-cultural communication*. Wellington: Victoria University Press/Price Milburn.

Michaels, S. (1981). "Sharing Time": Children's narrative styles and differential access to literacy. *Language in Society* 10, 423–42.

National Maori Language Survey (1995). Wellington: Maori Language Commission.

Riessman, C. (1990). *Divorce talk*. New Brunswick, NJ: Rutgers University Press.

Riessman, C. (1993). *Narrative analysis*. London: Sage.

Rymes, B. (1995). The construction of moral agency in the narratives of high-school drop-outs. *Discourse and Society* 6(3), 495–516.

Schiffrin, D. (1996). Narrative as self-portrait: sociolinguistic constructions of identity. *Language and Society* 25, 167–203.

Weedon, C. (1987). *Feminist practice and poststructuralist theory*. Oxford: Blackwell.

Ziv, A. (1988). *National styles of humor*. Westport, CT: Greenwood Press.

9

New York Jewish Conversational Style

Deborah Tannen

A pause in the wrong place, an intonation misunderstood, and a whole conversation went awry. (E. M. Forster, *A Passage to India*)

Conversation, New York's biggest cottage industry, doesn't exist in San Francisco in the sense of sustained discourse and friendly contentiousness. (Edmund White, *States of Desire*)[1]

Take, for example, the following conversation.[2]

F: How often does your acting group work?
M: Do you mean how often we rehearse or how often we perform.⌉
F: ⌊Both.
M: [Laughs uneasily.]
F: Why are you laughing?
M: Because of the way you said that. It was like a bullet.
    Is that why your marriage broke up?
F: What?
M: Because of your aggressiveness.

Of the many observations that could be made based on this interchange, I would like to focus on two: the general tendency to extrapolate personality from conversational style, and the specific attribution of aggressiveness to a speaker who uses fast pacing in conversation. In the discussion that follows, I will suggest that the stereotype of the 'pushy New York Jew' may result in part from discourse conventions practiced by some native New Yorkers of East European Jewish background. After examining some evidence for the existence of such a stereotype, I will (1) briefly present my notion of conversational style, (2) outline the linguistic and paralinguistic features that make up New York Jewish style and (3) demonstrate their use in cross-stylistic and co-stylistic interaction. In conclusion, I will (4) discuss the personal and social uses of conversational style.

Deborah Tannen, "New York Jewish conversational style" in *International Journal of the Sociology of Language* 30 (1981), pp. 133–49. Reprinted by permission of the author and Mouton de Gruyter, a division of Walter de Gruyter GmbH & Co publishers.

9.1　The Negative Stereotype

Evidence abounds of the negative stereotype of New York speech in general and New York Jewish speech in particular. The most widely recognized component of this speech is, of course, phonology. An Associated Press release (Boyer, 1979) reports on California therapists who help cure New York accents. One such therapist is quoted: 'It's really a drag listening to people from New York talk. It upsets me when I hear a New York accent. . . . We're here to offer a service to newcomers to this area, especially to New Yorkers. . . . When they open their mouths, they alienate everyone. We're here to help them adjust to life in Marin County.'

A third-grade teacher in Brooklyn wrote to Ann Landers complaining of native-born children who say, for example, 'Vot's the kvestion?', 'It's vorm ottside', and 'heppy as a boid'. Ann Landers advised the teacher, 'With consistent effort, bad speech habits can be unlearned. I hope you will have the patience to work with these students. It's a real challenge.'

Teachers in New York City have been rising to the challenge for a long time. Not so long ago one of the requirements for a license to teach in the New York City public schools was passing a speech exam, which entailed proving that one did not speak with the indigenous 'accent'. I myself recall being given a shockingly low midterm grade by a speech teacher in a Manhattan high school who promised that it would not be raised until I stopped 'dentalizing'. I am not aware of any other group whose members feel that their pronunciation is wrong, even when they are comfortably surrounded by others from the same group and have never lived anywhere else. Labov (1970) has documented the hypercorrection that results from the linguistic insecurity of middle-class Jewish New York women. I confronted this myself each time I recognized a fellow New Yorker in California by her or his accent. The most common response was, 'Oh is it THAT obvious?' or 'Gee, I thought I'd gotten rid of that'.

Unfortunately, moreover, evaluations of 'accent' are not applied merely to the speech itself but form the basis of personality judgments. In an attempt to evaluate the effect of Southern-accented speech on judgments of employability, Van Antwerp and Maxwell (1982) serendipitously tapped the negative valence of New York speech. One of their sample non-Southern speakers happened to be a woman from northern New Jersey whose speech approximated the dialect of New York City. Commentators from the Washington, D.C. area evaluated her employability negatively, attributing to her such characteristics as 'inability to articulate', 'disorganized and dull', 'seemed educated but not very together', 'a little too energetic, sort of in a hurry to get it over with', 'didn't seem to have things straight in her head before she spoke', 'sounded aggressive'. These findings demonstrate the possible consequences of negative evaluations based on speech style when cross-stylistic interaction takes place in 'gatekeeping' (Erickson, 1975) situations.

9.2　Background of the Study

My own findings on New York Jewish conversational style were in a way serendipitous as well. I had begun with the goal of discovering the features that made up the styles of each participant in two-and-a-half hours of naturally occurring conversation at dinner on Thanksgiving 1978. Analysis revealed, however, that three of the participants, all natives of New York of East European Jewish background, shared many stylistic features which could be seen to have a positive effect when used with each other and a negative effect when used with the three others. Moreover, the evening's interaction was later characterized by three of the participants (independently) as 'New York Jewish' or 'New York'. Finally, whereas the tapes contained many examples of interchanges between two or three of the New Yorkers, it had no examples of talk among non-New Yorkers in which the New Yorkers did not participate. Thus, what began as a general study of conversational style ended by becoming an analysis of New York Jewish conversational style (Tannen, 1979).

The dinner at which this conversation was taped took place in the home of Kurt, a native New Yorker living in Oakland, California. The guests who were also New Yorkers living in California were Kurt's brother, Peter, and myself.[3] The three other guests were Kurt's friend David, a native of Los Angeles of Irish, Scotch and English parents from Iowa and North Dakota; David's friend Chad, a native and resident of Los Angeles whose father was of Scotch/English extraction and whose mother was from New York, of Italian background; and Sally, born and raised in England, of a Jewish father and American mother.[4] Complex as these ethnic backgrounds are, the group split into two when looked at on the basis of conversational style.

9.3   Theoretical Background

My notion of conversational style grows out of R. Lakoff's (1973; 1979) work on communicative style and Gumperz' (1977; 1982) on conversational inference. 'Style' is not something extra, added on like frosting on a cake. It is the stuff of which the linguistic cake is made: pitch, amplitude, intonation, voice quality, lexical and syntactic choice, rate of speech and turntaking, as well as what is said and how discourse cohesion is achieved. In other words, style refers to all the ways speakers encode meaning in language and convey how they intend their talk to be understood. Insofar as speakers from similar speech communities share such linguistic conventions, style is a social phenomenon. Insofar as speakers use particular features in particular combinations and in various settings, to that extent style is an individual phenomenon. (See Gumperz and Tannen, 1979, for a discussion of individual vs. social differences.)

Lakoff (1973) observes that speakers regularly avoid saying precisely what they mean in the interest of social goals which they pursue by adhering to one of three *rules of politeness*, later renamed *rules of rapport* (Lakoff, 1979). Each rule is associated with a communicative style growing out of habitual application of that rule:

1. Don't impose (distance)
2. Give options (deference)
3. Be friendly (camaraderie)

To illustrate (with my own examples), if a guest responds to an offer of something to drink by saying, 'No thank you; I'm not thirsty', s/he is applying R1. If s/he says, 'Oh,

I'll have whatever you're having', s/he is applying R2. If s/he marches into the kitchen, throws open the refrigerator, and says, 'I'm thirsty. Got any juice?' s/he is applying R3. Individuals differ with regard to which sense of politeness they tend to observe, and cultural differences are reflected by the tendency of members of a group to observe one or the other sense of politeness in conventionalized ways.

These differing senses of politeness are associated as well with two goals of indirectness: *defensiveness* and *rapport*. Defensiveness, associated with R1 'don't impose', is the desire to be able to renege, to say 'I never said that', or 'That's not what I meant'. Rapport, associated with R3 'be friendly', refers to the fine feeling of being 'on the same wave length' which accrues when one gets what one wants without asking for it or feels understood without having explained.

Another deeply related strand of research in sociology is brilliantly elaborated by Goffman, building on the work of Durkheim. Durkheim (1915) distinguishes between negative and positive religious rites. Negative rites are 'a system of abstentions' which prepares one for 'access to the positive cult'. Goffman (1967: 72–3) builds upon this dichotomy in his notion of *deference*, 'the appreciation an individual shows of another to that other, whether through avoidance rituals or presentational rituals'. Presentational rituals include 'salutations, invitations, compliments, and minor services. Through all of these the recipient is told that he is not an island unto himself and that others are, or seek to be, involved with him . . .'. Avoidance rituals 'lead the actor to keep at a distance from the recipient' (Goffman, 1967: 62) and include 'rules regarding privacy and separateness' (Goffman, 1967: 67). Following Lakoff and Goffman, Brown and Levinson (1978) refer to two overriding goals motivating linguistic forms of politeness: negative face, 'the want of every adult member that his actions be unimpeded by others', and positive face, 'the want of every adult member that his actions be desirable to at least some others'.

All these schemata for understanding human interaction recognize two basic but conflicting needs to be involved with others and to be left alone. Linguistic systems, like other cultural systems, represent conventionalized ways of honoring these needs. I would like to suggest that the conversational style of the New Yorkers at Thanksgiving dinner can be seen as conventionalized strategies serving the need for involvement, whereas the non-New York participants expected strategies serving the need for independence.

9.4   Features of New York Jewish Conversational Style

Following are the main features found in the talk of three of the six Thanksgiving celebrants. (More detailed discussion of these can be found in Tannen, 1979; 1980a; 1981; 1987.)

1.   *Topic* (a) prefer personal topics, (b) shift topics abruptly, (c) introduce topics without hesitance, (d) persistence (if a new topic is not immediately picked up, reintroduce it, repeatedly if necessary).

2.   *Genre* (a) tell more stories, (b) tell stories in rounds, (c) internal evaluation (Labov, 1972) is preferred over external (i.e., the point of a story is dramatized rather than lexicalized), (d) preferred point of a story is teller's emotional experience.

3. *Pacing* (a) faster rate of speech, (b) inter-turn pauses avoided (silence is evidence of lack of rapport), (c) faster turntaking, (d) cooperative overlap and participatory listenership.

4. *Expressive paralinguistics* (a) expressive phonology, (b) pitch and amplitude shifts, (c) marked voice quality, (d) strategic within-turn pauses.

All of these features were combined to create linguistic devices which enhanced conversational flow when used among the New Yorkers, but they had an obstructive effect on conversation with those who were not from New York. Comments by all participants upon listening to the tape indicated that they misunderstood the intentions of members of the other group.

Perhaps the most easily perceived and characteristic feature of this style is the fast rate of speech and tendency to overlap (speak simultaneously) and latch (Sacks' term for allowing no pause before turntaking). I have demonstrated at length elsewhere (Tannen, 1979; 1980) that overlap is used cooperatively by the New Yorkers, as a way of showing enthusiasm and interest, but it is interpreted by non-New Yorkers as just the opposite: evidence of lack of attention. The tendency to use fast pace and overlap often combines, moreover, with preference for personal topics, focusing attention on another in a personal way. Both the pacing and the personal focus can be seen repeatedly to cause Sally, Chad and David to become more hesitant in their speech as they respond in classic complementary schismogenetic fashion (Bateson, 1972). That is, the verbal devices used by one group cause speakers of the other group to react by intensifying the opposing behavior, and vice versa.

9.5   Cross-Stylistic Interchange

The following conversation illustrates how both Peter and I use fast pacing and personal focus to show interest in David's discourse, with the result that he feels 'caught off guard' and 'on the spot'. (This is only one of many such examples.) David, a professional sign interpreter, has been talking about American Sign Language.

(1) D So: and thís is the one that's Bèrkeley. This is the Bérkeley . . . sign for . . for
     ⌈Christmas
     p
(2) T ⌊Do yòu figure oút those . . those um correspòndences?
     f
     Or do? when you learn the signs, /does/ somebody télls you.
(3) D Oh you mean ⌈watching it? like
(4) T   ⌊Cause I can imagine knówing that sign, . . . and not . . figur-
     ing out that it had anything to do with the decorátions.
     . . . .
(5) D No. Y you knów that it has to do with the
     decorátions.⌉
(6) T   ⌊Cause somebody télls you? Or you figure⌉it oút.
                            D: ⌊No⌋
(7) D Oh. . . . You you talking about mé, or a deàf person.⌉
(8) T   ⌊Yeah.⌋   ⌊You. You.

(9)   D   Me? uh: Someone télls me, ùsually. . . . But a lót of em I can tèll. I mean they're
óbvious. . . . The bétter I get the mòre I can tell. The lónger I do it the mòre
I can tell what they're talking about.
. . . . . Withoút knowing what the sign is.⌉
(10)   T   ⌊Huh:⌋   ⌊That's interesting.⌋
(11)   P   ⌊But how do you learn a
new sign.
. . . .
(12)   D   How do I learn a new sign?⌉
(13)   P   ⌊Yeah. I mean supposing ˏ . . . Víctor's
talking and all of a sudden he uses a sign for Thanksgíving, and you've never
séen it before.

My questions (2) (4) and (6) and Peter's questions (11) and (13) overlap or latch onto
David's preceding comments. In contrast, David's comments follow our questions after
'normal' or even noticeable (5, 12) pauses.

My question (2) about how David learns about the symbolism behind signs not only is
latched onto David's fading comment (1) but is spoken loudly and shifts the focus from a
general discourse about signs to focus on David personally. The abrupt question catches
him off guard, and he hesitates by rephrasing the question. I then interrupt David's rephrasing to supply more information (4), interpreting his hesitation as indication that I had
been unclear. The real trouble, however, was the suddenness of my question and its shift
from general to personal. Thus, I hoped to make David comfortable by acknowledging the
fault had been mine and rectifying the matter by supplying more information right away,
but the second interruption could only make him more uncomfortable; hence, the pause.

David answers my question (4) by commenting (5) 'You know that it has to do with
the decorations', but he avoids the more personal focus of my question (2) about *how*
he knows. I therefore become more specific (6) and again latch my question. David stalls
again, this time by asking (7) for clarification. His question comes after a filler, a pause,
a slight stutter: 'Oh. . . . You you talking about me . . .'. He expresses his surprise at the
shift in focus. Yet again, I clarify in machine-gun fashion: (8) 'Yeah. You. You.' David
then answers the question and my response (10) overlaps his answer.

Just as this interchange between David and me is settled, Peter uses precisely the
strategy that I was using, with the same results. Latching onto David's answer (9),
Peter asks another question focusing on David (11); David hesitates by rephrasing the
question after a pause (12); Peter barely waits for the rephrasing to finish before he
makes his question more specific (13).

The rhythm of this segment is most peculiar. Normally, a question–answer are
seen as an 'adjacency pair' (Sacks, Schegloff and Jefferson, 1974), and in a smooth
conversation they are rhythmically paired as well. The differences in David's pacing
on the one hand and Peter's and mine on the other, however, create pauses between our
questions and his delayed answers, so that the resultant rhythmic pairs are made up of
an answer and the next question. This is typical of how stylistic differences obstruct
conversational rhythm. While participants in this conversation were friends and disposed
to think well of each other, the operation of such differences in other settings can leave
participants with the conviction that the other was uncooperative or odd.

9.6   Co-stylistic Interchange

In the previous example, Peter and I directed similar questions to David, with unexpected results. The following segment shows how the same device serves to enhance conversational flow when used with each other. This segment begins when I turn to Peter suddenly and address a question to him.

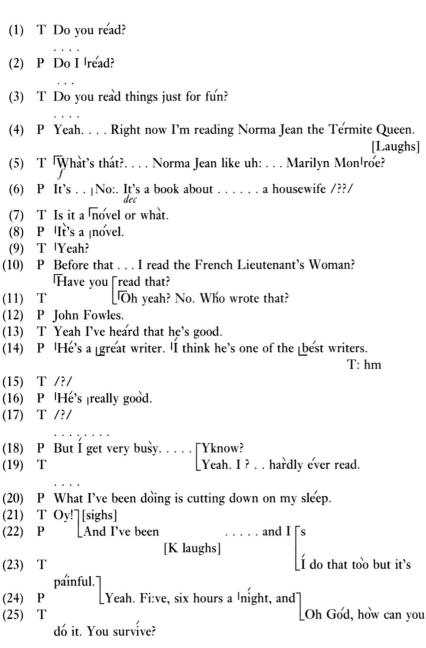

(1)   T   Do you réad?

   . . . .

(2)   P   Do I ˈréad?

   . . .

(3)   T   Do you reàd things just for fún?

   . . . .

(4)   P   Yeah. . . . Right now I'm reading Norma Jean the Térmite Queen.
            [Laughs]

(5)   T   ⌈Whàt's thát?. . . . Norma Jean like uh: . . . Marilyn Monˈróe?
            ʄ

(6)   P   It's . . ₁No:. It's a book about . . . . . . a housewife /??/
                      dec

(7)   T   Is it a ⌐nóvel or whàt.

(8)   P   ˈIt's a ₁nóvel.

(9)   T   ˈYeah?

(10) P   Before that . . . I read the French Lieutenant's Woman?
            ⌐Have you ⌐read that?

(11) T   ⌊⌐Oh yeah? No. Whó wrote that?

(12) P   John Fowles.

(13) T   Yeah I've heárd that he's good.

(14) P   ˈHé's a ₁gréat writer. ˈI think he's one of the ₗbést writers.
                                                      T: hm

(15) T   /?/

(16) P   ˈHé's ₁really goòd.

(17) T   /?/

   . . . . . ̠ . . . .

(18) P   But I get very busỳ. . . . . ⌐Yknow?

(19) T   ⌊Yeah. I ? . . haŕdly éver read.

   . . . .

(20) P   What I've been doìng is cutting down on my sléep.

(21) T   Oy!⌉ [sighs]

(22) P   ⌊And I've been   . . . . . and I ⌐s
                            [K laughs]

(23) T   ⌊I do that toò but it's
            paínful.⌉

(24) P   ⌊Yeah. Fi:ve, six hours a ˈníght, and⌉

(25) T   ⌊Oh Gód, hòw can you
            dó it. You survíve?

   . . . .

(26) P Yeah làte afternoon méetings are hàrd. . . . But outside of thát I

                                 T: mmm

      can keep goìng ⌈pretty well.

(27) T   ⌊Not sleeping enough is térrible. . . . I'd múch

      rather not eàt than not sleèp.

                   p

      [S laughs]

(28) P I próbably should not eàt so much, it would . . it would uh . . . sáve a lot of time.

(29) T If I'm /like really/ busy I don't I don't I don't eat. I don't yeah I just don't eat but ⌈I

(30) P   ⌊I ? I tend to spend a lòt of time eáting and preparing and ⌈/?/

(31) T   ⌊Oh: I néver prepare foòd. . . . . . . I eat whatéver I can get my hánds on.⌉

(32) P   ⌊Yeah.

This interchange exhibits many features of New York Jewish conversational style. In addition to the characteristic use of overlap, fast pacing and personal focus, it exhibits devices I have called (Tannen, 1979) persistence, mutual revelation and expressive paralinguistics.

Both Peter and I use overlap and latching in this segment: Peter's (22) (24) and (30) and my (19) (23) (25) (27) and (31). The interchange begins with a sudden focus of attention on him by my question (1). Like David, Peter is initially 'caught off guard', so he repeats the question after a pause. But then he not only answers the question but supplies specific information (4) about the book he is reading. A common feature of participatory listenership is seen in (5) and (6). While (6) is ostensibly an answer to my question (5), it is clear that Peter would have gone on to give that information in any case. He begins, 'It's . . .', has to stop in order to answer my question with 'No', and then repeats the beginning and continues, 'It's a book about a housewife'.

Persistence refers to the pattern by which speakers continue trying to say something despite lack of attention or interruption. In this example it can be seen in (22) and (24), in which Peter makes three attempts to say that he sleeps only five or six hours a night. Persistence is a necessary concomitant to overlap. It reflects a conversational economy in which it is not the business of a listener to make room for another speaker to speak. Rather, it is the business of the listener to show enthusiasm; the speaker, in this system, can be counted on to find room to speak. The conversational burden, in other words, is to serve the need for involvement at the risk of violating independence.

The mutual revelation device can be seen in the series of observations Peter and I make about our own habits. In (19) I state that I hardly ever read as a way of showing understanding of Peter's tight schedule (18). (23) is a similar response to his statement that he cuts down on sleep. (27) is a statement of my preference to balance his statement (26) about sleeping. In (28) Peter makes a statement about his eating habits; in (29) I describe mine; in (30) he reiterates his, and in (31) I reiterate mine. It might seem to some observers that we are not 'communicating' at all, since we both talk only about ourselves. But the juxtaposition of comments and the relationship of topics constitutes thematic cohesion and establishes rapport. In this system, the offer of personal information is encouragement to the other to volunteer the same, and volunteered information is highly valued.

Throughout the Thanksgiving conversation, Peter, Kurt and I use exaggerated phonological and paralinguistic cues. For example, my question (5) 'What's that?' is loud and high pitched. When any of the New Yorkers uses such features with Chad or David, the result is that they stop talking in surprise; wondering what caused the outburst. When used in talk among the New Yorkers, introduction of exaggerated paralinguistics spurs the others to follow suit, in a mutually escalating way such as Bateson (1972) has characterized as symmetrical. In the present segment, many of the words and phrases are uttered with extra high or low pitch as well as heavily colored voice quality.

It seems likely that my use of high pitch on 'What's that?' as well as on the last syllable of 'Monroe' in (5) was triggered by Peter's laughter while uttering the book title. In any case, Peter's response (6) uses sharp contrasts in pitch and pacing to signal the message, 'I know this is a silly book'. The pitch on 'No' is very low, the vowel is drawn out, the sentence is uttered slowly, and it contains a very long pause before the key word 'housewife' is uttered. Similar sharp shifts from high to low pitch can be seen repeatedly.

(8)   P ⌐It's a ⌐novel.
(14) P ⌐He's a ⌐great writer. ⌐I think he's one of the ⌐best writers.
(16) P ⌐He's really ⌐good.

These pitch shifts, together with voice quality, signal in (8) denigration of the book discussed and in (14) and (16) great earnestness.

Exaggerated paralinguistics can be seen as well in my expressions of concern for Peter's loss of sleep in (23) (25) and (27). These are all uttered with marked stress and breathy voice quality that demonstrate exaggerated and stylized concern.

Yet another stylized response to Peter's assertion that he doesn't sleep enough is a Yiddish non-verbal 'response cry' (Goffman, 1978), 'Oy!'. This utterance is rapport-building in a number of ways. Obviously, the choice of a Yiddish expression signals our shared ethnic background. At the same time, the exaggerated nature of my response – the utterance of a great sigh along with 'oy' – is a way of mocking my own usage, making the exclamation ironic in much the way Peter was mocking his own reading material while telling about it. (In a similar way, Kurt often mocks his own hosting behavior by offering food in an exaggerated Yiddish accent.) Finally, I utter this cry as if it were an expression of my own feeling, thus taking Peter's point of view as a show of empathy.

The interchange between Peter and me ends with another cooperative use of overlap and repetition. The conversation has turned to dating, and it has continued to be characterized by the features seen in the earlier segment. It ends this way:

(1)   P   And you just cán't get to know . . . . ten   people really well.
                                                 [breathy]

          ⌐You can't dó it.
          ⌐p
(2)   T   ⌐Yeah right. Y'have to there's no? Yeah there's ⌐no time.
(3)   P   ⌐There's not time.
(4)   T   Yeah . . . . 'strue.

Peter's statements (1) and (3) flow in a continuous stream, ending with 'You can't do it. There's not time'. However the last phrase echoes my words in (2). The end of the talk is signaled by a quieting down of voices as well as the pattern of blended voices and phrases.

9.7   The Opacity of Style

To those unfamiliar with the workings of particular stylistic strategies, their use seems like evidence of lack of communication – which is simply to say they don't see how they work. More often than not the features used have meaning in the speech habits of the different group, so conclusions are drawn based on what the signals would mean if the hearer had used them. To those who do not expect overlap to be used cooperatively, and would not use it in that way themselves, another's overlap will be interpreted as lack of attention. Thus an article in *New West* magazine (Esterly, 1979) tells of the work of a UCLA psychologist, Gerald Goodman, who believes that fast talkers are a conversational menace. Calling them 'crowders', he eloquently articulates the effect they have on those unaccustomed to this style:

> There's a dehumanizing aspect to being crowded; there's a lack of respect involved. Interrupting arises from a variety of factors – anxiety, a desire to dominate, boredom, the need to express freshly stimulated thoughts. . . . People walk away from conversations with crowders feeling upset or dissatisfied or incompetent, though they may not understand why. (p. 68)

Clearly, this is the interpretation of fast pacing made by David, Chad and Sally during Thanksgiving, at least at times. It is the feeling of being imposed upon, in violation of Brown and Levinson's (1978) negative politeness. However, the 'dehumanizing aspect', the vague feeling of dissatisfaction and incompetence, is not a response to others' use of specific linguistic features but rather to their use of such features in an unexpected way. It is the lack of sharedness of style that is disconcerting. Fast talkers walk away from those same conversations feeling similar discomfort, most likely having interpreted the slower pacing as a failure of positive politeness.

Style is often invisible. People tend to take their conversational habits as self-evident and draw conclusions not about others' linguistic devices but about their intentions or personalities. Moreover, few speakers are aware of ways in which others' linguistic behavior may be a reaction to their own.

9.8   The Coherence of Conversational Style

As Reisman (1974: 110) points out, 'The conventions which order speech interaction are meaningful not only in that they order and mediate verbal expression, but in that they participate in and express larger meanings in the society which uses them'. Becker (1979a: 18) explains, 'The figure a sentence makes is a strategy of interpretation' which 'helps the people it is used by understand and feel coherent in their worlds'. The structure and habits of language which seem self-evidently natural, serve not only as a way to communicate meaning but also to reestablish and ratify one's way of being in the world. In another paper, Becker (1979b: 241) explains:

> The universal source of language pathology is that people appear to say one thing and 'mean' another. It drives people mad (the closer it gets to home). An aesthetic response is quite simply the opposite of this pathology. . . . Schizophrenia, foreign language learning, and artistic expression in language all operate under the same set of linguistic variables – constraints on coherence, invention, intentionality, and reference. The difference is that in madness (and in the temporary madness of learning a new language or a new text) these constraints are misunderstood and often appear contradictory, while in an aesthetic response they are understood as a coherent integrated whole. . . . The integration of communication (art) is, hence, as essential to a sane community as clean air, good food, and, to cure errors, medicine.

The emotional/aesthetic experience of a perfectly tuned conversation is as ecstatic as an artistic experience. The satisfaction of having communicated successfully goes beyond the pleasure of being understood in the narrow sense. It is a ratification of one's place in the world and one's way of being human. It is, as Becker calls a well-performed shadow play, 'a vision of sanity'.

To some extent there is for everyone a discontinuity between the private code, i.e., communicative habits learned at home and on the block (or in the fields) around one's home, and the public code, i.e., the form of language used in formal settings. Hence the anxiety most people feel about communicating with strangers. But the degree of discontinuity may be greater or lesser. Those who learned and have reinforced at home norms of interaction which are relatively similar to those which are widely accepted in society at large have a certainty about their linguistic convictions. If they proclaim that it is rude to interrupt or that one ought to state the point of a story outright, it is without ambivalence. But those who have grown up hearing and using norms of interaction which differ significantly from more widely accepted ones may feel ambivalent about their own styles. Thus New Yorkers of Jewish background cannot complain 'Why don't you interrupt?'. On hearing a taperecording of a conversation they thoroughly enjoyed in the process, they often feel critical of themselves and slightly embarrassed. They, too, believe that it is rude to interrupt, to talk loudly, to talk too much. The 'interruption' may actually be the creation of the interlocutor who stopped when s/he was expected to continue talking over the overlap, but the cooperative overlapper is no more likely to realize this than the overlap-resistant speaker.

The greater the discontinuity between ingroup style and public expectations, the more difficult it is for one to feel sane in both worlds. Hence it is not surprising that many speakers reject one or the other style, and New York Jews who have moved away from New York may be heard to proclaim that they hate New York accents, hate to go back to New York or hate to go home, because 'no one listens to anyone else' or 'it's so loud' or 'people are so rude'. There are probably few speakers of this background who have not at times felt uncomfortable upon seeing through public eyes someone from their own background talking in a way that is attracting attention in an alien setting, just as American travelers may feel embarrassed on seeing another American tourist who fits too neatly the stereotype of the ugly American abroad. In contrast, the comfort of interaction in a setting in which one's home style predominates goes far to explain what often appears as clannishness – the preference for the company of those of similar ethnic background. The coherence principles (to borrow a term from Becker) that create conversational style operate on every level of discourse and contribute to, at the same time that they grow out of, people's attempts to achieve coherence in the world.

9.9   Afterword on Accountability

Perhaps a word is in order on the validity of the case-study method. How generalizable are findings based on close observation and interviews with six speakers? The most reassuring confirmation is a phenomenon I have called 'the aha factor' (Tannen, 1979). When I explain these style differences in public or private forums, a cry of relief goes up from many of my hearers – especially from intermarried couples, of whom only one partner is Jewish and from New York City. They invariably report that these style differences have been the cause of complaints; the non-New York spouse chronically complains of being interrupted, not listened to, not given a chance to talk, while the New York-bred partner feels unjustly accused and in turn complains that the other partner is unaccountably withholding. If the family does not live in New York City, the misunderstanding often extends as well to children who complain that the New York parent does not listen to them and overreacts to their talk.

In a recent column in *The Washington Post*, Judith Martin, assuming the persona of an etiquette expert named Miss Manners, addressed the question of conversational norms. A disgruntled reader wrote to complain that she is 'a good listener', but 'there are so many people in this world who will just talk right over me. Sometimes I'm halfway into a sentence or an idea when they burst in with their own'. Miss Manners responded in the spirit of cooperative overlap and participatory listenership:

> If you are, in fact, a practiced "good listener," you have not been traveling through life in silence. You have been asking questions, inserting relevant information and providing commentary on what the chief talkers to whom you have been listening are saying. A good listener is not someone who has to be checked every now and then by the speaker to see if he or she is awake. . . . Once in the driver's seat, you should try to be a good talker. That is to say, you must allow proper interruptions that are in the tradition of good listening, and even encourage them. . . .

Surprised to find such linguistic values articulated in the popular press, I contacted the writer and was not surprised to learn that Martin is Jewish.

This raises the question of the extent to which the linguistic conventions I have discussed are 'New York' and/or 'Jewish'. My hypothesis is that the style (i.e., the combination of linguistic devices used in the way described) I have discussed represents a prototype of a kind of conversation that is familiar to most New York Jews and unfamiliar to most midwestern and western Americans of non-Jewish background. My impression is that New Yorkers of non-Jewish background and Jews not from New York City use many of the devices I have described and that there are New York Jews who use few of them. I suspect that the existence of this style represents the influence of conversational norms of East European Jewish immigrants and that similar norms are probably general to the Levant.[5] I have not encountered evidence to indicate that Jews of German background necessarily share this style.

The precise distribution of these and related linguistic devices, like the distribution of dialect features, can only be determined by the painstaking research of many workers in many settings, if there turn out to be enough researchers who find this a thing worth doing. In any case, there is no doubt that the acquisition, maintenance and accommodation of conversational style is a crucial linguistic and social process.

Notes

1 My thanks to Stephen Murray for this reference.
2 This conversation was reconstructed from memory. Others presented are transcribed from taperecordings. The following transcription conventions are used, as gleaned from Schenkein (1978) and from those developed at the University of California, Berkeley, by Gumperz and Chafe and their respective collaborators.

. . .	half second pause. Each extra dot represents another half second of pause.
′	marks primary stress
`	marks secondary stress
underline	indicates emphatic stress
|	marks high pitch on word
⌐	marks high pitch on phrase, continuing until punctuation
|	marks low pitch on word
.	sentence-final falling intonation
,	clause-final intonation (more to come)
?	yes/no question rising intonation
ʔ	glottal stop
:	lengthened vowel sound
p	spoken softly (piano)
f	spoken loudly (forte)
dec	spoken slowly
/?/	inaudible segment

⌈Brackets connecting lines show overlapping speech.
⌊Two people talking at the same time.

Brackets with reversed flaps⌉
⌋indicate latching (no intraturn pause)

3 Thus I was both perpetrator and object of my analysis, making me not a participant observer (an observer who becomes a participant) but a participant who is also an observer. At the time of taping, I was in the habit of taping many interactions and had not decided to use this one, let alone what I would look for in analysis. Nonetheless there is a problem of objectivity which I have tried to correct for by painstaking review of the analysis with participants as well as others. I believe that the loss of objectivity is a disadvantage outweighed by the advantage of insight into what was going on which is impossible for a nonparticipant to recover, and that only by taping an event in which one is a natural participant can one gather data not distorted by the presence of an alien observer.
4 With the exception of my own, names have been changed. Now, as always, I want to express my gratitude to these friends who became my data, for their willingness and insight during taping

and later during playback. The transcripts will reflect initials of these pseudonyms, except for my own, which is rendered 'T' to avoid confusion with 'D' (David).

5   The use of cooperative overlap has been reported among American blacks, throughout the West Indies (see in particular Reisman, 1974), and the Middle and Near East.

References

Bateson, Gregory (1972). *Steps to an Ecology of Mind*. New York: Ballantine.

Becker, Alton (1979a). The figure a sentence makes. In *Discourse and Syntax*, T. Givon (ed.). New York: Academic Press.

—— (1979b). Text-building, epistemology and aesthetics in Javanese Shadow Theatre. In *The Imagination of Reality: Essays in Southeast Asian Coherence Systems*, A. L. Becker and A. A. Yengoyan (eds.). Norwood, N.J.: Ablex.

Boyer, Peter J. (1979). Therapists cure New York accents. *The Tribune*, Sunday February 4, 6E.

Brown, Penelope, and Levinson, Stephen (1978). Universals in language usage: Politeness phenomena. In *Questions and Politeness*, E. Goody (ed.), 56–289. Cambridge: Cambridge University Press.

Durkheim, Emile (1915). *The Elementary Forms of the Religious Life*. New York: The Free Press.

Erickson, Frederick (1975). Gatekeeping and the melting pot: Interaction in counseling interviews. *Harvard Education Review* 45(1), 44–70.

Esterly, Glenn (1979). Slow talking in the big city. *New West* 4(11) (May 21, 1979), 67–72.

Forster, E. M. (1924). *A Passage to India*. New York: Harcourt Brace Jovanovich.

Goffman, Erving (1967). *Interaction Ritual: Essays on Face-to-Face Behavior*. Garden City: Doubleday.

—— (1978). Response cries. *Language* 54(4), 787–815.

Gumperz, John (1977). Sociocultural knowledge in conversational inference. In *Georgetown University Round Table on Languages and Linguistics 1977*, M. Saville-Troike (ed.), 191–211. Washington, DC: Georgetown University.

—— (1982). *Discourse Strategies*. Cambridge: Cambridge University Press.

—— and Tannen, Deborah (1979). Individual and social differences in language use. In *Individual Differences in Language Ability and Language Behavior*, C. J. Fillmore, D. Kempler, and W. S.-Y. Wang (eds.). New York: Academic Press.

Labov, William (1970). The study of language in its social context. *Studium Generale* 23, 30–87.

—— (1972). Language in the inner city: Studies in the Black English Vernacular. Philadelphia: University of Pennsylvania Press.

Lakoff, Robin (1973). The logic of politeness; or, minding your p's and q's. *Papers from the Ninth Regional Meeting of the Chicago Linguistics Society*. Chicago: University of Chicago Department of Linguistics.

—— (1979). Stylistic strategies within a grammar of style. In *Language, Sex and Gender*, J. Orasanu, M. Slater, and L. Adler (eds.), 327. Annals of the New York Academy of Sciences.

Reisman, Karl (1974). Contrapuntal conversations in an Antiguan village. In *Explorations in the Ethnography of Speaking*, R. Bauman and J. Sherzer (eds.), 110–24. Cambridge: Cambridge University Press.

Sacks, Harvey, Schegloff, Emanuel, and Jefferson, Gail (1974). A simplest systematics for the organization of turn-taking for conversation. *Language* 50(4), 696–735.

Schenkein, Jim (1978). *Studies in the Organization of Conversational Interaction*. New York: Academic Press.

Tannen, Deborah (1979). Processes and consequences of conversational style. Unpublished thesis, University of California, Berkeley.

—— (1980). When is an overlap not an interruption? *First Delaware Symposium on Languages and Linguistics*. Newark, Del.: University of Delaware Press.

—— (1981). The machine-gun question: An example of conversational style. *Journal of Pragmatics* V(5), 383–97.

—— (1987). Conversational style. In *Psycholinguistic Models of Production*, H. Dechert and M. Raupach (eds.), 251–67. Norwood, N.J.: Erlbaum.

Van Antwerp, Caroline, and Maxwell, Monica (1982). Speaker sex, regional dialect, and employability: A study in language attitudes. In *Linguistics and the Professions*, R. DiPietro (ed.). Norwood, N.J.: Ablex.

White, Edmund (1980). *States of Desire: Travels in Gay America*. New York: Dutton.

10

Swedishness as an Obstacle in Cross-Cultural Interaction

Åke Daun

For a long time now, discussions about immigrants' difficulties in adapting to Swedish life have centered around the immigrants' cultures. Their customs and values make it difficult for them to fit into a Swedish environment. Swedish discrimination against immigrants has partially been explained in the same way; immigrants' strange behavior, language and appearance are the objects of Swedes' condescension, annoyance, insulting remarks, etc. Consequently, the remedy for Swedish prejudice against immigrants has been thought to be the need for more information about immigrants' backgrounds and cultures. The assumption is that knowledge makes for understanding.

It is at least as important, however, to discuss the Swedish culture (cf. Hannerz 1983). Immigrants' difficulties in adapting are also a result of the Swedish culture. Swedish customs and values are difficult to adjust to for a great many immigrants. The Swedish culture can be experienced as both disgusting and absurd by immigrants. Many simply maintain that Swedes don't have any "culture". Swedes are spiritually empty is one of the stereotypes expressed in the Discrimination Investigation ("Vittnesmålsstudien" (Bergman & Swedin 1982)).

10.1   A Swedish Culture – Does one Exist?

Is there a specifically Swedish culture? Well, by now the realization that this is the case is more widely understood. However, there still exists an unexpressed attitude among Swedes that it is immigrants who are tied to their culture and that immigrants' behavior is dictated by beliefs and traditions which are more or less irrational. They don't eat pork and the men forbid their wives to go out alone . . . Swedes, in contrast, are considered "modern". They belong to the "modern, urbanized, industrial society" and therefore possess no special culture other than the celebration of old holiday traditions such as Midsummer, for sentimental reasons. Especially modern, if you will, are our values

Åke Daun, "Swedishness as an obstacle in cross-cultural interaction" from *Ethnologia Europaea* 14:2 (1984), pp. 95–109. Copenhagen. Reprinted by permission of the author and editor and Museum of Tusculanum Press.

such as democracy, equality, rationalism and the love of peace. We believe that all countries can or should eventually come around to accepting the values we hold.

Such a perspective is ethnocentric. The Swedish mentality and way of life are just as culturally bound as any other people's. The fact that we call them "modern" doesn't make them less culturally bound. Labels are also a part of culture. In describing Swedish culture, it should also be pointed out that Swedes call their culture "modern". The interpretation of and the importance placed in Sweden on concepts such as democracy, equality, rationalism and peace are also Swedish.

Paul Britten Austin in a book on Swedishness (1968) sees this very reluctance among Swedes to view themselves as having any specific culture as being a characteristic of Swedish culture. History shows that for many years Swedes lacked any real opportunities for comparisons with other cultures. Germans in Stockholm and Visby during the middle ages and Walloon smiths working in forgeries during the 1600s were possibly the first to make Swedes reflect on what was typically Swedish. But in modern times, the population has been exceptionally homogeneous, right up until the large immigrations of workers beginning in the 1960s.

[. . .]

Which aspects of Swedishness do immigrants find (to a greater or lesser extent) difficult to accept when mixing with Swedes? I will mention some which I have come across so far.

10.2   Separating the Private from the Public

The linguist Jens Allwood is one of those who have pointed out the Swedish cultural characteristic of drawing a sharp line between life at work and private life (Allwood 1981). What this means is that Swedes find it completely natural not to socialize privately with colleagues, even if they have worked together for years. This doesn't conflict with the fact that many Swedes actually count those with whom they work as among their closest friends. What is uniquely Swedish is that a good friendship at work in no way necessarily leads to private socializing.

Generally, this surprises many foreigners. It also leads to the unfortunate consequence that immigrants find it difficult to make Swedish friends. Usually they have not been childhood chums or friends from school-days with Swedes. For most immigrants, their only place of contact with Swedes is at work.

Recently I met a woman from Uruguay who, after receiving an academic education in Sweden, had built up a well-established career. She had also developed friendly contacts with her colleagues, but she also stated how her suggestions about meeting socially outside of work had been negatively received. The Swedes appeared to have a nearly instinctive aversion to the idea of meeting privately. Only after one of them changed workplaces was there a change in attitude. After that they met strictly privately.

In this case, it was not the immigrant woman's background which presented an obstacle. She spoke perfect Swedish with almost no accent, and did not look particularly "foreign". Her colleagues were also well-educated. It is true that in some cases an indifferent or negative attitude towards foreigners is behind an aversion to socializing. There is much evidence to that effect, but such was not the case here. Even Swedes can – to the surprise of many foreign observers – work side by side for years without ever having been to each other's homes.

As I lack sufficient data, I am unable to comment on whether or not and to what extent this cultural characteristic exists in the other Nordic countries. I was struck, however, by the words of a Finn who was interviewed by one of my students:

> Foreigners are, of course, also often suspicious of Swedes. If they don't know that Sweden has been isolated for such a long time, then you often hear foreigners say, "Swedes are so incredibly strange, they're so cold and all, they only think of themselves. They just run home from work, lock their door, and don't open it until the next day", you hear that a lot. (Stigsgård-Blomster 1983: 39)

Jean Phillips-Martinsson in her book *Swedes As Others See Them* (1981) points out that this tendency to draw a distinct line between worklife and the other parts of their lives is a handicap for Swedish businessmen in their dealings with foreign customers. Swedes often restrict themselves completely to negotiating about business, but are close-mouthed when it comes to discussing themselves. They don't start business discussions as so many others do, by making "small talk", that is, chatting about their families, hobbies and so on. To many Swedes, this seems irrelevant, like wasted time and lack of discipline while working. In many other countries, however, this type of friendly interaction is seen as necessary for building up solid business contacts. Only when a person has first made a good impression as a human being can they then be relied on in business.

This feature of our culture does not, of course, mean that Swedes *are* cold and reserved, as they are often portrayed by others. On the contrary, foreigners sometimes talk about the unusually close friendships they have made with Swedes – what faithful friendships they have built up here. I once met an American professor of sociology whose family, during a sabbatical year in Sweden, had made friends with a Swedish dentist's family who happened to be their neighbors. They had never had such close friends in the US, he said.

Such closeness is, however, seldom achieved by immigrants in Sweden. An American guest-lecturer is of interest to many well-educated Swedes, whereas a Greek working in a car factory doesn't inspire the same interest among Swedes with whom he comes in contact, particularly not his workmates – not enough to invite him home.

[. . .]

10.3 Lack of Emotions/Emotionally Distant

One reason that Swedes seem cold in many foreigners' eyes is that they keep their feelings to themselves. It could be said that they express their feelings in other ways, for example faithfulness to their close friends. Even in that case they reveal the division between private and public. At home and possibly in front of his most intimate friends, a Swede can cry and argue in a loud voice, without inhibition. In a public place, such behavior would be unthinkable, a scandal or to say the least startling, depending on the context and the person's age, sex and position in society. Least self-discipline is expected of young women of low social status; most self-discipline is expected of older men in high social positions.

As immigrants generally never get near a Swede's private life, immigrants only experience – as they see it – a lack of emotion. Swedes gesticulate less than others, seldom change their facial expressions, and keep their voices low. Slowness of speech, punctuated by many silent pauses, reinforces the impression that Swedes' emotional lives are "low key". The expression "lagom är bäst" (not too much, not too little – just right) which foreigners quickly learn, can certainly be interpreted as a code-word for this behavioral pattern.

The fact that uninhibited emotional expression is taboo in Swedish culture can be witnessed in maternity hospitals. While in labor, many Swedish women groan as little as possible and, in many cases afterwards, ask if they yelled much. If they find out that they didn't, it is seen as positive. A midwife interviewed on TV stated among other things: "A midwife is asked a lot – Did I scream much and so on – did I make a fool of myself? And that's because it's so taboo to express strong feelings and childbirth is a situation where really – the natural thing to do is to express your strong feelings."

Another aspect of this cultural feature is that emotional arguments are ranked lowly when used in public debates. The fact that a person just really dislikes something such as free abortion, is hardly ever considered a legitimate argument. Only objective arguments are considered valid. For example, what facts could be used in an argument against free abortion: medical, psychological, population-planning, etc.? A debater who shows too much emotional involvement in an argument has lost, especially if his activities are political. A Swedish politician is supposed to keep cool and, without acting rashly, weigh the facts against each other.

This bias towards rational behavior can be experienced by foreigners as a repulsive emotional iciness.

In the eyes of Swedes, being temperamental is a special characteristic. Swedes nearly never refer to other Swedes as temperamental – no one is ever that "temperamental". From the Swedish perspective, it is not a question of degree of emotional expression, rather a specific distinction between either being or not being temperamental.

A Yugoslav who had lived in Sweden approximately 15 years described to Billy Ehn how "controlled" you have to be in Sweden.

"There is a Norwegian girl at work. And even though Norway and Sweden are similar, she feels a very long way from home. She told me she had a terrible time keeping control of her temper, but that she had to do so here. And I've had the same experience. I've had a really hard time keeping in my feelings. They're not temperamental like the Norwegians, but they are open. I show my feelings when I am sad and when I am happy. It's easy for me to laugh and say, 'Wow, we're having such a great time today!' But you can't say something like that in the employees' room. One time I was really happy and full of energy at work. I don't exactly remember what I said, but one of my workmates wondered what was wrong with me, if I was sick or something. Sick!? I was just *happy*. Since that day, I've become more careful." (Ehn & Arnstberg 1980: 146)

[. . .]

What I have termed emotional distance is difficult to define. In the minds of many immigrants, Swedes are "cold", as if they lack emotions. "I don't think Swedes feel very much", said the Yugoslav, when interviewed at another time. At present, I know too little about this matter of degree of feeling to comment, other than to say that Swedes certainly do experience strong emotional reactions in many situations, Swedes are struck, for example, by feelings of rage or joy, but because of cultural conventions, they express these feelings less explicitly, in another manner. It appears to be taboo in many situations, outside of the family, to openly discuss how happy you are or what a great time you are having with others, for example your colleagues, as the Yugoslavian woman above who said: "Wow, we're having such a great time today!"

Immigrants who go against norms and express happiness, naturally don't experience any terrible opposition, but they are reminded of their position as foreigners and can feel insecure. Such reminders can also reinforce their dislike of these features of the Swedish culture. It is more difficult when it comes to expressing aggressive emotions, as they are often directed *at* other individuals. These individuals, moreover, are in most cases, Swedes. An immigrant's psycho–socially inferior position is good cause for him to "bite his tongue" instead of venting his anger.

Swedish norms concerning emotional expression are reinforced by the tendency to avoid all conflict (except within the family). This means that Swedes steer clear of sensitive topics of conversation. "Don't talk politics", goes the saying. It can lead to argu-ments (to becoming "osams" with the other person), and a situation in which people are "osams" (in disagreement) is considered by probably most Swedes to be difficult to take. A common solution is to break off the conversation, stop speaking to each other. To feel that he can manage a relationship so that he doesn't experience discomfort and uncertainty, a Swede wants to be "sams" (in agreement) with those he meets. When he converses with a stranger and when making new acquaintances, a Swede looks for consensus, tries to agree with the views and values held by the other person.

According to Jean Phillips-Martinsson, this easily creates the impression for immi-grants, that Swedes never have dissenting views, that they possibly never think for them-selves, but just agree. She believes this is also the reason why Swedes are under the impression that they are kinder to one another than other nationalities are (1981: 112). Her assertion that Swedes are inclined to take it personally if others dare to criticize their views in front of others, is probably widely applicable to Swedes. It logically fol-lows that what an immigrant then incorrectly interprets as indifference is actually a Swede's way of being considerate. As a Swede takes it for granted that foreigners feel and react the same way he does, he prefers to keep his dissenting views to himself in order to avoid the risk of hurting a stranger's feelings.

The dominant Swedish value-system considers it adult to avoid conflicts, and thereby show respect to others. This attitude explains why Swedes think that many immigrants are "unruly". The loud voices characteristic of immigrants compared with Swedes are felt by many Swedes to be "unruly". This is because loud voices among Swedes are most often used in connection with fights, quarrels, conflicts. Swedes basic-ally only yell at each other when they are fighting, not when they are actively engaged in a discussion. Consequently, Swedes to a great extent value silence, quiet, unobtrus-ive voices and a calm tone in social situations.

In an ethnological study about Swedish attitudes towards immigrants, one quote reveals a prejudice against Assyrians: "They have a bad reputation because they fight and are rowdy . . . they are noisy and unruly . . ." (Öhlund 1982: 27). It was said about Italians:

"Italians, y'know, they have that hot temperament and fight and are stubborn, or whatever you want to call it" (ibid: 15). The author comments:

> Nearly all of the interviewees more or less divide up immigrants into those who are trouble-makers and those who are conscientious. One interviewee does this very categorically. She is highly critical of immigrants whom she classifies as "bothersome." (ibid: 42)

> "They are always shrieking and shouting. They can sit down on opposite sides of the subway car and sit there and yell at each other without being at all considerate." (ibid: 43)

[...]

This matter of drawing a line between the private and public in the Swedish culture, discussed earlier, is also involved in the Swedish aversion to speaking loudly and lively in, for example, the subway. Swedes in general feel that you shouldn't air your private conversations in public places. In public places, only public employees should speak loudly, such as the train conductor or subway driver speaking via loud-speakers, a lecturer (not the audience) in a lecture hall, or a nurse in a doctor's waiting room. Most Swedes' lack of experience in speaking loudly in public places helps to explain why an audience so unwillingly says anything in the discussion period following a lecture. Swedish students are afraid of expressing themselves in front of their friends, but not, however, in a private conversation with the teacher. This isn't just a question of their uncertainty about a subject and fear of making a fool of themselves, but probably also an uneasiness about mixing the private with the public.

As is so often the case, many features of a culture work together to form a pattern. The appreciation of silence is also connected with an attitude towards the quality of language, its content and function. Swedish culture looks down on people who talk without seeming to care about whether what they say is of any importance, on people who are unconcerned about the consequences of what they are saying and who could not care less about how what they say is interpreted. Here it is interesting to cite an example from the French culture for contrast. The concept of "kallprata" (talking about nothing in particular) lacks an equivalent in French, but expresses the Swedes' critical attitude towards talking for talking's sake.

According to Annik Sjögren, teacher of ethnology at Stockholm University, and French by birth, spoken words are "lightweight" in the French culture. Words disappear – they go with the wind – to use her own imagery. That's why you don't have to think about what you're saying; you don't have to be on guard, careful about what you say. The further south you go in France, the more language is seen as a vital part of socializing. The consequences of what you say are not very important, because afterwards you're not held to what you have said. Language is extremely important in conversational situations. Words and views are to be played with, and a person can express opinions which he doesn't really hold, just to liven the conversation. Talking is considered a pleasure in French culture, not in the Swedish.

In French there is no expression equivalent to the Swedish "tyst och fin" (nice and quiet) to describe a person. It's not considered a compliment to be quiet. When in France, as in Sweden, a child is told to keep quiet, it's not so that the child will become a quiet person, and not so that the child will learn to take a quieter conversational tone. The reason is that the child is interfering in the adults' pleasure, according to Sjögren. "You're bothering us. If you want to talk, go somewhere else" is why, in France, the children are asked to be quieter. In Sweden you can describe a child as a "nice, quiet little boy". In France this combination is unthinkable.

As language is an important instrument for expressing emotions between people, silence can sometimes be interpreted as a lack of feeling, or as a lack of strong feeling. There are, of course, various types of silence, which are considered positive, for example, lovers' non-verbal contact and mutually understood silence. But when silence and close-mouthed behavior fit into a pattern of – as interpreted by non-Swedes – social avoidance, then this quietness is viewed negatively.

[. . .]

In contrast to Sweden, where so many are raised to feel it is wrong to interrupt someone speaking, it is part of the German tradition for people to talk simultaneously. It is acceptable to both interrupt someone and to fill in for them with what you think that another person is going to say, both in order to show that you are following the conversation, and in order to fill in the silent pauses. Neither is it considered impolite, as it is in Sweden, to raise your voice and speak louder than someone who has the floor, in order to gain the floor.

Naturally there are many talkative individuals in Sweden, too. Most Swedes could probably point out talkative individuals in their own circle of friends. What is of interest here, as elsewhere in examining the Swedish culture, is what is considered typical or average, especially when compared with immigrants' backgrounds. What is typical among Swedes is the appreciation of quietness which is reflected in, for example, the expression "to be a good listener" as a description of a person who seldom speaks.

The theory among immigrants that Swedes lack feelings is reinforced by other features. The strongly held attitude in the Swedish culture and society in favor of objective argument actually means that emotional and thereby even artistic phenomena are lowly ranked. This appreciation of the objective means that Swedes particularly admire rational conduct. Rational behavior is equated with maturity or adulthood, in contrast to childish behavior which is ruled by emotions. Emotional discipline has long been viewed as a sign of true humanity and civilization. This attitude has developed above all among the bourgeoisie and from that class-perspective, both children and the working classes are seen to be closer to nature and farther from culture (Frykman & Löfgren 1979). But appreciation of objectively based as opposed to emotionally based judgments appears to be widespread. Naturally, though, it dominates behavior in Swedish public life, in politics and the bureaucratic system.

[. . .]

The population statistician Gustav Sundbärg in his well-known book about the Swedish mentality takes up another concept which sheds light on the planning philosophy, namely the Swedes' ability to organize:

> A highly developed ability to organize is another characteristic of the Swedes, and no doubt, to a large extent, explains the permanence and stability which Swedish society has displayed for hundreds of years. (Sundbärg 1911: 3)

Swedes are often thought to make suitable secretaries within international organizations, due to their abilities in organizing which stem from their emphasis on smoothness, reason, and the desire to mediate opposing interests in order to avoid conflicts (cf. Allwood 1981: 18).

Swedes' ambitions to plan and desire to control life with the aid of science and reason, carries with it the view of their own country as "way ahead", "modern", "future-oriented". That has also been Sweden's image abroad in the post-war period – "the Swedish model".

This view can, of course, be found in all of the industrialized Western world's attitude towards developing countries. The West believes that they stand for science and reason in contrast to the primitive superstitions and irrational ties to traditional values in the Third World. But in Sweden, people feel this way even when viewing other Western European countries, particularly Southern Europe. A "fiery temperament" is thought to be incompatible with good judgment. Rational ways of thinking do not include decisions made without a lot of consideration or under the influence of emotions.

If in Sweden a person wants to live according to the ideal image of his own country, then he has to let logic and rationalism guide him and put his emotions aside. A person considered a "true" Swede, as he or she has developed over the past decades, looks positively at recommendations and measures which go against so-called irrational phenomena.

Behind the eagerness for reforms (for example doing away with High School and Bachelor's degrees and former laws about surnames) lies the goal of equality and the achievement of job-equality.

High School certificates (degrees) were a symbol of class, and the struggle for equality was combined with and was even motivated by the rational perspective: since all people are of equal value – goes the argument – then class symbols are an anachronism. Since men and women are of equal value, it is then illogical to give the man higher status through surname, is the view. The laws concerning the rights of fathers to stay home with their children have also received strong support because of this special desire to follow through with arguments to their logical conclusions.

[...]

As implied by the above, it appears that from the Swedish perspective, many people throughout the world are irrational, more controlled by emotions, not least of all in politics. But also in the areas of sex roles, sexuality, raising children, etc., the general opinion in Sweden is that Swedes possess a special ability to look at things soberly and unsentimentally, and this is seen to be an advantage. Everyone "knows", then, that for example, men and women are "equal", which is why men as well as women should be allowed to be at home and take care of small children during paid worktime. All social rights should apply equally to both sexes. As this was not previously the case, such a reform is considered progress. This means a move in the direction of a higher state of *modernity* (Berger & Luckmann 1966/1979). Other countries, stuck in their traditional sex roles, are hindered in carrying out or even proposing such legal changes, and consequently are seen by Swedes to be less modern, and bound to a, in a sense, "primitive" culture. They are "behind" and less "developed".

[...]

I have so far been discussing emotions involved in decisionmaking. Another aspect of this theme is to consider what emotions a culture does allow and considers desirable. Swedes are often seen by foreigners as cool, emotionally cold. Those who have achieved closer relationships with Swedes constantly describe Swedes as suffering from their difficulties in expressing the strong emotions which they – like other people – do have.

In that case, the analysis should discuss the culturally accepted means of communicating, showing sympathy, joy, sorrow, pain, etc. It has been thought that alcoholism in Sweden serves the theoretically interesting function of legitimizing behavior which would otherwise be considered culturally unacceptable – that is, the type of behavior which goes directly against what I have so far described as typically Swedish – silence, seriousness, avoiding conflict and strong emotions, and oriented towards the rational. Even after an insignificant amount of alcohol, Swedes have the "right" to act boisterous and joke more than usual, to become aggressive and emotional – cry and even use emotional arguments – without risking making fools of themselves.

This rational approach characteristic of Swedes (prejudice against emotionalism) has been challenged more than anything else by *counter-cultural movements*. This opposition – strong and ideologically based – has taken place within alternative political movements, which in this case can be said to include the so-called new left, "the green wave" within and outside the center party, and in so-called extra-parliamentary movements, the environmental movement and the women's movement which has grown up during the 1970s. Much opposition has also occurred, in a general sense, among the young (the youth culture).

These groups voice an opposition to the (as they perceive it) coldly rational approach within the Swedish society, which places a low status on emotions and therefore even on poetry, art, etc. This gap was made particularly clear during the campaign before the nuclear referendum, where the "third line" tended to view the other two alternatives as voicing technocracy, while line three supporters were criticized as being a group of "dreamers and troubadours". Within the new women's movement, the value of emotions has been upheld in contrast to the "male" view of the world which is described as being oriented towards rationalism, organization and pragmatism. Lack of emotions is defined as "inhuman".

[...]

10.5 Tension in Social Relationships

Most Swedes are disinterested in immigrants and are not curious enough about strangers to make them desire closer contact. This they no doubt share with people throughout the world in countries where different cultures live side by side. Added to this, for Swedes there is the tension which exists in social relationships in general within Swedish culture. It is not at all easy or relaxing for Swedes to speak with strangers, or for that matter with anyone who doesn't belong to their closest family and circle of friends. Swedes appear to reflect more than many other nationalities on how others will react to what they are saying, about what is then suitable for them to say in each and every situation, what impression they are making on others, etc. Moreover, there is the added sense of respect for others, mentioned earlier, which makes them not want to express dissenting views. The long pauses in the Swedish manner of conversing make it possible for them to weigh their words and also mean that a listener is more secure than the one who is speaking. That is why many prefer to listen.

The emphasis on rationalism, lack of emotions, puts special demands on what should/shouldn't be said. Swedes reflect more than those other nationalities who are able to express their opinions without any factual basis – just if what's said is considered funny or adds to the discussion. A Swede could not afterwards forgive himself with the explanation, "that was just something I said – I didn't mean it." Along with rationalism goes seriousness in the Swedish culture. Naturally, Swedes joke often and happily, but underneath lies a basic quality of seriousness, which not only immigrants, but also Swedes themselves are aware of and point out. This seriousness appears in many areas and consequently has "paradigmatic power".

Jean Phillips-Martinsson gives one example in her book when she illustrates her visit to a Swedish tennis hall for the first time:

> If it had not been for people dressed in white scurrying after a little white ball, I should have thought I had entered a mausoleum. The pang pang of the ball cut the deathly silence like cannon shots. My British sportsmanship was offended when my good shots went unremarked. "Good shot! Well done! Bad luck!" I cried. "Sssh! Sssh!" came back at me from nearby courts. They must be playing the World Championships, I thought. However, my charming partner assured me that they were just friendly matches but that everyone took them dead seriously. (Phillips-Martinsson 1981: 24)

[. . .]

The American professor of sociology, Sharlene Hesse-Biber, who was a guest-researcher in Sweden in the early 1970s, described the Swedish academics with whom she came in contact as being "uptight", that is tense and afraid of making fools of themselves, and thus always seriously concerned with their own personalities. Many Swedes' relatively slow speech and numerous pauses in their speech can be explained, as suggested earlier, by the importance placed on words – the fear of saying "something rash". A Swede needs more time than, for example, a French speaker, to think out his next statement in a conversation. He thinks over his next comment and is naturally just as mentally active while waiting for his turn as the French speaker is, but the French speaker throws himself into the discussion, interrupting the others.

Swedes' desire to avoid conflicts makes conversations and contacts between people into a more serious matter among Swedes than among many other nationalities. Much greater care – guardedness – is required. You can't just "talk away". What has been written here about rationalism, seriousness and the desire to avoid conflicts all adds up to make socializing with others, in general, a highly tense situation. Many Swedes seem to get easily tired of socializing outside of the family, which explains a lot of everyday attempts to "get out of" talking, for example by avoiding taking the elevator with a neighbor.

A Yugoslav interviewed by Billy Ehn, described the difference he saw in Swedes in this respect: Swedes are "always sort of distant" even with each other. "Even if you are good friends, there is always a kind of distance between you. You have to be so controlled. Sure, it's all right to be controlled, but here everyone is too concerned about their customs and rules. You never can let up, you have to always be on your guard" (Ehn & Arnstberg 1980: 146).

[. . .]

Many immigrants' impression of Swedes is the one which was quoted earlier: "They just run home from work, lock their doors and don't open them until the next day"

(Stigsgård-Blomster 1983: 39). The woman interviewed, a Finn, came up with a theory about why Swedes are so "isolated". At the same time, she describes – in a few words – this Swedish mentality:

"...I believe that Sweden has been isolated for such a long time, during the war and so on, so isolated that they have forgotten one another. Now they are afraid to come out ... how shall I say ... not from Sweden, but from their Swedishness. At first I thought it was rather difficult. Okay, it's relatively easy to chat with Swedes, that's true. But to get any further than just chatting ... to become friends. Like at work in the beginning, that was difficult. They didn't want to open up right away. I didn't really understand; I thought at first 'they don't like me', 'it's because I come from Finland', but gradually I started understanding it all, that they're like that. That you have to come to them half way or a little more than half way." (Stigsgård-Blomster 1983: 39)

[. . .]

10.6   The Cultural Consequences of Modernization

Many features of Swedish culture which immigrants have difficulty in accepting stem from the growth of the industrial society and urbanization. Bergman and Swedin rightly point out in their book (1982) that the criticism which many immigrants aim at Sweden are in fact directed not against specifically Sweden, but against the "inhumanity" of an industrial society in general. Those immigrants see economic development as a contrast to what they label human underdevelopment. In their book, Bergman and Swedin point out that many immigrants' points of reference are derived from agrarian societies.

[. . .]

A Spaniard from Madrid, whom I interviewed, described how the earlier custom of taking care of aging parents – that is, letting them live with the younger generation – was on the way out in urban surroundings. In North America and Northern Europe, this division of the generations became common practice some time ago; but the treatment of the elderly is not something which is easy for immigrants to understand. The Yugoslavian woman interviewed above mentioned that her brother was now taking care of their elderly mother. "She has bad health, but she never needs to worry about ending up in a home for the elderly. It is the children's duty to take care of her as long as she lives" (Ehn & Arnstberg 1980: 122). A man from Ecuador, interviewed by Karl-Olov Arnstberg in the same book, stated that he might return to Ecuador when he started getting old. He didn't want to be a retired person in Sweden. "The old people don't have a very good life here" (ibid: 113).

A third aspect of modernization is childraising. The so-called liberal ("free") childraising methods practiced in Sweden since post-war times cause many problems for some immigrants. For them, liberal methods of childraising imply a lack of instruction, that is to say, Swedish parents simply don't teach their children what they will need to know as adults. To raise children is, for these immigrants, to mold the children so that they become good members of society, who are respected for good qualities and behavior. The Yugoslavian woman quoted above also stated:

"If a child goes past an adult and spits on him, I think it's wrong. Then I would like to say to the children that it's not nice for them to do things like that, couldn't they try to stop doing that, because it doesn't look nice. My workmates, on the other hand, don't worry about such things. They say that kids are kids and that children go through stages and will get over it. Stages? Well, kids don't just get over it by themselves, I'd like to say. It's through *us* that children learn to become human beings." (Ehn & Arnstberg 1980: 136)

Another woman from Yugoslavia said, as have so many other immigrants, that this same terrible freedom is also a part of the Swedish school system: "School, my, my, my. In my opinion, Swedish schools are bad. The children have no respect at all for their teachers . . ." (ibid: 256).

[. . .]

A fourth area of change which is the result of social modernization, is that of sexuality. As in the areas of childraising, sex roles and the relationship to the elderly, sexual attitudes and customs have undergone change in Sweden, especially over the past few decades. Sexual "liberalization" has also taken place in other Western industrialized countries, where even homosexuality has become, to some extent, accepted. In particular, the age of first sexual experience has lowered. This has also occurred in other parts of the world, even in Catholic areas, for example in Poland (from which many political refugees have come to Sweden). Among other immigrant nationality groups, however, this "dedramatization" of sexuality is an attack on their most basic moral views. A Yugoslavian man, interviewed by Ehn, discussed his discomfort with the idea of "freedom", even if this attitude had gained some acceptance in his own country. Whenever he was on bad terms with his Swedish wife, he thought that if he remarried it would be to a Yugoslav.

"I don't understand it, you see. My wife maybe says that she loves me and that she has a good life together with me and the children. But still she wants to go on vacation with a girlfriend. I can't understand it! If it is really love . . . then you want to share your happiness with each other.

"This has started happening in Yugoslavia, too. There are men who let their wives go to the Adriatic coast. Maybe this matter of liberation has gone too far if it leads to so many divorces." (Ehn & Arnstberg 1980: 56)

In summary, childraising and education, sex roles, relationships to the elderly, and sexuality are areas which have greatly changed over the last few decades. Similar types of changes are taking place and have come far in other countries, too – mainly Northern Europe and North America.

It should be made clear, however, that this is a question of real cultural change, that is to say, changes in basic values. The fact that similar changes are taking place in, for example, the Mediterranean countries, hardly makes it easier for immigrants here in Sweden to accept them. Moral views are linked with strong emotions. Furthermore, from an international perspective, the changes which have occurred in Sweden have been extreme. It is important to understand that these changes have gone more quickly and have been supported by features in the Swedish culture, mainly the appreciation of objectivity and the critical attitude towards emotional views.

[. . .]

Sex roles have become more equal, more similar, also as a result of the driving force of objective reasoning. Women's move into the workforce, of economic necessity, combined with the Women's Movement, has made women's liberation a relatively accepted idea in Sweden, particularly in political and social planning circles. The women's liberation movement is also connected to older traditions of individual freedom as an ideal in the Western world.

Since in Sweden only the idea of rational argument is by and large accepted – emotional reactions generally not accepted – any resistance to the Women's Movement has had little effect. Men who merely "instinctively" dislike the Movement have been seen, from a public perspective, as unworthy of debate. Arguments such as the one given by a Yugoslav married to a Swede would hardly be taken seriously:

> "I'm not saying that women who want more freedom are wrong, *I'm just talking about how I feel*. – My wife is great, she is OK, it's just when there are these cultural conflicts that the problems arise. Like this thing about the men helping their wives. I'm not saying that it's wrong to help in the house, but the truth is that a lot of women take advantage of that kind of help. Then everything gets turned around and the men become the housewives in the family . . ." (Ehn & Arnstberg 1980: 56)

[. . .]

Finally, when it comes to attitudes about the elderly, the pattern has been similar. Affluence in Sweden has made it possible to provide pensions and other financial aid, so that the elderly can live in special apartments and not need to rely economically on their children. The ideal of individual freedom has been valued both by the elderly themselves and by their children, but this has not, of course, prevented the fact that some elderly persons have also suffered from loneliness. The commonly held view is that the generations should live separately, be independent of each other and not "grate" on each other. When the older and younger members of a family meet, they should be in harmony, friendly with one another. Fights and conflicts should be avoided.

At the same time, respect for the elderly has decreased, possibly even disappeared. The sudden changes in society have made the elderly's life experiences irrelevant – in any case, that is the general view. The physical separation from the older generation has contributed to a social separation. The elderly are now seen as a separate category – the "retired persons" – who require special treatment. This treatment has also been "scientifically planned". Responsibility for the elderly is thus not mainly borne by the relatives, but is instead a matter of public (social) concern. The low value placed on emotional attitudes towards social planning has caused many immigrants to see Sweden as "inhuman".

In this discussion, where certain behavior and attitudes have been described as products of an industrial society as well as being reinforced by other features of the Swedish culture, it is important to understand that these cultural features are also subject to change. The emphasis on objectivity and rationalism which actually characterizes the Christian Western world, is unusually strong in the Swedish culture, but this strong emphasis on rationalism has not always been the case. It could possibly be shown that Swedes have long been viewed as a pragmatic people, but their objective, rational approach is perhaps no older than fifty years. In that case, this approach is essentially linked to the rise of the modern welfare state, with its, among other things, social democratic reforms.

I don't intend to go into the much more difficult discussion of the historical background and explanation of these cultural features which appear to be typically Swedish, such as silence and seriousness. The task here was to show how the Swedish culture – the Swedish mentality – can create special obstacles in cross-cultural interaction, and how the Swedish culture itself presents difficulties for immigrants in adjusting to life in Sweden. It is not merely immigrants' cultural values and traditions which create difficulties.

References

Allwood, Jens 1981: Finns det svenska kommunikationsmönster? in: *Vad är svensk kultur? Uppsatser från ett symposium i Göteborg i maj 1981. Papers in Anthropological Linguistics* 9: 6–50.

Anton, Thomas 1975: *Governing Greater Stockholm: A study of policy development and system change.* Berkeley: University of California Press.

Austin, Paul Britten 1968: *On being Swedish.* London: Secker and Warburg.

Berger, Peter & Thomas Luckmann 1966/1979: *Kunskapssociologi. Hur individen uppfattar och formar sin sociala verklighet.* Stockholm: Wahlström & Widstrand.

Bergman, Erland & Bo Swedin 1982: *Vittnesmål. Invandrares syn på diskriminering i Sverige. En rapport från Diskrimineringsutredningen.* Stockholm: Publica.

Daun, Åke 1980: *Boende och livsform.* Stockholm: Tiden/Folksam.

—— 1983: *Svensk mentalitet.* 23 Nordiska etnolog- och folkloristkongressen, Fuglsöcentret, Danmark. (Mimeo.)

Ehn, Billy 1983: *Ska vi leka tiger?* Stockholm: Liber.

—— & Karl-Olov Arnstberg 1980: *Det osynliga arvet. Sexton invandrare om sin bakgrund.* Stockholm: Författarförlaget.

Frykman, Jonas & Orvar Löfgren 1979: *Den kultiverade människan.* Lund: Liber.

Hannerz, Ulf 1983: *Den svenska kulturen.* Projektet Kulturteori för komplexa samhällen, rapport nr 9. Socialantropologiska institutionen, Stockholms universitet. (Mimeo.)

Huntford, Roland 1971: *The new totalitarians.* London: Allen Lane, the Penguin Press.

Kramer, Jane 1980: *Unsettling Europe.* New York: Random House.

Löfgren, Orvar 1982: Kulturbygge och kulturkonfrontation, in: *Kultur och medvetande.* Ulf Hannerz, Rita Liljeström, Orvar Löfgren. Stockholm: Akademilitteratur.

Öhlund, Marie-Louise 1982: *Har dom turban? En grupp svenskars attityder till invandrare.* (Uppsats för påbyggnadskurs. Vårterminen 1982. Institutet för folklivsforskning. Stockholm.) (Mimeo.)

Phillips-Martinsson, Jean 1981: *Swedes as others see them. Facts, myths or a communication complex?* Stockholm: Affärsförlaget.

Popenoe, David 1977: *The suburban environment. Sweden and the United States.* Chicago and London: The University of Chicago Press.

—— *Private pleasure and public plight.* (MS.)

Stigsgård-Blomster, Harriet 1983: *"Om man möter dom så hejar man väl." Om förutsättningar och effekter av ett gemenskapssträvande projekt i ett höghus- respektive radhusområde.* (Uppsats för påbyggnadskurs. Vårterminen 1983. Institutet för folklivsforskning. Stockholm.) (Mimeo.)

Suède. La reforme permanente. Livre-dossier. Paris: Stock 1977.

Sundbärg, Gustav 1911: *Det svenska folklynnet.* Stockholm: P A Norstedt & Söners förlag.

11

The Presence and Absence of Speech in the Communication of Gender

Penelope Harvey

11.1 Introduction

The events and practices described in this chapter took place in Ocongate, a small Andean town in Southern Peru. It is a relatively busy place, situated on an important though unpaved road which connects the highlands of Southern Peru to the tropical lowlands of Amazonia. Migrant workers, supplies and raw materials travel through daily on the lorries that work the route from Puerto Maldonado to the southern Peruvian cities of Cusco, Puno and Arequipa. The road is important to the livelihood of the villagers. Besides their basic subsistence from agriculture and herding, most people are involved in some way in business. They travel frequently in connection with these business activities, trading products from the local district, from the lowlands and from the cities. Many people also spend at least some time every year working as migrant labour in the cities or in the forest.

As a district capital Ocongate also has important administrative links to Cusco, the departmental capital.[1] Although the population of the village itself is relatively small, 1,300 approximately, it serves a district of some 8,500 people, who come into the village not only to trade but also to visit the town hall, the schools, the health post, the judge's office, the police post and the parish church. Until recently tourism has also played an important part in the local economy. At 3,600 metres the village lies at the foot of the highest snow peak in the area, Mt Ausangate, and climbers and walkers hire local guides and pack-horses in the cold summer months of the dry season.[2]

Ocongate is thus not an isolated town, and in the last three decades the expansion of education and communications has dramatically extended the access to Spanish by people from this area, and the vast majority of young people are fully bilingual in Spanish and Quechua.

Penelope Harvey, "The presence and absence of speech in the communication of gender," chapter 3 in *Bilingual Women: Anthropological Approaches to Second-Language Use*, edited by Pauline Burton, Ketaki Kushari Dyson, and Shirley Ardener (Oxford: Berg, 1994), pp. 44–64. Reprinted with permission of Berg Publishers. All rights reserved.

Despite the increased use of Spanish by the younger generations, bilingualism in the area appears at present to be stable. Quechua is still the first language of all adults who come from the district. Children continue to be brought up either as Quechua speakers or as bilinguals. Those few families who do not bring their children up as Quechua speakers are those who intend to educate them outside the district. This outside orientation is linked to economic possibility, and thus there is also a degree of correlation with economic status. Nevertheless, those who stay, even those who return, always know Quechua. As a result the only adult monolingual Spanish speakers living in Ocongate are found among the outsiders, the school-teachers, the police, the medical and mission workers.

However, when we look at the monolingual Quechua speakers the striking distinction is not between insiders and outsiders, but between men and women. Indeed, as illustrated in table 11.1, gender is a significant variable at all levels of bilingual competence.

Thus it can be seen that the majority of men (76 per cent) are either fully bilingual, or fluent in Spanish despite heavy influences from Quechua. This compares with 49 per cent of the women, of whom less than half are fully bilingual. Conversely 46 per cent of women are either monolingual Quechua speakers or have only extremely limited Spanish, as compared with a mere 10 per cent of men. Furthermore, it should be noted that among all categories of bilinguals, men actually use Spanish more than women. Women generally prefer to use Quechua.

There is one further distinctive difference in the use of Spanish by men and women which concerns a particular Spanish register, used exclusively by men, primarily for making speeches in formal public meetings. This register is characterised by long and complex utterances, with multiple clauses and qualifications. Special vocabulary is used which would rarely be heard in other circumstances, and there is a marked usage of

Table 11.1   Bilingual competence and gender

Competence	Gender			
	Men	%	Women	%
Category A	87	52	37	24
Category B	41	24	39	25
Category C	13	8	22	14
Category D	4	2	50	32
Unknown	23	14	9	5
Total	168	100	157	100

Note: 168 men and 157 women referred to in this table were drawn from 181 households.
The categories in this table are as follows:
Category A: Those who speak Spanish and Quechua with equal ease and fluency, although not necessarily with equal frequency, and who are recognised by others in the community as fully competent in both languages.
Category B: Those bilinguals who show a marked preference for speaking in Quechua and whose Spanish is strongly marked by Quechua influences in lexicon, phonetics, morphology and syntax.[3]
Category C: Quechua speakers who use Spanish for very limited functions. Such speakers will usually have a basic passive knowledge of Spanish.
Category D: Quechua monolinguals.

proverbs and clichés. Statements are qualified with the frequent citing of names and dates, and the intonation of the delivery is also distinctive. The formal meetings at which this register is used are concerned with the relationship between the community and the wider social environment, particularly the state and the church.

Women do not have an equivalent register for these public meetings and prefer not to speak at all; some even feel ashamed to attend. This is not to say that women are always silent or absent from political discussion. There are less formal meetings which take place in similar locales and under the direction of the same male authorities. These meetings refer to immediate practical issues, such as setting the prices of goods. Given the division of labour in this community, such meetings are attended primarily either by men or by women. In either case a similar style is employed: people speak when they feel like it, talk over each other, shout and show no inhibitions about dealing with the male village authorities. Women can be extremely vocal and forceful in these meetings but they will tend to speak in Quechua (Harvey, 1989).

The point I want to emphasise here is that women are not intimidated by the presence of men or village authorities. Women's silence in the formal meetings is associated with the nature of the meeting and the fact that a particular style of Spanish, which they do not command, is deemed not only appropriate but also authoritative.

In outlining these differences in the use of Spanish by men and women in Ocongate I do not intend to present a simple division of the population into two homogeneous groups. As I have indicated, there are important variations between men and women, according to age, future orientation and economic possibility. As I will discuss below, people may use more or less Spanish at different times of their lives, depending on the nature of the social relations in which they are engaged. Nevertheless, as table 11.1 indicates, there is a marked difference in the use of Spanish by women, emphasised by the fact that women do not use the formal Spanish register described above.

This difference in usage is critically dependent on women's attitudes towards the Spanish and Quechua languages. Spanish competence is generally thought of as an asset. Younger monolingual women go to adult literacy classes in the evenings, and parents will do whatever they can to ensure that their children receive some education, at least enough to learn Spanish. Older women are reluctant to learn, but not because they do not value the language. They say that they are too old, but that their children will learn and as a consequence will not have to suffer as they have had to. One woman said quite explicitly that if she were to try speaking Spanish, people would criticise, stare and make insulting comments. They would think that she was trying to pass herself off as a *mestiza*,[4] a more cultured or educated women than her background would allow. She had heard someone say about a friend of hers, who had put on *mestiza* clothes for a special festive occasion: 'A *mestiza* has come out of the dog shit; she doesn't even know how to talk Spanish.' She added that her friend actually spoke very good Spanish. However, to speak Spanish or to wear *mestiza* clothes is to make an explicit statement about your social identity, a statement which others will not necessarily allow you to make, however good your Spanish, whatever the quality of your clothes. This sense of shame at not speaking well enough is commonly given as a reason for not actively using Spanish. The young women who attend night classes are similarly afraid of ridicule. Consequently many of them have a good passive understanding, but seldom speak in Spanish. Young girls will use Spanish more frequently at those times in their lives when they are attending school, or when they are working as migrant labour, either in the cities or in Amazonia. However, when they return to the village, or when they finish their studies, they increasingly use Quechua, again retaining a passive knowledge of Spanish, but rarely using it in conversation.

11.2   Language and Gender

Discussion of speech differences such as those described above has generally taken place within the wider debate on the nature and workings of gender hierarchy.[5] Within this literature several distinctive positions have emerged, some more useful than others. The least useful, although perhaps the most common, explanation of gender difference is that the negative values associated with women's speech reflect women's subordinate position in society. The literature on gender and speech difference has shown that women's pronunciation is generally closer to the prestige standard than men's (see for example Cameron, 1988). Analyses for this gender-marked behaviour quite frequently point to the fact that women strive to speak correctly in order to counteract their low social status (Trudgill, 1972). Where gender hierarchy is salient, men are offered a greater range of ways to fuel their self-esteem and to gain prestige in the eyes of other people and thus do not have the same need to protect themselves with the use of prestige standard forms.

The problem with this type of explanation is that it offers a very passive model of the nature of social relatedness and in fact 'explains' very little. Hierarchy tends to be assumed as a social given, and thus little if any attention is given to looking at the nature of hierarchy, at how hierarchy is constituted and maintained in social relations and at the particular role of language in this social process.

More recently writers such as Milroy (1980) and Nichols (1984) have suggested that language use should be interpreted in terms of social networks. They have argued that people tend to speak most like those with whom they speak most frequently and interact with in a variety of different social roles. These dense, multiplex social networks constitute a supportive linguistic environment which allows speakers to use non-standard features which may be stigmatised by more powerful sectors of the population whose identities are constituted in very different networks of relatedness. Milroy and Nichols thus argue that it is not gender that determines the use of standard forms but rather the nature of the relationships in which men and women are involved. Thus Nichols (1984) argues that in her study of coastal South Carolina it was because the men had denser and more multiplex social networks within the community than women that they used more non-standard features in their speech. Analysis of gender differences in speech must therefore address the whole range of social relations in which men and women are involved.

This focus on the social relations within which gender differences are constituted and expressed is also evident in Brown's work on women's use of politeness in a Mayan community (1980). Expressions of politeness mediate the hierarchy and social distance between speakers by lessening imposition (attending to negative face) or asserting common ground (attending to positive face) (Brown and Levinson, 1978). The greater the insecurity on the part of the speaker, the more drastic the politeness strategy required, to the point where the speaker might not speak at all. Brown's discussion of why women use more politeness expressions than men looks carefully at the nature of social power and social distance in the community, at residence patterns, at networks of social interaction and at values associated with masculinity and femininity. She focuses on the notion of linguistic strategies, on looking at what men and women are doing by speaking in particular ways, at how they are using language to negotiate social relationships. This approach allows her to explore what the linguistic differences mean to speakers and how they are used to both maintain and undermine power differences. Language is thus no longer simply reflecting particular kinds of social relations, but is revealed as an active component in the constitution of those social relations.

This explanation of linguistic strategy links the use of particular linguistic forms to positions of relative powerlessness, but the emphasis on the active nature of this link, on the strategies adopted by speakers, generates a paradox. If politeness forms are generally interpreted as an expression of insecurity, as a relatively weak and indirect method of communication, it would appear that speakers are themselves perpetuating their powerlessness as they seek to protect themselves from the immediate threat raised by the linguistic interaction.

In Ocongate, as I will argue below, the demonstrated ability to use both Spanish and Quechua, together with competence in the formal Spanish register described above, are commonly used to constitute the authority of the speaker. Women have access to these forms: they recognise them as empowering, but are reluctant to use them. Thus by protecting themselves from ridicule and using Quechua instead of Spanish, women are in effect refusing to use the language which could constitute their authority. Why do women adopt the strategy that appears to perpetuate the need for this protection? Before moving on to look more closely at the set of assumptions that renders such practice meaningful, I first address certain standard explanations as to why those in relatively powerless positions do not use those linguistic forms that could confer prestige and authority.

In many cases speakers do not have access to prestige forms. Historically women's lesser bilingual competence in Ocongate was explicable to an extent in terms of their distinctive participation in those spheres of social relations in which Spanish was, and still is, most commonly acquired: education and migrant labour. Thus many poorer women over the age of thirty never went to school. If parents had to choose between their children as to who would receive education, it was deemed that men were more likely to have to deal with local Spanish-speaking authorities and with the Spanish-speaking world outside the village. In Ocongate this criterion is less relevant today. All children over the age of six are now required to attend school, and in the town itself where the school is accessible and absences noticeable, such gender differences are no longer salient.

Similarly, in terms of migration experience women still do not get drafted into the army, but as roads and transport have improved and wage labour has become more available, they frequently work in Spanish-speaking environments outside the village and also travel considerably for business purposes. Once a woman has children she is likely to travel less, but before this time both young men and women supplement family incomes and begin to find their own financial independence by working for periods outside the village. Indeed, many leave school in order to participate more fully in such work. Furthermore, women interact constantly with Spanish speakers in the village itself, even within their own homes. Women's unwillingness to use Spanish cannot therefore be explained in terms of opportunity to learn, and we thus have to consider how their attitudes towards Spanish are acquired and perpetuated.

Socialisation offers the standard explanatory paradigm for the acquisition of attitudes and behaviours. It has been argued by Coates (1986), for example, that young children are treated differently and are thus socialised into gender-specific practices. While I am not arguing against the notion that children learn gender-specific behaviour, I would emphasise here that children are themselves actively engaged in the process of acquisition. They are not socialised into a set of rules and practices that exist independently as a cohesive and commonly held set of values. Learning is an interactive process, and discussion of the acquisition of norms and values must show how people come to acquire and normalise patterns of behaviour that ostensibly work against their interests. The appeal to ideology, the argument that social actors are mystified, operating on the basis of a false consciousness, still leaves unanswered the question of how the misrecognised values are acquired.[6]

The women of Ocongate quite clearly recognise that their inability to use Spanish has negative implications for their social position. This brings me back to a discussion of value and prestige. The notion of covert prestige in sociolinguistics has been extremely useful in demonstrating that speakers are not simply socialised into a dominant set of values which they adopt and seek to emulate. For example, men as much as women seek prestige and recognition through their language use, but frequently do not appeal to standard forms, but rather rely on the validation offered by an appeal to an alternative 'vernacular culture' (Labov, 1972a, 1972b). Covert prestige refers to the oppositional values that emerge in response to the imposition of hierarchy. These values are sustained in the dense multiplex social networks which Milroy and Nichols have described. Thus a particular language usage, such as Black English Vernacular, can operate to constitute and perpetuate a powerless position in certain relationships with powerful white speakers, but in such a way as to produce a sense of autonomy and difference from which to resist domination and which thus subverts the values by which powerlessness itself is constituted and experienced. In this case to speak Black English Vernacular is not a direct attack on white power, but a process of disarticulation from the values that constitute the language of the white speakers as powerful. The fact that women more commonly use standard prestige forms than men indicates that they are in some sense excluded from the social relations that generate and sustain the values of covert prestige.

In Ocongate women's speech does not appeal to an alternative covert prestige, nor do women speak more 'correctly' than men. In general terms, women's pronunciation of Spanish demonstrates a higher level of Quechua influence and thus does not approximate the prestige standard of the higher-ranking monolingual Spanish speakers in the village. It is more difficult to estimate whether women's Quechua pronunciation could be said to be more or less standard as there is no accepted outside standard, Quechua itself being a minority, non-prestige language. In more general terms women's lesser Spanish competence is obviously further from the national standard than men's. Although Quechua has the status of an official language in Peru, Spanish is the language of government, law and education, and all official business of the state is conducted in Spanish.

However, women's language use is not more prestigious in terms of an alternative vernacular culture, despite the fact that women are involved in dense, multiplex social networks within the community that should uphold such an alternative. These women have considerable economic autonomy and do not see themselves as subservient to men in the ways that Brown described for the Mayan community. Labov refers to vernacular culture as the source of covert prestige, and claims that 'men are the chief exemplars of the vernacular culture' (Labov et al., 1968:41). Despite Labov's unwarranted generalisation,[7] this statement is in fact appropriate to the Ocongate case if the vernacular is understood as a prestigious alternative rather than as simply a non-standard one.

The subsequent sections of this chapter demonstrate how certain discursive practices associated with the constitution of racial or ethnic identities articulate with salient representations of masculinity and femininity. The use of a gendered idiom to articulate racial domination, negatively affects the ways in which women's speech is understood, undermines the possibility of constituting such speech as an instance of covert prestige and makes it difficult for women to become confident bilingual speakers.

11.3   Latent Meaning in Talk and Silence

In this section it is argued that the important differences in the speech of men and women lie in the latent meanings that affect the way in which talk is interpreted. Spanish and Quechua are not semantically equivalent, nor are the utterances of men and women. Their meanings are constituted in social interactions that are themselves historically situated and thus relate to previously constituted meanings. The speech of men and women thus reproduces rather than reflects gender difference, constantly articulating anew the ways in which such difference can be understood.

Before looking in detail at Quechua and Spanish usage, it is worth considering the ways in which silence operates as a meaningful aspect of communication. Silence is obviously not a gendered feature of discourse *per se*, as the use of silence is an essential aspect of any communicative repertoire. However, silence can communicate many different meanings. I will here concentrate on four inter-related meanings that commonly attach to silence in Ocongate: power, powerlessness, resistance and respect.

Silence can be understood as an expression of power, a refusal to enter into the intercourse that a social inferior is demanding. In face-to-face interactions such silence communicates its meaning in association with particular body postures, facial expressions, eye movements, gestures and so forth. Silence also holds meaning in non-face-to-face interaction, and in Ocongate this is particularly relevant to the experience of communication with the supernatural world. The Awkis, powerful hill spirits who control the natural fertility essential to the agricultural and herding economy, are believed to communicate verbally among themselves and when represented in ritual, are invariably noisy, somewhat disruptive characters. However, they do not speak to human beings. Their silence is noted with regret as an indication of the difficulties involved in maintaining satisfactory contact with this source of power. The silence with which appeals to secular power are often received is frequently interpreted in a similar fashion.

The classic Andean silence of resistance is related to the idea of silence as power. Silence in the face of authority can signify the absence of agreement, a refusal to participate, an act of defiance.

Silence as lack of power refers to a submissive silence, intrinsically connected to non-linguistic symbols such as body posture. Silence here denotes recognition of another's superiority and a simultaneous sense of shame (*verguenza*) in one's own inferior posi-tion. An extreme of this meaning is silence as stupidity, silence as indication that a poten-tial speaker can think of nothing to say.

Finally, there is the silence of respect, a silence which I feel depends to some degree on both power and powerlessness for its meaning. Respectful silence essentially consti-tutes the silent participant as powerless and thus gives status to other participants, yet respect does not imply a sense of shame in oneself. Such respectful silence can be observed, for example, during Andean wedding celebrations when the bride and groom are expected to show extreme respect to their god-parents who have sponsored the marriage. The couple sit silent and sober amidst the noisy drunken partying of their god-parents, family and friends. Respect in a situation such as this is about not saying everything that you might feel; people emphasise that one of the problems with drinking alcohol is that things that should remain unsaid are voiced and problems arise as a result.

Perhaps the most interesting feature of silence is precisely the lack of material content which heightens the ambiguity of its meaning. Silence can thus be seen as potential antagonism, as submission and recognition of inferiority, as respect, or as distraction and lack of interest. Silence marks the calm, self-contained *tranquilo* as opposed to the crazy *loco*, but also the stupid, slow *sonso* as opposed to the lively, quick-witted *vivo*.

The use of Quechua and Spanish is similarly multivocalic. Quechua is associated with insider status. The indigenous deities that reside in the local landscape, the hill spirits and the earth powers, the Awkis and Pachamama, are the source of regeneration for this local social space. These spirits are always addressed in Quechua and are reported to speak Quechua among themselves. The Quechua-speaking world is organised through networks of kin and spiritual kin relations, networks in which these supernatural powers also have their place as pre-Hispanic ancestors. It is thus through reference to a pre-Hispanic past that people establish their enduring right to the land of the locality and to the benefits that the Pachamama and the Awkis can bring by ensuring its fertility. Here we come close to the source of an alternative prestige, the identification of a con-quered people with a glorious past – a past that goes back in time beyond the Inkas to the land itself and the original source of productive social life. Their present status as moral, worthy human beings is sustained through kinship relations which extend to and embrace these supernatural forces. It is in terms of these meanings that Quechua comes to be the most appropriate language for the home, for affection and love-making, and for ritual. However, this past also has a negative image which concerns beliefs in Quechua people's ultimate inferiority in the face of the Spanish-speaking state.

The positive image of Quechua speakers co-exists with a representation of the pre-Hispanic past as a time of ignorance and barbarity. The Inkas could not read and write, and in these terms ignorance of Spanish implies ignorance both of modern technology and of the material comforts that money can buy. It also implies a sense of weakness: for all their power, indigenous deities were defeated by the Spanish God. This feeling is exacerbated by the notion that the Quechua spoken locally is not real Quechua, but a degenerate Hispanised version of some imagined 'pure', 'traditional' form.

To be a monolingual Quechua speaker thus implies insider status, legitimacy and a certain access to the regenerative powers of the animate landscape, but at the same time this identity carries with it a sense of disadvantage and discrimination in the modern world, vulnerability, innocence and ignorance in the face of dominant, powerful outsiders.

Spanish by contrast is the language through which contact can be made with the powers of the state and the material goods produced in the market economy. Spanish is also the language of education and the kinds of knowledge that allow people to function effectively in the modern world. However, a monolingual Spanish identity is problematic to the people of Ocongate because Spanish is ultimately associated with outsider status, and with a world organised around impersonal relations of production which do not respect the moral values inscribed in kinship. Monolingual Spanish speakers thus have a certain knowledge and power, but as outsiders they have no moral basis for the exercise of authority in the locality.

It is in terms of the salient meanings outlined above that bilingualism operates as the language of legitimate authority in the village. In bilingual discourse the positive aspects of both forms of power and/or history can be evoked, while the negative implications are simultaneously denied. To speak Spanish cannot imply the illegitimate abuse of the outsider if the speaker simultaneously invokes insider status through the use of Quechua. Similarly, to use Quechua does not imply ignorance if reference is made to an ability to speak Spanish and to operate effectively outside the village.

Thus, Quechua in this community only operates as a prestigious vernacular in so far as it articulates with, or implies a facility in, the Spanish culture of urban areas and state institutions. The use of Quechua must carry the possibility of choice, implying a decision to distance oneself from the Hispanic. Given that everyone in this community is a first-language Quechua speaker, it is thus understandable that it is Spanish rather than Quechua competence that is emphasised in public, particularly in those formal political meetings that most directly refer to the world outside the village. Quechua is the more suitable language for use at home or among kin, as it refers directly to moral, friendly, insider relationships.

The implicit meanings in Quechua and Spanish and in their combination obviously have implications in terms of women's lesser bilingual competence and consequent lesser authority in all matters that link the village to the wider social context of the outside world. In theory the linking of bilingualism to efficacy in certain political tasks has no negative implications for women. Women can remain forceful and authoritative in other spheres. As Quechua speakers and as women, they are the guardians of indigenous culture and exemplify the source of moral attachment, while men as bilinguals stress their Spanish competence in negotiating inter-community, even inter-household status.[8]

However, the prestige of bilingual discourse emerges in response to the weakness of the Quechua sphere. Women are very aware of this. Their lack of Spanish competence evokes feelings of inadequacy and inferiority and a sense of exclusion from certain levels of prestige within their community. So why the reluctance to use their Spanish? The reason appears to relate to the fact that femininity as a value in terms of which individual women can construct positive subjective identities is very closely connected to the inner world of the family and the community. It is by raising children and by interacting effectively in kinship networks, however wide, that women both value themselves and are valued. The importance of the role of women as mothers and nurturers is emphasised in the dominant images of femininity from both inside and outside the community. It is virtually impossible for women to have access to contraception, but both church and state institutions celebrate motherhood, and indeed women gain adult status from the birth of their first child. This femininity is closely connected to a

Quechua-speaking social world and cannot easily co-exist with alternative, more urban images of women as autonomous and oriented towards the Spanish-speaking world. Autonomy and individualism are not necessarily attractive options for these women.

Dominant notions of masculinity, however, present no such conflict for men. Men can legitimately both be autonomous and express an affiliation to the moral relations of kinship, because their most valued achievement is a mediating role between households and between communities.

This pattern of difference is common in many cultures. The question it raises here is why women feel inadequate in their sphere of social life, why they interpret their own actions in a way that validates male experience at their expense. Bilingualism works for men; why do women not have an alternative, more positive concept of their use of Quechua?

To answer this question we have to take into account the fact that the notions of power, hierarchy and language which I have been describing are essentially experienced in a racial, not a gendered idiom. Spanish and Quechua are primarily understood as indicators of ethnic (and by implication class) status. Bilingualism essentially deals with the problem of colonial, i.e. racial, domination. In the following section of this paper I describe the ways in which gender is used as a metaphor to express other power differences; and I suggest that the use of this gender metaphor allows men to negotiate the ambiguity of their racial status, but at the expense of women. To do this, I look at a particular set of rituals which not only use a gendered idiom, but which explicitly connect representations of gender to the use of speech and silence.

The rituals to which I refer and which occur on various occasions in the ritual calendar of Ocongate all involve men dressing up as women and enacting female roles in ritual dramas. The occasions on which these events occur are: (1) the festival of the Immaculate Conception of the Virgin (8 December), (2) the festival of Saint Isidore (15 May) and (3) the Corpus Christi pilgrimage to the shrine of the miraculous Christ of the Snow Star (May/June).

The drama of the first festival involves a man dressing up as a soldier and another man blacking his face and dressing as a woman, a *mestiza*. Considerable entertainment for the onlookers is provided by this visual spectacle, but is increased when the soldier makes love to the 'woman', attempting to kiss and fondle her. The 'woman' attempts to evade the attentions of the man but remains silent throughout her ordeal.

At the festival of Saint Isidore teams of bulls are brought into the village square in an enactment of the ritually and materially important maize-sowing. Men, ideally dressed in traditional *bayeta* clothing, direct the bulls, while other men dressed as women place the seed in the ground. The character of the overseer, the *mandón*, mounted on a horse, directs the operations which are constantly disrupted by two other men, who represent the Awkis and whose task it is to place the fertilising ash on top of the seeds that the women have placed in the ground. However, they actually spend their time noisily molesting the 'women' and the onlooking crowds. The men and 'women' involved in the act of sowing do not react to the antagonism of the Awkis.

There are several ritual personae, either female or ambiguously male/female, performed by men during the festival for the Christ of the Snow Star. The *ukukus*, or bear dancers, carry an ambiguous symbolism in many respects (Allen, 1983). They fulfil various functions: they are the guardians of authority at the shrine, acting as a kind of police force, making sure that pilgrims behave with appropriate decorum; they are buffoons who entertain the pilgrims with their antics; and they act as general dogsbodies in the various dance groups to which they are attached. Their ritual status is on the one hand high and autonomous – they lead an independent pilgrimage onto the glaciers above the shrine where they keep an all-night vigil – and on the other hand low and dependent, in that they are the servants of their particular dance troupes.

Finally, concerning the *ukukus*, I suggest that their gender is also ambiguous. As they march round the shrine, brandishing their whips and keeping order, and when they climb the glacier and risk death on the freezing ice, they are unmistakably fulfilling masculine roles, imposing order and demonstrating physical strength and endurance. However, they also spend a considerable amount of time begging from the people in high falsetto voices, brandishing small images of themselves, little *ukuku* dolls which they claim are their babies and for whom they need money or food. The language register they use for this begging is very similar to a preferred female register of request (rapid, high-pitched and with distinctive intonation). Finally, there are both the "'external go-betweens' between the spectators and the dance group, and 'internal go-betweens', between the dancers and themselves" (Poole, 1985:15) – a combination of the ideal behaviours of men and women.

The Qolla dance troupes who represent alpaca herders from the *punas* of Puno have among their number a female role, the *imilla* who is quite frequently danced by a man, although the Ocongate Qollas always use a woman for this role. On their return from the shrine, a ritual battle is enacted between the Qollas and another dance group, the Chunchus, who represent the inhabitants of the jungle and are distinguished by their feathered headdresses and *chonta* sticks.[9] On one occasion (the festival of Exaltation, 1987) the male dancers of the Qolla group dressed themselves as women, putting on homespun skirts and adopting the high-pitched falsetto voices of the *ukuku* dancers. The ritual battle centred on the depiction of sexual activity between the Chunchus and the Qollas, but most particularly between the Qollas themselves, until finally all the Qollas had been killed by the *chonta* sticks of the Chunchus, which had been used to represent the phallus in the antics performed throughout the fight. The Qollas were extremely active and noisy, in stark contrast to the female figures of the first two festivals I have described.

An interesting point of similarity in all these male representations of femininity is that the symbolism associated with the 'female' characters is as closely related to ideas about indigenous identity as it is to those about gender. In some cases the female characters are unambiguously female indigenous peasants, and in the festival of the Virgin the 'woman' appears with a black face and in clothes which mark the wearer as *mestiza* and thus more closely connected to an Andean than to a Hispanic identity, especially in contrast to the soldier. The 'women' in the Saint Isidore festival directly represent indigenous peasant women, wearing homespun clothing and performing the same functions that a female peasant would perform while sowing maize. Similarly the Qollas wore homespun skirts to identify themselves as indigenous women, and whatever the ambiguities over the gender of the *ukukus*, there is no doubt that they represent an indigenous presence among the huge variety of ritual figures portrayed in the Corpus Christi festival.

These ritual female characters are also closely connected to depictions of sexuality and implied notions of fertility. The jokes that surround the performances of the female characters at the festivals of the Virgin and of Saint Isidore always concern their having silently to put up with explicit sexual advances on the part of the male characters. The Qollas also engaged in explicit representations of sexual intercourse. The *ukukus* have a less explicit connection to sexuality, but the general symbolism of their characters firmly connects them to ideas about natural fertility and regeneration in that they are themselves supernatural figures associated with the animate powers of the local landscape.

Gender is a potent metaphor for other levels of social relations. It is an extremely strong representation of difference, and is also a concept which here succinctly juxtaposes both the idea of indigenous fertility and that of conquest or submission. Femininity as a concept has long been used as an image of defeat and power difference in the Andes. The Inka conquest hierarchy described ruling lineages as male while conquered peoples were conceptually female. Such a representation of gender obviously parallels the representation of a Quechua monolingual identity, with which the female is also associated. In what ways does the male representation of silent, as opposed to vocal, femininity relate to these other structures of gender and race?

The silent female characters are represented as extremely passive in the ritual dramas. The female character in the Virgin drama simply allows herself to be bothered by the soldier for the entertainment of the crowd. The female sowers in the Saint Isidore festival play an active role in the sowing, yet in the ritual as a whole it is the characters of the Awkis and the overseer who actively generate the ritual activity; the overseer orders the silent male peasants, on whose actions the women's sowing is dependent, and the Awkis make a huge amount of noise molesting the female sowers.

Referring back to the possible ways in which silence could be interpreted, I would suggest that this portrayal of passive feminine silence is not a portrayal of feminine power. Given that the male characters these 'females' are made to interact with are both representatives of outside power, the soldier (state) and the Awkis (animate landscape), I also suggest that it is improbable that their silence communicates respect. Thus we are left with the options which again connect femaleness with racial oppression – silence as both subordination and resistance. These female ritual characters thus appear to harness the metaphor of gender to express the subordination and insecurity of the local population in the face of both the state and the animate landscape.

To turn now to the other female characters, the Qollas and the *ukukus*, these characters are female in a far more ambiguous sense than the others, and the symbolism that attaches to them is thus somewhat more complex. Both have certain silent passive characteristics. The Qollas end their ritual drama lying silent, feigning death, heaped on top of each other in the village square – a very direct image of silent conquest. The *ukukus* are also silent in their subordinate role as dogsbodies, where they occupy a very low rank in the dance group hierarchy. The strength of these characters is represented partly through their masculine characteristics and partly through their noise. In both cases their noise is confrontational and demanding, and in the case of the *ukukus* the falsetto register they employ is unequivocally female. Thus we are not simply faced with a male/female opposition that can be equated to a noise/silence opposition. While silent passive indigenous resistance is female, noisy active indigenous confrontation combines the male and the female.

The female thus invokes the negative aspects of racial identity while a male/female combination presents insider identity as an altogether more positive concept. Finally, I come to the question of why men are used to represent these female characteristics.

It appears that the combination of the male and the female that the male performance provides stops the dramas from becoming simply a representation of female – and by extension, indigenous – humiliation. It permits the expression of these sentiments without the experience of them in the enactment of the role itself. Men and women say that men have to act the parts because if women were to do so, then the male characters would have to be more restrained in their behaviour. In that case the gender interaction which I have analysed here simply would not occur. Such was indeed the case on one occasion when I witnessed the festival of Saint Isidore and the Awkis paid no attention to the female characters who sowed the seed. This was not without regret; people said the festival was much better when the Awkis could molest the 'women' by pulling their skirts up over their heads. Paradoxically, then, the male cannot interact with the female and create the necessary male/female combination unless the 'female' is a male.

11.4   Conclusions

I come finally to some conclusions on the original question of why women speak less Spanish than men. A traditional theory of complementary and separate spheres might suggest that the best hope women have for some degree of autonomy and authority in the local community would be through their involvement with spheres of activity that relate more directly to the autonomous powers of the landscape in order to construct an identity that did not rely on validation from the male-dominated, outsider-oriented public sphere. Women's insistent monolingualism could be interpreted in this light. Their monolingualism does perhaps offer a degree of protection in so far as it isolates them from the Spanish-speaking state, or rather constitutes a statement of non-collaboration and lack of interest in this sphere of power. However, as we have seen, women themselves feel dissatisfied with this monolingual option.

I have tried to show how Quechua monolingualism is associated with subordination, oppression and ignorance and that this is an image associated with race and colonial domination and is one with which both male and female monolinguals identify. Their Quechua on its own is not sufficient to secure them a valued place in the contemporary world. Their monolingualism offers them no distance from the negative evaluation of their indigenous past.

The animate landscape, the physical focus of indigenous identity in terms of which Quechua holds positive connotations, is a source not of female power, but rather of indigenous power. Indigenous power in turn is an ambiguous concept that embraces the possibilities of regeneration as well as those of defeat. Men attempt to avoid the implications of the association between a Quechua identity and the subordinate status of a conquered people through cultural practices which involve articulations with the Spanish-speaking world. Their bilingualism is an example of such practices which reinforce the positive image of masculinity in which men act as mediators between the inside world of kinship and community and the outside world of finance and knowledge. The dominant image of femininity places women firmly inside the community, even if this is understood as the larger community of the business/trading networks. Speaking Spanish does nothing to validate this position, yet neither does association with the Quechua sphere offer women a strong and positive female identity. Where human gender is represented in relation to this sphere, women are at best the silent partners of men, at worst the objects of male ridicule, often only represented through the burlesque figures of disguised men.

All human beings construct their subjective identities in terms of the discursive representations which surround them and which constitute their social world. What I have tried to show in this paper is that while bilingualism offers a possibility for a degree of local autonomy and authority to indigenous men, it does not offer the same possibilities to women. Male representation and subsequent cultural association of femininity with the silent, dominated aspect of indigenous identity in fact constitutes a male appropriation of the alternative prestige culture at the expense of women.

These male representations, which are also crucially the central indigenous representations of female gender, make it far more difficult for women than it is for men to escape the implications of racial defeat. An appeal to non-indigenous cultural symbols such as speaking Spanish does not cancel the negative side of Quechua culture for women, because femininity itself is so strongly associated with the notions of defeat and subordination. Women cannot negotiate the ambiguity of insider indigenous status through *language* as men can, because as women they themselves embody their position. Their disarticulation thus has to be more far-reaching than the use of verbal symbolism.

Nevertheless more and more women are learning Spanish, in recognition of the connection between bilingualism and positions of authority in the community. However, they are simultaneously aware that such changes in language use have more to do with confronting power structures than with actually acquiring such authority.

Authority must to some extent be based on the ability to communicate – that is the ability to be heard, for your message to be understood and accepted. Language in itself does not guarantee communication. If women's Spanish already has an overlay of other meanings – as illustrated by the woman who was told so violently that her language came out of dog shit – even a woman's Spanish can impede her ability to communicate. Thus it is in those areas of Peruvian life where women have begun to organise and find a political voice that they have registered the experience of a changing relationship to their language. They say that they become more aware of language as they come across their language as an obstacle in their political practice, as they become aware that part of their oppression was an alienation from language, not in the sense of being forced to speak a male language, but in the sense that as women they had been excluded from communication in the language of power.

Notes

This article is based on three periods of fieldwork in the village of Ocongate, the first in 1983–5 (funded by the Economic and Social Research Council), the second in 1987 (funded by the British Academy) and the third in 1988 (funded by the Nuffield Foundation). Earlier drafts of the paper have been presented to the XIV Congress of the Latin American Studies Association, New Orleans, the Women's Studies seminar at the Charles Center, Williamsburg and to the London Institute of Latin American Studies workshop on Andean discourse. I am particularly grateful to Meryl Altman, Cecilia Blondet, Deborah Cameron, Cecilia McCallum and Maria Phylactou for their comments and suggestions. I would also like to thank my former colleagues at Liverpool University who supported all the research on which this paper is based.

1   Peru is divided into twenty-three departments, in turn subdivided into provinces and districts. Ocongate is a district capital in the Province of Quisipcanchis, Department of Cusco.

2   The escalation of guerrilla activity in the Cusco region in the mid-1980s led to a dramatic decline in tourism in this area.

3   Quechua influence on local Spanish is particularly evident in the following aspects of speech: intonation (for example, Quechua has no rising intonation for interrogatives), accentuation (Quechua has a firm rule of accentuation of the penultimate syllable), phonetics (Quechua has three vowel phonemes while Spanish has five, which leads to a correspondence of e/i and o/u sounds in local Spanish), grammar (distinctive variations in local Spanish include a lack of number and gender concordance, generalisation of rules for conjugating verbs which produces 'regular' forms of standard Spanish 'irregular' verbs, distinctive uses of the gerund and the pluperfect which follow Quechua grammar and syntax), lexical borrowings and calques.

4   *Mestizo* was originally a term used to refer to people of mixed race, while the Spaniards referred to the indigenous population as Indians. In contemporary Peru these terms carry complex and ambiguous meanings. They refer primarily to cultural and class distinctions rather than racial difference. In the context of a small town such as Ocongate, those with money or political influence, with some education and/or urban contacts are referred to as *mestizo*. Nevertheless, despite the fact that the terms denote distinctive cultural orientation and experience, they are also used to naturalise and validate social hierarchy through an appeal to racial difference which firmly distinguished the *mestizo* from the indigenous peasant, the *campesino*.

5   See for example Daly (1978), Lakoff (1975) and Spender (1980). Useful overviews of this literature are provided by Cameron (1985), Coates & Cameron (1988), and Graddol & Swann (1989).

6   Bourdieu, despite his sophisticated demonstration of how such values are maintained, does not provide a clear account of acquisition (Bourdieu, 1977).

7   Labov is apparently unaware of those cases where women can and do embody the prestige of vernacular culture. See for example McCallum (1990) and Harris (1980).

8   Harris's work on the Bolivian Laymi provides a comparable case for Aymara speakers (Harris, 1980).

9   'Chonta' (Sp.) 'Bactris ciliata is a small palm tree with a hard black elastic ebony-like wood growing in the montana below 1,200 metres. In Inka times it was used for making spears and other weapons, and it was an important trade item from the tropical forest people to the highlands' (Sallnow, 1987:309).

References

Allen, C., 1983, 'Of Bear-men and He-men: Bear Metaphors and Male Self-perception in a Peruvian Community', *Latin American Indian Literatures* 7(1) 38–51.

Bourdieu, P., 1977, *Outline of a Theory of Practice*, Cambridge: Cambridge University Press.

Brown, P., 1980, 'How and Why are Women more Polite: Some Evidence from a Mayan Community' in S. McConnell-Ginet, R. Borker and N. Furman (eds.), *Women and Language in Literature and Society*, New York: Praeger.

Brown, P. and Levinson, S., 1978, 'Universals in Language Usage: Politeness Phenomena' in E. Goody (ed.), *Questions and Politeness*, Cambridge: Cambridge University Press.

Cameron, D., 1985, *Feminism & Linguistic Theory*, London: Macmillan.

—— , 1988, 'Language and Sex in the Quantitative Paradigm: Introduction' in J. Coates and D. Cameron (eds.), *Women in their Speech Communities*, London: Longman.

Coates, J., 1986, *Women, Men and Language*, London: Longman.

Coates, J. and Cameron, D., 1988, 'Some Problems in the Sociolinguistic Explanation of Sex Differences' in J. Coates and D. Cameron (eds.), *Women in their Speech Communities*, London: Longman.

Daly, M., 1978, *Gyn/Ecology: the Metaethics of Radical Feminism*, Boston: Beacon Press.

Graddol, D. and Swann, J., 1989, *Gender Voices*, Oxford: Basil Blackwell.

Harris, O., 1980, 'The Power of Signs: Gender, Culture and the Wild in the Bolivian Andes' in C. MacCormack and M. Strathern (eds.), *Nature, Culture and Gender*, Cambridge: Cambridge University Press.

Harvey, P., 1989, 'Genero, autoridad y competencia linguistica: participación politica de la mujer en pueblos andinos', *Documento de Trabajo* no. 33, Lima: Instituto de Estudios Peruanos.

Labov, W., 1972a, *Sociolinguistic Patterns*, Philadelphia: University of Pennsylvania Press.

—— , 1972b, *Language in the Inner City*, Oxford: Basil Blackwell.

Labov, W., P. Cohen, C. Robins and J. Lewis, 1968, *A Study of the Non-standard English of Negro and Puerto Rican Speakers in New York City*, US Office of Education Co-operative Research Project 3288–1.

Lakoff, R., 1975, *Language and Woman's Place*, New York: Harper & Row.

McCallum, C., 1990, 'Language, Kinship and Politics in Amazonia', *Man* 25(3) 412–33.

Milroy, L., 1980, *Language and Social Networks*, Oxford: Basil Blackwell.

Nichols, P. 1984, 'Networks and Hierarchies: Language and Social Stratification' in C. Kramarae, M. Schulz and W. O'Barr (eds.), *Language and Power*, Beverly Hills, California: Sage Publications.

Poole, D., 1985, 'The Choreography of History in Andean Dance' (unpublished manuscript).

Sallnow, M., 1987, *Pilgrims of the Andes: Regional Cults in Cusco*, Washington, D.C.: Smithsonian Institution Press.

Spender, D., 1980, *Man Made Language*, London: Routledge and Kegan Paul.

Trudgill, P., 1972, 'Sex, Covert Prestige and Linguistic Change in the Urban British English of Norwich', *Language in Society*, 1 179–95.

12

Hearing What's Not Said and Missing What Is: Black Language in White Public Space

H. Samy Alim

I mean, I think the thing that teachers work with, or combat *the most at Haven High, is definitely like issues with standard English versus vernacular English.* (Teacher at Haven High in Sunnyside, USA (2003))

Studies of discourse and intercultural communication, or intergroup communication, often examine communicative misunderstandings or conflicts that occur when speakers of different language backgrounds come into contact. These misunderstandings usually occur not because the languages have different syntactic structures, but because they have different rules of language use. For example, in the US, misunderstandings or conflicts may not occur between a native Arabic speaker learning English and a native speaker of English simply because Arabic does not use the copula (*is* or *are*) in sentences like "She excellent" for "She is excellent" (Bahloul 1993). However, misunderstandings or conflicts may occur between the same two speakers as a result of fundamental differences in their native speech communities' rules of language use regarding social distance, formality and age, among other variables (Hussein 1995). Intergroup conflict can occur between speakers of the same language group (but perhaps different ethnicity, gender, social class, religious affiliation, regional background or other grouping) when speaker intent (illocutionary force) is misinterpreted by the hearer.

Any study of Black–White intercultural communication must take into account the persistent racial tensions that exist between the communities in the US. Wolfram's (1974) paper on the controversial nature of Black–White speech relations begins with a comment that observed Black–White speech differences are "still interpreted by some" through the White ideological lens of Black inferiority. This is a point that has been understated in the literature and is now beginning to be newly interrogated by studies of "whiteness" (see below). Further, to my knowledge, no study of Black–White intercultural communication directly examines the multiple reasons – historic and contemporary – for interracial tensions between the two groups in a given community. The next section provides the

H. Samy Alim, "Hearing what's not said and missing what is: Black language in White public space." © 2004 by Blackwell Publishing Ltd. This essay was specially commissioned for this volume.

community context as a necessary precondition for examining Black Language in White public space. It is within this context that the following sections are to be interpreted.

12.1   The Gentrification of Speech and Speakers

The data presented in this chapter stems from a multi-year ethnographic study of Sunnyside, a diverse, working-class suburb of about 20,000, which has experienced a dramatic increase in ethnic diversity and economic development within the last decade. The community was once a thriving Black community that led the nation in Black consciousness and nationalism, establishing the nation's only independent Black pre-school through college educational system in the 1960s and 1970s. Since the government's forced closure of the city's only high school in the 1970s, the Black community has experienced an increasing sense of displacement in what was once known as "a Black city," as the Latino population rises and Whites begin to move in slowly. For two decades, the community did not have a high school and Black students experienced a 65% drop-out rate in the schools of the neighboring suburbs, all of which were predominantly White and upper-middle-class. The gentrification of the community by White real estate developers is directly linked to educational concerns, since the city's new 28-acre, high-end shopping plaza (and several expensive hotels) stands on the grounds of the former high school (similar situations are occurring nationwide from Oakland to Atlanta to New York).

While it is not possible to do justice to the community context in this chapter (see Alim 2004a for an in-depth account), it is helpful to present the perspectives of the current generation of Black youth juxtaposed with a perspective from the previous generation. The previous generation, after experiencing the rise and fall of Black nationhood, illegal real estate practices, land annexation, lack of job opportunities and a serious crack epidemic – all of which were debilitating – saw the interest shown by White developers as perhaps one of the only ways to save the city from a withering tax base. Below, we present two generations' views of this recent gentrification:

Male: C'mon, cele*BRATE*!	Bilal: This is the, the, the white part of
Female: Yeah, we gon celebrate this day!	Sunnyside now . . .
Reporter: What are you celebrating?	Researcher: Yeah, so what *is* all of this?
F: We are celebrating the demolition of	Yesmina: The *white* part!
Raven High School.	B: This *bullshit* right here!
M: We're celebrating hope for the city!	R: Is this Sunnyside?
That's right, a *major* milestone. It's	B: Hell naw! This is, this is corporate
the beginning of our economic	America takin over . . .
independence, which we hope.	Aqiyla: Yeah . . .
That's what it seems like, a great	B: This is the sunnyside of Sunnyside . . .
opportunity for us.	Amira: This whole area, right here, where
F: Right. Right on!	*all* this new, all these new buildings are,
[Clapping and cheering]	this useta be Raven High School . . .
50-year-old Black couple in	17-year-old Black youths in
Sunnyside (1996)	Sunnyside (2002)

While one generation celebrates the demolition of the old, dilapidated structure of the city's only high school, another is lamenting the displacement of Black people from a city that no longer *has* a public high school. As the city continues to raise revenue through the continued development, rent control legislation is being overturned and more and more Blacks are being forced out of the area (the community is now about 20% Black in 2004, and needless to say, the economic independence of Black people in Sunnyside has not been attained). Tensions between Blacks and Whites, and other ethnic groups, continue to rise in this small city, as well as distrust for Whites, as we see in the dialogue between me and several Black youth below. In this conversation, I commented on how the only place I see White people is in the newly developed area of Sunnyside, and I asked if Whites (driving in their fancy cars) have always been in Sunnyside:

Bilal: *Hellll naw!*
Researcher: . . . , the Volvo station wagon . . .
Amira: Never!
R: . . . , and the Mercedes and all that?
B: Never . . .
R: Never? Forreal?
A: Mm-mm . . .
B: *Ever*! Only time you . . .
A: They scared or they buyin drugs . . .
B: Only time you see them, only time you see them is when they crossin over the
            bridge, if they commute . . .
            Yesmina: Oh, yeah, the commuting . . .
B: [suck-teeth], that's *all* they do . . .
A: And they got they doors on *lock*! [Laughter] . . .
R: Oh, yeah? [Laughter]
A: Yep . . .
R: How you know they got they doors locked? You can't see . . .
A: They don't look – they don't look at you. They be like this [making a scared
            face] . . .
Y: *Mm-hmm!*
A: . . . and start flyyyin!
Voice: . . . [suck-teeth]
R: Man, that's crazy, so people just basically be ridin through . . .
Y: Mm-hmm . . .
A: Usin our streets . . .
B: We should put a damn toll on *them*, *shiiitt!*
Y: [Laughter] . . .
R: [Laughter], a toll every time you drive through . . .
B: *Yeahhh,* I'll toll they ass two dollars, [Laughter] . . .
Y: We'd make a lot of money . . .

Whites are seen as outsiders ("usin our streets") who are "scared" of Blacks and who are only in Sunnyside to either commute to work or if "they buyin drugs." Also, one can see that Whites are also viewed as having the economic upper hand in the way Bilal insists: "We should put a damn toll on *them, shiiitt!*"

In this context, Black youth in Haven High will often comment on how they only see their teachers (mostly White) when they are exiting or entering the community on the nearby freeway ramp. The fact that White teachers don't spend time in the community only reifies feelings of social distance and distrust between students and teachers, which can be a major source of tension in the schooling experiences of Black youth. As one student put it, "Man, they don't know what it's like here – they act like they know, but they don't know . . . they *can't* know."

Just as economic institutions are gentrifying and removing Black communities around the nation and offering unfulfilled promises of economic independence, one can also say that educational institutions have been attempting (since integration) to gentrify and remove Black Language from its speakers with similarly unfulfilled promises of economic mobility. In both cases, the message is: "Economic opportunities will be opened up to you if you just let us clean up your neighborhoods and your language." Most Blacks in the US since integration can testify that they have experienced teachers' attempts to eradicate their language and linguistic practices (see Morgan 2003 on "outing schools") in favor of the adoption of White cultural and linguistic norms. I'll return to this point at the end of the chapter.

12.2   Black Language Structure and Use

Turning our focus to language within this context, this chapter focuses on Black Language (BL, sometimes referred to in the literature as "Ebonics," "African American Language," "African American English," or "African American Vernacular English," among other labels) as a complex system of structure and use that is distinct from White Mainstream English (WME) in the US. While it is true that BL shares much of its structure with WME, there are many aspects of the BL syntactic (grammar) and phonological (pronunciation) systems that mark it as distinct from that variety. If we examine syntax alone, sociolinguists have described numerous distinctive features of BL, such as copula absence (as we saw in the Arabic example in the beginning of this chapter, Labov 1969), invariant *be* for habitual aspect ("He *be* actin crazy," meaning "He usually/regularly/sometimes acts crazy," Fasold 1972) and equatives ("We *be* them Bay boys" for "We are them Bay boys," Alim 2004a), *steady* as an intensified continuative ("She *steady* prayin her son come home," meaning "She is intensely, consistently and continuously hoping her son comes home," Baugh 1983), stressed *BIN* to mark remote past ("I *BIN* told you not to trust that woman," meaning "I told you a long time ago not to trust that woman"), *be done* to mark future/conditional perfect ("By the end of the day, I *be done* collected $600!" meaning "By the end of the day, I will have collected $600!", Baugh 1983), aspectual *stay* ("She *stay* up in my business" meaning "She is always getting into my business," Spears 2000), 3rd person singular present tense -*s* absence ("I know who run *this* household!" for "I know who runs *this* household," Fasold 1972), possessive -*s* absence ("I'm braidin Talesha hair," for "I'm braidin Talesha's hair"), multiple negation ("I ain't never heard about no riot big as the one we had in LA" for "I have never heard about a riot as big as the one we had in LA," Labov 1972), negative inversion ("Can't nobody touch

E-40!" meaning "Nobody can touch E-40!", Sells, Rickford and Wasow 1996), and several other features (see Rickford 1999). It is important to note that many of these distinct BL features are used in variation with WME features as most speakers possess an ability to shift their speech styles, to varying degrees (not all BL speakers have the same stylistic range). I am conceptualizing BL to include the full range of styles, including WME, as speakers deem appropriate.

While much of the sociolinguistics literature has focused on distinctive phonological and syntactic features of BL, most researchers are aware that BL cannot simply be defined as a checklist of features that are distinct from WME (Morgan 1994). Aside from having an ever-evolving *lexicon* (Turner 1949, Major 1970 [1994], Dillard 1977, Folb 1980, Anderson 1994, Smitherman 1994 [2000], Stavsky, Mozeson and Mozeson 1995, Holloway and Vass 1997), speakers of BL may participate in numerous linguistic practices and cultural modes of discourse such as *signifyin* (and *bustin, crackin, cappin* and *dissin*, Abrahams 1964, Kochman 1969, Kernan 1971, 1972, Labov 1972, Smitherman 1973, 1977, Morgan 1996), *playin the dozens* (Abrahams 1970, Brown 1972), *call and response* (Daniel and Smitherman 1976, Smitherman 1977, Alim 2004b), *tonal semantics* (Smitherman 1977, Keyes 1984, Alim 2004c), *battlin* and *entering the cipher* (Norfleet 1997, Newman 2001, Alim 2004c), and the use of direct and indirect speech (Spears 1998, Morgan 1998), among others.

BL, then, refers to both linguistic features and rules of language use that are germane to Black speech communities in the US. In the following sections, we see how the richness of BL goes completely unnoticed and is regularly censored in White public space. We also see how speakers manipulate BL and how use of BL can often lead to misinterpretation and conflict for Blacks languaging in White public space, particularly educational institutions. While differing rules of language use are certainly part of what sometimes creates misunderstandings in intercultural communication, miscommunication often occurs in sociopolitical and sociohistorical contexts where communities (and their languages) are in conflict for economic, political and social reasons as we touched on above (see Lippi-Green 1997).

12.3   Black Language in White Public Space

The racial segregation present in American society has led some scholars to use the term "American apartheid" to describe the deliberate isolation and exclusion of Blacks from educational, occupational and social institutions in the US (Massey and Denton 1993). Perhaps it is centuries of persistent segregation between Blacks and Whites that accounts for the dearth of significant studies of Black–White intercultural communication, with the notable exception of Kochman's (1981) *Black and White Styles in Conflict*. Additionally, when Blacks and Whites do interact, as Kochman (1981: 7) points out, "Black and white cultural differences are generally ignored when attempts are made to understand how and why black and white communication fails." One could argue that most Black–White intercultural communication occurs either in schools or on the job, where Blacks and Whites are "forced" into contact and Whites tend to be in the position of power. In this sense, I will draw on "White public space" as used by Page and Thomas (1994, cited in Hill 1998: 683): "a morally significant set of contexts that are the most important sites of the practices of racializing hegemony, in which Whites are invisibly normal, and in which racialized populations are visibly marginal and the objects of monitoring ranging from individual judgment to Official English legislation." Whites in educational and occupational settings may exercise their power in obvious ways (such as giving an order or firing an employee) and less obvious ways. As research on "whiteness" argues (Frankenberg 1993, Yancy 2000), Whites exercise power through overt and covert racist practices, which often reveal racist ideologies that even the "racist" may be unaware of (Hill 1998). In our case, WME and White ways of speaking become the invisible and unmarked norms of what becomes glossed as "communicating in academic settings." Further, White public space in this chapter not only refers to physical space, but also to most interactional spaces in which Blacks encounter Whites, particularly White strangers or Whites in positions of power over them. In both cases, Blacks work to maintain a social face (Goffman 1967) – or the "mask," as poet Paul Laurence Dunbar described in his 1895 poem and rappers The Fugees rhymed 101 years later – "the image and impression that a person conveys during encounters, along with others' evaluation of that image" (Morgan 2002: 23).

The fact that it is the language and communicative norms of those in power, in any society, that tend to be labeled as "standard," "official," "normal," "appropriate," "respectful," and so on, often goes unrecognized, particularly by the members of the dominating group. This dialogue with a teacher from Haven High in Sunnyside serves as the entry point to our discussion of how BL (and its speakers) are viewed in American educational institutions. We enter the dialogue as the teacher describes the "communication" goals of the school, and the language and communication behavior of her Black students. We return to some of the key words and phrases underlined in this passage:

Teacher: They [Haven High] have a lot of presentation standards, so like this list of, you know, what you *should* be doing when you're having like an oral presentation – like you should speak slowly, speak loudly, speak clearly, make eye contact, use body language, those kinds of things, and it's all written out into a rubric, so when the kids have a presentation, you grade on each element. And so, I mean, in that sense, they've worked with developing communication. I mean, I think the thing that teachers work with, or combat the most at Haven High, is definitely like issues with standard English versus vernacular English. Um, like, if there was like one of the *few* goals I had this year was to get kids to stop sayin, um, "he was, she was . . ."
Alim: They was?
T: "They was. We be." Like, those kinds of things and so we spent a lot of time working with that and like recognizing, "Okay, when you're with your friends you can say *whatever you want* but . . . this is the way it is. I'm sorry, but that's just the way." And they're like, "Well, you know, it doesn't make sense to me. This sounds right." "She was." Like, and that's just what they've been used to and it's just . . .
A: Well, "she was" is right, right? You mean, like, "They was"?
T: "They was."
A: And "we was" and that kinda thing . . .
T: Yeah, "we was." Everything is just "was."
A: [Laughter] . . .

T: And like, just trying to help them to be able to differentiate between what's <u>acceptable</u> . . . There's a lot of "ain't", "they was," "we ain't not . . ."

A: [Laughter] . . .

T: And <u>they can't codeswitch</u> that well . . .

A: Uh-huh . . .

T: Um, and I have to say it's kind of <u>disheartening</u> because like despite <u>*all* that time that's been spent focusing on grammar</u>, like, I don't really see it having helped enormously. Like, if I stop them in class and they're like, you know, "The Europeans, they was really blah-de-blah . . ." and I'd be like, "<u>Oh, they *was?*</u>" And they'd be like, "they were," like they'll correct themselves, but it's not to the point where it's <u>natural</u> . . . They're like, "Why does it matter?"

A: "You knew what I said, right?"

T: Yeah . . . I'm not sure they understand *why* it's necessary . . .

A: Do you have any other ideas about language at the school, like maybe the way the kids speak to themselves versus they way they speak in class, or do you notice . . .

T: Well, I mean, of course, they're not gonna be as <u>free</u> as when they're speaking to each other when they're speaking to me. I mean, I guess the only thing is not so much spoken language as it's like unspoken language, like tone, like a lot of attention is paid to like tone and body language, in terms of <u>respectful attitudes</u> . . . For a lot of kids, they don't see the difference. They're like [loud voice and direct speech] "Yeah, I just asked you to give me my grade. Like, what's the big deal?" And I'm like, "You just ordered me. I mean, you talked to me like that." Like, it's like, [loud again] "You didn't give me a grade!" like that, it's very <u>abrasive</u>, but they don't realize that it's abrasive. And so, I mean, it's just like, I guess, teaching them like the nuances of like when you're talking with people, what's <u>appropriate</u>? Should you be sitting up, or should you be kinda be leaning over [and she leans in her chair] . . .

A: [Laughter] . . .

T: Like that your body language and your facial features like speak just as loudly if not *more* loudly than what you *actually* say . . . I mean, just even bringing awareness to that, like, it's upsetting to them and it's like shocking to them that we'll comment on that, like, <u>maybe their parents let them get away with that and speak to them that way</u> and having to be like, "Hey, you know what, like, maybe your parents let you, but here that's never acceptable." Like, there's just so many – I mean, thinking about it, it's just, it's asking a lot of them to do, not only to speak standard English but to know all these other like smaller nuances that they've never experienced before and never had to think about. Like, it's probably on some level pretty overwhelming to them to have to deal with all of these things at once. Because, I mean, their parents say "they was" . . .

A: Yeah, is there any talk about what they're being expected to do, and what they do ordinarily, in the community, in the home, or anything?

T: Um, I mean, not officially or regularly, but I'll always be like, "I know you might speak this way at home, but in an academic setting, or if you're interviewing for a job, or if you're applying to college, and you talk to someone like that, they will like not even give you the time of day" . . .

A: Do they ever ask why?

T: Yeah, they're just like, you know, "Why?" and I'm like, "I don't know!" [Laughter!] "You know, that's just the way that it is! You have to learn how to play the game guys! I'm sorry."

A: Right, and I can see that being such an inadequate answer for a student who doesn't care about "they was" or "they were," being like, "What's the difference? What's the big deal? Like what's the overall picture?"

T: Right, and I don't know how to provide that . . .

A: Yeah . . .

After two years of ethnographic research as a teacher–researcher at Haven High, and several years of experience as a teacher–researcher in Philadelphia schools, I marvel at how remarkably consistent teachers' ideologies of language are, particularly in response to the language of their Black students. The language of the Black child is consistently viewed as something to eradicate, even by the most well-meaning of teachers. In fact, this particular teacher is genuine about her commitment in seeing as many of her students attend four-year colleges as possible. And when she states, "I have to say it's kind of disheartening because like despite *all* that time that's been spent focusing on grammar, like, I don't really see it having helped enormously," one gets the sense that she is actually disheartened and saddened by her lack of results.

What teachers like this one are probably not aware of is how they are enacting whiteness and subscribing to an ideology of linguistic supremacy within a system of daily cultural combat. It is revealing that the teacher describes the language of her Black students as the thing that teachers at Haven High "*combat* the most." In fact, her attempt to eradicate the language pattern of her Black students has been "one of the *few* goals" she has had throughout that academic year. The teacher not only works to eradicate the language pattern of her Black students, but responds negatively to what she calls "unspoken language," or the students' "tone." Black students and their ways of speaking are described with adjectives like "abrasive" and not "respectful." This attribution of negative characteristics due to cultural differences has been noted frequently in studies of intercultural communication (Gumperz 1982a, 1982b).

Interestingly, the teacher notes her students' failure to speak "standard English" – particularly in the case of what's known as the generalization of *was* to use with plural and second person subjects (Wolfram 1993) – while she fails to make several linguistic distinctions herself (her own language being only marginally "standard"). Not only does the teacher erroneously point out "he was" and "she was" as cases of BL (this is actually WME) and imply that BL has a random system of negation ("we ain't not" is actually not found in BL or any other language variety in the US), but she is clearly not aware of the stylistic sensitivity in the use of *was* and *were*. When the teacher says, rather exasperatedly, "Everything is just 'was'," she is not recognizing the subtle stylistic alternation of *was* and *were* that is employed by BL speakers, where speakers alternate their use of *was* and *were* based upon various contextual and situation factors, including the race of the person with whom they are speaking. In fact, the teacher goes as far as to say that her Black students do not have the ability to "codeswitch." Somehow, despite the vitality of BL, teachers continue hearing what's not said and missing what is (see Piestrup 1973 and Smitherman 1981).

We will return to the teacher's comments at the end of this chapter, but for now we take up her claim that her Black students do not possess stylistic sensitivity in speech (what she calls "codeswitching," and I will call "styleshifting"). The next section reveals how Black youth shift their speech style when speaking with Whites and Blacks, and the following section reports on misunderstood Black linguistic practices and the resulting conflicts with Whites. These sections report on findings from a larger ethnographic and sociolinguistic study of styleshifting in Sunnyside (Alim 2004a).

12.4   Black Stylistic Flexibility

Contrary to the teacher's comments that her Black students could not styleshift – that is, shift their speech style according to various contextual and situational factors – sociolinguistic research at Haven High reveals that Black youth possess a wide range of linguistic styles. Following Labov's (1969) research on Black teenagers in New York City, Baugh's (1979, 1983) research on the styleshifting of Black adults in LA and other urban centers, and Rickford and McNair-Knox's (1994) reporting of the styleshifting of one 18-year-old Black female, I designed a sociolinguistic study of style to determine what factors influenced that speech style of Black youth. Focusing on the impact of the interlocutor's identity characteristics, I recorded conversations between youth in Haven High (Sunnysidaz) and unfamiliar interlocutors from a university (Stanfordians). In this study, I asked the question: How do Black youth vary their speech style based on the race, gender and level of Hip Hop cultural knowledge of their interlocutors? Figure 12.1 presents a grid that identifies the characteristics of the participating interlocutors.

The grid shows that there are only two types of Sunnysidaz, Black Male Hip Hoppers and Black Female Hip Hoppers. It also shows that the Stanfordians vary in terms of race, gender and Hip Hop cultural knowledge. Within these three factor groups, there are two factors each, allowing for eight different types of Stanfordians ($2^3 = 8$ possible combinations). So, each type of Sunnysida speaks to eight different Stanfordians,

			Stanfordians		
			Race	Gender	Hip Hop
Sunnysidaz		Black Male Hip Hopper	Black/White	Male/Female	Hip Hop/ No Hip Hop
		Black Female Hip Hopper	Black/White	Male/Female	Hip Hop/ No Hip Hop

Figure 12.1   Interlocutor characteristics of Sunnysidaz and Stanfordians.

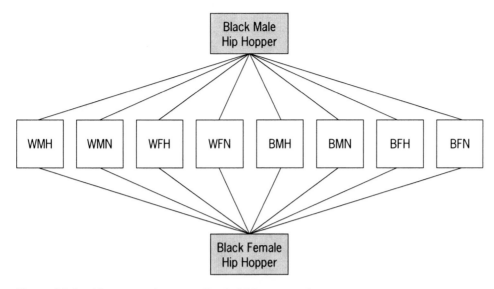

Figure 12.2   16 conversation types. Total of 32 conversations.

making for 16 conversation types as shown in figure 12.2. So, the total corpus for this portion of the study consisted of 4 Sunnysidaz – two Black Male Hip Hoppers and two Black Female Hip Hoppers – and eight Stanfordians for a total of 32 conversations (4 Sunnysidaz × 8 Stanfordians = 32 conversations).

The 32 conversations averaged 40 minutes per interview for a total of approximately 1280 minutes of talk, or over 21 hours. All transcripts were transcribed verbatim, resulting in approximately 1300 pages. In addition to these 32 conversations, I have recorded the speakers' peer, in-group talk, which will serve as an additional point of comparison.

All three identity characteristics proved to be significant factors in the styleshifting of Black youth in Sunnyside. One student, for example, shows a remarkable range of stylistic flexibility. Figure 12.3 shows Bilal's varying rates of copula absence across each Stanfordian interlocutor and for his peer group.

In this remarkable case of styleshifting, Bilal displays an *extremely* broad stylistic range of copula absence. He goes from exhibiting 0% absence when talking with the WFN Stanfordian to 88.37% absence in his peer group! (Δ 88.37%).

12.5 Black Linguistic Practices

Not only do Black youth possess and deploy a variety of sociolinguistic styles, but there are numerous Black linguistic practices that are misunderstood and misinterpreted in White public space. As part of my experience as a teacher–researcher in Sunnyside, I trained students to become "hiphopographers" – that is, ethnographers of Hip Hop Culture and communication. As such, they were responsible for documenting and describing the linguistic practices of the most recent instantiation of Black American expressive culture, i.e., Hip Hop Culture. Several examples of linguistic practices that they described

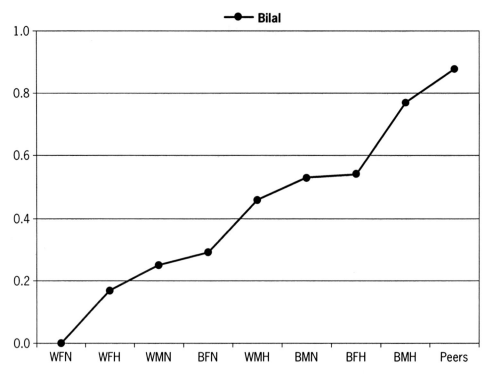

Figure 12.3   Frequencies of copula absence for Bilal across eight Stanfordian interlocutors and his peer group.

follow. Terms in upper case indicate other practices and lexical items also described by the class. The first practice is *battlin*, a form of Black verbal dueling associated with Hip Hop Culture and the verbal art of rhyming (Spady, Lee and Alim 1999). The second is *hush mode* and *scratch that green off yo neck*, two phrases associated mostly closely with Black female interaction, argumentation and play. Both of these entries highlight the value placed on verbal creativity and competition in the Black speech community. The third is *rogue*, a localized example of semantic inversion (where the negative meaning prescribed by the dominating group is flipped on its head) used *only* within the 2.5 square miles of Sunnyside. All of the examples below are taken from student writing that is part of a larger project where students describe and document their own linguistic practices.

BATTLIN (noun) (verb) and FLOW (noun) (verb)
   Battlin involves more than one person. A **FREESTYLE** rapping contest when a group of people take turns rapping lyrics. They don't write the lyrics; they say them as they think of them off the top of their heads. As they take turns rapping back and forth, they're actually competing. In the end, the judges or the people watching the competition vote who won the competition and who had the better lyrics. Sometimes it is just obvious to the contenders who won by who **DISSED/CLOWNED** the other better.
   *Also judged by who had the better meaning behind his/her words.

Example: JT and T-Reezy were battlin in the grass last week; they got on each other. JT got on T-Reezy's braids and face and T-Reezy got on JT about his height and women/girls.

The term comes from the idea of fighting with words. A battle is set up like a fight. One contender takes one side and the other takes the other. They rap at each other (in turn, though) until one <u>gives up</u> or a specific winner is announced. Usually done by males – those who tend to be street-affiliated. Males talk about guns, women and **SETS** (areas of affiliation) and other topics. Done at clubs, social events, on street corners, etc. Takes the place of actual fights at parties where people **FLOW** – to have a smooth current of rap lyrics. If a person messes up their rap lyrics while saying them, then they ain't flowin. Flowin does not necessarily have to rhyme, as long as your words go good together.

HUSH MODE and SCRATCH THAT GREEN OFF YO NECK (phrase)

Hush mode is when you get **CLOWNED** (to get talked about rudely) and not have a remark or comeback for that person. To be dumbfounded. Usually used when instigating or talking about a fight or argument.

Example 1:
Aisha: Shut up, Tee!
Tee: [doesn't say anything]
Tereese: She got you on hush mode!

When somebody get **CAPPED ON**, and that person don't have anything to come back with, then the person who capped on them would say, "I got you on hush mode."

Example 2:
For example, say Shahira and Bibi are capping on each other and Shahira says to Bibi, "Yo mamma so old she used to gang bang with the Hebrews." If Bibi can't come back with something, then Shahira would say to her, "I got you on hush mode."

While we were defining the word, Jamal got on Tereese nerves and she said she was gon hit him . . .

Example 3:
Tereese: I'mma bust you in yo mouth.
Jamal: [silent]
Aisha: Oooh, Jamal, she got you on hush mode.
Jamal: She ain't got me on hush mode.
Tereese: I'mma hit you in yo mouth.
Jamal: **I WISH YOU WOULD**.

Females use this phrase a lot because they tend to instigate more than males. Males sometimes use it when they want to start something. Someone might tell you to "scratch that green off yo neck" after you been hush moded. Not sure of the origin of this phrase, but it's used after someone has been proven wrong.

Example 4:
For example, say two people are arguing and one of them got proven wrong, then someone would say to them, "Oooh, scratch that green off yo neck."

ROGUE (noun)

A word that people use as a substitute for another person's name. Originated in Sunnyside, California and mainly used in Sunnyside. JT uses it a lot to say hi to people. "What's up rogue?"

Example 1: Waz up rogue?
Example 2: Dang, rogue, what you doing?!

Males use it more, but females do often use it. Used by all races in Sunnyside. Used mainly with the younger generation.

Example 3: Aisha was **CONVERSATIN** with Shahira on the phone and at the end she said, "alright, rogue." Then her mom asked her why they call each other rogue.

(from students' writings)

All of these linguistic practices can be misunderstood by Whites not familiar with Black culture and language. For example, while Black youth place extreme value on the verbal inventiveness and competition involved in battlin, teachers broke up the biggest rhyme battle in the school because, as one student relayed, "Whenever they see a group of Black folks they automatically think it's a fight!" One teacher described the event in these words, "Whatever they were doing, it wasn't appropriate on school grounds." If Whites were more aware of the verbal creativity of Black youth and their penchant for verbal games, perhaps their linguistic practices would not be so misunderstood. Rather, they would be utilized for pedagogical purposes. As Labov (1972: 212–13) wrote plainly decades ago:

> The view of the black speech community which we obtain from our work in the ghetto areas is precisely the opposite from that reported by Deutsch or by Bereiter and Englemann [verbal deprivation]. We see a child bathed in verbal stimulation from morning to night. We see many speech events that depend on the competitive exhibition of verbal skills – sounding, singing, toasts, rifting, louding [and battlin] – a whole range of activities in which the individual gains status through his use of language. We see the younger child trying to acquire these skills from older children, hanging around on the outskirts of older peer groups, and imitating this behavior to the best of his ability. We see no connection between verbal skill in the speech events characteristic of the street culture and success in the schoolroom.

The incident above is not merely a matter of communicative misunderstanding. An issue that is often not taken up by studies of intercultural communication, but is certainly central to them, is the fact that Black verbal competition was interpreted as *violence*. This interpretation must be understood in relation to the White racist view of Blacks as violent, despite the fact that it is Whites who commit most of the violent crimes in American society. This misunderstanding is particularly poignant when the students' definition of *battlin* includes the notion that it often "takes the place of actual fights at parties."

Several questions for studies of Black–White intercultural communication remain: Why is it that, despite ample evidence from sociolinguistic studies and theory that different speech communities possess different, yet theoretically equivalent, linguistic rules and rules of language use, BL and linguistic practices continue to be denigrated and under-appreciated by Whites, particularly in educational institutions? What is at the *root* of this denigration and misinterpretation? How is it that the ideology and practice of *linguistic supremacy* – the unsubstantiated notion that White linguistic norms are inherently superior to the linguistic norms of other communities, and the practice of mapping White norms onto "the language of school," "the language of economic mobility," and "the language of success" – persists, even *within* the subjugated group? What is the role of communicative misunderstanding in maintaining and perpetuating tensions between communities? How do we understand communicative differences not as the source of tensions but as a means of perpetuating and reinforcing those tensions? How do we move beyond searching for communicative mismatches to explain intercultural tensions and conflicts that already exist due to the larger and systematic social, political and economic subjugation of a group? Or worse yet, as we see in Eades (this volume, chapter 20), will greater knowledge of communicative differences be used *for* or *against* justice? As overt forms of racism begin to be publicly sanctioned in most areas of the US, linguistic differences are currently being used to exclude Blacks from full participation in society in a number of ways (see Baugh 2003 on *linguistic profiling* in housing discrimination based on "Black-sounding" voices, and Bertrand and Mullainathan 2003 on differential access to employment based on "Black-sounding" names). Studies of intercultural communication need to address these questions if the field is to remain relevant to dominated populations. Such studies are essential since the problem with BL has more to do with Black *people* than Black *language*. Given the emerging studies addressing the role of BL in various forms of discrimination, more scholars are beginning to see the BL "problem" as one that is part and parcel of a socio-structural system of White racism in the US.

For this population of Black youth, how do we avoid explanations of Black academic failure as the result of Black "opposition" to formal schooling and begin interrogating the daily cultural combat (conscious or unconscious) against Black language and culture in White public space? How do we go beyond the oft-heard and inadequate teachers' response to Black resistance to White cultural and linguistic norming: "I don't know!" [Laughter!] "You know, that's just the way that it is! You have to learn how to play the game guys! I'm sorry"? Responses of this type are enactments of whiteness that put the onus on the oppressed group at the same time as they alleviate the dominating group of any responsibility. In this case, when pushed, the teacher is willing to admit that she is not equipped to provide an answer for the underlying reasons of what I have called the gentrification of BL – this is a start. The continued gentrification of BL is the cultural analogy to the physical removal of Black communities by White developers. As one of my students so passionately expressed her resistance to the gentrification of the community in which she was born and raised, "I mean, that's takin part of our heritage outta there, cuz I mean, we, we, that's where people was *raised* and stuff! [She pauses for a brief second, glaring over the freeway ramp, and adds] . . . and now the hotels."

While Blacks around the nation continue to be removed from their communities, BL persists despite every attempt by Whites to eradicate it. The community continues to resist these efforts to "renew" its language for reasons so clearly articulated by Black writers and artists.

The language, only the language . . . It is the thing that black people love so much – the saying of words, holding them on the tongue, experimenting with them, playing with them. It's a love, a passion. Its function is like a preacher's: to make you stand up out of your seat, make you lose yourself and hear yourself. The worst of all possible things that could happen would be to lose that language . . . It's terrible to think that a child with five different present tenses comes to school to be faced with books that are less than his own language. And then to be told things about his language, which is him, that are sometimes permanently damaging . . . This is a really cruel fallout of racism. (Toni Morrison (1981))

A Black teacher in Philadelphia provides a different perspective: "The reason why Black students continue to speak their language is because, really, if you think about it, it's the *one thing* that they own in this world. It's the one thing that *noooobody* can take away from them. NO–body."

12.6   Conclusion: Facing and Fighting the Challenge

By this point, if the responses to my teacher workshops are any indication, there are probably many of you that are asking: "What are you saying, Alim – are you proposing that teachers should *not* teach 'standard English'"? Here's what I'm proposing. First and foremost, we must begin with an understanding that there is nothing *standard* about "standard English." Standard simply means that this is the language variety that those in authority have constructed as the variety needed to gain access to resources. What we have, then, for a "standard" in the US is nothing short of the imposition of White linguistic norms and ways of speaking in the service of granting access to resources to Whites and denying those same resources to as many others as possible, including poor Whites (*linguistic supremacy* goes for *varieties* of a language as well as languages other than the dominating language, whatever that may be).

Secondly, I take the statement that I've heard from so many teachers, linguists, and scholars – "Well, fair or unfair, that's just the way the world works" – as a *starting* point for the discussion that we need to be having, not as an *end* point. This is truly where philosophical interrogation begins. Rather than agreeing, for one reason or another, that we *have* to provide "these students" with "standard English," I ask: By what processes are we all involved in the construction and maintenance of the notion of a "standard" language, and further, that the "standard" is somehow better, more intelligent, more appropriate, more important, etc., than other varieties? In other words, how, when and why are we all implicated in *linguistic supremacy*?

Thirdly, many well-meaning teachers and scholars who insist on the teaching of "standard English" to Black youth are under the assumption that BL is a monostyle, i.e., that BL can be described as one style of speaking that is identifiably Black. As these data have shown, Black youth possess a broad range of speech styles (review Bilal's stylistic flexibility when talking with a White female non-Hip Hopper and in his peer group, for example). It makes more sense, that is, it is more in line with the data on Black stylistic variation, to consider BL as the whole range of styles within speakers' linguistic repertoires. Part of speaking BL is possessing the ability to styleshift in and out of in–group ways of speaking. This is not astonishing. But somehow, when it comes to Black youth, some are under the impression that they are mired in this monostylistic linguistic ghetto (this is certainly a contemporary strain of linguistic depravation thinking). But the ghetto is a beautiful thang – that is, speakers such as Bilal, who have had a full range of experiences as Black youth, naturally (and quite obviously) vary their speech styles in different situations and contexts. Any time spent in Black communities would reveal that Bilal speaks to his Minister in the Nation of Islam mosque in one way, to his White teachers in another, to his grandmother in another, to his girlfriend, father, brothas on the block in yet another. And certainly, since he's forced to look for employment outside of his community, as a sporting goods store employee he will speak to White customers and non-English speaking customers in yet another style. And why should we expect him not to? The question is: If the Black speech community possesses a range of styles that are suitable for all of its communicative needs, then why the coercion and imposition of White styles?

Lastly, while it may be true that many Blacks would resist a pedagogical approach that did *not* focus on "standard English," it is *also* true that there are many Blacks who view access to White ways of speaking as part of "playing the game" (Urrieta 2004). That is, as one of my informants put it, "If you livin in the White man's world, you gotta play by the White man's rules. At least as long as *they* runnin shit." As is often the case, subjugated populations develop survival strategies that seem antithetical to linguistic emancipation. This does not mean that it is futile to attempt to develop ways to eradicate *linguistic supremacy*. It means that scholars dedicated to *linguistic equanimity* – the structural and social equality of languages – have to work equally hard among the oppressors and the oppressed. This is the challenge – and it is one worth taking up.

Note

I thank Christina Paulston for her critical reading and editing and for the lively intellectual exchanges that most certainly produced a better chapter. I also thank Ray McDermott, Geneva Smitherman, John Baugh, Donielle Prince (Dee) and Luis Urrieta, Jr., for their encouragement, insights, and readings of early drafts of this work. This paper was first presented at the annual meeting of the American Educational Research Association 2003 in Chicago on a panel with Angela Rickford, John Rickford, Sonja Lanehart, and Arnetha Ball, all of whom were helpful. The research reported in this paper was supported by a Spencer Foundation grant. Much love to the Sunnysidaz.

References

Abrahams, Roger. 1964. *Deep Down in the Jungle: Negro Narrative Folklore from the Streets of Philadelphia*. Chicago: Aldine Publishing Co.

Abrahams, Roger. 1970. Rapping and capping: Black talk as art. In John Swzed (ed.), *In Black America*. New York: Basic Books.

Alim, H. Samy. 2004a. You know my steez: An ethnographic and sociolinguistic study of styleshifting in a Black American speech community. Publications of the American Dialect Society No. 89. Durham, NC: Duke University Press.

Alim, H. Samy. 2004b. Hip Hop Nation Language. In Edward Finegan and John Rickford (eds.), *Language in the USA: Perspectives for the 21st Century*. Cambridge: Cambridge University Press.

Alim, H. Samy. 2004c. Nation language in the African diaspora: Language use in contemporary African American expressive culture. In Arthur Spears (ed.), *Black Languages in the US and the Caribbean: Structure, History, Use and Education*.

Anderson, Monica. 1994. *Black English Vernacular (From "Ain't" to "Yo Mama": the Words Politically Correct Americans Should Know)*. Highland City, FL: Rainbow Books.

Bahloul, Maher. 1993. The copula in Modern Standard Arabic. In Mushira Eid and Clive Holes (eds.), *Perspectives on Arabic Linguistics V: Papers from the fifth annual symposium on Arabic linguistics*. Amsterdam, The Netherlands: John Benjamins, 209–29.

Baugh, John. 1979. Linguistic style-shifting in Black English. PhD dissertation, University of Pennsylvania.

Baugh, John. 1983. *Black Street Speech: Its History, Structure, and Survival*. Austin, Texas: University of Texas Press.

Baugh, John. 2003. Linguistic profiling. In S. Makoni, G. Smitherman, F. Ball and A. Spears (eds.), *Black Linguistics: Language, Politics and Society in Africa and the Americas*. London: Routledge.

Bertrand, Marianne and Sendhil Mullainathan. 2003. Are Emily and Greg more employable than Lakisha and Jamal? A field experiment on labor market discrimination. NBER Working Paper No. 9873.

Brown, H. Rap. 1972. Street talk. In Thomas Kochman (ed.), *Rappin' and Stylin' Out: Communication in Urban Black America*. Urbana, IL: University of Illinois Press, 203–8.

Daniel, Jack and Geneva Smitherman. 1976. How I got over: Communication dynamics in the Black community. *Quarterly Journal of Speech* 62, February.

Dillard, J. L. 1977. *Lexicon of Black English*. New York: Seabury.

Fasold, Ralph W. 1972. *Tense Marking in Black English: A Linguistic and Social Analysis*, Washington, DC: Center for Applied Linguistics.

Folb, Edith. 1980. *Runnin' Down Some Lines: the Language and Culture of Black Teenagers*. Cambridge, MA: Harvard University Press.

Frankenberg, Ruth. 1993. *White Women, Race Matters: The Social Construction of Whiteness*. Minneapolis: University of Minnesota Press.

Goffman, Erving. 1967. *Interaction Ritual: Essays in Face to Face Behavior*. Garden City, NY: Doubleday.

Gumperz, John. 1982a. *Discourse Strategies*. Cambridge: Cambridge University Press.

Gumperz, John. 1982b. *Language and Social Identity*. Cambridge: Cambridge University Press.

Hill, Jane. 1998. Language, race, and White public space. *American Anthropologist* 100(3), 680–9.

Holloway, Joseph and W. Vass. 1997. *The African Heritage of American English*. Bloomington: University of Indiana Press.

Hussein, Anwar A. 1995. The sociolinguistic patterns of native Arabic speakers: Implications for teaching Arabic as a foreign language. *Applied Language Learning* 6(1–2), 65–87.

Keyes, Cheryl. 1984. Verbal art performance in rap music: The conversation of the 80's. *Folklore Forum* 17(2), Fall, 143–52.

Kochman, Thomas. 1969. 'Rapping' in the Black ghetto. *Trans-Action*, February, 26–34.

Kochman, Thomas. 1981. *Black and White Styles in Conflict*. Chicago: University of Chicago Press.

Labov, William. 1969. Contraction, deletion, and inherent variability of the English copula. *Language* 45, 715–62.

Labov, William. 1972. *Language in the Inner City: Studies in the Black English Vernacular*. Philadelphia: University of Pennsylvania Press.

Lippi-Green, Rosina. 1997. *English with an Accent: Language, Ideology and Discrimination in the United States*. London and New York: Routledge.

Major, Clarence. 1970 [1994]. *Juba to Jive: A Dictionary of African-American Slang*. New York and London: Penguin.

Massey, Douglas and Nancy Denton. 1993. *American Apartheid: Segregation and the Making of the Underclass*. Cambridge, MA: Harvard University Press.

Mitchell-Kernan, Claudia. 1971. *Language Behavior in a Black Urban Community*. University of California, Berkeley: Language Behavior Research Laboratory.

Mitchell-Kernan, Claudia. 1972. Signifying and marking: Two Afro-American speech acts. In John J. Gumperz and Dell Hymes (eds.), *Directions in Sociolinguistics*. New York: Holt, Rinehart & Winston.

Morgan, Marcyliena. 1994. The African American speech community: Reality and sociolinguistics. In Marcyliena Morgan (ed.), *Language and the Social Construction of Identity in Creole Situations*, 121–48. Los Angeles: Center for Afro-American Studies, UCLA.

Morgan, Marcyliena. 1996. Conversational signifying: Grammar and indirectness among African American women. In E. Ochs, E. Schegloff and S. Thompson (eds.), *Grammar and Interaction*. Cambridge: Cambridge University Press.

Morgan, Marcyliena. 1998. More than a mood or an attitude: Discourse and verbal genres in African-American culture. In S. Mufwene, J. Rickford, G. Bailey and J. Baugh (eds.), *African American English: Structure, History, and Usage*. New York: Routledge, 251–81.

Morgan, Marcyliena. 2002. *Language, Discourse and Power in African American Culture*. Cambridge: Cambridge University Press.

Morrison, Toni. 1981. Interview with Thomas LeClair in *The New Republic*, March 21st, 1981, 25–9, cited in John Rickford and Russell Rickford, 2000. *Spoken Soul: The Story of Black English*. New York: John Wiley & Sons, Inc.

Newman, Michael. 2001. "Not dogmatically/It's all about me": Ideological conflict in a high school rap crew. *Taboo: A Journal of Culture and Education*.

Norfleet, Dawn. 1997. Hip-hop culture in New York City: the role of verbal music performance in defining a community. PhD dissertation, Columbia University, New York.

Page, Helan E. and Brooke Thomas. 1994. White public space and the construction of White privilege in U.S. Health Care: Fresh concepts and a new model of analysis. *Medical Anthropology Quarterly* 8, 109–16.

Piestrup, Ann McCormick. 1973. Black Dialect interference and accommodation of reading instruction in first grade. University of California, Berkeley: Monographs of the Language Behavior Research Laboratory, 4.

Rickford, John. 1999. *African American Vernacular English: Features and Use, Evolution, and Educational Implications*. Oxford: Blackwell.

Rickford, John and Faye McKnair-Knox. 1994. Addressee- and topic-influenced style shift: A quantitative sociolinguistic study. In Douglas Biber and Edward Finegan (eds.), *Sociolinguistic Perspectives on Register*, 235–76. Oxford: Oxford University Press.

Sells, Peter, John Rickford, and Thomas Wasow. 1996. Negative inversion in African American Vernacular English. *Natural Language and Linguistic Theory* 14(3), 591–627.

Smitherman, Geneva. 1973. The power of the rap: The Black idiom and the new Black poetry. *Twentieth Century Literature: A Scholarly and Critical Journal* 19: 259–74.

Smitherman, Geneva. 1977 [1986]. *Talkin and Testifyin: the Language of Black America*. Houghton Mifflin; reissued, with revisions, Detroit: Wayne State University Press.

Smitherman, Geneva. 1981. *Black English and the Education of Black Children and Youth: Proceedings of the National Invitational Symposium on the King Decision*. Detroit: Wayne State University, Center for Black Studies.

Smitherman, Geneva. 1994 [2000]. *Black Talk: Words and Phrases from the Hood to the Amen Corner*. Boston and New York: Houghton Mifflin.

Spady, James, Charles Lee, and H. Samy Alim. 1999. *Street Conscious Rap*. Philadelphia: Black History Museum/Umum Loh Publishers.

Spears, Arthur. 1998. African-American language use: Ideology and so-called obscenity. In S. Mufwene, J. Rickford, G. Bailey and J. Baugh (eds.), *African American English: Structure, History, and Usage*. New York: Routledge, 226–50.

Spears, Arthur. 2000. Stressed *Stay*: A new African-American English aspect marker. Paper presented at the Linguistic Society of America Convention, Washington, D.C., January.

Stavsky, Lois, Isaac Mozeson and Dani R. Mozeson. 1995. *A 2 Z: The Book of Rap and Hip-Hop Slang*. New York: Boulevard Books.

Turner, Lorenzo. 1949. *Africanisms in the Gullah Dialect*. Chicago: The University of Chicago Press.

Urrieta, Luis, Jr. 2004. "Performing success" and "successful performances": Chicanas and Chicanos "playing the game" or "selling-out" in education. In B. K. Alexander, G. Anderson and B. Gallegos (eds.), *Performance in Education: Teaching, Reform, and Identities as Social Performance*. Mahwah, NJ: Lawrence Erlbaum Associates.

Wolfram, Walt. 1974. The relationship of white southern speech to Vernacular Black English. *Language* 50, 498–527.

Wolfram, Walt. 1993. A proactive role for speech–language pathologists in sociolinguistic education. *Language, Speech and Hearing Service in Schools* 24, 181–5.

Yancy, George. 2000. Feminism and the subtext of whiteness: Black women's experiences as a site of identity formation and contestation of whiteness. *The Western Journal of Black Studies* 24(3), 155–65.

13

Pronouns of Address in Swedish: Social Class Semantics and a Changing System

Christina Bratt Paulston

13.1 Introduction

The purpose of this chapter is to describe the forms of address in Swedish and the patterning of their usage. When I stated this purpose of my fieldwork in Sweden, a very common reaction was *Det kan du aldrig göra*, 'you'll never do it, it can't be done'. The Swedish address system is in rapid change, and, although Swedes have found difficulties in their address system for the last hundred years, they are sensitive now more than ever to seeming lack of generally accepted rules of usage. Indeed, for some type of encounters the rules are so vague that people may report (I noticed it in my own usage as well) that choice of a particular form of address simply depended on one's mood that day, whether one is feeling cheerful or cranky. Nevertheless, there exists considerably more order than Swedes at present give themselves and their language credit for. This paper is an attempt to delineate that order.

In Sweden, the Social Democratic party has been in power off and on since 1932 and through its programs for social, economic, and educational reforms has consistently stressed egalitarian relations among all members of society. [. . .] Politically induced social structural change does not necessarily result in a change in the cultural value system. Söderberg (1972), a social historian, posits the change in address forms as an indicator of social change with concomitant cultural change. Sweden still remains a country highly stratified in terms of social class but her cultural values are changing and some of the friction between speakers and confusion about usage which stem from the address system can best be understood in terms of the lag between slow cultural change in the wake of rapid social change. The viewpoint from which this paper is written is that linguistic description of the Swedish address system is not possible unless one takes into account the social and historical factors of the society.

[. . .]

Christina Bratt Paulston, abridged version of "Pronouns of address in Swedish: Social class semantics and a changing system" in *Language in Society* 5 (1976), pp. 359–60, 362–75, 377–86. © by Cambridge University Press, reproduced with permission.

13.2   The Forms of Address

13.2.1   Background

Swedish possesses two second person singular pronouns of address, with the typical distinction in European languages between the familiar, *du*, and the formal, *ni*. Because of a reluctance in the past by many Swedes to use *ni*, Swedish also has several other forms of address. [. . .]

1.	Vad vill du ha?	'What do you want?' (familiar form)
2.	Vad vill ni ha?	'What do you want?' (formal form)
3.	Vad vill hon ha?	'What do you want?' (third person singular feminine)
4.	Vad vill Christina ha?	'What does Christina want?' (in direct address)

5. Vad vill {fru Paulston / Professor / Paulston} ha? 'What does {Mrs Paulston / Professor / Paulston} want?'

6.	Vad vill fröken ha?	'What does the Miss want?' (to female stranger, married or unmarried, a status one can only guess at from the presence or absence of a wedding band)
7.	Vad vill frun ha?	'What does the Mrs want?' (only from sales madam in the market place, to female stranger, married or unmarried)
8.	Vad vill professorn ha?	'What does the professor want?'
9.	Vad vill man ha?	'What does one want?'
10.	Vad vill vi ha?	'What do we want?'
11.	Vad får det vara?	'What may it be?'
12.	Vad behagas (det)?	'What is pleased?'
13.	Vad skulle det vara för någonting?	'What would it be?'

To this list should be added one more form: Vad vill du ha, fröken Lundgren? This curious usage of informal *du* plus formal title + last name (TLN) is the mode of addressal between clerks (otherwise on first name terms) in better shops in the presence of a customer. The existence of this usage is frequently denied by Swedes but it occurs in my data both as self-report and in my own observations.

There are strict co-occurrence rules (Ervin-Tripp 1973) of the pronouns with the type of fillers which can occupy the frames in which the pronouns occur. *Du* typically co-occurs with name, usually first name (FN), nickname (NN) or kinship title (KT) but occasionally with last name (LN). *Du* may also occur with no name (Ø). It normally never occurs with T(LN), and hence the discredence of *du* + fröken Lundgren. TØ or TLN co-occurs with *ni* or is used in third person address. The reverse is not true; *ni* may in regional usage co-occur with kinship title (KT), actual or honorary. *Hon* can co-occur with either (T)LN or FN; its use is rural and disappearing. Although I can remember being so addressed in my youth and there are frequent references to this usage in the archive data (Nordiska Museet 1969), there is not one incidence of it in my Stockholm data.

All forms in 3 through 13 in the list above represent a relationship between speakers where *du* is not appropriate, i.e. where an expression of 'condescension or intimacy' in Brown and Gilman's terms (1960) is not called for. These forms also represent a way of avoiding the use of *ni*, an avoidance of which Swedes are very conscious. [. . .]

The major argument of this chapter is that one can describe the Swedish address system adequately only if one recognizes that the social classes have different rules of use due to different 'semantics'[1] for the pronouns *du* and *ni*. This difference, I believe, can primarily be accounted for by the historical development of the language and by political ideology. The corollary to that argument is that such different rule systems within a single speech community cannot be discovered, understood or described by analyzing only the single pronominal forms. Beyond (non-)reciprocity (Brown & Gilman 1960) and dispensation rights (Ervin-Tripp 1973), one needs to consider *inter alia* co-variance of address forms, change of options and the direction of such change, initiation procedures, external versus internal systems of address, but most specifically the particular frames or formulae within which the pronouns occur (Hymes 1974), i.e. with the non-pronominal forms of address with which they do or, just as importantly, do not co-occur. When Swedes discuss their address system, they typically talk about *du*, in and of itself, without looking at the other factors, and this practice is a contributing factor to the confusion and feeling that no rules exist.

13.2.2   Historical background

Old Swedish had only one singular pronoun of address *du*, used to friend and stranger alike. In the 1600s, under influence of usage at the Byzantine court says Wellander (1952: 1; cf. Brown & Gilman 1960), the plural pronoun *I* came to be used in address to a single person. This pronoun *I* developed into *ni* from the plural suffix *n* of the preceding verb as in *haven I* 'do you have'. During the 1700s the Swedish elite was under strong French influence, and the *du/ni* dichotomy seems to have developed in the upper classes then under influence of French *tu* and *vous*.

The lower classes, especially the peasant class (Sweden remained a primarily rural society much longer than continental Europe) did not adopt this usage but maintained *du* as the mutual form of address to both known and unknown of their equals. To their superiors they used titles which proliferated *ad absurdum*. Americans are familiar with the euphemism of maintenance engineer for janitor but in Sweden such titles were used seriously in direct address; *Herr Mattnedläggaren* 'Mr Rug-installer' and *Herr Tågbefälhavaren* 'Mr Train-commander' occur from the 1930s in my archive data.

It would give a wrong impression to imply that there was no social stratification within the peasant class. At the turn of the century on the large estates, the womenfolk carefully observed social niceties. Informant KU 2525[2] writes 'At the coffee clatches (by and for the wives of the peasants who worked the estate) the wife of the head gardener was to serve herself first, next the wife of the smith, followed by the coachman's wife.' They did not use *du* to each other but *hon*.

The guilds too were careful to maintain the social distance created by skill and age, and apprentice learners were specifically forbidden the use of *du* to their superior fellow workers.

But among full-fledged workers and ordinary peasants *du* was the common form of address, and this peasant *du* survived within the labor class and became a hallmark of membership in the Social Democratic party (many informants say they would address the Prime Minister as *du* because he is a fellow social democrat) and the unions. Its semantic now is that of solidarity.

Because of the idiocy and cumbersomeness of the titles there have been repeated attempts at address reforms during the last hundred years. The first attempts were in the latter part of the 1800s and well in advance of any political ideological change; indeed, members of the royalty were among the co-signers of the public declarations. This movement was referred to as *ni-reformen* and advocated the use of *ni* instead of titles in third person. It failed.

There were further attempts throughout the first half of the twentieth century. Schools and hospitals carried signs which said 'Here we say *ni*'. Many informants comment on a doctor or dentist below such a sign who addressed the nurse as *syster* 'sister, nurse' in third person. I have no evidence which establishes a causal relationship between these reforms and today's practice where the younger generations do not hesitate to use *ni*. But when a people which has over a hundred years been intermittently exposed to editorials and articles in the press on the virtue of *ni* with no result finally changes its address behavior it makes more sense to look for other causes than the repeatedly ineffectual *ni*-reforms. Whatever other purpose the *ni*-reforms served, they certainly helped to make Swedes conscious of their address system and aware that it often was awkward.

The change toward increased *ni*-usage is becoming obscured by what most accurately can only be described as the *du*-landslide. *Alla säger du nu för tiden* 'all and everyone says du nowadays' was the common rejoinder when people heard I was studying the address forms. Although this is far from true, it is a very frequently stated belief, especially among older members of the upper class with whose own usage the increased use of *du* contrasts most sharply.

'*Du* was and is the form of address among the workers' writes a retired railroad worker (KU 2768) who clearly sees the relationship between *du* and the social democratic movement. But in addition to the leftist political parties, organizations such as Red Cross and the Home Guard with its auxiliaries institutionalized the use of *du* among its members. It is easy to imagine the sense of emergency such organizations must have experienced during the two World Wars. Sweden managed to remain neutral, and the correlation between state of emergency and the T-form is well documented (Brown & Gilman, 1960; Friedrich, 1972; Jonz, 1975). Many informants comment on the formative effect of such experiences.

There certainly was opposition to the use of *du*. Informant KU 2604 writes of the angry speech the rector of his school addressed to the students in 1915 on the 'demoralizing tendencies in an evil time'. The students, age 16–30, had suggested they be allowed to address each other with *du*.

The earliest attempt at a *du*-reform in the private sector I have come across took place in the early fifties in a department of the Swedish Employers Association. That the director and the janitor were on *du*-terms (+LN) was considered sufficiently newsworthy to be written up in the public press. In those days, however, the janitor delicately changed to Director X in third person in the presence of others outside the department. Not so today. The 1960s saw widespread institutionalized *du*-reform, at first in the public institutions like hospitals and universities. Stockholms Spårvägar (public transportation, later Storstockholms Lokaltrafik) 1965–72 carried through a *du*-reform, and my informants directly related this change to membership by management in the Social Democratic party. Around 1968, the public schools began to follow suit, with the vocational schools beginning the trend.

The private sector is also changing and all factories with which I am familiar have instituted a general use of reciprocal *du* from management to lowest worker. Management's motivation, however, is not the same as that underlying the Social Democratic party. Big business finds it more effective to be on *du* terms with its workers. A case will illustrate. One of the companies whose factory I visited had been in the red five years previously due to faulty management. One of the problems had been poor relations with the union, which had been forced into *underdànig ställning*, 'subservient obeisant posture'. The then president of the company did not believe in a strong union. On his daily round he reportedly addressed the workers with first name in third person and received a polite TØ, an illustration of the classical non-reciprocal power-relationship, in Brown and Gilman's terms.

The present management had faced the task of having 'to create a climate in which one could exist'. One of their recommendations was general, reciprocal use of *du* throughout the company, and against considerable doubt 'a president is after all a president, not proper (from the workers' side)' the *du*-reform was institutionalized and successful. While I was in Stockholm, a leading journal ran an article on the recovered economic success of the company, and it would be naïve to believe that either success stemmed from egalitarian motives. Swedish management certainly are not ogres, but it makes good capitalistic sense to be on good terms with the labor force, and management clearly conceives the use of *du* as promoting such feelings. It can, however, be argued that the workers previous unhappiness and subsequent acceptance of the *du*-reform was partially grounded in egalitarian ideology; I am merely arguing that management clearly acted from profit-making motives, and that these coincided with the workers' wishes.

The comments on the *du*-reform by the 60-year-old company physician cannot be laid at any political door: 'Listen, it's great; one can reach them so much better'. Swedes for whom personal interrelationships tend to be difficult (Garbo's 'I vant to be alone' remark is never cited in Sweden, presumably because it is typical of all) feel closer and warmer with the use of *du*. Whatever the reasons, egalitarian, manipulative, or just humanitarian, all agree on the positive aspects of the spreading *du*-usage. Even some 70-year-old upper-class ladies find it agreeable to be addressed as *du* in the street; they say it makes them feel younger.

The change is also observable on an individual level. Many informants comment that their children did not address them as *du* but that their grandchildren do. One informant had sons with an age difference of 20 years; the elder had addressed him with KT in third person, the younger said *du*. There are repeated anecdotes of people who had known each other as youths and not exchanged *du*; on meeting 20 or 30 or 40 years later, they either spontaneously used *du* or promptly initiated *du*-usage. The difficulty lies not in demonstrating increased usage of *du* but rather in delineating the new rules which accompany the shift toward *du*, the change in options as context for the specific linguistic expressions.

13.3   Uses of *Du*

There are two distinct uses of *du* with two different semantics: intimacy–familiarity and solidarity. The two uses overlap and may well eventually become merged, but at this time the two are distinguishable.

13.3.1   *Du* + FN

The pattern for intimacy–familiarity use of *du* is distinct in this way: (1) it always co-occurs with FN or KT, and (2) its use among adults is always preceded by the speech act of *lägga bort titlarna* 'putting the titles away' which follows ritualized dispensation rules (Ervin-Tripp 1963).[3] This is an elaborate set of rules as to whose right it is to initiate the use of *du* (primarily from *ni* and/or title–last name (TLN) usage but there are also occurrences from (KT)FN in third person), and worries and misunderstandings about this initiation rite occur frequently in the data. The rules, which are found in the Swedish etiquette books, involve the variables of sex, age, and rank in that order of importance. It is always the prerogative of a woman to initiate *du* with age and rank deciding if the speakers are of the same sex. Age is not necessarily chronological but may involve other factors, such as year of high school matriculation or number of years spent with a company or institution. But note that these are the rules of the educated elite. From the responses to the questionnaire of an ethnological investigation which the Nordic Museum undertook in 1969 on terms of address, it is overwhelmingly clear that for members of social group 2 and especially 3, rank is the all over-ruling factor:

> If a *överordnad* (superior in rank) says *ni* or Fru Angquist, then I address him with the title which is owed him. That person will himself have to suggest if there is to be any change. (KU 2411)

Next to rank comes age: 'because he was of middle age, and in that case it was not the lady who should suggest'. The informant was 20 (KU 2854).

More often than not, social group 3 lacks a rule which involves sex as a variable. In my interviews with 18 low-salaried female factory-workers, ten claimed that there was no rule, and eight said that it was a man's prerogative to initiate *du*.

The highly formalized ritual of *dricka du-skål* 'drinking a *du* toast' has now become much simplified although it still can occur. A member of the high nobility writes as follows:

> Now it is much easier to become *du*. I usually propose it as soon as it is practical. I usually say something like: '*Skall vi inte lägga bort titlarna*' 'shan't we put titles away,' it is much easier so. (KU 2418)

The act of becoming on *du* terms is called *lägga bort titlarna* ('put the titles away') and so reflects its origin in the higher classes which had titles. There are other linguistic correlates which help define this speech act: *stå fadder* 'stand godfather' (if such hesitation exists that neither partner can bring themselves to initiate as in the case of a young woman and an old man of high rank, a third party may be brought in to break the ice), *du-broder* 'du-brother' etc.

Finally, the attitudes of the speakers themselves are clear indications that there are semantics of *du* which vary according to the speaker. They say so. Typical remarks are 'I want to keep *du* only for those I am very close to' versus 'It feels like a relief when that happens' (being addressed by *du*). 'One feels equal' (KU 2920). There are of course exceptions, but in general intimacy use of *du* is associated with social group 1 usage and solidarity use of *du* with social group 3. In the Nordic Museum investigation, the last question inquires about the informants' attitudes towards the various reforms of address suggested during the last hundred years in Sweden. Of the 26 responses from members of social group 1, all with only one exception want to keep *ni* and/or titles. Of the 55 responses from social group 3, all with four exceptions wanted general usage of *du* to all people. (Of the four exceptions, three are upwardly socially mobile as measured by occupation or children's occupation.) Social group 2, on the other hand, showed no clear trend: of the 50 responses, 29 favored the maintained use of *ni* while 14 were in favor of a *du*-reform, i.e. general use of *du* to everyone. The maintained use of *ni* of course implies an intimacy semantic for *du*.

The fact that two distinct usages of *du* exist, with a tendency to separate along class lines, is not recognized, and there are constant complaints from encounters where the speakers apply different sets of rules with no recognition of the difference. An anecdote will serve to illustrate. Herr and fru (Mr and Mrs) Nilsson, members of social group 2 with origin in 3, are caretakers of a farm, owned by Lennart B., a member of the Stockholm upper class. The men are approximately of the same age, and because of his social rank, Mr B. initiated the use of *du* with Mr Nilsson and the two now freely exchange *du* and FN. But with Fru Nilsson, Mr B. was stuck. His rules say that a woman initiates *du* no matter what, while Mrs Nilsson has no such rule. Her rule gives rank precedence and if she does have a rule regarding precedence of sex, it will be that the male initiates. Nor does she use *ni* (see the discussion below) with the result that she addresses Mr B. as *Direktör B.* in the third person, a practice Mr B. dislikes intensely.

Mrs B., on the other hand, who knows perfectly well that Mr and Mrs Nilsson would prefer to use *du* with her and that it is up to her to initiate as woman and older, refuses to do so. She does not realize that to Mrs Nilsson *du* means solidarity, not intimacy, and that it is her rank, not her age which keeps Mrs Nilsson from initiating. To Mrs B., the semantic of *du* is strongly one of intimacy, and when pressed by her social-democratic children for reasons of egalitarianism to become *du* with the Nilssons, she will say 'But I don't know them that well'. Mrs Nilsson is likely to perceive that distance as one of social class rather than as of personal friendship. And certainly neither of them realizes that they don't share the same set of rules.[4]

Upper-class speakers of course think that their rules are the only appropriate ones. But they fully expect the rest of the world not to know these rules since it is only by being one of them (upper class) that one gains access to social niceties. Swedish upper-class children are socialized by stigmatizing their unwanted behavior as lower class: 'Don't drink from a cup without a saucer; that's lower class'. Upper-class speakers expect lower-class speakers not to know their rules, only they don't realize that lower-class behavior also is rule-governed, but rather see it as an absence of rules. Lower-class speakers on the other hand have not spent as much time learning arbitrary rules at a conscious level and are not as likely to realize that their behavior also is rule-governed.

The typical reaction to upper-class speech patterns is that it is 'stuck up', but lower-class speakers are not likely to question the 'correctness' of upper-class speakers.

Even though the rules for dispensation rights differ between the social classes, it is generally recognized that such rights exist. Consequently people develop strategies for forcing dispensation, for manipulating the other into suggesting *du*. [. . .] One informant commented that he would pretend to misspeak and say *du*, and then apologize. He said it never failed that the addressee would ask him to please continue with *du*. Another strategy is constant and repeated use of T + LN (once or twice in each sentence) which marks the address system for attention. This is the strategy Mrs Nilsson used. A common strategy is some teasing remark like 'Well, you are oldest, I wouldn't dare suggest *du*.' [. . .]

Intimacy is not signalled by the use of *du* or by the use of first name but exactly by the combination of *du* + FN. First name by itself does not imply intimacy, and its usage in third person, i.e. repetition of the name instead of the pronoun in direct address, denotes familiarity and often social distance. This usage is disappearing and I have no instances of it in my data although I well remember being so addressed, especially in the country from the servants and the local population who had seen me grow up from childhood. Totally gone is the usage of my grandfather's generation to third person first name among relatives although that may primarily have been between the sexes.

Nor does the use of *du* by itself signal intimacy.

13.3.2   *Du* + Ø or solidarity, yes, intimacy, no

When the form *I* and titles came into usage, *du* remained within the peasant population as the mutual form of address of equals to both known and unknown, and this manner of address has survived until the present day within the labor class. The semantic of this usage of *du* is one of solidarity, an expression of membership in the same group. It is this usage of *du* which has spread so rapidly and so widely. In 1965, for instance, police officers in patrol cars addressed each other by TLN in third person; today they all use *du*. This increased usage of *du* resulted in a change of available options of address as well as in a change of the frames in which *du* occurs, the latter presumably as a result of the former.

In this use, *du* may co-occur with FN but more frequently with no name (Ø), even when the name is known. The use of first name is often avoided since it is felt to express intimacy. Solidarity use of *du* is now extended to strangers and people with whom one cannot presume an intimate relationship. This development of *du* + Ø reflects the upper-class reciprocal use of *du* which is one of intimacy and which always co-occurs with first name. *Du* by itself, then, expresses solidarity but not intimacy, maintaining a personal but not social distance. By institutional decree, university students now address their professors with *du* as an expression of group membership. Said my Swedish colleague: 'Well, I have gotten used to *du* but when they come and say *Hör du Bengt* (i.e. *du* + FN) – that's going too far.'

My students freely addressed me as *du*, even at guest lectures, but even my regular students *never* referred to me by name. It was of course difficult for them since it meant that they had to have eye contact with me before they could be recognized to speak, lacking a linguistic means by which they could call my attention, since *du* co-occurs with

FN but not with T. [. . .] Other informants, from social groups 2 and 3, have commented on the difficulty of first naming with solidarity *du*. They frequently resort to some kind of made up name or nickname (NN). Swedish last names commonly end in -sson, 'son of,' and there are several occurrences in the data where someone with the name, say, of Valter Danielsson, is addressed as *du* and Daniel in the attempt to avoid the use of *du* + FN.

The development of *du* + Ø is recent, [. . .] and has resulted, I believe, from the increased use of *du* in relationships which cannot be characterized as intimate. This increased usage is a result of a national policy of social egalitarianism which in turn has brought about a definite change in the value system. In addition, the alternative options to solidarity *du* have been so cumbersome or considered not acceptable with the result that the linguistic system has supported the pressures of the social system. One is reminded of Labov's 'theme that internal, structural pressures and sociolinguistic pressures act in systematic alternation in the mechanism of linguistic change' (Labov 1972: 537).

13.3.3   Solidarity use of *du* – individual usage

The working class has always been very clear on the solidarity function of *du* and clearly sees its relationship to social class: [. . .]

> There is a clear line between what we call social group 1 and 3. I heard on one occasion an old woman who claimed that it was not suitable for workers to buy *wienerbröd* 'a type of elegant coffee bread'. It is that kind of mentality one finds when people are classified as 'fine folk' and 'ordinary folk'. The respect for fine folk is still great for many among social group 3. One 'degrades' oneself before others who have done well and one really cannot blame them for this. Heard at the hospital how a physician asked a patient of his own age who had been his childhood chum to address him as *du*. The patient who was 'only' a worker answered: 'It is not proper!' and continued to say 'Doctor'. A hopeless case. (Retired typesetter, informant KU 2341)

But attitudes are changing with the younger generations. Within social group 3, such change is often difficult and accompanied by a feeling of conflict. The secretary, born 1936 into a rural family of carpenters and smiths, who wrote the following is typical of the informants:

> And myself, I have also changed my attitude to using *du* - I react with pleased gratitude if I am addressed with *du* by strangers and sex makes no difference. I know that others in my age group can easily feel depressed about this, feel that it is below their dignity to be *duad* by the landlord. I think they seem so small and afraid in their attitude, am so proud to have changed. I try also myself to say *du* to everyone but meet certain difficulties and feel at times uncertainty. [She comments that she uses *du* to everyone everywhere of her own age but not to older people.] The uncertainty comes when I am struck dumb by respect before a high imposing title and I forsake my good resolutions. I also avoid using *ni*; at a visit to the doctor's office recently, e.g. I said *du* to the nurse but then said *Professorn, Professorn* [T-third person]. I want so very much to say *du* to everyone and make no distinction and I get into a conflict when I all the same make a difference between folk and folk on the basis of their social position. (Informant KU 2854)

The use of solidarity *du* has now spread to members of all social classes, in social group 1 primarily among the younger members who frequently comment that they use it as an expression of their egalitarian ideology. This is very similar to the situation Bates and Benigni (1975) found in Italy and Morford (1997) in France. The solidarity *du* is always intended by the addressor to be reciprocal, but there are numerous instances in my observed data that *du* is not returned. Several taxi cab drivers, for instance, who claimed that they virtually always addressed their clients with *du*, carefully avoided any pronoun reference to me, even when I addressed them as *du*. (The use of *ni* by the cab driver would have been insulting in such a situation as it would blatantly have denied my claims to solidarity.) Throughout my conversations with the cab drivers runs a clear awareness on their part of social class, which speech and appearance are used to determine. Generally the informants claimed that they waited to see how they were addressed, meaning they would reciprocate the same address form which in fact they didn't. 'It also depends on how they talk,' said one, 'if they are *bildade*.' *Bildade* roughly corresponds to *educated* and is a frequent euphemism for membership in social group 1. This sentiment was echoed by many informants. In other words, although members of social group 1 are increasingly adopting the use of solidarity *du*, this usage is many times met with distrust by members of social group 3 who do not return it, and the result is a condescending *du*, i.e. the non-reciprocal *du* in Brown and Gilman's terms, the very opposite of what was intended.

Although solidarity occurs primarily with social class, there are instances of *du* as an expression of other types of solidarity. When a police chief in a 'speech by the coffin' addressed the deceased as *ni*, the editorial commented the following day that he should have used *du* because 'in the face of death we are all alike', i.e. *du* as an expression of common human frailty and mortality (informant KU 2448).

One informant links these two themes of solidarity in the following folk poem from a church yard:

Att döden han ser inte te personen	*Death he does not look to the individual*
For döden han är demokrat	*For Death he is a democrat*
Så direcktören och fabrikören	*So the director and the factory owner*
A rätt om di forsmädlitt mot mig le	*Even if they scoff me with a sneer*
Sa kanske de få legga breve me	*May end up lying next to me.*

(KU 2768)

The archbishop, a man of charisma, told me that, although he in general does not encourage the use of *du*, there exists a group of high school and theology students with whom he works closely, who do address him as *du*. They are profoundly religious and see their work as that of a 'guerrilla group' (the archbishop's term) in a profoundly irreligious country. The use of the T-form is common as an expression of religious solidarity (cf. the Quakers) but its usage is almost always institutionalized rather than as here in an individual case.

13.3.4   Solidarity use of *du* – institutional usage

The most widespread use of solidarity *du* occurs in institutionalized usage, *du* as a function of membership in a formal group, such as social institutions of occupation, recreation, organizations, and the like. The decreed use of *du* now occurs in hospitals, factories, universities, offices, clubs, etc. (but not in the military or in the police force). The *du* usage in an institution like the Swedish Employers Association on the immediate surface looks like institutional solidarity *du* and indeed the receptionist addressed me as *du*, as is their custom, over the telephone. But among its professional members, lawyers by training, reciprocal *du* is always preceded by *titelbortläggning* according to upper-class dispensation rules or disapprovingly commented on as deviant usage when those rules are not adhered to. Nor is there any FN avoidance among the upper-class members, and in fact their usage among themselves retains its intimacy–familiarity function albeit more widely extended than fifteen years ago. But between lawyer and janitor there is clear change: solidarity *du* with no first name and no initiation rights.

One of the young lawyers commented that in her work at court among her own political group there is automatic use of *du* as distinct from her usage at the Swedish Employers Association, where she begins with *ni* + TLN and proceeds to *titelbortläggning* and *du*. In their individual usage, people will tend toward a perception of *du* either as a function of intimacy–familiarity or of solidarity. In institutionalized usage of *du* this is not so and upper-class speakers will, as the young lawyer, switch between functions. She exemplifies a system in change as she was brought up with the upper-class intimacy–familiarity semantic of *du*, functions with its rules when they are imposed on her, but has come to prefer solidarity usage of *du*.

One more example to illustrate the switch between the two semantics of *du*. At a visit to the *Kungliga Biblioteket*, Royal Library, to fill out application forms, I was addressed as *du* by the librarian, a woman older than myself. She knew from the forms my occupation as professor and this did not impress her (professors rank very highly in the social order in Sweden) sufficiently to avoid *du* + ØN. Her use was clearly that of solidarity *du* to strangers. In the course of the interview of filling out the cards she discovered my Stockholm identity, as it were; she had known my father and for some years lived in the same apartment house as my family. At this point she changed to *ni*. (It is considered the height of rudeness to switch back to *ni* after an initiation ritual to intimacy *du*.) *Du*, at this stage, when I had ceased to be an anonymous stranger, would to her imply an intimacy *du*, and she changed to the mode of address we would mutually employ, had we been introduced in the street.

The University of Stockholm changed to institutional *du* around 1963 and many informants complained that it was difficult, especially for the older secretaries. Within a department, there is now general use of *du* + ØN by all, chairman, students and secretary. The chairman of linguistics addressed me as *du* with no further ado even though I had addressed him as *ni*. The students all say *du* + ØN to everyone. However, across departments there is considerable uncertainty. The secretaries do not say *du* to professors in other departments without a great deal of caution. Most of interdepartmental contact is by telephone which makes age difficult to judge, and in institutions with decreed *du*-usage, age especially but not necessarily when paired with rank, is the most important variable in choosing options. The secretaries never initiate address form, and their basic strategy is one of wait and see. They observe the greeting: from an older janitor *goddag* will to them indicate *ni* while *hej* will signal go ahead and use *du*. If the caller introduces himself as Professor X, they respond formally with *ni* or TLN, which is exactly what happened the first time I called the linguistics department. But when I appeared in person and the secretary saw that she was older than I, she changed to *du* + ØN without any hesitation.

Most uncertainty appears in the communication between the academic departments and the bureaucratic non-academic administration with its civil servants. One senses a strain on the feeling of solidarity and there is considerable hesitation and address avoidance from professors and secretaries alike.

Neither do professors automatically address their colleagues in other departments with *du*. Swedish professors can look very old and imposing and to these 'greying men' my informant–professors said they would most certainly not use *du*. Their general policy then is one of address avoidance.

What the students then observe and disseminate to the larger society is the mutual *du* + ØN between student/student and student/professor as well as frequently between professor/professor. They are not likely to notice the address avoidance between professors (avoidance is very difficult to observe) or be party to the administrative communications between departments and even less between departments and the administration. It is easy to understand then that the general perception is that every-one says *du* at the university when in fact they don't.

The solidarity usage of *du* is only extended to members of a group when their social intercourse is a function of group membership. At the Nobel Awards banquet, a formal dinner at which the king presides and to which only scholars and their spouses (besides the Nobel Foundation officials) are invited, there was a general use of *ni* and titles among the academicians.

[. . .]

13.4 Uses of *Ni*

While the two semantics of *du* are not recognized at all, the different semantics of *ni* are described in the literature and accounted for by the historical development of the linguistic form. There is, however, considerable confusion in the century-long public debate in the press over the use of the pronoun and, as late as 1963, Rosengren could write: 'The Swedish language still lacks a generally accepted word of address' (1963: 109). He was referring to *ni*. The general uncertainty regarding the semantics of *ni* no doubt has contributed to the recent rapid spread of *du*.

Ni derives from *I* which was originally the second person plural form. This *I* developed along three different lines.

13.4.1 *Ni* + (KT) (FN); peasant *ni*

Among the peasant population, *ni* (with regional variations of *I* and *ji*) became an address of respect reserved for parents, older relatives and worthy elders within the community. It occurred typically with KT and/or FN and tended to be non-reciprocal with the speaker receiving *du*. This *ni* took the place of *du* as evidenced by the gradual replacement of *ni* by *du* as the children grew up and reached adult status, and also by the fact that *ni* was occasionally refused with 'I'm not so old you'll have to say *ni*' (Ahlgren 1973: 78).

This use of *ni* is today rural and rapidly disappearing. I myself have never heard it, but several of my students said they had called their parents by *ni*.

13.4.2   *Ni* + Ø; polite and impolite *ni*

Given this development, it is unclear and curious how *ni* came to be received with such very negative connotations that its usage would be conceived as an insult by parts of the population. A multitude of folk sayings arose as a rejoinder to *ni*: 'Do you think I am lousy?' (meaning that with fleas the addressee would have been plural), '*Ni* the farmer called his mare when he didn't know her name' etc. (Ahlgren 1973: 75, 76). Wellander and Ahlgren account for this development by the fact that *ni* came to be used by the upper classes downward to their inferiors while they expected to be addressed by their titles, and that this non-reciprocity was the cause of the bad reputation of *ni*.

> When the new time came in [1800s] and the *du* of the old *ståndsamhället* 'estate society' by politeness was substituted with the modern *ni*, the mark of social class was transferred from *du* to *ni* which naturally follows with non-reciprocal address forms: he addressed by *ni* got an inferiority complex vis-à-vis the titled person. (Wellander 1952: 7)

But by this argument the earlier non-reciprocal condescending *du* might have been expected to share the same fate. Ahlgren reasons that a downward *ni* would be felt more distancing, more haughty, more arrogant than downward *du* because the inferiors knew that the speaker used *ni* to strangers and *du* to friends: 'A downward directed form of address also used between friends has larger possibilities to survive than a downward directed form also used between strangers' (1973: 121). I am not convinced.[5]

It is beyond a doubt that *ni* came to be considered as a rude form of address by parts of the population and in all social classes although by very few in social group 1. In the Nordic Museum questionnaire, only two members (both ministers of the church) from social group 1 objected to the use of *ni* while only two (of 55 responses) from social group 3 were for *ni*. For whatever reasons, people who acquiesced at an endless use of titles, which certainly marked the status relationship, balked at *ni* on the grounds that it was impolite. One of the informants to the Nordic Museum survey from social group 3 writes:

> Already in primary school, our teacher warned us against the use of *ni* as term of address because it was considered as a cussword. He said that in coarse language there was an expression '*Ni* kan kyssa mig där bak'. '*Ni* can kiss me behind.' For this reason he advised us to use *ni* only when we spoke to *bildat folk* 'educated people' so that no misunderstandings would occur. (KU 2930)

He had an unusually sensitive teacher. Especially the folkschool teachers show wide variance in their acceptance of *ni*, and many children were categorically taught never to use *ni* while others were taught that it was perfectly acceptable (apparently by teachers of strong egalitarian convictions), and according to many informants such teachings remained with them throughout life.

This considered rudeness of *ni* is no doubt the major reason for the extreme address avoidance and circumscriptions that one finds in Swedish. From my notes on address to customers in department stores I have:

Skall det betalas kontant	'Shall it be paid in cash?'
Vad skall vi ha?	'What shall we have?'
Om damen går . . .	'If the lady goes . . .', etc.

with only two occurrences of *ni* (during five months' observation), one by a much older woman and the second, interestingly enough, *after* I had completed my purchase – no need to be polite any more, I suppose.

By necessity, I visited one of the same department stores on December 27, the first day stores were open after the Christmas holidays. The store was crowded, with the majority of customers trying to exchange or return gifts. The clerks gave an impression, say my notes, of cranky sullenness and I heard so many *ni*'s that I lost count. Clearly *ni* is an integral part of Swedish clerks' linguistic competence but in some situations carefully avoided.

In my study of the department stores, I had expected to find a difference in the address systems of the clerks between the expensive and inexpensive store. I found no difference between the three but a lot of difference between the various departments within the store. The clerks in sporting goods, toys and teenage clothes tended toward solidarity use of *du* + ØN, but virtually no clerks used *ni*. Their attitude is that *ni* is not polite. The personnel manager of the expensive store (who did address me as *ni*) told me several anecdotes about women customers whose name and title (husband's title in feminine form) were known to the clerk and who had protested at being addressed as *ni* 'I am not *ni* with you'. I suppose after such an episode one is careful to avoid the use of *ni*. From the titles and names cited, like *kunsulinnan Petersson*, I suspect such customers would belong to a class my grandmother would have labelled as *nouveau riche*, i.e. recently upwardly mobile speakers with pretensions to upper-class behavior which they knew imperfectly.

Peasant use of *ni* is clearly distinguishable from impolite use of *ni* in that the former always co-occurs with KT and/or FN while the latter never does, but there is no linguistic distinction between polite and impolite use of *ni* + Ø. I have looked very diligently for social settings, scenes, even channels (Hymes 1972) which might mark the meaning of the interaction between linguistic form and social setting. The only vector I have been able to identify is the use of anonymous *ni* to a stranger in public when dressed in street clothes, a usage which is now generally accepted as polite by the younger generation.

The police, for example, freely use *ni* to strangers, but only to those they take to be members of social group 1 and 2; to members of 3 and to the young they use solidarity *du*. However, the lower ranks do not use *ni* to their own superiors whom they address with TLN in third person. *Ni* in that situation is considered disrespectful and impolite.

But I can't tell when someone first addresses me as *ni* whether that person considers such usage to be polite or not. The rector of the Police Academy addressed me as Professor Paulston in third person over the telephone, switched to *ni* when he saw me (I was some fifteen years younger than he), and sighed with relief when I initiated to *du*. Clearly he does not consider *ni* as impolite but still as less polite than TLN in third person as is reflected in the general usage of the police. There is however no social setting which can inform me that he considers *ni* as less polite than TLN if he had addressed me with *ni* from the beginning; the only clue lies in the direction of his change of address within the formal range.

[. . .]

13.4.3   *Ni* + TLN; polite *ni*

The third development of *ni* took place in the elite where *du* and *ni* became patterned after French *tu* and *vous* (cf. Russian, Friedrich 1972). Ahlgren writes: 'Apparently *ni* during the earlier half of the 1800s has had its strongest support within the aristocracy – where it was perceived as corresponding to French *vous* – and within the peasant class, whereas the growing middle class more often used titles' (1973: 135). Certainly, the spokesmen for the *ni*-reforms advocated during the 1800s and 1900s were all members of the aristocracy and/or the intelligentsia.

[. . .] The free use of *ni* + TLN has now become common (maybe because *ni* + ØN to strangers is in frequent use) in the intercourse between the public and the many federal institutions like the post office, transportation, communications, etc. Although more formal and definitely class-linked, the use of *ni* + TLN marks the same meaning in personal interrelationship as solidarity *du* + Ø: a maintenance of personal but not social distance. My own address system underwent a drastic change as a result of my findings, and I virtually never use *ni* + TLN any more. When I did, it was invariably with upper-class speakers whom I either disliked or felt to be cool and distant.

Because of the widespread institutional use of *du*, I have fairly few direct observations of reciprocal *ni* + TLN but without exception they all involve members of social group 1. A typical example is the Nobel Awards banquet where the guests addressed each other by *ni* + TLN. Some may, like my own group, have switched to familiarity *du* after proper toasting ceremonies, but those I know of did not. At the banquet I promptly initiated *du* with the professor on my right but the one on my left was much older than I, grey-haired and so distinguished that I hesitated. When I pointed out my dilemma to him, adding teasingly that he could not very well initiate, he delightedly said: *Det är vad du tror* 'That's what you think' and raised his glass in the ritual toast. A younger gentleman across the table then raised his glass and said, 'May I join you?' The three men then prompted the woman across from me to follow my example and initiate *du* with them which she did. Clearly the men were more than willing to use *du* but the women were reluctant to initiate and so in most groups *ni* + TLN prevailed. But note that the use of *ni* + TLN and the ritual initiation ceremony for switching to *du* were partially a function of the occasion. According to both my partners at table, had I met them at the university they would have addressed me as *du* without further ado.

13.5   Choosing Options

Present at the musical soiree which followed the dinner and mingling with the guests were technicians from radio/TV, by official order also dressed in white tie. In my conversation with them, there was mutual use of solidarity *du* + ØN. This episode can be taken to illustrate the ruling principle of all encounters in Swedish in normal situations: the speaker attempts to speak in a fashion he believes will please the addressee (not necessarily consciously so). The sequence followed by the dinner guests of (1) intro-duction of self which consisted of saying one's first and last name aloud followed by a handshake, (2) use of *ni* + TLN (in order to know which title to use one must either study the place lists carefully before dinner or else find out surreptitiously), (3) initiation ceremony, and (4) use of *du* + FN, I felt would be considered putting on airs by the working-class technicians so I omitted all of that sequence and simply used *du* and no name to them. Certainly I made no such conscious analysis at the time. And certainly one can never be sure that one guesses correctly how the other would like to be addressed; hence all the agony Swedes experience in addressing their fellow man. The following lament from a worker is typical:

> But you can't tell, and you don't want to use titles if they are workers and one doesn't dare use *du* in case they aren't. (KU 2932)

He is an older man, and the younger working-class generation is more likely to use *ni* to strangers, which they consider perfectly polite, or practice address avoidance, but note that the criteria for choice of option have not changed. The following comments on why they would choose *du* rather than *ni* are culled from my interviews with young factory workers: 'if he looks kind; age; to "simple" folk; I look at the general style; which social class; those who don't seem arrogant and superior; people I like; not large.' *Ni* is offered to 'older people; in order to be polite; not to irritate someone; to those with snotty manners; and to Östermalms-women.' In other words, social class and age still remain the basic criteria. Rather, what has changed is the situation and the range of options.

[. . .]

Indeed, choice of option can be so delicate a matter that one of the personnel man-agers of an international business firm, whom I interviewed, uses address choice as a test in hiring salesmen. At the job interview, one was disqualified for greeting the per-sonnel manager with *hej* (marked for *du*) instead of *goddag* (unmarked). Another was disqualified for addressing him as Herr Johansson. The third passed the test; he care-fully avoided until he was addressed as *du* which he unostentatiously reciprocated. On the whole, that is the general rule: let the other initiate and then reciprocate. Indeed, there is a court ruling on the matter. Engineer T. had been arrested by the police for disturbing the peace (he was drunk). He complained to the court about his treatment and pointed out he had been addressed as *du*. The court cleared the police, acknow-ledged the recent change in address system but added that the police had been remiss, they should have waited until they were addressed with *du* or *ni* and then recipro-cated – 'restrictivity' in the matter of address was essential. [. . .]

Obviously, such general strategies strain the rules for dispensation rights to the utmost as someone must initiate. As a matter of fact, the court's ruling violates the rules of the etiquette books (variables of sex, age, and rank in that order of importance) as some policemen will be older than their male clients but still cannot initiate. It seems there are two distinct initiation acts.

One is the clearly recognized initiation to *du* by *titelbortläggning*. This is the speech act which follows the dispensation rights discussed above and which vary according to social class. But there is also an initiation act which does not involve dispensation, sim-ply an initiation of choice of option, primarily *ni* + Ø or *du* + Ø but any form of address is possible. Everyone is aware of the existence of this initiation act, but it is not recognized that its rule occasionally conflicts with those for dispensation rights, another cause of the Swedes' confusion. This initiation act rule says simply that the customer or client initiates. At the hairdresser and the post office, in the bus and the department store, to the police and the bank clerk, the customer is granted choice of option. The exception will be upper class 'patrons', like bank officers and librarians, who will not hesitate to initiate and who tend to use the dispensation rule-variables in choice of option as will strangers who are not in a client–patron relationship.

[. . .]

The initiation act as distinct from the dispensation act is a recent development, and I was not aware at the time I collected the data that the two did not conform to the same rules. Consequently I did not investigate specifically the parameters of the client–patron relationship. I think what is happening is as follows. When the address system was stable, prior to the present change, form of address was fairly predictable: speakers from social group 1 used *ni* or third person to such patrons as police, bank clerks and sales personnel while members from social group 3 used *du* to patrons from their own social class and *ni*, third person, or avoidance to patrons from social groups 1 and 2. Patrons knew what to expect, and could perfectly well predict and therefore *initiate* address form. Whatever hesitation existed lay only in accurately ascertaining the dispensation rule-variables.

There is today no way of predicting form of address between strangers. As a result, patrons from social groups 2 and 3 are developing an 'avoid – let the other initiate – then reciprocate' strategy, and the change in choice of options with the present uncertainty in predicting choice is accompanied by new rules, i.e. not a change in rules but additional rules, for who chooses option. Application of the dispensation rules requires some familiarity with the addressee in order to determine sex, age, and rank in whatever order they are applied. With the rapidly increased use of *du* + Ø between strangers and clients' fluctuation between this *du* and anonymous *ni*, it makes sense in service relationships to grant the customer the opportunity to miscalculate rather than to offend by one's own faulty estimation of the situation.[6]

It is especially this alternation between anonymous *ni* and solidarity *du* between strangers which leads Swedes to believe that their address system is totally irregular. Anonymous *ni* is being replaced so rapidly by *du* + Ø that an individual's usage will vary from day to day depending on his mood that day. When I was cheerful and happy with the world, I would address many more strangers as *du* than when I felt tired and irritated in which case I would use *ni*. I was not aware of this variation in my own usage until several informants commented on the influence of mood on their own usage.

There are, however, certain factors which do influence an individual's alternation so there is not totally free variation. I would never use *du* to somebody much older than I or *ni* to somebody younger. The librarian I overheard at the Royal Library constitutes a perfect example. He was filling out cards for two customers. As upper-class patron, he did not hesitate to initiate, which he did. To the man of his own age, about 30, he said *Vad heter du?* 'What is your name?' while to the reader who was fifteen–twenty years older than he was, he said *Vad är Ert namn?*

The setting of similar transactions may influence choice of pronoun. Many informants commented that they would address the sales clerk in a *boutique* with *du* but that they would never do so at NK, the expensive department store. Gas station attendants are repeatedly singled out by upper-class informants for their uninhibited address form; although working-class patrons, they frequently initiate *du* + Ø, but they too are sensitive to social class. One amused informant reports that when he drove up in a small car he was addressed with *du* only to be addressed as *ni* later in the day when he returned in a big expensive car. The same informant also reports that the Lutheran minister, who was known to the attendant, in mufti was addressed as *du* but in clerical garb received a polite *Pastorn*, i.e. T-third person.

But individual usage will vary between individuals in the same identical setting, and one cannot predict such usage. My friend, around 40, writes me that the other day two plumbers around 25 came to fix something in her apartment. One of them addressed her as *du*, the other as *ni*. At a cash register in a sports clothes store where I was paying for my purchase, there were two clerks; one addressed me as *du*, the other as *damen*. The *du*-speaker in this case was the younger, and the *du*-usage clearly is spread by the younger generation. But the impossibility of delineating rules of address which will accurately predict choice of address is limited to the interaction of strangers, of *opresenterade* (Andersson et al. 1970) 'people who are not introduced to each other', and all other interactions are clearly rule-governed.

13.6   Conclusion

The Swedish address system is in a stage of rapid change with an increased use of solidarity *du* + ØN, brought about by the dominant political ideology, and no doubt facilitated by the awkwardness of the previous usage which most Swedes are relieved to escape. Swedes are given to generalizations that (1) today everyone uses *du* and (2) there are no stateable rules for address usage. Neither proposition is true, and I have attempted in this paper to account for those rules. The major argument has been that an adequate description of the Swedish address system is possible only through the recognition that the social classes have different rules due to different semantics of the pronouns *du* and *ni*.

Notes

1   'Semantic' is the term used by Brown and Gilman to refer to the 'covariation between the pronoun used and the objective relationship existing between speaker and addressee', p. 253.
2   Quotations with a KU number are from the archives of the Nordiska Museet, 'the Nordic (Scandinavian) Museum' which undertook an ethnological investigation on words of address in 1969. The informants are not randomly selected and are not representative of the Swedish population at large as they are especially selected for their ability to express themselves in writing. In reading through the responses from the 290 informants, one is forcibly impressed by their intelligence and power of observation and recall. As a source, say, for investigation of working-class lexicon they would not be valid; for my purposes these informants proved an invaluable source, and I have no doubt as to the validity of the archive data.
3   Children may use *du* + KT without any initial ritual. They also learn the communicative competence rules much later than the linguistic forms, i.e. the appropriateness of their usage. I am grateful to Are Mörner for the example of a child's *du* + *vinnan* (from grevinnan, 'countess'), totally inappropriate in adult speech.

4   At a visit two years later, I found that Mrs B. had indeed initiated *du* with Mrs Nilsson and thought nothing remarkable of it. If anything is an indicator of sociocultural change, Mrs B.'s change of attitude and use of *du* + FN with the caretaker wife is. It would have been not only unthinkable but unimaginable in my childhood.

5   Ahlgren's argument is contradicted by the case in English where the T form disappeared and the V form survived. There is one comment from a Medelpad farmer: '*Ni* from someone of my own age I take as intended: as an insult' (KU 2600) which leads me to speculate. Peasant *ni* was never used to an equal so that its usage in such a case would have been sarcastic just as I might address my husband as Professor Paulston when I think he deals with me as an ignorant student. As upper-class usage of *ni* to equals spread, it would not be surprising if such usage was misunderstood by the peasants who themselves would never use *ni* downwards or to equals (see also Haugen 1975).

6   This approach is reflected in the following excerpt from *Trafikhandboken*, Storstockholms *Lokaltrafik* 1974, the manual for employees of the local transportation company: 'Between employees, we usually say *Du* to each other. Avoid, however, saying *du* to customers. Word of address is a personal matter which one ought to agree on. Older persons usually don't like to be addressed as *du*.'

References

Ahlgren, P. (1973). Tilltalsordet Ni:s historia, unpublished Phil. Lic. dissertation, University of Uppsala.

Andersson, B., Holmquist, B., Ljungquist, L. & Lund, K. (1970). Om tilltalsskicket i modern Svenska. Unpublished MS, University of Lund.

Bates, E. & Benigni, L. (1975). Rules of address in Italy: a sociological survey. *LinS* 4. 271–88.

Beckman, N. (1947). Rang och pronomen. *Nysvenska Studier* 27 årgången. 99–112.

Brown, R. & Gilman, A. (1960). The pronouns of power and solidarity. In T. Sebeok (ed.) *Style in language*. Cambridge, Mass.: The MIT Press. 253–376.

Ervin-Tripp, S. (1973). *Language acquisition and communicative choice*. Stanford: Stanford University Press.

Friedrich, P. (1972). Social context and semantic feature: The Russian pronominal usage. In J. Gumperz & D. Hymes (eds.) *Directions in sociolinguistics*. New York: Holt, Rinehart and Winston. 270–300.

Haugen, E. (1975). Pronominal address in Icelandic: from you-two to you-all. *LinS* 4. 323–39.

Hymes, D. (1972). Models of the interaction of language and social life. In J. Gumperz & D. Hymes (eds.) *Directions in sociolinguistics*. New York: Holt, Rinehart and Winston. 35–71.

Hymes, D. (1974). *Foundations in sociolinguistics*. Philadelphia: University of Pennsylvania Press.

Jonz, J. (1975). Situated address in the United States Marine Corps. *Anthropological Linguistics* 17. 68–77.

Labov, W. (1972). On the mechanism of linguistic change. In J. Gumperz and D. Hymes (eds.) *Directions in sociolinguistics*. New York: Holt, Rinehart and Winston. 512–37.

Morford, Janet. 1997. Social indexicality in French pronominal address. *Journal of Linguistic Anthropology* 7. 3–37.

Nordiska Museet (1969). *Etnologiska undersökningen*, Frågelista 194, Tilltalsord, Stockholm.

Paulston, C. B. (1975). Language universals and socio-cultural implications in deviant usage: personal questions in Swedish. *Studia Linguistica* XXIX. 1–11. 1–15.

Paulston, R. G. (1968). *Educational change in Sweden*. New York: Teachers College Press.

Rosengren, K. E. (1963). Ni-reform nit. *Studiekamraten* 6. 109–12.

Svenska Dagbladet (1970). Sociala structuren lika efter 60 år. August 15, 1970.

Söderberg, T. (1972). *Två sekler svensk medelklass*. Stockholm: Bonniers.

Uthorn, N. (1959). Om *NI* i läroverk och seminar *Modersmålslärarnas Förening*. Årsskrift 1959. Lund: Skånska Central Tryckeriet. 113–25.

Wellander, E. (1952). Ni eller Du? *Svenska Dagbladet*, August 13, 1952.

Wellander, E. (1964). *Språk och Språkvård*. Stockholm: Norstedts.

14

Off-Record Indirectness and
the Notion of Imposition

Maria Sifianou

Abstract

Off-record utterances are polite ways of requesting, but encode their politeness in situationally and culturally specific ways. Off-record requests have been largely seen as devices deriving their politeness force from minimizing impositions by leaving the options open for the addressee to interpret them. This paper presents some preliminary observations and findings which associate off-record requests with offers in familial and familiar contexts in Greek. It is thus argued that another equally strong motivation for their employment is the opportunity they provide the addressee to offer instead of being requested. Bearing in mind differences between the Greeks and the English concerning the variable importance attached to the notions of involvement and independence, it appears that the motivation for offering is stronger in Greek than that of non-imposition, which appears to be stronger in English.

14.1 Introduction

Indirectness is a multifunctional linguistic phenomenon, and has been closely associated with politeness in relevant current theories (Brown and Levinson 1978, 1987; Leech 1983). I will not go into its various functions, such as teasing, joking, rebuking or illustrating what Ervin-Tripp (1976: 44) calls 'communicative abbreviation' or its various motivations, such as shyness or reluctance or lack of necessity to be explicit, since my aim here is to present the relationship between off-record requests and politeness from a different angle.

In most current theories, politeness has been conceptualized as strategic conflict avoidance (Lakoff 1973; Leech 1983; Brown and Levinson 1978, 1987). It has been widely assumed that politeness is the main motivation for people's using indirectness. Off-record

Maria Sifianou, "Off-record indirectness and the notion of imposition" from *Multilingua* 12:1 (1993), pp. 69–79. Reprinted by permission of the author and Mouton de Gruyter, a division of Walter de Gruyter GmbH & Co publishers.

strategies, in particular, have been regarded as more polite than on-record strategies (Brown and Levinson 1987: 73). The main justification offered for this view is simple and straight-forward. Since off-record devices have more than one plausible interpretation, they enable the speaker to avoid responsibility for having committed a particular act, while also leaving the addressee more freedom to decide how to interpret the utterance. Consequently, the decisive factor in choosing an off-record construction is assumed to be the degree of imposition involved in the act: the higher the degree of imposition, the more indirect the utterance to minimize it.

It is worth mentioning here that these views have been contested by Blum-Kulka (1987), among others, who states that on-record rather than off-record indirect requests were judged as more polite by her Hebrew and American informants. The convincing inter-pretation offered is that for an utterance to count as polite a certain balance between pragmatic clarity and non-coerciveness is required. This balance is retained in the case of conventional indirectness, whereas it is destroyed in off-record indirectness, since high inferential demands are placed on the addressee.

Brown and Levinson (1987: 71) also note that 'off-recordness' may be motivated by the speaker's wish to avoid committing a face-threatening act, while providing the addressee with the opportunity to appear caring, co-operative and bounteous if he or she decides to take up the implied meaning of the utterance. They illustrate this with the much-quoted example 'It's hot in here.' If the addressee responds to this with, 'Oh, I'll open the window then!', he or she 'may get credit for being generous and cooperative' and the speaker will thus avoid 'the potential threat of ordering . . . [the addressee] around'. However, even in this account, which Brown and Levinson do not discuss any further, the speaker's primary concern appears to be the need to avoid committing the face-threatening act, and thus the imposition.

The question which naturally arises here is whether minimizing impositions is the only or even the most basic motivation for off-record indirectness, both intra-culturally and cross-culturally, and this is what I will proceed to consider.

In examining the relationship between politeness and off-record indirectness cross-culturally, I would like to concentrate on some common types of off-record requests in familial and familiar contexts and to suggest that although they are frequent in both Greek and English, their primary motivation seems to be different in each of these languages. In Greek, off-record requests are not used for the purpose of avoiding intrusion on the addressee's freedom of action, thus minimizing the imposition; instead, they are employed in order to provide addressees with an opportunity to express their generosity and solicitude for the interlocutor by offering. This choice prevents the actual request from occurring and paves the way for an offer to be made. And offers are intrinsically polite acts in Leech's (1983: 83) 'absolute' politeness terms, and in the ethnomethodological literature (Schegloff 1979: 49) they are structurally more preferred sequences than requests.

Preliminary observations and findings (Sifianou 1992) indicate that the Greeks and the English move on similar levels of off-record indirectness in familial and familiar contexts (65.7% versus 63.5%, respectively). Given the different politeness orienta-tions of the two societies (more positive politeness strategies are preferred in Greece, more negative politeness in England; Sifianou 1987), this finding seems surprising and even contradictory at first sight. However, a closer look reveals that even the different politeness orientations are mainly the result of different views about the concept of imposition. Thus, similar surface structures with apparently similar functions seem to conceal different underlying motivations. In order to substantiate this claim, I will briefly review Greek social structure.

14.2   Greek Social Structure

For historical and geographical reasons, Greek society attaches great importance to the distinction between *(e)δiki* 'in-group' and *kseni* 'out-group', and both verbal and non-verbal behavior is largely determined by which group others fall into.[1] 'In-group' is defined as one's 'family, relatives, friends, and friends of friends'. Moreover, anybody else who is perceived as showing concern for one is also viewed as a member of the in-group. By contrast, the 'out-group' consists of anyone who falls outside this in-group perception (Triandis and Vassiliou 1972: 305). Appropriate behavior among members of the same in-group requires intimacy, support and generosity, whereas that towards members of out-groups requires competition, indifference and perhaps formality (see, for instance, Herzfeld 1983; Triandis 1972).

The culturally specific concept of *filotimo*, which requires self-sacrificing helpfulness to in-group members, is revealing. This concept is difficult to define and translate, but as Triandis and Vassiliou (1972: 308) state, 'a person who has this characteristic is polite, virtuous, reliable, proud, has a "good soul", behaves correctly, meets his obligations, does his duty, is truthful, generous, self-sacrificing, tactful, respectful and grateful'. Thus, for the Greeks, who see personal achievements in relation to group success, since they stem from the support of the group, the limits of personal territories are looser than those of the English. The Greeks seem to emphasize involvement and in-group relationships, which are based on mutual dependence rather than on independence, and on a series of shared reciprocal rights and obligations. In such a framework the idea of distance is hardly relevant and, consequently, that of imposition cannot be prevalent. For the Greeks, as Triandis and Vassiliou (1972: 305) observe, the functional significance of this close bondage among members of the in-group is obvious: 'It is easier to survive in a highly competitive world as a member of a group of people who cooperate and help one another.' By contrast, the English seem to define their in-group differently. The distinction between in-group and out-group is less salient and the individual's privacy and independence is of greater concern than that of closer in-group relationships (see Matsumoto 1988; Triandis and Vassiliou 1972; Wierzbicka 1985).

Consequently, in a society such as that in Greece where members of an in-group depend on each other a lot, sometimes even more than on institutions (for instance, in obtaining a loan), the definition of what counts as an imposition, as well as how serious a particular imposition is, will differ from that in societies where the notion of an individual's right to freedom plays a determining role in the social structure. For instance, in England one cannot, generally speaking, expect to be provided with accommodation or a meal, even by family members, when no specific arrangements have been made in advance. However, in Greece it would be unthinkable in such cases to consider going outside the family circle, since that would violate the unwritten laws of Greek hospitality and would be perceived as an insult rather than as concern for non-imposition.

14.3　The Notion of Imposition

Imposition could be defined as the extent of interference in the recipient's autonomy of action. Brown and Levinson (1987) allow for situational and cross-cultural variability in the weight of impositions, but they imply that some degree of imposition is always involved when they say that small impositions are found in requests for 'free goods' (1987: 80). Thus, minimizing the imposition in some way will be necessary, and the constructions and mitigating devices used will, consequently, primarily serve this function. In Greek, on the other hand, requests are more frequent, and the 'free goods' available, such as a cigarette, more coffee or something small to nibble can be obtained without even asking for them, but rather by just taking them, and perhaps stating what one is doing. For example:

(1)　[in a gathering of friends][2]
　　　A: *Perno ena tsiɣaro. Pjanu ine?*
　　　　'I'm taking a cigarette. Whose are they?'
　　　B: *Δika mu. Pare osa θelis.*
　　　　'Mine. Have as many as you like.'

Again jokingly, in the case of a colleague who saw some biscuits in the librarian's office: 'Oh, these are for the taking, eh? Thank you very much.' Since the exchange of biscuits and other goodies is common among colleagues, the speaker felt it more appropriate to help herself in a jocular manner rather than employ any kind of requesting construction. The laughter of all those present clearly indicated that her choice was successful.

Requesting such things, then, cannot be perceived as a face-threatening, imposing action and, consequently, off-record requests in such contexts do not function to soften an imposition, since there is no imposition involved.[3] Such acts are understood as part of sharing whatever is available, which is the behavior expected from all members of the in-group. This social obligation for reciprocity is not restricted to specific acts or even to particular individuals, that is, not just to those who have done one an immediate favor. In other words, recompense is not calculated on a one-to-one basis. Given that the small group rather than the individual is the basic unit of Greek social structure, it seems highly unlikely that the Greeks behave as individuals who like imposing on others or that they 'actually *enjoy* being imposed upon in some way' (Brown and Levinson 1987: 77).

In this framework, the Greek tendency to be generous, comparatively speaking, is easily understood. Sometimes even a compliment may result in the recipient sincerely offering the item concerned as a gift to the person who expressed admiration. Durrell (1978: 60) describes this gift-giving generosity of Cretans very vividly. He says that 'it is dangerous to express admiration for something, for you will certainly find it in your baggage as a farewell gift when you leave. You cannot refuse. They are adamant. I knew of a lady who got a baby this way.'

This giving behavior is not restricted to tangible goods, but also covers various ways of volunteering to do things for others, which indicates knowledge of and consideration for their needs. The main aim of all members of the same in-group is to retain the group bond, and this can be achieved by treating others the way you would like to be treated by them or even the way you treat yourself. The group is part of the image of self, and its success counts more heavily than the success of each individual, as Triandis and Vassiliou (1972: 326) contend. Thus, members feel free, perhaps even obliged, to express both their positive and negative feelings and opinions openly (1972: 319), since they believe that this will contribute to the improvement of the image of their in-group.

It is not unreasonable, therefore, to see the opportunity to be helpful or to perform particular duties as the prime motivation for off-record requests, especially in in-group contexts. Thus, off-record utterances are expressions of politeness and a means of 'preserving face', but in situationally and culturally specific ways and not necessarily just as a means of avoiding impositions. In this social background, where strong dependency relations prevail, it is hard to see in what sense a husband or father who requests his glasses or his newspaper, using a question concerning their location, feels inferior in status or is committing a serious face-threatening act that would lead him to use the highest degree of politeness to perform this act. What is necessary for the success of such utterances is the participants' shared knowledge of the culturally specific rights and obligations, or more specifically of beliefs and habits, likes and dislikes. For example, a couple are getting ready to go out and the wife has put on a black dress:

(2)   H: *To mavro forema θa foresis?*
           'Are you going to wear the black dress?'
      W: *Ande. Na su kano to χatiri n' alakso.*
           'O.K. I'll do you the favor and change.'

The husband asks a question, which does not make much sense as such. The wife, who obviously shares her husband's code of communication, understands the implied meaning that her husband does not like that particular dress, and responds with an offer to change in order to please him. Of course, the wife could have chosen to ignore or question the hint, knowing, however, that such a choice could have caused dissatisfaction. We may assume that since she decides to conform, the husband's request is not in any great conflict with her own likes and that she feels it is more important to maintain the balance of their interpersonal relationship.

One could, of course, argue here that the husband is indirect because he does not want to risk a more explicit imposition. This is possible. However, given the positive politeness orientation of Greek society, in which opinions, feelings, requests, etcetera, tend to be expressed directly rather than in a conventionally indirect way, such an interpretation becomes highly unlikely. It seems more plausible that the husband has chosen a hint rather than a direct construction in order to give his wife the opportunity to show her solicitude. Such choices are, to a great extent, subconscious and reciprocal between in-group members.

Relations between parents and children deserve special attention. Very briefly, parents feel obliged to control their children's decisions, assuming that in this way they protect and help them and show their concern and love. They see them as extensions of themselves and take every opportunity to furnish them with all the material and intellectual means that they believe will contribute to their success, means which were denied to them because of the harder times they grew up in. For example, a father can see that his daughter is getting ready to go out.

(3)   F: *Θα vγis?*
      'Are you going out?'
    D: *Ne, ala δe θ' arγiso.*
       'Yes, but I won't be late.'

The father's question is unnecessary. However, by asking, he implicitly communicates his desire, which is the norm, that girls in particular should not stay out late. The daughter interprets this apparently unnecessary question correctly, and politely responds to both the literal and the implied senses. In this context, the participants share specific knowledge which renders their communication successful. This is demonstrated by the fact that there is no further requesting or commanding on the part of the father. By being indirect here, the father clearly does not try to grant her any extra freedom, since they both know and follow the established patterns which govern their relationship. In so doing, what the daughter is offered is more important – the opportunity to feel satisfaction that her conformity is the result of her own free will. Consider the following example between mother and daughter:

(4)   D: *To sinema ine panakrivo.*
      'The cinema is extremely expensive.'
    M: *Poso ine?*
      'How much is it?'
    D: *700 δraχmes.*
      '700 drachmas.'
    M: *Pare lefta apo to portofoli mu.*
      'Take money from my purse.'

Here, the daughter asks for money by making a general statement which the mother correctly conceives as a hint, and so offers the amount required. The daughter has not decided to be indirect in order to minimize any imposition because she knows that her parents are socially obliged to provide her not only with the essentials but also with various 'luxuries'. The daughter is following the established pattern of indirectness and by doing so offers the mother the opportunity to express her concern and generosity overtly.

If, however, the addressee does not grasp the implied requestive force of an utterance, or decides, for whatever reasons, to ignore it, then a possible follow-up request will frequently be used to indicate annoyance. For example:

(5)   [between father and daughter]
    F: *Eχis δi puθena tin efimeriδa?*
      'Have you seen the newspaper anywhere?'
    D: *Ine sto trapezaki.*
      'It's on the small table.'
    F: *Θα pas na mu ti feris?*
      'Will you go and get it for me?'

The annoyance here is the result of violating the principle which requires obedience from children in response to the self-sacrificing support they receive from their parents.

In other words, the addressee is in reality not free to decide how to interpret the utterance. The assumption is that it should be clear for both that the utterance is a request. In those cases in which ambiguous utterances of this type are meant and expected to be interpreted as directives, non-compliance causes annoyance. Questions concerning location have been conventionalized and function as requests in many contexts. Results (Sifianou 1992) indicate that a considerable number of English and Greek informants would be inclined to construe this question concerning location as a request to give the speaker the newspaper (45.7% and 40.0%, respectively). Thus, it would appear that the difference between Greek and English is not located in the indirectness of the request itself, but rather in the motive for employing such indirectness.

Among equals, a response to the literal meaning can indicate joking, as in the following exchange between friends:

(6)   A: *Mipos ftiaχnis kafe δaki?*
         'Are you making coffee by any chance?'
      B: *Oχi vevea.*
         'Certainly not.'

The speaker intended the question as a request for coffee. The addressee pretends that she has not recognized the speaker's intention and responds to the literal sense, but prepares two cups of coffee (see Ervin-Tripp 1976: 45). There are also cases in which the reverse can happen; that is, an utterance not intended as a request can be interpreted as such. For example:

(7)   [between colleagues/close friends]
      A: *Θa pas sto panepistimio avrio?*
         'Are you going to the university tomorrow?'
      B: *Ne. Ti ora na peraso na se paro?*
         'Yes. What time shall I pick you up?'

Since on many occasions this addressee gives a lift to the person asking the question, it is natural to interpret the question in this particular case as a request and to make the offer immediately. Although the addressee's interpretation is fully justified, the speaker's intention was not that of a directive.

Although such cases in which the speaker's intentions are not perceived correctly may cause misunderstandings, they do not necessarily do so. What is interesting to note is that many simple questions and statements, whether interpreted as requests or not, provide the addressee with the opportunity to express his or her readiness to satisfy the speaker's needs by offering or even by apologizing for being unable to do so. For example:

(8)   [between friends/colleagues]
      A: *Pali kseχasa ta tsiγara mu.*
         'Again I've forgotten my cigarettes.'
      B: *Δen pirazi eχo eγo.*
         'It doesn't matter, I have (enough for both).'

Alternatively, B might equally have responded with 'I'm sorry but I haven't got any, either.' Although in this case the speaker is most probably making a statement of fact (being an absent-minded person), one of the hearers grasps the opportunity to indicate her eagerness and inclination to share her cigarettes with the speaker.

14.4 Concluding Remarks

It seems, therefore, that although one motivation for off-recordness is to soften impositions, this is not the only one, nor even the most basic. It is necessary to go beyond this observation and look at the type of social relationships prevalent in a particular society and the values which inform them before arriving at conclusions concerning the type and degree of politeness encoded in off-record requests. More specifically, it is not unreasonable to suggest that in societies where the principles of distance and non-imposition prevail in daily encounters, it will be essential to take all linguistic measures to ensure minimization of coerciveness. Thus, it may be the case that in English the primary motivation for such off-record requests is to guarantee the addressee's autonomy of action. Nevertheless, it is questionable if and to what extent they encode the highest degree of politeness, especially when employed among family members and close friends.

However, in societies where greater importance is attached to closer relationships, such as in Greece, impositions will be assessed differently. The main concern will be to satisfy the need for involvement rather than that of independence. Thus, off-record indirect acts will not be chosen by participants eager to avoid intrusion but primarily by speakers willing to provide the addressee with the opportunity to make an offer to express their similarity of desires and solidarity. It appears that in Greek the primary motivation of off-record requests is not to guarantee non-imposition but rather to ensure eagerness to be of service or to indicate solicitude.

Thus, off-record utterances are perceived as polite ways of requesting in both cultures, but they are used to encode politeness in situationally and culturally specific ways.

Notes

I would like to record my indebtedness and gratitude to Peter Trudgill and Jean Hannah for their valuable advice on this paper, for their constant support and encouragement, and above all for the sense of confidence in my work they have always given me. Similarly, my very special thanks are also due to Robert F. Halls for his instructive comments on various aspects of this paper and to Richard W. Janney for giving me the opportunity to participate in the workshop on politeness phenomena at Innsbruck and to meet many interesting people. I am also grateful to Angeliki Tzanne, who helped me with the collection of data on indirectness.

1 It should be noted that *kseni* means both 'strangers' and 'foreigners'. For an explanation of some of the Greek characters here and in the examples, see footnote 2.
2 The examples used in this chapter come from the naturally occurring data for the study of indirectness I have been collecting for over two years. The interpretations given here, as is the case with any interpretation, are unavoidably subjective, but the large amount of data examined and the discussions I have had with various informants made these generalizations possible.

Although the examples are given in Latin characters, I have used the Greek characters 'γ' (velar voiced fricative), 'δ' (interdental voiced fricative), 'θ' (interdental voiceless fricative), and 'χ' (voiceless velar fricative) since they best render the equivalent Greek sounds.

3   My personal experience also illustrates the claim made. Many of my students (who are Greek) find it very hard at first to conceive of requests for 'free goods' as face-threatening, imposing actions.

References

Blum-Kulka, Shoshana. 1987. Indirectness and politeness in requests: Same or different? *Journal of Pragmatics* 11, 131–46.

Brown, Penelope and Stephen Levinson. 1978. Universals in language usage: Politeness phenomena. In Goody, Esther (ed.), *Questions and Politeness*. Cambridge: Cambridge University Press, 56–324.

Brown, Penelope and Stephen Levinson. 1987. *Politeness: Some Universals in Language Usage*. Cambridge: Cambridge University Press.

Durrell, Lawrence. 1978. *The Greek Islands*. London: Faber and Faber.

Ervin-Tripp, Susan. 1976. Is Sybil there? The structure of some American English directives. *Language in Society* 5, 25–66.

Herzfeld, Michael. 1983. Looking both ways: The ethnographer in the text. *Semiotica* 46, 151–66.

Lakoff, Robin. 1973. The logic of politeness; Or, minding your p's and q's. *Chicago Linguistics Society* 9, 292–305.

Leech, Geoffrey. 1983. *Principles of Pragmatics*. London and New York: Longman.

Matsumoto, Yoshiko. 1988. Reexamination of the universality of face: Politeness phenomena in Japanese. *Journal of Pragmatics* 12, 403–26.

Schegloff, Emanuel. 1979. Identification and recognition in telephone conversation openings. In Psathas, George (ed.), *Everyday Language: Studies in Ethnomethodology*. New York: Irvington, 23–78.

Sifianou, Maria. 1987. Politeness markers in Greek and in English. Unpublished PhD thesis. University of Reading.

Sifianou, Maria. 1992. *Politeness Phenomena in England and Greece: A Cross-Cultural Perspective*. Oxford: Clarendon Press.

Triandis, Harry (ed.). 1972. *The Analysis of Subjective Culture: Comparative Studies in Behavioral Science*. New York: Wiley.

Triandis, Harry and Vasso Vassiliou. 1972. A comparative analysis of subjective culture. In Triandis, Harry (ed.), *The Analysis of Subjective Culture: Comparative Studies in Behavioral Science*. New York: Wiley, 299–335.

Wierzbicka, Anna. 1985. Different cultures, different languages, different speech acts. *Journal of Pragmatics* 9, 145–78.

15

Cultural Differences in Framing: American and Japanese Group Discussions

Suwako Watanabe

15.1 Introduction

As relations between the United States and Japan become close and important, more interactions between Americans and Japanese are seen in ordinary, informal situations than in those involving government officials or business executives. In the past several years, the number of Japanese who study in the United States has increased rapidly. Some Japanese are enrolled in EFL programs, and others are in regular programs at undergraduate or graduate levels. As a matter of course, they experience cross-cultural communication, whether it is successful or unsuccessful, as everyday occurrences in their public and private lives.

Among the many speech events in which Japanese students may experience cross-cultural miscommunication, this study will examine a particular speech event in the school setting, that is, group discussion. The communication problems in this speech event occur not only because of the language difference but also because Japanese students are accustomed to different framing strategies for group discussion than American students. In other words, they have a set of expectations about how to interact in a group discussion that is different from American students'. According to Japanese students studying in the United States, they tend to get lost in the middle of discussion because sometimes opinions, questions, and so forth, expressed by American students are not as relevant to the topic or what has preceded as they expect these utterances to be, and they lose track of what is going on in a discussion and/or view the group discussion as incoherent and disorganized.

This chapter attempts to shed light on a cultural aspect of framing by demonstrating differences between American and Japanese university students in their framing of the speech event, group discussion. A further aim of this chapter is to demonstrate the application of theories of frames to the study of cross-cultural communication.

Suwako Watanabe, abridged version of "Cultural differences in framing: American and Japanese group discussions," chapter 6 in *Framing in Discourse*, edited by Deborah Tannen (Oxford: Oxford University Press, 1993), pp. 176–86, 191–9, 203–9. © 1993 by Deborah Tannen. Used by permission of Oxford University Press, Inc.

I have found the following differences between Americans and Japanese in their framings in the group discussions: (1) Americans promptly began and ended group discussions while Japanese were deliberate as they talked about procedural matters before discussions and, when ending, a leader punctuated the end by checking and announcing it. (2) When the participants were asked to give reasons, Americans framed their giving of reasons as "briefing" while Japanese framed theirs as "storytelling." (3) When they discussed a controversial topic, Americans used a "single-account" argumentation strategy (one account per discussant at a time) while Japanese used a "multiple-accounts" argumentation strategy (multiple accounts per discussant at a time).

In this chapter, I first discuss relationships among theories of frames, communication process, and cross-cultural communication; second, I discuss two characteristics of Japanese communication: nonreciprocality of language use and the tendency toward nonconfrontational communication, both of which are most relevant to the findings in this study. Then I demonstrate the analyses of the beginnings and the endings of the group discussions, presentation of reasons, and argumentation strategies. After this, I suggest the sources of these differences in discourse strategies at the level of framing. Finally, I discuss some theoretical and practical implications of my findings.

15.2   Theoretical Background

The notion of frames goes back to Bateson (1972), who identified three different levels of communication: (1) the denotative level (i.e., referential level), (2) the metalinguistic level (i.e., the purpose of communication is to talk about language), and (3) the metacommunicative level (i.e., communication concerning the relationship between the speakers). On the metacommunicative level, people send, intentionally or unintentionally, a message that tells the intention of the communication. For example, when one says, "I hate you," on the denotative level, s/he may send signals telling that the communication is intended to be "joking." The term "frame" is used to refer to messages defining intentions of communication in the sense that a picture frame delimits the picture within it and distinguishes the picture from the surrounding wall. Accordingly, Tannen (1984:23) defines "frame" as "a superordinate message about how the communication is intended." [...]

15.2.1   Frames and the communication process

Tannen (1986) writes that, in interaction, "meaning is never totally determinate but rather is . . . a joint production" (146). This suggests that, even in a verbal exchange between two people, the interactive process consists of not only two utterances produced by the two but also the hearer/addressee's interpretation appropriate at that particular moment. Without the addressee's proper interpretation, communication may fail in the worst case. In this sense, meaning is a joint production. However, the question arises, "How do we arrive at a proper interpretation?" An example of an exchange between two secretaries given in Gumperz (1981) suggests that sharing a language is not sufficient. The following is the exchange:

A: Are you going to be here for ten minutes?
B: Go ahead and take your break.

                    (Gumperz 1981:326)

Gumperz (1981) points out that although A's first utterance is a yes–no question, B does not give a yes–no answer, but an imperative one. This is because B interprets A's utterance as requesting B to stay while A takes a break, and, accordingly, B suggests that A take her break. The appropriateness of B's interpretation is confirmed by A's later line: "I won't take long." What is it, then, that is shared by the two secretaries? According to Goffman (1986:10–11), people within a society share frames, defined as "principles of organization which govern events – at least social ones – and our subjective involvement in them." It is because the two secretaries shared, besides the language, principles of organization which govern the event of "taking a break" that they understood each other and made appropriate moves.

In situations, interactants are always figuring out what it is that is going on, and on the basis of the interpretation, they act accordingly. Frames guide interactants to appropriate interpretations of what is going on in situations at each moment. Tannen (1985) and Tannen and Wallat (1993) have incorporated the various notions of frame and redefined frame as "sets of expectations about people, objects, events, settings, and ways to interact." [. . .]

Gumperz (1982:132) further points out that "conversationalists have *conventional* expectations about" interaction (italics mine). To the extent that these sets of expectations about people, objects, events, settings, and ways to interact are conventional, some parts of them may vary from culture to culture. [. . .]

If two people from different cultures do not share the same expectations about how to interact, that is, perceive differently the unmarked or marked linguistic features that signal a superordinate definition of what is being done by the talk, it is possible that differing interpretations of the situated meaning of what is said are processed by the interactants. On the surface, it looks as if they understand each other, but it is likely that they will find later that they have misunderstood each other. For the study of cross-cultural communication, it is useful to analyze various speech events from the perspective of the theories of frames. By closely examining communication, linguistic cues signaling frames in a given culture can be identified. The frames that are found in one culture can be, then, compared with those found in another.

15.2.2   Characteristics of Japanese communication

In this section, two characteristics of Japanese communication, nonreciprocality of language use and a tendency toward nonconfrontational communication, will be discussed. First, it has been repeatedly confirmed that Japanese communication is nonreciprocal. It is reflected in the vast variety of honorifics which are an essential part of the Japanese language (Harada 1976). Benedict (1946:47) writes that in Japanese "Every time a man says to another 'Eat' or 'Sit down' he uses different words if he is addressing someone familiarly or is speaking to an inferior or to a superior." The choice of language is strictly determined by the hierarchical social structure. According to Nakane (1972:30), a social anthropologist, the Japanese social structure is based on vertical hierarchy, and a

Japanese is always expected to use appropriate language according to his/her rank in relation to the addressee. Thus, information about the interactants such as age, social rank, occupation, gender, the schools they have graduated from, and the social profile of their families is drawn together to determine the relational position to others in every situation, which enables individual interactants to interpret the communicative intent of others and to make an appropriate move toward it.

The second characteristic of Japanese communication that is relevant to this study is the tendency toward nonconfrontational communication which is reflected in indirect and ambiguous communication (Tsujimura 1987, Ramsey 1985). The social motivations for nonconfrontational communication are strong emphasis on harmony within a group and sensitivity to face. An ethnographic study of interpersonal relations and behaviors of employees in a Japanese bank revealed that harmony was a high-ranking value (Rohlen 1974). Studies of management in Japanese companies (Stewart 1985) also found that "group orientation," which puts a strong emphasis on "consensus," is the key to their success. In Japanese society, confrontation is to be avoided since it disrupts harmony within a group. Moreover, it is considered almost prohibited when it is against the superior in the social hierarchy because it causes the superior's loss of face. Hirokawa (1987:146–7), in his study of communication in Japanese business, attributes deliberate ambiguity to the Japanese "desire to avoid embarrassing both themselves and others." He continues: "The Japanese appear to be particularly sensitive to the concept of 'face' (i.e., one's dignity and self-respect) and thus make every effort to avoid or prevent the 'loss of one's face' (i.e., the loss of self-respect and dignity resulting from public humiliation and embarrassment)." [. . .]

In sum, (1) nonreciprocal language use and (2) confrontational communication are characteristics of Japanese communication. These two characteristics, along with the social motivations underlying them, are important to relating the communicative behaviors of the Japanese participants in the group discussions to their expectations about interactions in that speech event.

15.3   The Data and the Analytic Focuses

Seven group discussions were set up and tape-recorded.[1] Each group discussion was made up of four participants who spent approximately fifteen to twenty minutes, in a school setting, spontaneously discussing three topics without formally appointing a leader. Depending on circumstances, some of the conditions were modified. For example, if a group felt the topics were not exhausted, they could spend more than twenty minutes discussing them.

There were four American groups and three Japanese groups, labeled A-1, A-2, A-3, A-4, J-1, J-2, and J-3.[2] All the participants were students of Georgetown University, Washington, D.C. Each group consisted of two males and two females, except A-2, which consisted of one male and three females.[3] All American participants were undergraduates, ranging from freshmen to seniors, studying Japanese in the intensive courses I taught. Members of J-1 were students in the EFL program at Georgetown University. Both the J-2 and J-3 groups consisted of one undergraduate and three graduate students.[4]

The three topics that were discussed are as follows:

1. Why did you decide to learn Japanese? (for A-1, A-2, A-3) Why did you decide to study abroad? (for J-1, J-2, J-3, and A-4)[5]
2. Many people say that, for Americans, Japanese is hard to learn compared to European languages. Do you agree or disagree? Why?
3. Discuss misunderstandings that are likely to occur between Americans and Japanese because of the language and cultural differences, giving specific examples of misunderstandings.

The transcripts were analyzed in order to identify linguistic features signaling framing differences. Analysis indicated two kinds of framing. One kind is found in the beginning and ending phases of the group discussions. It is what Goffman (1986:251) calls brackets, defined as "a set of boundary markers" that mark off a social activity from other ongoing events. Bracketing is another way of framing in the sense that, just like brackets used as punctuation in writing, they frame what is between them. The beginning and ending phases, in one sense, mark off the actual discussion frame; yet, in another, they are partial elements of the speech event as a whole. The analyses of these beginning and ending phases have revealed that the Americans and the Japanese bracketed the discussion frame differently.

The other kind of framing is identified in what is termed a communicative act such as requesting or joking. The assigned topics triggered two communicative acts in all the group discussions. One is to present reasons for a certain decision made in the past, in relation to the first topic; the other is to argue, in relation to the second topic. The Americans and the Japanese framed these two communicative acts differently.

In the following three sections, I analyze the beginning and ending phases, presentation of reasons, and argumentation, in turn.

15.4   How They Began the Discussion

The American and Japanese participants began discussions differently. The Japanese participants took a longer time than the American participants getting into the actual discussion frame as the Japanese talked about the order of turns and/or the procedure in which they would discuss the topics while the Americans did not. In every group, after I explained the procedures and turned on the tape recorder(s), I told the participants to begin, saying something like "Go ahead" or "Please." The American participants, on one hand, directly began to discuss without talking about procedural matters. In groups A-1 and A-2, the participants acknowledged my telling them to start with "Okay," then one participant began telling his/her reason for studying Japanese. In group A-3, when I was out of the discussion room, one member said, "Okay::," signaling the discussion frame. The discussion was immediately begun by another's directly asking a topic question. In general, the American groups gave the impression that the discussions started promptly.

The following excerpt is from the A-3 group discussion, which starts from Jenny's beginning her comment about the tape recorders, which was interrupted by my telling the participants to begin. Before then, Mike, pointing to the tape recorder in front of him, said, "Tsk, tsk, tsk." He had already indicated that he did not like being tape-recorded, the experience of which reminded him of taking an oral test. Immediately after Mike's reaction to the tape recorder, Jenny began as follows:

[Excerpt 1]
```
1  Jenny:   I hate-┐           ┌Oops.
2  Suwako:        └ Go ahead.─┘
3                  [pause:3.5 seconds; sounds of opening and closing a door as I left the dis-
                   cussion room]
4  Beth:    Okay::┐
5  Mike:          └So, Beth, why ┌did you decide to learn →
6  Sean:                         └Why.
                  Japanese.
7  Beth:    Uhm . . . I guess I decided to learn Japanese [Beth continues.]
```

During the pause (3), I was leaving the discussion room. When the door was closed and I was out, Beth said, "Okay::" (4), which signaled the discussion frame. Immediately, Mike called on Beth and asked her a question: "So, Beth, why did you decide to learn Japanese?" (6). Beth simply took up the turn and started with a hedge: "I guess I decided to learn Japanese . . ." (7). There was no discussion about how the group would go about discussing the given topics. Instead, there was a three-and-a-half-second pause during which the participation alignment changed from that of a prediscussion frame, mostly concerning the procedural matter of the experimental group discussion involving the four participants and me, to that of a discussion frame in which the four participants engaged in discussing the given topics.

In the A-1 discussion one member, Stan, asked the group who would talk first. However, it was very brief and did not turn immediately into a discussion:

[Excerpt 2]
```
(1)  Suwako:  Begin:: whenever you're ready::
(2)  Kris:    Okay.┐
(3)  Joan:         └Okay.┐
(4)  Stan:                └Who's first... I'll go.
```

When Stan asked the others, "Who's first?" they remained silent for one second. Stan interpreted the silence to mean that he should talk first, so he took a turn: "I'll go," (4).

In contrast to the American groups' prompt beginning, the Japanese groups took more time getting into discussion frame as they talked about procedural matters, such as the order in which they would take turns and the order of the topics to be discussed. For example, in the J-1 discussion, after I told them to begin, one member (Satoko, female) raised the question of how they would begin each topic. After discussion, they decided that one member (Teruo, male) would read each topic to the group. In the J-2 discussion, there was negotiation in terms of who would speak first. The most extensive beginning was that of group J-3 because they talked about both the turn order and a way of conducting the discussion. Let us look at their segment which begins with a line in which I told the participants to begin on their own. (An English translation follows the Japanese.)

[Excerpt 3]
[Japanese]

  (1) Suwako: JA   ONEGAI SHIMASU.
                     then ask

  (2) Yasuo: EETO, YAPPARI ANO ICHIOO JUNBAN-O FUNDE
                     well   as you see uhm   number-OP following

  (3) Keiko: SOODESUNE, ICHIBAN, NIBAN,   SANBAN TO.
                     right   number one number two number three

  (4) Fumiko: H-H-H-H

  (5) Yasuo: HN. HAIRI-YASUIDESU-NE.
                     hm enter-easy-FP

  (6) Keiko: SOODESU-NE. JAA.. MAA U-
                                right   -FP   then uhm
                ICHIBAN UE-WA HITORI HITORI HANASU
                number one top-TP one   one   talk
                SHIKA NAI KASHIRA.
                only   NEG wonder

  (7) Fumiko: SOO-NE.
                           right

  (8) Yasuo: SOODESU-NE.. JUNBAN KARA. DOO-SHIMASU-KA...
                     right-FP   turn   from   how-do   -QP

  (9) Ikuo: REDII FAASUTO.
                     lady   first

  (10) Fumiko: DOOZO.
                         please

  (11) Yasuo: AA IIDESU-NE, SORE-WA.
                     oh good-FP   that-TP

  (12) Fumiko: [laugh]

  (13) Keiko: [laugh]

  (14) Keiko: JA   WAKAI KATA KARA [laugh]
                     then young   person from

  (15) Fumiko: DOOZO.   [laugh]
                     please

  (16) Fumiko: IYA IYA ONEESAMA [laugh]
                     no   no   big sister

  (17) Keiko: EE::?
                     what

  (18) Ikuo: DOTCHIDEMO II-JA NAI DESU-KA.
                     either one   okay NEG   -QP

  (19) Keiko: YAPPASHI [Keiko takes turn.]
                     as you see

[English]

  (1) Suwako: Then, please.

  (2) Yasuo: Let's see, as you see, uhm, basically we'll follow
                  the number.⌐

  (3) Keiko: ⌐That's right. Number one, number →

  (4) Fumiko: ⌊H-h-h-h.
                  two, and number three.

  (5) Yasuo: Hm. It's easy to get in.⌐

  (6) Keiko: ⌊ That's right. Then..
                  well, the top one, each one of us has to talk in
                  turn, I wonder.⌐

  (7) Fumiko: ⌊That is so.⌐

  (8) Yasuo: ⌊That's right...
                  following numbers, how are we going to do...

  (9) Ikuo: Ladies first.⌐

 (10) Fumiko: ⌊ Please.

 (11) Yasuo: Oh, that sounds good.⌐

 (12) Fumiko: │ [laugh]

 (13) Keiko: ⌊[laugh]

 (14) Keiko: Then, from ⌈the younger one. ⌈[laugh]

 (15) Fumiko: ⌊Please   ⌊[laugh]

 (16) Fumiko: No, no. Big sister. [laugh]

 (17) Keiko: What?

 (18) Ikuo: It doesn't matter, does it.

 (19) Keiko: As you see, [Keiko takes turn]

First, in line 2, Yasuo suggested a discussion method by saying that the group would discuss according to the topic number. Keiko confirmed this and elaborated it: "Like number one . . . number three" (3). Second, in line 6, Keiko suggested a way to discuss the first topic: "each one of us just has to talk in turn," as in a round-robin system instead of a free discussion. Keiko's suggestion was immediately confirmed by Fumiko (7) and Yasuo (8).

Then, third, Yasuo raised the question of turn-taking order, saying, "how are we going to do . . ." (8). Ikuo suggested that ladies should go first (9). Almost at the same time, Fumiko said, "Please" (10), indicating that she conceded the first turn to someone else. Here, both Ikuo and Fumiko are making a concession. Yasuo, then, enthusiastically agreed with Ikuo, saying, "Oh, that sounds good" (11). Fumiko and Keiko interpreted this as meaning that one of them was to talk first, and they mutually made a concession in lines 14–17. Keiko invited "the younger one," Fumiko, to go first (14), and Fumiko invited "big sister," Keiko, to go first (15 and 16). It was when Ikuo said, "It doesn't matter, does it," in line 18, that Keiko volunteered to be the first speaker and began to tell her reason (19).

The pattern of the beginnings of the Japanese group discussions suggests that they did not want to be engaged in discussion unless procedural matters were agreed upon within the group. Because of this, the Japanese groups appeared to be deliberate in beginning the discussions. The question of who speaks first seems to be very important. No one simply decided to speak first; instead, there were invitations to take the first turn, concessions to others, and suggestions of who should talk first. In the end, in all the Japanese group discussions, a female member started, followed by the other female member, then by the younger male member, and last by the oldest male member. This consistent pattern of the turn-taking order in the Japanese group discussions further suggests that in the beginning segments, the Japanese members were negotiating not only the procedural matters but also a hierarchical order within a group. The hierarchical order is an essential part of Japanese communication to the extent that language style and vocabulary are carefully chosen according to the hierarchical relationship between the speaker and the addressee. It seems very natural for a Japanese to discern rank order within a given group because it is important information which enables him/her to choose appropriate linguistic forms with which to communicate.[6]

Furthermore, the importance of hierarchy is also reflected in the sequence of turns. One result of failing to use an appropriate linguistic form is loss of face. In general, the face of a highly respectable person is to be protected at any cost. This tendency was observed in the negotiation of turn-taking order in the Japanese group discussions in the sense that the oldest male member, who is considered the most superior, was given the last turn. From the Japanese perspective, in a meeting like these group discussions, in which the contents of the discussion are spontaneous and unplanned, the first turn entails the chance of making premature, wrong, or ignorant statements, resulting in loss of face, since it is too early to know what would be an appropriate statement. Thus, turn-taking order is indirectly arranged in the way that juniors/inferiors take earlier turns perhaps because their face is considered dispensable while seniors/superiors take later turns when they can express their opinions without losing face.

In brief, the American participants began group discussions promptly without talking about procedural matters, while the Japanese participants negotiated the discussion procedures and the turn-taking order before they began the actual discussion.

[. . .]

15.5   Expectations about Presenting Reasons in a Group Discussion

The first topic, "Why did you decide to learn Japanese or study abroad?" directly asked the discussants to present reasons. Every group, both American and Japanese, decided that each member should take a turn as in a round-robin system. Although the turn-taking system was the same, the average time of each member's presentation in the Japanese group discussions was much longer (71.5 seconds) than that in the American group discussions (23.1 seconds). When I closely examined the transcripts, I found that the time difference is the result of differences in expectations about the presentation of reasons between the American and Japanese participants. The Japanese participants framed their reasons as "stories." They seemed to have the expectation that they should present details as fully as possible, in chronological order, which built up to the situation in which they decided to study abroad. Telling small details and presenting them in chronological order made their reasons "stories." On the other hand, the American participants framed their presentations of reasons as "briefing" or "reporting." Their reasons were short and to the point, and they tended to use flat intonation. [. . .]

In the following section, I will first demonstrate the two characteristics of the Japanese members' presentation: organizing in chronological order and describing contexts in detail. Then, I will demonstrate two characteristics of the American members' presentations: keeping to the point and using flat intonation.

15.5.1   Japanese presentation of reasons

First, the Japanese participants tended to organize their reasons according to chronological order. They followed the chronological sequence of the process in which they decided to study abroad. Moreover, the most directly and immediately related reason was postponed until the end since presentation began from an original past event and built up to the point at which they made a decision. The following excerpt is Satoko's presentation, which contained a chronological sequence.

[Excerpt 7]
[Japanese]
(1) WATASHI -WA   JUUHAS-SAI   NO   TOKO-NI..
    I   -TP   18-years old   of   time-at
    ANO..   ASOBIDE..   LOS ANGELES-NO   HOO-E
    uhm   for fun   Los Angeles-of   area-to
    IKKAGETSUKAN   HOOMUSTEE   SHITA-NO-NE.
    for one month   homestay   did   -you know
(2) SOREDE   NANKA..
    and then   uhm
    IROIRO   KOTCHI-NO   REGYURAA-NO-HITO-TO
    various   this-of   regular-of-people-with
    TOMODACHI-NI   NATTE...
    friends   became
(3) DE..   NANKA   SOOYUUNO   MITETE
    and   uhm   that things   seeing
    NANKA   EIGO   HONTOONI
    somehow   English   seriously
    BENKYOO-SHI-TAKU   NATTE-NE
    study   -want   became-FP
(4) ZUTTO..   KOYOO TOKA   OMOTTE
    long   come   thought
    SORE-
    and

[English]
(1) In my case, when I was eighteen years old,
    uhm.. I went to Los Angeles.. for fun,
    homestayed for a month, you know.

(2)   And then, somehow..
       I became friends with people from the regular courses.
(3)   And.. as seeing things like that,
       I became seriously wanting to study English, you know.
(4)   For all those years, I was determined to come.
       And–

Satoko's most direct reason is that she wanted to study English seriously. Instead of directly stating so, she referred to a time when she went to Los Angeles. This event further unfolds in (2). She said that she became acquainted with some (Japanese) students who were studying in a regular college program. In (3), she stated that she was influenced by these students and what they were doing ("things like that") and became serious about studying English until she actually came back to the United States to study. The events in (1), (2), and (3) are chronologically sequenced.

Furthermore, the beginning of her statement of her reason was an orientation to a time in the past, in the expression "When I was eighteen years old" (1). A similar kind of orientation to a time was found in other Japanese participants' comments. Beginning with a particular point in the past is a way to set up a context for a story to unfold, and it is one way of framing a reason as a "story" in the sense that the audience is led to expect something to happen.

It also should be noted that Satoko used temporal connectives and phrases. First, in (2), she used *sorede* (and then); second, she began (3) with *de* (and). In the reasons presented by other Japanese participants, there was frequent use of temporal connectives and phrases, which indicates their tendency to follow a chronological sequence.

Second, the Japanese participants tended to describe contexts in detail, as if they were explaining each step in the process of reaching the decision. These details include background information directly or indirectly related to the point such as names of schools, the kind of company one had worked for, one's age, and psychological states, such as how one was eager to go abroad or was concerned about past circumstances.

The difference between the Japanese and American styles is illustrated by the following two examples. I will compare Minako's discourse in J-2 with Jill's in A-2 because their reasons are similar in that both referred to their fathers' experiences. Jill, on one hand, mentioned her father's experience in Japan briefly; Minako, on the other, extensively described her father's experience in the United States. In the following, the first excerpt is Jill's reason, and the second is Minako's.

[Excerpt 8]
Jill: And my dad went over to Japan
      to set up exchange programs
      and he really liked it.
      So I decided to take Japanese.

[Excerpt 9]
(Japanese)
Minako: EETOO, WATASHI-WA CHIISAI-KORO-KARA
        well   I   -TP little   -when-from

GAIKOKU-NI IKI-TAI-TTEYUU KIMOCHI-WA
abroad   -to go -want-that   feeling-TP
ATTAN-DESU-YO-NE.
had   -P -FP
DE, WATASHI-NO CHICHI-GA.. MOO NANTE YUUKA
and I   -of father-SP   what   say
AMERIKA-BIIKI TTEYUUKA..
America-fan   that say
ANO.. UCHI-NO CHICHI-JISHIN-GA KOTCHI-DE
uhm I   -of father   self   -SP here   -in
BENKYOOSHI-TAKUTE ...
study   -wanting
DEE, U OF M, UNIVERSITY OF MISHIGAN TO
and   U of M University   of Michigan   and
ATO UCLA TO NI ANO
also   UCLA and to uhm
KENKYUUSHI-NI ITTARI TOKA SHITE
research   -to go   etc.   did
MO TONIKAKU SOTCHI-NO-HOO-NI
    anyway   that-of-direction-in
ANO WATASHITACHI-NO-KOTO-MO
uhm we   -of-thing-too
IKASE-TAI   TTEYUUKA
make go-want or
SOOYUU-KANJI DATTA-NODE,
so   -like   was   -so
SOREDE JOJONI-NE
therefore gradually-FP
KOTCHI-NO-HOO-NI IKOO-KANA
this-of-direction-in   go   -wonder
TTE KANJI-NI NATTE KITE.
that like-P   become   came

(English)

Well, I, since when I was little...
had had a desire to go to a foreign country.
And my father was..
what should I say,
an American fan, if I could say..
y'know.. my father himself
wanted to study here...
And he went to U of M, University of Michigan
and, also UCLA, y'know,
to do research or did things like that.
Anyway, in that direction, y'know,
he wanted to make us go, or

> since it /he was like that,
> therefore, gradually, y'know,
> I had come to feel like
> "How about going this way?"

Jill's reference to her father's account is very succinct ("And my dad went over to Japan to set up exchange programs and he really liked it.."). In contrast, Minako's reason is extensive in that she explains her father's motivation for going to the United States ("my father himself wanted to study here"), mentions which US universities he attended (U of M and UCLA), and tells of his hopes for his children ("he wanted to make us go").

In Jill's segment, the fact that her father influenced her was expressed only through a logical connective "so" in "he really liked it. *So* I decided to take Japanese." In contrast, Minako explicitly stated how she was influenced in "therefore, gradually, y'know, I had come to feel like 'How about going this way?' "

Furthermore, in Minako's segment, it is observed that the main point was presented toward the end. In the beginning, she explained her father's experience. Then, at the end, she stated that she had come to consider studying in the United States. From the viewpoints of the speaker who was telling what happened in the past and the other participants who expected to hear a story, it was natural that the main event was postponed until the end.

I have shown in the previous section that the reasons of the Japanese participants contained the features of (1) chronological organization and (2) detailed description of past contexts. These features suggest that the Japanese participants framed their reasons as "stories."

15.5.2 American presentation of reasons

While the reasons presented by the Japanese participants were extensive, the reasons presented by the American participants were relatively brief. The best term with which to characterize the way in which the American participants presented reasons is "briefing" or "reporting." They tended to use flat intonation and to keep their reasons short by directly making the point. The following comparison of two deliveries by the same person (Mark in the A–3 group discussion) demonstrates the way he differentiated the use of intonation according to his perception of the ongoing communicative task. The first excerpt is a segment from Mark's episodic example of a cross–cultural misunderstanding in response to the third topic ("Discuss misunderstandings that are likely to occur between a Japanese and an American because of the language and cultural differences. Give specific examples of misunderstanding."). The episode concerned his difficulty in arranging to send flowers to his mother, who was living in Japan, on Valentine's Day. In Japan, it is the custom for girls to give chocolates to boys on Valentine's Day, which is the opposite of the custom in the United States. To make the situation more complicated, Mark was in the United States when he called a flower shop which was near his parents' house in Japan.

[Excerpt 10]
(1) So I was calling up this flower shop..
     near my house[7]

(2) and I was trying to like
     all the Japanese I could /?/
     to convince this guy to send like uh..
     five thousand or eight thousand yen,
     take flowers to my mom's house on Valentine's Day.
(3) And he was like, you know, basically, he-,
     I had to go through like three people
     and eluding me all around,
(4) and they couldn't conceive the concept
     that I was sending,
     me a guy,
     sending flowers,
     why flowers,
     on Valentine's Day you send chocolate, you know,
     to a girl, you know,
(5) he was-, couldn't conceive it at all.
(6) And I tried and tried,
     finally he gave up, you know,
     and he, uhm, and uh,
     I just, I had like someone else deal with
     the whole thing.
(7) But it's, it was really hard...

When Mark was telling this episode, his intonation rose and fell frequently. For example, in (2) he used an exaggerated tone for "convince." He also emphasized
"flowers," "mom's," and "Valentine's," which were key words for the point of the story.
In (4), after he said, "I was sending," he put emphasis on "me" and more emphasis
on "guy," by quickly raising and dropping intonation on each word, to explain that
the concept of a male sender was contrary to the Japanese expectation. Furthermore,
the intonation he used when saying, "Why flowers," was a skeptical one, not the one
for innocently asking for a reason, because from the Japanese perspective, it was obvious that the flowers made no sense. He also emphasized contrastive key words such as
"chocolate" and "girl."

The second excerpt is Mark's presentation of the reasons why he decided to learn
Japanese, in which he used flat intonation.

[Excerpt 11]
(Mark)
(1) I decided .. when I was, I spent a summer over there, visiting friends.
(2) And I've never taken a language /where/ I can speak.
(3) And uhm.. people seem nice.
(4) [Beth: [laughter] People. [as if she were saying Mark's line] "I like people."]
(5) [laughter] So I.. went back to.. decided to take it.
(6) And my parents got a job there...
     which gave me more incentive...
(7) That's why.

Compared to the various uses of intonation in the previous excerpt, the intonation contour in this presentation is weak in its rise and fall. The intonation is, in a sense, flattened. For example, in the last word "friends" in (1), the intonation fell on the primary stressed syllable instead of rising.

When Mark remarked about the Japanese people, "people seem nice" (3), Beth laughed and said, "I like people," teasingly, as if she were reminded of a funny story which she and Mark shared.[8] She used dramatic intonation, putting strong emphasis on "like" and dramatically differentiating the stress level on the two syllables in "people." The intonation that Beth used was different from the one which Mark had been using. Beth's remark also prompted Mark's laughter (5), but as he immediately resumed what he had been saying, his intonation became flat again.

Second, the American participants tended to keep their reasons short by reaching the point directly. An extreme example is Linda's reason in the A-4 group discussion, when the participants were asked of their reasons for deciding to study abroad. She said:

[Excerpt 12]
To figure stuff out for going to college..
waste a year before I went to college..

The point of Linda's reason was a purpose for studying abroad. She directly reached her point by starting with the infinitive "to," the function of which is to express a purpose. In contrast to the Japanese ways of telling reasons, Linda did not describe what the circumstances were, nor give specific information such as names, nor explain how she had felt about going to college before she ultimately decided not to begin college at that time.

Another way of briefly expressing one's reason is to summarize details. An example of this is found in Steve's presentation. He was the only one of the American participants who organized a reason in chronological order. In the following excerpt, Steve began by referring to an exchange program and explained the process, from applying for the scholarship to arriving in Japan.

[Excerpt 13]
	1	Well, I went on YFU also.
	2	And.. it was just the opportunity,
	3	I was interested in Japan,
	4	and the opportunity came up...
	5	So the, uh, scholarship to spend a year there,
	6	so .. I just applied for it..
→	7	One thing led to another, and..
	8	then, I was there

In (6), Steve said that he applied for a scholarship. Then, in (7), he summarized details of many events that might have happened by using the expression "One thing led to another." Instead of describing in detail how he was selected as an exchange student before he arrived in Japan, he used a shortcut expression to bridge the gap between the point of application and the point of his arriving in Japan. This short-cut enabled him to keep to the point and make the reason clear without going into a lengthy story.

The previous two sections have shown characteristics of the ways in which the American and the Japanese participants presented reasons. The chronological organization and the elaboration with details found in the Japanese participants' reasons suggest that they framed their reasons as "stories." On the other hand, the flat intonation and briefness found in the reasons presented by the American participants indicate that they framed their presentation of reasons as "briefing" or "reporting."

Being given the same or a similar topic, the participants from the different cultures framed their task differently. The communicative task that they shared in common, in this case, may be termed as "responding to a why-question, which asked reasons why certain kinds of decisions were made in the past, within a group discussion." If this question were asked in a casual conversation, perhaps Americans would have framed reasons as "stories." However, the speech event of "group discussion in a classroom setting" seems to be a major factor in their framing reasons as "briefing" rather than "stories" because it is expected they should reach the point directly. In a situation in which two or more people get together to get a job done within a certain time limit, the American expectation is that one should "get to the point" instead of "beating around the bush." To the Japanese participants, getting to the point seemed to have little impact on their ways of presentation. From the Japanese perspective, direct point making is generally avoided, while its opposite trait, indirectness, is preferred as it is considered a convenient tool for preventing frictions or conflicts from damaging harmony within a group. The Japanese participants, thus, seemed to have used the framing of "storytelling" as in talk shows, interviews, and casual forum/roundtable-type discussions which are commonly set up by the media in order to elicit personalized stories.

[. . .]

15.6 Conclusion

This study has demonstrated framing differences between the American and Japanese students as they interacted in group discussions. The analyses of the beginning phases of the group discussions revealed that the American discussants entered the discussion frame promptly while the Japanese discussants began gradually and deliberately, because, in the beginning, they talked about how they would discuss and only then began the discussion. The analysis of presenting reasons showed that the Japanese participants framed their reasons as "stories" as they tended to organize reasons according to chronological order and to give detailed contexts. In contrast, the American discussants framed their giving of reasons as "briefing" or "reporting" by their use of flat intonation (which was completely different from the intonation used when telling stories) and their tendency to keep reasons to the point. [. . .]

Each of the analyses on the discourse level revealed cross-cultural differences on the framing level. The differences in the way Americans and Japanese began and ended suggest differences in their frames for group discussion. The Americans perceived the discussion as an activity which binds four individuals only in terms of the purpose of discussing, so they began their group discussions when they were told to do so and ended them when the purpose was fulfilled. In contrast, the Japanese perceived the activity as one they should carry out as a group rather than as co-present individuals. They perceived themselves as group members in a hierarchy established within a given group. Thus, they negotiated to establish the hierarchy when beginning discussion and punctuated the end of the activity in order to get out of the discussion frame as a group, all at once.

When discussing the first topic, which asked the participants to give reasons for a decision, the Americans framed the presenting of reasons as briefing or reporting while the Japanese framed the same act as storytelling. It should be pointed out again that the Americans chose to frame their presentations as briefing in spite of the fact that Americans, in general, often tell stories when asked the same type of question in a different situation such as casual conversation. I suggest that they framed the giving of reasons as briefing because they perceived that the speech event "group discussion" required them to get to the point without using too much time of the limited time available. For the Japanese, the time limit was not as important as sharing what one went through when deciding to study abroad.

[. . .]

Founded on Goffman's (1986) notion of frame, that is, that people within a society (or a culture) share, to a certain extent, principles of organization that govern social events, this study investigated some governing principles of group discussion shared among American students, on the one hand, and among Japanese students, on the other. I found that, in the same kind of speech event, participants from different cultures interact differently, and this is partially due to differences in expectations about interaction, in general, or specific to the speech event.

I have shown, then, that some elements of frames are specific to a culture. This has significant implications for cross-cultural communication. For instance, the finding of the differences between the Americans and the Japanese in their expectations about how to argue enables us to predict that when Japanese and Americans are to discuss a controversial issue, the Japanese may experience frustration, being unable to participate in the argument because they find the one-at-a-time argumentation of the Americans too fast. At the same time, the Americans may perceive the Japanese as illogical and elusive because they give both supportive and contradictory accounts. In giving of a reason for a decision made in the past, Japanese, hearing Americans' brief reasons, may be unsatisfied, asking, "Is that all?" as they expect to hear personalized stories. In contrast, Americans may feel frustrated hearing Japanese give trivial, irrelevant details without reaching the main point immediately. Americans may perceive Japanese as overly cautious, prearranging the discussion manner and asking one another whether the discussion should be ended. In contrast, Japanese may perceive Americans as too individualistic, ignoring the importance of hierarchy within a group.

In conclusion, this chapter has shown cultural differences between Americans and Japanese in their expectations about interaction in group discussions. It also demonstrates that a frame analysis provides a strong foundation for explicating the mechanism of cross-cultural communication. Theories of frames help identify what is shared among interactants, while they can also be the basis for the identification of causes of miscommunication among those from different cultures. Finally, the notion of frames, along with discourse analysis, enables us to connect cultural knowledge at the macrolevel to individuals' communicative behaviors at the microlevel, in the sense that the former is considered a resource for interactants as they rely on it to come up with a plausible interpretation of what is going on at a particular moment and make a proper move.

Appendix A: Transcription conventions

Transcription conventions follow those used in Tannen (1984).

.. noticeable pause or break in rhythm (less than 0.5 second)
... 0.5 second pause
.... 1.0 second pause

Highlight marks emphatic stress, but, in some cases where so indicated, it indicates a point of analysis

. marks sentence-final falling intonation
? marks yes/no question rising intonation
– marks a glottal stop or abrupt cutting off of sound
: marks elongated vowel sound
/?/ indicates transcription impossible
/Words/ in slashes indicate uncertain transcription
[Brackets] are used for comments on quality of speech and context
⌈Brackets between lines indicate
⌊overlapping speech
Brackets on two lines indicate second utterance
latched ⌉
         ⌊onto first, without perceptible pause
→ left arrows indicate points of the analysis
An arrow at right indicates speaker's turn →
continues without interruption and a succeeding line is anticipated

Appendix B: Abbreviations used in Japanese transcription

TP for *wa* = topic particle marking the preceding noun phrase as a theme or a topic
SP for *ga* = subject particle marking the preceding noun phrase as a subject
Q for *ka* = question particle which marks the sentence as a question
QT for *to, toka,* and *-tte* = quotation particles which are equivalent to "that" for English verbs "think," "feel," "seem," "say," etc.
FP for *yo* (I tell you,) *ne* (isn't it (?)), *naa* (interjection) = sentence-final particles which assign extra meaning to the preceding sentence
ONO. = onomatopoeic expressions

Appendix C: Ethnographic profiles of the participants

Group A-1

Name	Sex	Age	Grade	Ethnic Background
Kris	F	N/A	Senior	Anglo-Saxon
Joan	F	22	Senior	Korean
Stan	M	18	Freshman	Anglo-Saxon/Japanese
Ken	M	N/A	Junior	Anglo-Saxon

Group A-2

Name	Sex	Age	Grade	Ethnic Background
Katy	F	19	Freshman	Anglo-Saxon
Jill	F	N/A	Freshman	Anglo-Saxon
Mary	F	18	Freshman	Anglo-Saxon
John	M	18	Freshman	Anglo-Saxon

Group A-3

Name	Sex	Age	Grade	Ethnic Background
Beth	F	19	Sophomore	Anglo-Saxon
Jenny	F	19	Sophomore	Anglo-Saxon
Sean	M	21	Senior	Anglo-Saxon
Mark	M	20	Sophomore	Anglo-Saxon

Group A-4

Name	Sex	Age	Grade	Ethnic Background
Cindy	F	20	Sophomore	Anglo-Saxon
Linda	F	19	Freshman	Anglo-Saxon
Paul	M	19	Sophomore	Anglo-Saxon
Steve	M	20	Sophomore	Anglo-Saxon

Group J-1

Name	Sex	Age	Subject of Study	Length of Stay in the United States
Hiroko	F	23	EFL*	1 month+
Satoko	F	20	EFL	1 month+
Teruo	M	22	EFL	1 month+
Jiro	M	20	EFL	1 month+

*EFL is English as a Foreign Language.

Group J-2

Name	Sex	Age	Subject of Study	Length of Stay in the United States
Kazuko	F	23	linguistics	1 year+
Minako	F	22*	government	7 years+
Masao	M	26	linguistics	1 year+
Kiyoshi	M	32	linguistics	1 year+

*Minako was an undergraduate student, and the others were graduate students.

Group J-3

Name	Sex	Age	Subject of Study	Length of Stay in the United States
Keiko	F	28	linguistics	6 months+
Fumiko	F	23	linguistics	6 months+
Yasuo	M	29	linguistics	1 year+
Ikuo	M	N/A*	Foreign Service	6 months+

*Ikuo was an undergraduate student, and the others were graduate students.

Notes

I am greatly indebted to Deborah Tannen, who offered valuable suggestions and comments in the course of writing this chapter as well as my dissertation, "Framing in American and Japanese Group Discussions," from which this chapter has been adapted. I am also grateful to Deborah Schiffrin and Miwa Nishimura for their helpful comments on the dissertation; to all the students who participated in the group discussions; and to Sarah Koch, who helped me with editing. Nevertheless, all remaining errors are my responsibility.

1   The tape recorders that were used were SONY TC-2 and TC-11.
2   The A-1 and A-2 group discussions took place in a Japanese drill session in which I was a drill instructor. The other group discussions were set up in discussion rooms in the university library.
3   Since I used a portion of a Japanese drill session which was naturally going on, I could not control gender ratio of group A-2.
4   Ethnographic profiles of the participants are shown in Appendix C.
5   Although the predicate parts of the first topics are different, both were designed to ask discussants to give reasons for something that they chose to do. In addition, analysis will focus on how discussants presented reasons rather than on the nature of the reasons. Thus, it was assumed that the two versions of the first topic can be treated as similar in terms of the objective of the questions.
6   A paradigm of polite forms is prescribed in the language. An appropriate form is selected according to whether the speaker wants to exalt a superior or lower an inferior (including oneself). If the speaker chooses not to exalt or lower the addressee, neutral forms are used. For instance, *imasu*, *irasshaimasu*, and *orimasu* all refer to an animate kind of existence. When I am talking to my teacher, I use *irasshaimasu* in reference to my addressee:

Irasshaimasu.   S/he (the teacher) is (here/there).

On the other hand, when referring to myself, I use *orimasu*.

Orimasu.   I am (here/there).

However, when I am talking to my colleague who is of equal status, I use *imasu* in reference to my colleague or myself.

Imasu.   I am (here/there) *or* S/he is (here/there).

7   "My house" in this context means his parents' house in Japan.
8   Or it is also possible that Beth interpreted Mark's remark as a shallow comment and she teased him about it.

References

Bateson, Gregory. 1972. *Steps to an ecology of mind*. New York: Ballantine.

Benedict, Ruth. 1946. *The chrysanthemum and the sword*. New York: New American Library.

Goffman, Erving. 1986. Frame analysis: An essay on the organization of experience. Reprint. Boston: Northeastern University Press.

Gumperz, John J. 1981. The linguistic bases of communicative competence. *Analyzing discourse: Text and talk*, ed. by Deborah Tannen, pp. 323–34. Washington, DC: Georgetown University Press.

Harada, S. I. 1976. Honorifics. *Syntax and semantics: Japanese generative grammar*, ed. by Masayoshi Shibatani, 449–561. New York: Academic Press.

Hirokawa, Randy Y. 1987. Communication within the Japanese business organization. *Communication theory: Eastern and western perspectives*, ed. by D. Lawrence Kincaid, 137–49. San Diego, CA: Academic Press.

Nakane, Chie. 1972. *Japanese society*. Berkeley, CA: University of Califormia Press.

Ouchi, William G. 1981. *Theory Z*. Reading, MA: Addison-Wesley.

Ramsey, Sheila. 1985. To hear one and understand ten: Nonverbal behavior in Japan. *Intercultural communication: A reader*, ed. by Larry A. Samovar and Richard E. Porter, 307–21. Belmont, CA: Wadsworth.

Rohlen, Thomas P. 1974. *For harmony and strength: Japanese white-collar organization in anthropological perspective*. Berkeley, CA: University of California.

Stewart, Lea P. 1985. Japanese and American management: Participative decision making. *Intercultural communication: A reader*, ed. by Larry A. Samovar and Richard E. Porter, 186–9. Belmont, CA: Wadsworth Publishing Company.

Tannen, Deborah. 1984. *Conversational style: Analyzing talk among friends*. Norwood, NJ: Ablex.

Tannen, Deborah. 1985. Frames and schemas in interaction. *Quaderni di Semantica's round table discussion on frame/script semantics*, ed. by Victor Raskin. Quaderni di Semantica 6:326–35.

Tannen, Deborah. 1986. Discourse in cross-cultural communication. *Text* 6(2):143–51.

Tannen, Deborah and C. Wallat. 1993. Interactive frames and knowledge schemas in interaction: Examples from a medical examination/interview. *Framing in discourse*, ed. by Deborah Tannen, 57–76. New York: Oxford University Press.

Tsujimura, Akira. 1987. Some characteristics of the Japanese way of communication. *Communication theory: Eastern and western perspectives*, ed. by D. Lawrence Kincaid, 115–26. San Diego, CA: Academic Press.

Yamada, Haru. 1992. *American and Japanese business discourse: A comparison of interactional styles*. Norwood, NJ: Ablex.

Discussion Questions

1. If you have had an experience in which you thought someone from another culture was rude, try to analyze that interaction from the approaches in this part. Do any of the approaches help explain the "rudeness" of the person you spoke to? Which approaches work the best?

2. For one or more of the case studies, suggest what theoretical approach (or approaches) from Part I is being used by the author. What specific features of the reading make it an example of that approach?

3. Use a different approach to try to account for the data in one of the articles. For example, can one use an Ethnography of Speaking or Politeness approach to account for the data presented by Tannen?

4. Collect a narrative yourself and compare it to the descriptions given by Holmes. You can audiotape a friend or acquaintance, or you could use email, instant messaging, or chats to save stories people tell online. Can you find the different parts of the story? Are your narratives more like the Maori or the Pakeha stories outlined by Holmes?

5. Alim's reading raises the question of what to do when a minority culture's different ways of speaking are part of the way disadvantage is perpetuated. Do you think a minority culture should have to learn the majority culture's way of speaking, or do they have the right to their own way of speaking in every instance? For example, should a student be able to write a term paper in Black English? Why or why not?

6. Collect opinions about the interactional style of a particular culture, either in print or from friends and acquaintances. Using an approach similar to Tannen's and Watanabe's, can you account for the differences? Can you think of a way that this culture may have different contextualization cues than yours? What is different?

7. How is emotionality expressed in language? Compare the characterization of Swedish culture described by Daun with those described by Tannen in her chapter. What do you think would happen if a Swede were present at the Thanksgiving dinner?

8. Outline the range of ways requests (or another speech act) can be accomplished in your language, and characterize them as direct or indirect. In what situations would you use each one? Compare these to another person's, either from the same culture or a different culture. What similarities and differences are there? Can Politeness Theory account for these differences? Do any other approaches work better? Why or why not?

9. How should gender differences be thought of in a culture? Are the differences discussed by Harvey similar to subcultural differences? If so, how? If not, why not?

10. Summarize the address terms that different people use with you, and the kinds of relationships each address term indexes. Does it create power, solidarity, intimacy, or something more specific? Compare your address terms with others. Are there differences in the address terms used? Are they cultural differences? Does using a particular address term in a specific place tell people anything about your culture? What?

Part III

Cultural Contact: Issues of Identity

Introduction

Most research on intercultural discourse focuses on the differences between groups of speakers, from a variety of perspectives as was explored in part I. But cultures also come into contact within the individual, within individuals who have to live and function in two languages and two cultures simultaneously. Such research is much more scarce and the questions, the problematization, are different. The issue is no longer miscommunication but rather identity: Who am I? What sociocultural, sociolinguistic rules do I use?

We have collected three such studies here. Karen Ogulnick reflects on the acquisition of a second language and a second culture in "Learning language/learning self." You might call this a postmodern approach; it tells no big story with sweeping generalizations. As a matter of fact, we can draw no universal generalizations from her account at all – it is her little story, a personal story. And yet, any reader who has lived for a year or two in another culture, learning the language, will feel a strong empathy.

Benjamin Bailey in "The language of multiple identities among Dominican Americans" does pursue group identity or rather, the identity of members of a group of a visible minority. Speaking English, they are perceived as African American, speaking Spanish they become Hispanic and so they can situationally activate various facets of their multiple identities. This multilinguistic construction of identity undermines implicit assumptions of uniformity and essentialism of US racial categories.

Christina Bratt Paulston's "Biculturalism: Some reflections and speculations" is just that – reflections on what it is like to be both Swedish and American. What is it like to function with two sets of rules? Can you in fact have two sets of rules? Are all bicultural individuals the same? These are some of the questions which she addresses. It should be added that this was not a very popular piece with the most adamant proponents of bilingual education who argued that to become bilingual was the same as to become bicultural – presumably as a political argument for the Bilingual Education Act of 1968 and the legislation which followed it.

16

Learning Language/Learning Self

Karen Ogulnick

One of my first childhood friends in Flushing, New York, was a Chinese girl named Wendy who lived next door. Except for my grandparents' house, where Yiddish was spoken frequently, Wendy's house was the only place where I recall hearing a language other than English. I experimented with my own version of "Chinese" at home, stringing together the Chinese sounds I heard at Wendy's house. My grandfather heard me and became intrigued. "Can you really speak Chinese?" he asked me. When I insisted that I was really speaking Chinese, he proceeded to quiz me, just to be sure: "How do you say this in Chinese?" he'd ask as he pointed to various household objects, and I'd promptly come up with my own Chinese version. "Mary, she's speaking Chinese!" My grandmother nodded her head and smiled in a way that said she wasn't convinced. But Grandpa's enthusiasm remained strong, and became an even greater source of amusement to the rest of the family than my newly discovered linguistic talent. Every once in a while someone in my family recalls the time "when Grandpa really believed [I] could speak Chinese."

Ever since I was very young, I wanted to travel. When I was 19 I finally had my first chance to travel abroad. As a college student in London, I lived in an international hostel with other foreign students, most of whom were from Asia and Africa. We would take turns cooking and tasting one another's cultures – Indonesian, Indian, Malaysian, Thai, Chinese, Iranian, Tunisian, Ethiopian. I also contributed a dish of my own: spaghetti à la Bronx. After four months of our dinners together not only did I develop a taste for hotter and spicier foods, but the many stories I heard about the faraway places and the people my friends were so homesick for gave me a craving to travel more extensively. A few months later, I did. What began as an invitation to spend the Chinese New Year with friends in Hong Kong turned into a 13-month journey through Southeast Asia.

As I traveled from one country to another, I enjoyed communicating primarily through gestures. I imagined that I could read minds and send telepathic messages. I focused on

Karen Ogulnick, "Learning language/learning self," chapter 25 in *Language Crossings: Negotiating the Self in a Multicultural World*, edited by Karen Ogulnick (New York: Teachers College Press, 2000), pp. 166–70. Reprinted by permission of the publisher. All rights reserved.

facial expressions and zoomed in on eye contact. There were many times when I wanted to know what people were actually saying; however, I also often sensed that I was at a distinct advantage not knowing. Ambiguity felt liberating. I didn't have to conform as much to expectations or behavior that I might consider restrictive. I could move in and out of culturally imposed definitions more freely.

While being a traveler gave me an enormous sense of freedom, living in a foreign country for an extended period of time was a different experience altogether. I first went to Japan in 1985 to teach English in Japanese high schools. Before my departure, I spoke not even one word of Japanese. (Well, maybe "sushi".) I convinced myself that people in Japan could speak English, and if they couldn't, I was planning on teaching it to them. Almost immediately upon my arrival on that cold, wet July day, I realized, when nobody spoke English, that learning Japanese might be a good idea. In spite of what I understood logically, I made very little if any effort to do so. On one level, I wanted to be included in the culture, but on another, I felt comfortable remaining outside it. I also was convinced that it would be almost impossible for me to learn Japanese. Aside from my stint at Chinese, I did not consider myself a good language learner.

To my surprise, my extremely limited Japanese did not prevent me from making friends with people who didn't speak English. I even learned, to some degree, *sado* (tea ceremony) and *ikenebo* (flower arrangement). These classes were recommended to me by my supervising teacher at the high school because they were considered appropriate for young single women. They were conducted entirely in Japanese. I also watched a lot of TV. Without understanding a word, I was thoroughly engrossed in the soap operas, samurai dramas, sumo wrestling matches, *animé* (cartoons), even the commercials.

I worked six long days a week in Japanese schools. On the seventh day I was usually invited to attend an outing with Japanese colleagues or friends. I spent months not understanding most of what people said. (This was often the case even when they spoke English.) At this point I was becoming more confident in my interpretations of body language, pitch, tone, volume, and silence. I felt I could sense the emotional climate – when an interaction was harmonious and when I thought someone was being overly polite, stiff, and compliant. It was reassuring to think that I had at least *some* idea of what was going on.

The first time I realized I was absorbing Japanese occurred about three months after I first arrived in Japan. One day while I was riding on a streetcar on my way to work, an elderly woman entered at one of the stops and sat down right next to me in the empty car. When she began to speak to me in Japanese I cut her off with an expression I memorized – *zenzen wakarimasen* – I can't understand a word of what you're saying. This didn't seem to discourage her, however, from continuing to talk to me. I just smiled and nodded as she spoke and felt relieved when we arrived at her stop, at which point I waved her off with the one other word (in addition to *sushi*) that comprised my entire active Japanese vocabulary – *sayonara*. Once alone with my thoughts, I realized that I had understood some of what she had said, something about the weather, and that the entire conversation was in Japanese. This sudden awareness – that I was beginning to learn Japanese – was exhilarating. From that moment on, I could no longer resist being swept up in the current of Japanese language and culture.

The first stage of my verbal ability consisted of imitating what I heard. This posed several problems, since it is not always appropriate for two speakers to use the same level of politeness and formality with one another. For instance, when speaking with my landlord, an elderly grandmother, I repeated words and expressions that are typically spoken to children. Similarly, I responded to shopkeepers and other people providing services with the same extremely polite expressions with which they greeted me, such as *irrashaimase* (welcome), which prompted some startled looks from people who apparently were not used to customers, greeting them back in honorific language. I also picked up some "male" and regional expressions from friends and colleagues, which may have sounded cute and funny in some contexts, such as when we were out drinking, but in more serious situations, these same expressions became crude and dis-respectful. I could tell by the grimaces on people's faces. People rarely corrected me directly; on the contrary, they showered me with praise: "*Nihongo ga o-jouzu desu ne*" (your Japanese is very good), to which I often responded by saying, "Thank you." Another no-no. It took me a while, but finally I realized that the compliments were intended as an indirect way of correcting me.

One of these occasions was when I met a high school principal for the first time. Before leaving his office I bowed and said *gokuroosamadeshita* (thank you very much). He responded by telling me how well I spoke Japanese, which prompted me to thank him again. He bowed and responded with a different thank you, *osukaresamadeshita*. Outside his office, a Japanese English teacher was kind enough to enlighten me on the many different "thank you"s in Japanese, depending on whom you are thanking for what. Apparently, I thanked the principal for doing some demeaning work for me. That's when he told me how well I spoke Japanese. The second time he thanked me for my trouble (realizing I was having a hard time learning the language). It would have been more appro-priate to use a polite expression that is used in a formal context: *domo arigato gozaimasu*. It didn't take long for me to learn the ubiquitous *sumimasen* (*thank you* that also means *excuse me*), and the more humble and polite *osoreirimasu* (*thank you* that also means *I'm sorry*). With friends I learned to be more casual with *arigato*, or even more intimately, *domo* (thanks). And (this one took me a while) I learned that when someone compli-ments you, it is more appropriate to modestly reject it, *iie, sono koto wa arimasen* (oh no, not at all), than to say "thank you."

Even in the use of directions, the Japanese have still found a way to express their status and humility. As a world traveler, I had developed some confidence in my sense of direction. This was shaken when I began to travel independently in Japan. I've always taken for granted that "up" means north and "down" means south, but that is not always the case in Japan, which made train travel confusing, since trains are referred to as "up" or "down" trains. Since all trains arriving at Tokyo are called "up" trains, the important thing to know, apparently, is not the actual direction you are going, but whether the city of your destination has a higher or lower socioeconomic status than the one you started from.

Status is also marked in the psychological and geographical division of Japan into two parts: eastern Japan (the side facing China), also known as "the backside," and western Japan, "the frontside." The contradiction one faces is that with all the lip service given to "tradition" in Japanese culture, it is the more modern and future-oriented "frontside" of Japan that is afforded higher status, as people who reside in Japan's "backside" self-effacingly refer to themselves as "country bumpkins."

Because my job required a lot of traveling, I had many opportunities to meet people. If I had my own car, I probably wouldn't have learned as much Japanese. The trains and buses were the best language laboratories. While in transit, it might have looked as though I was reading an English newspaper, but more often I'd be eavesdropping on the conversation behind me, sometimes even taking notes. I also had to ask for directions often and found it very encouraging when people not only understood me, but responded and sometimes initiated further conversation in Japanese. There were even a few surprising occasions when I became involved in deep discussions.

Similar to the way people sometimes tell fellow travelers their life stories, women I barely knew shared intimate details of their lives with me. While being invited in this way into people's lives helped to make me feel more inside the culture, telling me their stories may have been a way for Japanese women to connect with the outside world. I was told tales of forced arranged marriages that made me feel relieved to be American. I believed I was freer than these Japanese women I had met. In contrast to the supermodern image that the American press promoted of Japan prior to my initial departure in 1984, the society in which I was living reminded me more of an ancient time when women were controlled and constrained to activities and roles revolving around the household.

When I returned to Japan for the third time in 1993, I saw things quite differently. This time, looking at Japanese women seemed more like looking into a mirror, not one that reflected back my exact image, but one that revealed, even where there were differences, much about the condition of being a woman in my own culture. As a thirty-two year-old single Jewish American woman living in Hiroshima, I contemplated the contradictions of learning to speak and of being silenced by a culture. My inside/outside location as a participant–observer in Japan gave me a vantage point from where I could notice oppressive structures in both Japan and the United States, particularly how they pertain to women, which is difficult to do from a space within the culture. The glass ceiling became more visible.

Ironically, learning the importance that role status plays in communication – that levels of politeness and formality are governed by such factors as age, class, social position, and gender – inhibited me: I felt self-conscious and afraid of making mistakes that would make me look like a stupid, unrefined American in many Japanese people's eyes. My desire to fit in as much as possible to the society that was nurturing my new Japanese persona motivated me to work on producing softer, more polite and refined ways of speaking. The way Japanese was affecting me physically did not occur to me until the first time I saw myself on a video, which a friend taped at the end of my second year in Japan. I watched this non-Japanese woman, sitting demurely on her knees, delicately covering her mouth with her hands as she giggled, speaking in a high-pitched tone of voice. She seemed so Japanese. I knew that she had my face and hair, but I could hardly recognize the rest of myself.

Through learning Japanese I learned something about my first language and culture, which leads me to conclude that there is a dialectic between language learning and identity that is inextricably linked to our historical experiences and the sociopolitical contexts in which we find ourselves. Beyond knowing words and grammar, learning a language involves acquiring a role, and knowing how to act according to that social definition. It is knowing, sometimes tacitly, sometimes consciously, what others approve and disapprove of, how to sit, how to enter a room, how to read nuances, when to speak and when to be silent, how to accept a gift, how to ask for a favor, how to ward off unwanted invitations. Knowing this is also inhabiting, willingly and unwillingly, consciously and subconsciously, a location in the hierarchy. In other words, language learning entails a process of fitting into one's place in society, or rather, one's imposed place.

17

The Language of Multiple Identities among Dominican Americans

Benjamin Bailey

Abstract

As a group whose members are Hispanic, American, and largely of African descent, Dominican Americans must negotiate distinctive issues of identity in the United States. Language is central to these negotiations, both as a symbol of identity and as a medium through which to construct and display local social meanings. Dominican Americans use linguistic forms from multiple varieties of two codes, Spanish and English, to situationally activate various facets of their multiple identities. This multi-variety linguistic and inter-actional construction of identities undermines implicit assumptions of uniformity and essentialism in United States linguistic and ethnic/racial categories, particularly in the construction of the category "African American."

17.1   Introduction

The language and identities of Dominican second-generation high school students in Providence, Rhode Island reflect a social reality of growing up in Dominican families with Dominican social networks, but residing and going to school in a low-income, multi-ethnic American inner city. As a group whose members are both Hispanic *and* largely of African descent, Dominican Americans[1] must negotiate distinctive issues of identity in the United States. Up to 90% of Dominicans have sub-Saharan African ancestry (Haggerty 1991), which would make them African American by historical United States "one-drop" rules of racial classification (Davis 1991). Dominican Americans, how-ever, do not think of themselves as "Black," but rather as "Dominican," "Spanish," or "Hispanic," and their Spanish language makes this ethnolinguistic identity situationally

Benjamin Bailey, "The language of multiple identities among Dominican Americans." This is a shortened version of an article which appeared under the same title in *Journal of Linguistic Anthropology* 10:2 (December 2000), pp. 190–223. Reproduced by permission of the American Anthropological Association. Not for sale or further reproduction.

salient to outsiders. Everyday enactment of a Dominican American identity thus involves negotiating multiple and conflicting ascriptions of identity and resisting American Black–White racial categorization, a fundamental form of social organization in the United States (Omi and Winant 1994; cf. Rodríguez 1994; Smedley 1993).

Second-generation language alternates among linguistic forms drawn from varieties of Dominican Spanish, African American English, local English sociolects, and hybrid forms resulting from contact among these varieties. Members of the second generation use these diverse linguistic resources to situationally align themselves with, and differentiate themselves from, European Americans, African Americans, and even other Dominicans. This situational, linguistic enactment of identity challenges received social categories such as "Black," "White," and "Hispanic," and undermines the essentialized assumptions on which they are based. Dominican American enactment of ethnolinguistic identity highlights contradictions in the category "African American" particularly clearly because African American *race* and African American *ethnicity* have historically and popularly been treated as one and the same (Waters 1991).

Many members of the second generation in Providence identify strongly with African American peers, with whom they share a structural position characterized by low-income,[2] segregated neighborhoods, substandard schools, and non-White/African-descent phenotype ascription. This affiliation is reflected and reconstituted in part through extensive adoption of lexical and syntactic forms from African American English, which serves many young Dominican Americans as a language of resistance to dominant disparaging discourses, just as it does for many African American youth (e.g. Morgan 1994a). At the same time, however, the Dominican second generation emphasize that they are "not Black." In contrast to non-Hispanic second-generation immigrants of African descent (Bryce-Laporte 1972, Woldemikael 1989, Waters 1994), members of the Dominican second generation don't identify themselves in terms of phenotype – as African American or Black – but rather in terms of language – as "Spanish." The many second-generation Dominicans who are phenotypically indistinguishable from African Americans, for example, "speak Spanish" in order to counter others' assumptions that they are African American. Dominican ethnic/racial identity in the second generation is simultaneously a "reactive ethnicity" – in which significant aspects of identity are a reaction to being defined as a minority in a hierarchical United States society – and a "linear ethnicity" – in which identity is based on continuation of linguistic and cultural practices from the Dominican Republic (cf. Portes 1995).

In this chapter I explore how Dominican Americans use language to construct and make sense of their social identities, focusing on boundaries that are situationally activated between in-group and out-group. The term "identity" comes from Latin, *idem*, meaning "the same." Identities are constituted by socially counting as "the same" as others or counting as "different" from others. All individuals have multiple characteristics and allegiances, so it is the situational and selective highlighting of commonalties and differences – rather than the existence of underlying, essential natures – that is characteristic of identity groupings (Evans-Pritchard 1940, Moerman 1965, Barth 1969).

Cohen (1978:387) emphasizes that there are multiple levels at which commonalty or difference can be constructed or activated. He defines ethnicity as "a series of nesting dichotomizations of inclusiveness and exclusiveness" that are activated at different levels at different times:

Group A can be labeled A in relation to B, C, and D. But among themselves, A people are keenly aware of subgroup differences in which groups X, Y, and Z all understand the ethnic distinctions among themselves and the possibility of greater or lesser differences in the future, depending upon a large range of factors. (Cohen 1978:388)

Analysis of identity thus revolves around the questions of how, when, and why individuals count as members of particular groups. Analysis of language and naturally occurring discourse is a means to understanding how individuals, as social actors, highlight social boundaries and activate facets of identity.

In this chapter, I focus on the boundaries that are activated between in-group and out-group at two nested levels of specificity. First I show how Dominican Americans linguistically claim a "non-Black" Spanish/Dominican identity – made evident through Spanish use and represented by the ethnolinguistic label "Spanish" – that differentiates them from other African-descent Americans. Although Dominican Americans situationally align themselves with African Americans – as non-Whites – they also see themselves as distinct from African Americans, and they situationally highlight this distinction.

Then, I illustrate a way that Dominican immigrants situationally highlight boundaries among themselves. United States-raised Dominican teenagers see themselves as different from more recently immigrated Dominican teenagers (cf. Zentella 1990 among New York and island Puerto Ricans), and differences in language practices between United States- and Dominican-raised individuals can serve to highlight these differences. Language can function as an emblem of identity – as in the common Dominican usage of the term "Spanish" as an ascription of ethnic/racial identity – but it is also a tool used to instantiate multiple, shifting alignments and oppositions that are situationally activated or backgrounded vis-à-vis other individuals or groups. Individuals use multiple Spanish and English resources to activate aspects of identities in ways that belie reified dichotomies, monolithic identities, and the one-to-one correspondences between linguistic code and social affiliation that have been emphasized in some research on language and ethnicity (e.g. Fishman 1989).

17.2   Methods

Fieldwork for this study took place in Providence, Rhode Island and the Dominican Republic between July 1996 and July 1997. Data collection methods included ethnographic observation, audiorecorded interviews, and videorecording of naturally occurring interaction in school, home, and community contexts.

Transcripts of naturally occurring interaction in this article come from videorecordings made of students from Central High School, a Providence city school of 1350 students, which is over 20% Dominican. Roughly 60% of the student body is Hispanic, with Puerto Ricans and Guatemalans comprising the second and third largest Hispanic groups. About 16% of the students are non-Hispanic African-descent, 16% are Southeast Asian, primarily first and second generation Cambodian and Laotian refugees, and about 5% are White American. Central is one of four major high schools in the city of Providence system, which tracks its high-achieving students into one academic-magnet school. Central has the problems typical of many inner-city public schools. Almost 90% of the students are categorized as poor according to federal guidelines, and more than half of the students officially enrolled in the 9th grade drop out by the 11th grade.

Six principal subjects, aged 16 to 18, were repeatedly observed and interviewed, and were videorecorded throughout a school day and in one non-school context. Selected segments were transcribed in detail following conversation analytic conventions (Heritage and Atkinson 1984; see Appendix A). Bilingual Dominican American consultants, including the six principal subjects, aided in the transcription and translation of talk and offered interpretations and explanations of interactions.

17.3   Multiple Dominican Identities and Heteroglossic Language

Social and linguistic categories, e.g. "African American," "White," "Spanish," and "English," suggest uniformity, masking internal variation and the diachronic change that is characteristic of both available social categories (e.g. Lee 1993) and language (e.g. Thomason and Kaufman 1988). While the label "Dominican American" similarly suggests a degree of uniformity, the range of identities enacted by Dominican Americans, and the explicit heteroglossia (Bakhtin 1981) of their language, embody and recreate a social world that undermines assumptions of unitary categories particularly clearly.

The multiple and multifaceted identities of Dominican Americans are reflected and reconstituted through their broad linguistic *repertoire* (Gumperz 1964). The linguistic resources comprising Dominican American language are not monolithic codes of English and Spanish, but include forms drawn from multiple varieties of each, e.g. Standard Providence English, Non-Standard Providence English (e.g. "yous guys"), African American Vernacular English (e.g. "He be working"), Standard Dominican Spanish, and Regional Non-Standard Dominican Spanish (e.g. /puelta/ for puerta 'door' and /poike/ for porque 'why') (cf. Zentella 1993, 1997 among New York Puerto Ricans). Dominican American language includes both the alternation of forms associated with diverse varieties and also the use of distinct, convergent forms resulting from language contact, e.g. word and phrasal calques (Otheguy, García, and Fernández 1989) and syntactic transference and convergence (Clyne 1967, 1987). These categories of forms are discrete from an etic, analytical perspective, but in the communicative practices of Dominican Americans, these features form part of a seamless whole.

The variety of linguistic forms used by Dominican Americans in Providence, and their unmarked juxtaposition in everyday interaction, provide a window into Dominican American social reality. All language, including that of monolinguals, is heteroglot, shot through with multiple and competing sociohistorical voices and ideologies (Bakhtin 1981). This heteroglossia is particularly salient in the language of Dominican Americans, however. There are two main reasons for this: (1) Dominican Americans draw forms from grammatical codes that count as distinct languages and from varieties with implications of stark social difference, e.g. African American Vernacular English (hereafter AAVE) and American English, and (2) use of these forms is not tied to domains in one-to-one fashion (Fishman, Cooper, and Ma 1971). Explicitly heteroglossic Dominican American language practices both reflect and help reconstitute the Dominican American *repertoire of identities* (Kroskrity 1993). Single utterances or short exchanges that include forms with diverse provenances index the multiple social forces and processes, e.g. immigration, regional Dominican origins, economic class, and United States racial/ethnic formation processes, that inform aspects of the identities of Dominican Americans in Providence.

The following segment of transcript documents some of the juxtaposition of linguistic features of the language used by Dominican American high school students in everyday intra-group interaction:

(10)

[(JS #2 12:26:40) Isabella and Janelle are sitting on steps outside of the main school building at the end of their lunch period. Isabella has returned from eating lunch at a diner near the school, and she has been describing the generous size of the turkey club sandwich she has just eaten.]

J: Only with that turkey thingee //*ya yo (es)toy llena*.
                                        'I'm already full'
I: //Two dollars and fifty cent.
J: That's good. That's like a meal at //Burger King.
I: //That's better than going to Burger King, you
   know what I'm saying? And you got a Whopper, french fries,
   //and a drink. And=
J: //Yeah
I: =the french fries cost a dollar over there.
J: For real?
I: *Sí, sí cómo no?*
   'Yes, really.'
J: *Mirale el ombligo. Miralo. Se le ve, ya se lo tapó.* ((looking at a passerby))
   'Look at her belly button. Look. You can see it, she already covered it.'
   (.5)
I: *Seguro porque se lo enseñó.* ((laughing))
   'She must have showed it.'
   (1.5)
J: //( )
I: //But it's slamming, though, oh my God, mad ['a lot of'] turkey she puts in there.
J: That's one thing I l-, I love the way *como l-* =
                                        'how th-'
   =the American ['White Americans'] be doing sandwich, they be <u>rocking</u> ['are excellent'], them things, yo, they put <u>everything</u> up in there, yo.

This segment of transcript illustrates several aspects of the multi-variety language of Dominican Americans. The exchange is primarily in English, which is typical of the interactions among English-dominant Dominican Americans that I observed and recorded, but it includes distinctive alternation of forms indexing a Dominican American identity. Most salient of these, perhaps, is the alternation between English and Spanish in code switching (Bailey 2000a). Isabella and Janelle use Spanish phrases (*ya yo estoy llena* and *como l-*) in turns that are otherwise in English, and some of their turns are entirely in Spanish (e.g., *Sí, sí cómo no?*).

Janelle and Isabella are also using a third grammatical variety in this exchange, African American Vernacular English (AAVE). In the stretch of speech *the American be doing sandwich, they be rocking, them things, yo* Janelle uses grammatical structures unique to AAVE. She uses the AAVE habitual "be" to capture the recurring way White Americans make sandwiches (*the American be making sandwich*) and the on-going, excellent character of those sandwiches (*they be rocking*). This habitual "be" is one of the most researched features of AAVE (Labov 1972a, Morgan 1994b), and it is a component of the tense/aspect system of AAVE that sociolinguists use to define AAVE (Labov 1980). A second form characteristic of AAVE that both Janelle and Isabella use is plural nouns without overt plural marking (Baugh 1983:95). Janelle elides the /s/ and /əs/ in *American* and *sandwich*, respectively, while Isabella elides the /s/ in *cents*. (Further AAVE forms used by Dominican Americans will be discussed in a separate section below.)

In addition to using syntax associated with Spanish, standard American English, and AAVE, Janelle and Isabella use lexical items and expressions that some scholars have defined as AAVE (e.g. Smitherman 1994) and that are popularly associated with the speech of urban, African American youth. Isabella uses the adjectives *slamming* ('great') and *mad* ('a lot of') and the expression *you know what I'm saying* (described by Smitherman (1994:151) as a "call for a response from the listener"), while Janelle uses the verb *to be rocking* ('to be great') and the interjection *yo*, which has crossed over from its AAVE origins to the wider population.

Constellations of linguistic features that are officially authorized as codes or languages, e.g. "English" or "Spanish," are often implicitly treated as if they were of monolithic, uniform character in the context of bilingualism. This veils the diversity of linguistic resources available to speakers within codes. The English that Isabella and Janelle use in the exchange above, for example, includes prescriptivist standard American English forms, non-standard vernacular forms, lexical forms associated with AAVE, and grammatical forms that occur only in AAVE, indexing a particular urban American background. Their Spanish similarly indexes particular linguistic histories. Their pronunciation of word-initial *y* as an affricate /dʒ/ (e.g. in *ya yo*), and their elision of syllable final /s/ (e.g. in *e(s)toy*), for example, are characteristic of Caribbean Spanish, particularly Dominican and lower-class varieties (Lipski 1994, Alba 1995). Variation among forms within officially authorized codes has social implications – as does code switching – both as a reflection of social identity and as an expanded set of linguistic resources which members can use to enact their identities.

As a result of language contact, Dominican American language also includes novel forms, the result of, e.g. syntactic transference (Clyne 1967) or convergence (Clyne 1987, Gumperz and Wilson 1971), and forms used in novel ways, e.g. calques. Forms used above by Isabella suggest the influence of Spanish discourse patterns on her English. She preposes the direct object of the verb in this segment in what has been called fronting, focal object construction (Silva-Corvalán 1983:135), or focus-movement (Prince 1981) (DO=Direct Object; S=Subject; V=Verb):

(11)
mad **turkey she puts** in there
     DO   S   V

In Spanish such preverbal Objects can serve various discourse functions, depending in part on intonation contour (Silva-Corvalán 1983). Use of this preverbal-Object structure in English allows Isabella to highlight her point – the large amount of turkey put on her sandwich – in a linguistically creative way.

The variety and juxtaposition of linguistic resources by Janelle and Isabella in the above exchange reflect their specific life experiences and aspects of their social world. The alternation of English and Spanish reflects their dual socialization as does Isabella's use of a characteristically Spanish discourse pattern. Their use of forms associated with urban African American youth – particularly Janelle's use of AAVE syntax – suggests longer-term contact with African Americans and identification with African American experiences. Janelle's use of the term "American" to mean "White people" indicates that she identifies herself with reference to another nation-state and in terms of racial/ethnic categories in which she doesn't count as "American."[3] The juxtaposition of these diverse linguistic elements in single utterances, e.g. *I love the way como l- the American be doing sandwich* reflects and instantiates a social reality in which both linguistic practices and social identities fit poorly into received, unitary categories of language and identity.

17.4   Spanish as Resistance to Phenotype-based Racialization: "We all Speak Spanish, so we're Spanish"

Dominican Americans' use of AAVE has a paradoxical effect on their efforts to resist dominant discourses that misrepresent or disparage them. While AAVE serves as a form of resistance to White denigration of non-Whites, it makes many Dominican Americans increasingly subject to another United States form of symbolic domination: the Black–White racial dichotomy.[4] In the Dominican Republic, Dominicans consider their nationality, ethnicity, and race [*raza*] to be Dominican, and they do not generally think of themselves as "Black" or of significant African descent (Hoetink 1967, Del Castillo and Murphy 1987, Davis 1994:119, Moya Pons 1996). Dominican American teenagers in Providence, Rhode Island also self-ascribe racial identities that are outside the historical United States Black–White dichotomy. When I surveyed Dominican Americans in Providence, "What is your *race?*" they answered "Dominican," "Hispanic," and "Latino," but never "Black" or "White" (Bailey 2000b, 2001).

Dominican Spanish language serves as a resource for resisting Black–White dichotomization and ascription on several levels. In terms of identity ascription in everyday encounters, it is the primary means by which Dominican Americans display an ethnolinguistic identity that can counter phenotype-based ascriptions. In a broader sense, it encompasses an alternate model of the social world in which African/European phenotype is less important in terms of social differentiation, and it links individual Dominican Americans to a wider Dominican community who share and recreate this world. Spanish language is so central to identity for Dominican Americans in Providence that many use the term "Spanish" as a label for their race, culture, and ethnicity, even when active fluency in Spanish has been lost.

The significance of Spanish language for countering phenotype-racial identity ascriptions and communicating an ethnolinguistic identity in everyday encounters is evident in both (1) Dominican Americans' explanations of how outsiders know that they are

Dominican/Hispanic rather than, e.g. "Black" or "White," and (2) the common proof procedure that Dominicans use to counter others' assumptions that they are Black or White American: they show that they can speak Spanish. Dominican Americans from the ten to fifteen percent segment of the Dominican population who are of overwhelmingly European ancestry are sometimes perceived as White Americans, for example:

(29)

Martin: I don't really look Spanish. . . . People don't think that I'm Spanish until I tell them I speak Spanish, or whatever. If they just look at me, "Oh, it doesn't look like he's Spanish."

BB: Do Dominicans tease you and say, "Oh you're White"?

Martin: No – sometimes that'll happen. Sometimes they don't know I'm Spanish, and they'll say something or whatever and I'll say something back in Spanish but not directly to them, but just so they can hear it, though. . . . And then I have like my friends, after they've known me for a couple of years, and we'll just reminisce and talk about things from before, they be like "I always knew you were Spanish." I tell 'em, "No you didn't. I remember telling you I was Spanish." They're like "For real?" After a while you get used to it, I guess. And they're like "You look Spanish" and I'm like "No I don't. You never thought that before."

A much larger percentage of Dominican Americans are regularly perceived to be African American. Even at Central High School, where Caribbean Hispanics out-number non-Hispanic African-descent students by more than two to one, many Dominican Americans are assumed to be African American until they are heard speaking Spanish:

(30)

BB: If somebody asks you "What are you?", what do you say?

Janelle: I usually say Spanish, Dominican. I'll usually say Dominican first, cause most people – most people think I'm Black though. A lot of people think I'm Black. A lot of people! . . . .

BB: Can you think of a specific time when someone thought you were Black?

Janelle: I was in the gym, and usually in school I don't really talk in Spanish, and I was talking to some kid in English, and some girl, I guess she was listening, and I said a word in Spanish, and she goes "Oh my god, you're Spanish." No she goes, "You know Spanish." She thought I was just a Black who knew Spanish. I was like "I am Spanish." She's like, "Oh my god, I thought you was Cape Verdean or Black." I was like "No." A lot of people think I'm Black. I don't know, it's usually just little things like that, just people be like "What are you, Black?" I'm like "No, I'm Spanish."

In this exchange between Dominican American Janelle and an African American class-mate, "Spanish" is treated not just as a language, but as an ethnic/racial identity.

Being "Spanish," in local terms, does not mean that one is from Spain, but rather that one is Spanish-speaking and ethnically/culturally/racially Hispanic:

(31)

BB: When people ask you what you are, what do you say?

Nanette: I say I'm Spanish. I've had disputes over that one, "What do you call
          Spanish, you're not from Spain." When you're not Spanish, you don't really
          understand it, and I don't know if I really understand it myself. When
          people ask me, I'm Spanish. They're like, "What's Spanish? Where are you
          from then if you're just Spanish?" Well, there's tons of different Spanish
          people, but we just come from all different places. But we all speak Spanish,
          so we're Spanish. And they're like, "But no we speak English, and we're not
          all English." But it's just so different. There's something different. We all say
          we're Spanish.

Spanish language in the United States is a defining symbol of common origins in
former Spanish colonies, and the label for the language becomes a label for the social
identity indexed by speaking it (cf. Urciuoli (1991) among New York Puerto Ricans).

In Janelle's reported exchange about being perceived as Black, Janelle and her interlocutor treat the social category "Spanish" as parallel in type to the folk-racial category
"Black," but mutually exclusive from it. In local terms, if one is Dominican or Spanish-
speaking, one doesn't count as "Black," regardless of phenotype. An individual only counts
as Black *and Spanish* if he or she has a Spanish parent and a non-Hispanic African-descent
parent. This local system of classification does not necessarily privilege identities based
on phenotype – specifically, perceived degrees of European and African ancestry – over
those based on other social criteria such as language or national origins. This African
American classmate of Janelle treats Janelle's Spanish language (and subsequent self-
ascription as Spanish) as valid evidence that Janelle is *not* Black or Cape Verdean, even
though she had initially perceived Janelle to be Black or Cape Verdean. Race is thus
treated not as a static attribute of individuals, but rather as a locally and linguistically
achieved identity.

This primacy of Spanish ethnolinguistic identity over African-descent phenotype-racial
identity can be seen in the discursive, interactional negotiation of identity. In the segment of interaction transcribed below, a student of Southeast Asian descent, Pam, tells
an African-descent Dominican American, Wilson, that she didn't think he was Spanish
when she first saw him – she assumed he was African American – but she then came to
realize that he was Spanish when she heard him speak Spanish. As a joke, Wilson and
a Dominican confederate, JB, pretend that Wilson *is* Black or African American, and
not Spanish.[5] Although Wilson never identifies himself as Black or African American,
he and JB know that Wilson is regularly perceived to be African American. This enables
them to try to fool Pam by getting her to believe that Wilson is Black, a social category
attribution that is implausible from a Dominican perspective. The humor of this put-
on depends on tensions and disparities between Dominican and United States socio-
cultural frameworks for understanding race and social categories.

When Pam cites Wilson's speaking of Spanish as evidence that he is Spanish, rather
than Black, JB and Wilson initially deny that he can speak Spanish and then devise scenarios that could explain his apparent Spanish use. They falsely claim, for example, that
Wilson's father is Black and that his mother is Black *and* Spanish and was born in America.
(Wilson was born of Dominican parents in the Dominican Republic and came to live in

Providence with his father as a seven-year-old.) Wilson and JB are engaged in an adolescent put-on about Wilson's race, ethnicity, and language, but analysis of their talk reveals much about local criteria, and ordering of criteria, for defining a person as "Black" or "Spanish."

(32)
[(WR #2 1:34:57) Wilson, Pam, and JB are sitting in class. The teacher is absent and students are treating the period as an opportunity to socialize, ignoring the substitute teacher's written assignment.]

Pam: Yo, the first time I saw you, I never thought you were Spanish.
          (.5)
Wilson: //Who ?
JB: //(He's) Black.
Pam: I never-
Wilson: Cause I'm Black.
JB: (   )
Wilson: Cause I'm Black.
Pam: No
JB: His father //is Black , her mother is-, his mother is uh–
Wilson: //I'm Black
Pam: (Can he) speak Spanish?
JB: No
Wilson: Cause I was – //I was
Pam: //Yeah!
JB: So why (d-   ?)
Wilson: No, no seriously, I'm Black and I was raised in the Dominican Republic.
          (.5)
Wilson: For real.
Pam: Your mother's Black?
Wilson: My mom? No, my father.
Pam: Your father's Black, your //mother's Spanish?
Wilson: //My mom's Spanish
JB: His mom is Black – and she's Spanish
Wilson: Is mix(ed)
JB: His mom was born over here.
          (2.0) ((Wilson smiles at Pam and throws a piece of paper at her))
JB: Wilson, don't t(h)row anything to her.
Wilson: *Excusa me, se me olvidó, que es la jeva tuya*
          'Sorry, I forgot that she is your girlfriend.'
JB: *Cállate, todavía no.*
          'Be quiet, not yet!'
Pam: English!
JB: English, yeah!
Wilson: I said I'm sorry.
JB: He can't speak Spanish.
Pam: I saw you were talking to him (   )

Wilson: I understand, but I don't speak everything.
            (2.2) ((Wilson smiles broadly at Pam))
JB: I'm teaching him.
            (5.5)
Wilson: *Qué tú vas (a) hacer en tu casa hoy, loco?* ((slaps JB on the back))
            'What are you going to do at your house today, man?'

Spanish language is being treated in this segment as the key to racial/ethnic identity, preceding phenotype. When JB and Wilson claim that Wilson is not Spanish, but Black, Pam asks if he can speak Spanish. The implication is that if Wilson can *speak* Spanish, then he *is* Spanish, rather than Black. Wilson and JB also treat Spanish language as the key to determining social identity, both for ratification as Spanish and for disqualification from the category "Black." JB initially denies that Wilson can speak Spanish, despite immediately available counterevidence. Admitting that Wilson can speak Spanish would invalidate JB and Wilson's story that Wilson is not Spanish but Black.

Individuals of African descent in the United States have historically been categorized on the basis of phenotype and treated as ethnically undifferentiated. Dominican Americans in Providence successfully resist this form of classification by defining themselves in terms of national and/or ethnolinguistic origins rather than phenotype. Their use of Spanish language is a salient, everyday way of constituting communicative contexts in which they do not count as Black. This linguistic enactment of race highlights the processual and contingent nature of race, thereby undermining the dominant United States Black–White dichotomy, which rests on assumptions of inherent and unchanging difference. Individual Dominican American's freedom to define themselves as something other than Black, despite African–descent features, thus represents a transformation of United States racial categories, if only at the local level.

17.5   Intra-Group Boundaries: "He's Like a Hick, he Talks so much Spanish"

I have thus far argued that Dominican Americans (1) use varieties of language associated with Black and White Americans to mark boundaries between themselves and White Americans, and (2) use Spanish to mark boundaries between themselves and African Americans. In the first instance, use of AAVE serves to align Dominican Americans with African Americans and other non-Whites. In the second instance, use of Spanish serves to align individuals with other Spanish speakers and differentiate them from non-Spanish speakers. These nested "we"/"they" dichotomizations operate at different levels of specificity, i.e. the White/non-White is more general, while the Spanish/not Spanish is a subgroup boundary among members of the non-White group. Within the group "Spanish," there are many additional subgroupings, e.g. between Caribbean Hispanics and other Latin Americans, and between Puerto Ricans and Dominicans.

Salient among these intra-Hispanic boundaries are divisions between Dominican Americans who were raised primarily in the United States, and more recent Dominican immigrants, who are more *Dominican* and less urban *American* in their language, dress, and cultural framework (cf. Zentella 1990 among island and New York Puerto Ricans). While Spanish language is a *unifying* diacritic (Barth 1969) of Spanish or Dominican identity in contexts involving non-Hispanics, it can be a key index of *difference* in local, intra-Hispanic contexts. Some Dominican Spanish forms used by recent immigrants, for example, are seen by Dominican American teenagers as indexing a lack of urban American sophistication.

The ways in which such intra-group boundaries are situationally highlighted belie static one-to-one correspondences between code and social affiliation. Language and social identities in the context of bilingualism or code switching in the United States have often been treated as dichotomous, focusing on two languages and the ways in which alternation between these languages corresponds to expression or enactment of one of two identities (e.g. Gumperz 1982:73–5; Fishman, Cooper, and Ma 1971).[6] As described above, however, the linguistic resources of Dominican Americans and the identities variously available to them do not fall into two categories, and innumerable "we"/ "they" dichotomies can be situationally activated through discourse.

In the following segments Isabella and Janelle use language to display shifting stances toward various Spanish language forms and various Dominican/Dominican American identities. In the first segment Isabella gives an account of how she came to be dating a recently arrived Dominican immigrant, Sammy, and why she is going to break up with him. Her explanations of why she eventually found him to be undesirable – including a code-switched direct quote of his Spanish – reveal the local and interactional negotiation of code meanings in the construction of Dominican American identities.

(35)
[(JS #2 11:56) Isabella and Janelle are sitting outside, skipping class, discussing their weekend plans. Isabella has been dating Sammy for about 10 days.]

Isabella: . . . . And then I started going out with him. And I couldn't believe that he would like me because he was so cute.

Janelle: Uh huh.

Isabella: And then I got to know him? And I'm like – ((wrinkles face))

Janelle: ((of disgust)) /u::::::/! ((both laugh))

Isabella: He's like – I don't kno:w. He's- he's so jealous.

Janelle: Oh

Isabella: This kid is sickening! He- he tells me to call him before I go to the club. He- I'm like, I don't have time to call you, pick up the phone, call you while my friends are outside beeping the horn at me so I can jet with them to the club. And he's like- I don't know, he talks- he's like a <u>hick</u>, he talks so <u>much</u> Spanish! And he //(   )

Janelle: //O::h! ((while looking away))

Isabella: No, but he speaks Spanish, but- I- the reason- I talk to him- when he talks on the phone he speaks English a lot because I speak English. More. I tell him, speak English, speak English. (I go *loco* ['honey']), ((wrinkled face)) *lo::ca, lo::ca* ['honey, honey']. He goes, you know, *ni:ña* ['girl'], and you know, and I don't want to hear it.

Janelle: You should have found that out before you went out with him.

Isabella: I know, he's rushing into it . . .

Sammy is initially described as very attractive (*he was so cute*) and desirable, but then subsequently construed as very unappealing. This lack of appeal is constructed in terms of a constellation of associated traits that are sequentially revealed and interactionally assessed. This construction of negative traits begins with a very general characterization of his personality, proceeds through a specific trait (jealousy), and ends with highly specific examples of his linguistic behavior (*lo::ca, ni:ña*) that index negative social attributes.

Sammy's biophysical cuteness – a desirable trait – contrasts with aspects of his person that were revealed to Isabella as she got to know him. Isabella specifies a particular personality deficiency from which Sammy suffers – *he's so jealous* – and gives an example of the effects of this jealousy, his displeasure that she went to a club without first calling him. In this same turn, Isabella specifies two further, negative characteristics of Sammy: *he's like a hick* and *he talks so much Spanish*.

Janelle responds to these two assessments (Goodwin & Goodwin 1992) with an emphatic *O::h!* and vertical head nods, suggesting a shared understanding of the undesirable nature of a male who is like a hick and speaks so much Spanish. Isabella, however, treats some aspect of Janelle's second assessment (*O::h!*) – perhaps her turning away – as problematic (*No, but....*). The fact that Sammy is like a hick and speaks so much Spanish is not the last word on him and why Isabella is breaking up with him. Isabella then describes specifics of Sammy's language use – that he speaks a lot of English on the telephone at Isabella's insistence. She then enacts, through direct quotation, particular Spanish forms – *lo:ca, lo:ca* 'honey, honey' and *ni:ña* 'girl' – that Sammy uses. Isabella wrinkles her face and uses a slightly nasal voice quality, drawing out the /o/ of *loca* and the /i/ of *niña*. In viewing this tape, Isabella translated *loca* as 'honey' and *niña* as 'girl,' i.e. address forms of endearment. She said that she didn't like being addressed with these terms in Spanish, although there was "nothing wrong with them," and that she wanted boyfriends to use their English equivalents.

The use of code switching to set off quotations from surrounding talk has often been noted as a function of code switching, and many have noted that the code used for the quotation is not necessarily the same one that the speaker originally used. In this case, the code match between the quoted speech and Sammy's original speech is of significance. Code switching here is not just a means of marking off the directly quoted speech, but a means of displaying a stance toward a particular use of a code and constructing such use as an index of negative social attributes.

This code switch – and the prosodic and visual features of the quoted speech (cf. Mitchell-Kernan 1972 on "marking" among African Americans) – serves to index a stereotyped island Dominican style that is being constructed as inappropriate for an American urban youth context. These expressions may index traditional Dominican gender roles associated with island Dominican male identities. Isabella identifies Sammy as jealous, like a hick, and speaking so much Spanish all in the same turn at talk. Consultants as well as literature on Dominican gender roles (e.g. Pessar 1984, 1987, Grasmuck and Pessar 1991, 1996) indicate that Dominican males have traditionally exercised a great degree of control over their girlfriends' and wives' interactions and social contacts outside of the home. For Isabella, Sammy's addressing her as *loca* and *niña* may invoke a traditional Dominican social framework for their relationship, a framework that she wishes to avoid. In this case, Isabella code switches to display a particular stance toward particular Dominican male ways of talking to her, a stance that is at least partly shared by

Janelle. This stance, in turn, serves to index aspects of a particular Dominican American teenage female identity.

Much of the literature on code switching has emphasized the in-group connotations of the code used by the non–dominant/minority group in informal and family situations. In this case, in contrast, Spanish is being used to mock a fellow Spanish-speaker and differentiate between a positive self and a disparaged other, even though the other is a fellow Dominican immigrant and Spanish-speaker. Although Isabella lived in the Dominican Republic until age 6, speaks fluent Spanish, and has a mono-lingual mother, Spanish language forms are treated as indexing *negative* attributes in this interaction.

The social indexicality of language is locally negotiated, and indexical meanings are locally brought about (Silverstein 1976). In the above segment, for example, Isabella and Janelle use negative social associations of particular Spanish forms to align themselves in opposition to characteristics of a recent male immigrant. In the segment below, in contrast, Spanish and English forms are used by Isabella to differentiate herself from Janelle. In this case, Isabella's greater familiarity with the language (and institutions) of the island are treated as favorable characteristics of a positive social identity that includes greater Dominican authenticity.

(36)
[(JS #2 12:39:33) Isabella and Janelle are outside skipping class and have been talking about a couple that just walked by. Isabella tries to ascertain the relationships between Daniel and Sammy, the boyfriend she described as a "hick" in the prior segment of tran-script, by asking Dominican American female Basil ("B:"), who is standing nearby.]

Isabella: And I go out with his-
           (.5)
Isabella: (->B) Sammy and Daniel are cousins? ((Janelle looks away))
Basil: They're friends
Isabella: They're friends
Basil: They know each other //(   )
Isabella: //(*de*/from) *Santo* <*Domi:ngo*>,
                                'from the Dominican Republic'
Janelle: Are they really- //they're brothers, (   )?
Isabella: //<*del ca:mpo*>
                              'from the countryside'
Janelle: *Son hermanos?*
           'Are they brothers?'
Isabella: (->B) *Son hermanos?*
           'Are they brothers?'
Basil: They used to go to school together.
Isabella: They used to go to school together in *Santo Domi:ngo. En el-* (.) *asilo.*
                              '. . . the Dominican Republic. At a (.) boarding school'
           (2.2)
Isabella: *el-* (.8) ((Isabella frowns)) *colegio.* >Yeah, that.<
           'a (.8) private high school.'
           (.2)

Janelle: I know, I hate that with *colegio*. It sounds like- (.2) some Catholic- or I don't
know ((Isabella quietly mouths *colegio* during Janelle's turn))
Isabella: I used to- (you know-) Oh, //(now) I understand]
Janelle: //(   )], hmm.
           (.2)
Isabella: You're a bootleg, //I forgot.
Janelle: //(yeah, man)
Janelle: But what?
Isabella: I used to- I used to- when I //used to go over there?
Basil: //(going inside)
           (.5)
Isabella: (->B) Get out of here!
Janelle: What time is it?

As in the prior segment, Isabella adopts a markedly slow and slightly nasal pronunciation as she switches into Spanish (*Santo Domi:ngo, del ca:mpo*). This register – her version of a rural Dominican/recent immigrant variety[7] – is distinct from the variety that she uses in code switching with friends (e.g. in her subsequent *Son hermanos?*) or speaking Spanish to her mother. Although she is not using Spanish for direct quotation here, she is still assuming the voice of a recent Dominican immigrant from the countryside, inspired by her perceptions of Sammy, to talk about Sammy. This distinctive register serves as a contextualization cue (Gumperz 1982, 1992), suggesting that Isabella's "alignment, or set, or stance, or posture, or projected self is somehow at issue" (Goffman 1981:128). Isabella uses this code switch with marked prosodic features to distance herself from particular recent immigrant identities.

Isabella hesitates in specifying the institution where Sammy and Daniel met, with a cut-off and a beat of silence before saying *asilo*, which, she later told me, she thought was a kind of school. (It can mean 'boarding school' or 'old-age home.') After a gap of 2.2 seconds, she self-corrects with *El-* (.8) *colegio*, again with a cut-off and a pause after *el-*. Before saying *colegio* she displays a dramatic frown as if trying to come up with a word or concept with which she was unfamiliar, even though *colegio* is the everyday word for (non-public) high school in the Dominican Republic. Her subsequent accelerated pronunciation and code switch (*Yeah, that*), helps instantiate a separate speech activity, a comment on *colegio* that displays her stance toward it, one of distance and unfamiliarity.

Janelle treats Isabella's utterance as displaying this outsider stance toward *colegio*, by addressing that aspect of Isabella's utterance in her own subsequent turn. Janelle's *I know* is not oriented toward the propositional content of Isabella's turn, but the social stance (e.g. "These are strange words and institutions") that she displays in it. Janelle is aligning herself with Isabella in this outsider perspective on island Dominican institutions, and she gives an example of her own unfamiliarity and confusion regarding the term *colegio*.

In her next turn, Isabella begins to give an account of when she used to go *over there* (the Dominican Republic), but then cuts herself off to address Janelle's associations of the word "*colegio*" with "Catholic" (*Oh, ( ) I understand.*). Rather than displaying alignment with the stance displayed by Janelle, she chooses to socially differentiate herself, identifying Janelle as belonging to a separate social category based on Janelle's displayed stance toward *colegio* and Catholic: *You're a bootleg, I forgot.*

Dominican Americans in Providence who speak little Spanish and are unfamiliar with institutions and geography on the island are sometimes accused of being "bootleg" Dominicans. The term bootleg, commonly used to identify products such as cassette tapes or CDs that are illegally produced or distributed, suggests a lack of authenticity. Thus, "bootleg Dominicans" are those individuals who are Dominican by parentage but who lack the traits of true, authentic Dominicans. Paradoxically, Isabella publicly displays her own unfamiliarity with the Dominican secondary school system through hesitation in saying *colegio* and metadiscursive comment (*Yeah, that*), but then differentiates herself from Janelle in terms of linguistic-cultural knowledge and authenticity. Isabella had spent her first six years on the island and visited several times. Janelle, in contrast, was United States-born and had been to the Dominican Republic only once, as a baby.

Isabella's identification of Janelle as a "bootleg" is preceded by Isabella's incipient reference to trips to the Dominican Republic. After calling Janelle a bootleg, Janelle other-initiates repair (*But what?*) (Schegloff 1979, Schegloff, Jefferson, and Sacks 1977), leading to Isabella's self-repair of her uncompleted utterance: (*When I used to go over there?*). Isabella's reference to trips to the Dominican Republic is consistent with her ascription of Janelle to the category bootleg, as both serve to differentiate between authentic Dominicans with knowledge and experience of the island and inauthentic ones. Even within a single sequence of talk, Dominican Americans display shifting stances toward the island and Spanish language, which can be both a source of stigma and a source of positive esteem and identity.

In these two segments, Isabella and Janelle use language both referentially and indexically to situationally invoke commonalties and differences between themselves and others, and between each other. Enactment of these varying "dichotomizations of inclusiveness and exclusiveness" (Cohen 1978:387) is the basic realization of identity, marking who counts as the same and who counts as different. As is evident in these segments, social categories, their linguistic indexes, and the ways individuals fit into categories are not static and predetermined but are negotiated and constructed at the local level.

17.6 Conclusions

In this article I have analyzed the discursive construction of identity through in-group/out-group dichotomies that Dominicans situationally activate through language. Linguistic means of highlighting a specifically non-White identity include extensive adoption of AAVE. Paradoxically, use of AAVE – a form of resistance to White cultural and linguistic hegemony – makes many Dominican Americans of African descent increasingly subject to another form of hegemony: the dichotomous Black–White racial classification system in the United States. Dominican Americans use Spanish language to resist such classification and highlight their ethnolinguistic identity, differentiating themselves from African Americans, and many use the term "Spanish" as a label for ethnic and racial self-ascription. Finally, Spanish language, which is commonly a unifying emblem of identity among Dominican immigrants, can also be used situationally to mark intra-group boundaries among Dominicans. United States-raised Dominican Americans situationally mock aspects of the Spanish speaking of more recent immigrants, using linguistic means to socially differentiate between themselves and such relative newcomers.

Heteroglossia and multiplicity of identities are particularly salient in the language and lives of the contemporary Dominican second generation. Dominican American language juxtaposes forms from grammatical codes, Spanish and English, that count as distinct languages and from language varieties with implications of stark social difference, e.g. AAVE and American English. In terms of social identities, individual Dominicans match popular stereotypes of Black and White phenotypes, but Dominicans also claim the widely and officially recognized identity "Hispanic" (or "Spanish" or "Latino"). The bilingual, multi-variety repertoire of many Dominican Americans challenges unitary notions of what it means to speak a language, and Dominican American enactment of Hispanic identities serves to undermine United States assumptions of a primordial unity among language, phenotype, and identity, particularly in constructions of the category African American.[8]

The particular issues of identity faced by contemporary second-generation Dominicans and the particular linguistic resources with which they confront these issues are a function of the sociohistorical moment and this group's generational position in immigration. The bilingualism of second-generation immigrants is overwhelmingly a transitional second-generation phenomenon. The third and fourth generations will likely find it more difficult to differentiate themselves from non–Hispanics, both Black and White, as they lose even passive knowledge of Spanish. The new second generations, in turn, will grow up in a social landscape that has been partly transformed through the activities and agency of their predecessors, who have made "Spanish" a locally available ethnic/racial category (within a larger national context that is increasingly Latino). Dominican language and identities in the United States will thus increasingly vary by generation, with the first generations confronting different issues of identity, with different linguistic resources, than the third and fourth generations.

In this article I have attempted to illustrate a few of the ways in which analysis of talk and interaction can serve as a window onto the workings of sociocultural worlds. The details of everyday talk – whether descriptions of turkey club sandwiches, jokes played on a classmate, or gossip about a date – can be linked to larger questions of power, intergroup relations, and social identity formation processes. Analysis of language can tell us how individuals both experience and negotiate their sociohistorical circumstances. Language reflects particular circumstances, such as positions in economic and ethnic/racial hierarchies, but it is also a tool used by individuals to respond to or resist such hierarchies. Through their talk, individuals display and negotiate social meanings and construct social worlds. Analysis of such talk-as-social-action can thus shed light on the processes by which larger-scale constellations such as ethnic/racial identity groupings are reproduced, resisted, and/or transformed.

Appendix: Transcription Conventions

Wilson: The speaker is indicated with a name or abbreviation on the left of the page.
como   Italics indicate words spoken in Spanish. I have used standard Spanish orthography to represent Dominican Spanish even though pronunciation of Dominican Spanish, e.g. in elision of syllable- and word-final /s/, systematically differs from the Castilian varieties (e.g. Henríquez Ureña 1940) that written Spanish more closely reflects. I choose not to represent

these divergences, e.g. *e'toy* or *e(s)toy* for *estoy*, because, as Duranti notes, "Speakers of other [non-dominant] varieties are implicitly characterized as deviant, proportionally to the number of modifications necessary to represent their speech" (Duranti 1997:139).

['Jerk.']   Text surrounded by single quotation marks and brackets indicates a translation of the immediately preceding language.

( )   Empty parentheses indicate material that couldn't be heard clearly enough to transcribe.

(I can)   Words in parentheses indicate uncertainty about accuracy of transcribed words.

((smiling))   Double parentheses indicate nonverbal, visual, or background information.

//I don't-   Text after double slashes that is directly above or below other text after
//He said   double slashes indicates words spoken in overlap.

(1.5)   Numerals in parentheses indicate periods of time, in seconds, during which there is no speech.

Da::mn   A colon indicates that the preceding sound was elongated in a marked pronunciation.

rocking   Text that is underlined is pronounced with emphasis, i.e. some combination of higher volume, pitch, and greater vowel length.

como l–   A hyphen or dash indicates that speech was suddenly cut off during or after the word preceding the hyphen or dash.

(->Wilson)   An arrow to a person's name indicates to whom a speaker's gaze and upper body are oriented during that turn, i.e. the ostensible primary recipient of the utterance.

?   A question mark indicates a marked rising pitch.

.   A period indicates a falling pitch.

!   An exclamation point indicates an exclamatory tone.

,   A comma indicates a continuing intonation in the sound(s) preceding the comma.

< .... >   Speech between outward brackets is elongated.

> .... <   Speech between inward brackets is rushed.

Notes

For further reference, see Bailey's (2002) book *Language, Race, and Negotiation of Identity: A Study of Dominican Americans.*

1   I use the term "second generation" to refer both to the United States-born children of Dominican immigrants, and to Dominican-born children who came to the United States by age eight. By their mid- to late teens, such Dominican-born individuals are very similar to their American-born peers in terms of being English-dominant, seeing themselves as American minorities, and planning to spend their lives in the United States. I use the term "Dominican American" to refer to the same group, i.e. the second generation, rather than third- and fourth-generation Dominican Americans who experience a much more American than Dominican socialization.

2   According to 1990 census data, the Dominican unemployment rate in Providence was 17.4%, 38.5% of households were below the federal poverty line, and the median household income was $17,533.

3 In everyday Dominican American usage, the term "American" (or *americano*) refers to "White American" (cf. Urciuoli 1996 among New York Puerto Ricans). United States-born Dominican Americans such as Janelle identify themselves as "American" in some contexts, e.g. in referring to citizenship or the passport they have, but they identify "what they are" as Dominican/Spanish/ Hispanic. These categories are mutually exclusive from the category White/American in local terms. Dominican Americans refer to other non-White groups in similarly marked terms: African Americans are not "Americans" (or *americanos*) but "Blacks" (or *negros/prietos/morenos*), and Asian Americans are not Americans but rather "Asians" (or *chinos*).

4 In the Dominican Republic there is no binary division among Dominicans into social categories based on the perceived presence/absence of sub-Saharan African ancestry and no notion of race that differentiates among Dominicans in the same way the United States folk-notion of Black/White differentiates among Americans. Individual differences in phenotype, i.e. relative degrees of African/European phenotype, do not covary with language, culture, religion or other markers of social identity. When I surveyed Dominican teenagers in Santiago, Dominican Republic, *Cuál es tú raza?* 'What race are you?', they answered *dominicano/a* 'Dominican' without regard to individual phenotype, and many treated it as a statement of the obvious (Bailey 2001).

5 I use the terms "Spanish," "Black," and "African American" in their local, emic senses, following the usage of participants in this interaction. The terms "Black" and "African American" refer only to non-Hispanic African-descent individuals. "Spanish" refers to individuals of Latin American descent. While "Spanish" individuals may be phenotypically indistinguishable from "Blacks," they do not belong to the same social category in this local context.

6 Kroskrity's (1993) repertoire of identity among trilingual Arizona Tewa and Zentella's (1993, 1997) emphasis on the multi-variety linguistic repertoire of New York Puerto Ricans represent prominent exceptions to this tendency.

7 Dominican Americans' characterizations of individuals as "hicks" or references to the *campo* do not mean an individual is actually from the countryside in the Dominican Republic, but rather serve as a metaphor for a perceived lack of urban *American* sophistication.

8 Assumptions of a unity among African-descent language, phenotype, and identity underlie even contemporary descriptions of AAVE. Morgan (1994a:327; see also 1996:428), for example, defines African American English as "the language varieties used by people in the United States whose major socialization has been with US residents of African descent." This definition is clearly problematic given the hundreds of thousands of African-descent residents of the United States who socialize their children in Spanish, Haitian creole, African languages, etc. With the large numbers of African-descent immigrants to the United States since 1965, African descent clearly does not imply homogeneity of language, culture, or identity.

References

Alba, Orlando. 1995. *El Español Dominicano dentro del Contexto Americano*. Santo Domingo, DR: Librería La Trinitaria.

Bakhtin, M. M. 1981. *The Dialogic Imagination*. Austin: University of Texas Press.

Bailey, Benjamin. 2000a. Social and interactional functions of code switching among Dominican Americans. *IPra Pragmatics* 10(2), 165–93.

Bailey, Benjamin. 2000b. Language and negotiation of ethnic/racial identity among Dominican Americans. *Language in Society* 29(4), 555–82.

Bailey, Benjamin. 2001. Dominican American ethnic/racial identities and United States social categories. *International Migration Review* 35(2), 677–708.

Bailey, Benjamin. 2002. *Language, Race, and Negotiation of Identity: A Study of Dominican Americans*. New York: LFB Scholarly Publishing.

Barth, Frederik. 1969. Introduction. In F. Barth (ed.), *Ethnic Groups and Boundaries: The Social Organization of Culture Difference*, pp. 9–38. Boston: Little Brown and Co.

Baugh, John. 1983. *Black Street Speech: Its History, Structure, and Survival.* Austin: University of Texas Press.

Bryce-Laporte, Roy Simón. 1972. Black immigrants: The experience of invisibility and inequality. *Journal of Black Studies* 4(1), 29–56.

Clyne, Michael. 1987. Constraints on code switching: How universal are they? *Linguistics* 25, 739–64.

Clyne, Michael. 1967. *Transference and Triggering.* The Hague: Martinus Nijhoff.

Cohen, Ronald. 1978. Ethnicity: Problem and focus in anthropology. *Annual Review of Anthropology* 7, 379–403.

Davis, F. James. 1991. *Who Is Black?: One Nation's Definition.* University Park, PA: The Pennsylvania State University Press.

Davis, Martha Ellen. 1994. Music and black ethnicity in the Dominican Republic. In Gerhard Behague (ed.), *Music and Black Ethnicity: The Caribbean and South America*, pp. 119–55. New Brunswick, NJ: Transaction Publishers.

Del Castillo, José and Martin Murphy. 1987. Migration, national identity and cultural policy in the Dominican Republic. *The Journal of Ethnic Studies* 15(3), 49–69.

Duranti, Alessandro. 1997. *Linguistic Anthropology.* New York: Cambridge University Press.

Evans-Pritchard, E. E. 1940. *The Nuer.* New York: Oxford University Press.

Fishman, Joshua. 1989. *Language and Ethnicity in Minority Sociolinguistic Perspective.* Philadelphia: Multilingual Matters.

Fishman, Joshua, Robert L. Cooper, and Roxanne Ma. 1971. *Bilingualism in the Barrio.* Bloomington: Indiana University Press.

Goffman, Erving. 1981. *Forms of Talk.* Philadelphia: University of Pennsylvania Press.

Goodwin, Charles and Marjorie H. Goodwin. 1992. Assessments and the construction of context. In A. Duranti and C. Goodwin (eds.), *Rethinking Context: Language as an Interactive Phenomenon*, pp. 147–89. Cambridge: University of Cambridge Press.

Grasmuck, Sherri and Patricia Pessar. 1991. *Between Two Islands: Dominican International Migration.* Berkeley: University of California.

Grasmuck, Sherri and Patricia Pessar. 1996. Dominicans in the United States: First- and second-generation settlement. In S. Pedraza and R. Rumbaut (eds.), *Origins and Destinies: Immigration, Race, and Ethnicity in America*, pp. 280–92. Belmont, CA: Wadsworth.

Gumperz, John. 1964. Linguistic and social interaction in two communities. *American Anthropologist* 66(6), 137–53.

Gumperz, John. 1982. *Discourse Strategies.* New York: Cambridge University Press.

Gumperz, John. 1992. Contextualization and understanding. In A. Duranti and C. Goodwin (eds.), *Rethinking Context: Language as an Interactive Phenomenon*, pp. 229–52. Cambridge: University of Cambridge Press.

Gumperz, John and Robert D. Wilson. 1971. Convergence and creolization: a case from the Indo-Aryan-Dravidian border. In D. Hymes (ed.), *Pidginization and Creolization of Languages*, pp. 151–69. Cambridge: Cambridge University Press.

Haggerty, Richard (ed.). 1991. *Dominican Republic and Haiti: Country Studies.* Washington, DC: Library of Congress (US Government Printing Office #550–36).

Henríquez Ureña, Pedro. 1940. *El Español en Santo Domingo.* Buenos Aires: Biblioteca de Dialectología Hispanoamericana, vol. 5.

Heritage, John and J. Maxwell Atkinson. 1984. Introduction. In J. M. Atkinson and J. Heritage (eds.), *Structures of Social Action: Studies in Conversation Analysis*, pp. 1–15. Cambridge: University of Cambridge Press.

Hoetink, Harry. 1967. *Caribbean Race Relations: A Study of Two Variants.* New York: Oxford University Press.

Kroskrity, Paul. 1993. *Language, History, and Identity: Ethnolinguistic Studies of the Arizona Tewa.* Tucson: University of Arizona Press.

Labov, William. 1972a. *Language in the Inner City: Studies in the Black English Vernacular.* Philadelphia: University of Pennsylvania Press.

Labov, William. 1972b. *Sociolinguistic Patterns*. Philadelphia: University of Pennsylvania Press.

Labov, William. 1980. Is there a Creole speech community? In A. Valdman and A. Highfield (eds.), *Theoretical Orientations in Creole Studies*, pp. 389–424. New York: Academic Press.

Lee, Sharon. 1993. Racial classifications in the US census: 1890–1990. *Ethnic and Racial Studies* 16(1), 75–94.

Lipski, John. 1974. *Latin American Spanish*. New York: Longman.

Mitchell-Kernan, Claudia. 1972. Signifying, loud-talking, and marking. In T. Kochman (ed.), *Rappin' and Stylin' Out: Communication in Urban Black America*, pp. 315–35. Champaign: University of Illinois Press.

Moerman, Michael. 1965. Ethnic identification in a complex civilization. *American Anthropologist*, 67, 1215–30.

Morgan, Marcyliena. 1994a. The African American speech community: Reality and sociolinguists. In Marcyliena Morgan (ed.), *Language and the Social Construction of Identity in Creole Situations*, pp. 121–48. Los Angeles: Center for Afro-American Studies, UCLA.

Morgan, Marcyliena. 1994b. Theories and politics in African American English. *Annual Review of Anthropology* 23, 325–45.

Morgan, Marcyliena. 1996. Conversational signifying: grammar and indirectness among African American women. In E. Ochs, E. A. Schegloff, and S. A. Thompson (eds.), *Interaction and Grammar*, pp. 405–34. New York: Cambridge University Press.

Moya Pons, Frank. 1996. Dominican national identity: A historical perspective. *Punto 7 Review: A Journal of Marginal Discourse* 3(1), 14–25.

Omi, Michael and Howard Winant. 1994. *Racial Formation in the United States: From the 1960's to the 1990's*. New York: Routledge.

Otheguy, Ricardo, Ofelia García, and Mariela Fernández. 1989. Transferring, switching, and modeling in West New York Spanish: An intergenerational study. *International Journal of the Sociology of Language* 79, 41–52.

Pessar, Patricia. 1984. The linkage between the household and workplace of Dominican women in the U.S. *International Migration Review* 18, 1188–211.

Pessar, Patricia. 1987. The Dominicans: Women in the household and the garment industry. In Nancy Foner (ed.), *New Immigrants in New York*, pp. 103–29. New York: Columbia University Press.

Portes, Alejandro. 1995. Children of immigrants: Segmented assimilation and its determinants. In A. Portes (ed.), *The Economic Sociology of Immigration: Essays on Networks, Ethnicity, and Entrepreneurship*, pp. 248–79. New York: Russell Sage.

Prince, Ellen. 1981. Topicalization, focus-movement and Yiddish-movement: A pragmatic differentiation. *Proceedings of the Seventh Annual Meeting of the Berkeley Linguistics Society*, pp. 249–64.

Rodríguez, Clara. 1994. Challenging racial hegemony: Puerto Ricans in the United States. In S. Gregory and R. Sanjek (eds.), *Race*, pp. 131–45. New Brunswick, NJ: Rutgers University Press.

Schegloff, Emanuel. 1979. The relevance of repair for syntax-for-conversation. In T. Givon (ed.), *Syntax and Semantics 12: Discourse and Syntax*, pp. 261–88. New York: Academic Press.

Schegloff, Emanuel, Gail Jefferson and Harvey Sacks. 1977. The preference for self-correction in the organization of repair in conversation. *Language* 53, 361–82.

Silva-Corvalán, Carmen. 1983. On the interaction of word order and intonation: Some OV constructions in Spanish. In Flora Klein-Andreu (ed.), *Discourse Perspectives on Syntax*, pp. 117–40. New York: Academic Press.

Silverstein, Michael. 1976. Shifters, linguistic categories, and cultural description. In Keith Basso and Henry Selby (eds.), *Meaning in Anthropology*, pp. 11–56. Albuquerque: University of New Mexico Press.

Smedley, Audrey. 1993. *Race in North America: Origin and Evolution of a Worldview*. Boulder, CO: Westview Press.

Smitherman, Geneva. 1994. *Black Talk: Words and Phrases from the Hood to the Amen Corner*. New York: Houghton Mifflin Company.

Thomason, Sarah Grey and Terrence Kaufman. 1988. *Language Contact, Creolization, and Genetic Linguistics*. Berkeley: University of California Press.

Urciuoli, Bonnie. 1991. The political topography of Spanish and English: The view from a New York Puerto Rican neighborhood. *American Ethnologist* 18, 295–310.

Urciuoli, Bonnie. 1996. *Exposing Prejudice: Puerto Rican Experiences of Language, Race, and Class*. Boulder, CO: Westview Press.

Waters, Mary. 1991. The role of lineage in identity formation among Black Americans. *Qualitative Sociology* 14(1), 57–76.

Waters, Mary. 1994. Ethnic and racial identities of second-generation Black immigrants in New York City. *International Migration Review* 28(4), 795–820.

Williams, Raymond. 1977. *Marxism and Literature*. Oxford: Oxford University Press.

Woldemikael, Tekle. 1989. *Becoming Black American: Haitians and American Institutions in Evanston, Illinois*. New York: AMS Press.

Zentella, Ana Celia. 1990. Returned migration, language, and identity: Puerto Rican bilinguals in dos worlds/two mundos. In F. Coulmas (ed.), *Spanish in the USA: New Quandaries and Prospects*. *International Journal of the Sociology of Language* 84, 81–100.

Zentella, Ana Celia. 1993. The new diversity: Bilingual and multilingual repertoires in one New York Puerto Rican community. Paper presented at the American Anthropological Association Annual Meeting, Washington, DC, November, 1993.

Zentella, Ana Celia. 1997. *Growing Up Bilingual: Puerto Rican Children in New York*. Malden, MA: Blackwell Publishers.

18

Biculturalism: Some Reflections and Speculations

Christina Bratt Paulston

18.1 Introduction

[...]

In this chapter[1] I want to consider three questions:

(1)   Is there, and can there be, such a thing as being bicultural in a fashion similar to that in which one can be bilingual?
(2)   If there is, and it is far from as obvious as one might think, then what is it?
(3)   Finally and briefly, what are the implications for the schools, for the universities, for any institutions which deal with members from another culture?

I must point out that these are very elusive topics and I readily admit the speculative nature of my comments. In my readings, I have drawn primarily on anthropology, social psychology and clinical psychiatry, all of which share the problem of soft data. When social psychology does get down to hard data, I find that for my purposes the results become trivial. I have found insightful interpretations along the lines of Seward's (1958) *Clinical Studies in Culture Conflict* and Brislin, Bochner & Lonner's (1975) *Cross-Cultural Perspectives on Learning* by far more helpful in sorting out the issues involved.

Just as helpful have been the numerous interviews and discussions I have had with other bicultural individuals, as they have crossed my path during the two, three years this paper has been in the writing. I have been careful not just to introspect and generalize from my own experience because two facts have become clear from these interviews: (1) bicultural individuals do not agree on whether one can be bicultural, and (2) there are different types of bicultural individuals.

Christina Bratt Paulston, abridged version of "Biculturalism: Some reflections and speculations" which originally appeared as chapter 5 in Paulston's *Sociolinguistic Perspectives on Bilingual Education* (Clevedon, UK: Multilingual Matters, 1992), pp. 116–30.

18.2   Some Considerations of Culture

Definitions are boring, but one cannot very well consider biculturalism without first considering what is meant by culture. Anthropology deals exhaustively with culture and, as we will see, defines it in various ways; but the caution needed is that the emphasis is always on the patterned behavior of the group – not on the behavior of individuals who cross the boundaries of ethnic groups.

Roger Keesing (1974) in 'Theories of culture' reviews the conflicting theories of culture within the discipline of anthropology. He distinguishes between two major paradigms. The first, those theories of culture which see culture as an adaptive system which serves to relate human communities to their ecological settings and cultural change primarily as a process of adaptation and what amounts to natural selection. In order to reach an understanding of biculturalism, such an approach is clearly not fruitful.

The other major paradigm, according to Keesing, includes the ideational theories of culture where culture can be interpreted either as (a) a cognitive system, as inferred ideational codes lying behind the realm of observable events (Goodenough, Frake, Metzger & Williams, Wallace), or as (b) a structural system. Levi-Strauss 'views cultures as shared symbolic systems that are cumulative creations of mind; he seeks to discover in the structuring of cultural domains – myth, art, kinship, language – the principles of mind that generate these cultural elaborations' (Keesing, 1974: 78). (c) Finally there is the view of culture as a symbolic system of shared symbols of meanings:

[. . .]

> Where the normative system . . . is Ego centered and particularly appropriate to decision-making or interaction models of analysis, culture is system-centered . . . Culture takes man's position vis-a-vis the world rather than a man's position on how to get along in this world as it is given . . . Culture concerns the stage, the stage setting, and the cast of characters; the normative system consists in the stage directions for the actors and how the actors should play their parts on the stage that is so set (Schneider, 1972: 38). (Keesing, 1974: 81)

However theoretically interesting all this is, it is still not very helpful to our particular problem. In fact, in using most of these theories as a conceptual framework, one would be forced to conclude that logically a person cannot be bicultural. But Keesing goes on to what he calls a conceptual sorting out, where he distinguishes between a cultural and sociocultural system:

> Sociocultural systems represent the social realizations or enactments of ideational designs-for-living in particular environments. A settlement pattern is an element of a sociocultural system, not an element of a cultural system in this sense. (The same conceptual principles might yield densely clustered villages or scattered homesteads, depending on water sources, terrain, arable land, demography, and the peaceful or headhunting predilections of the neighboring tribe.) A mode of subsistence technology similarly is part of a sociocultural system, but not strictly speaking part of a cultural system (people with the same knowledge and set of strategies for subsisting might be primarily horticulturalists in one setting and primarily fishermen in another, might make adzes of flint in one setting or shells in another, might plant taro on one side of a mountain range or yams on the other side). (Keesing, 1974: 82)

This is beginning to sound very much like *langue* and *parole* and indeed the conceptual untangling Keesing suggests for 'culture' is very familiar to us: he suggests the notion of *cultural competence* as an analog to *linguistic competence*:

> Culture, conceived as a system of competence shared in its broad design and deeper principles, and varying between individuals in its specificities, is then not all of what an individual knows and thinks and feels about his world. It is his theory of what his fellows know, believe, and mean, his theory of the code being followed, the game being played, in the society into which he was born. It is this theory to which a native actor refers in interpreting the unfamiliar or the ambiguous, in interacting with strangers (or supernaturals), and in other settings peripheral to the familiarity of mundane everyday life space; and with which he creates the stage on which the games of life are played. We can account for the individual actor's perception of his culture as external (and as potentially constraining and frustrating); and we can account for the way individuals then can consciously use, manipulate, violate, and try to change what they conceive to be the rules of the game. But note that the actor's 'theory' of his culture, like his theory of his language, may be in large measure unconscious. Actors follow rules of which they are not consciously aware, and assume a world to be 'out there' that they have in fact created with culturally shaped and shaded patterns of mind.
>
> We can recognize that not every individual shares precisely the same theory of the cultural code, that not every individual knows about all sectors of the culture. Thus a cultural description is always an abstracted composite. Depending on the heuristic purposes at hand, we, like the linguists, can plot the distribution of variant versions of competence among subgroups, roles, and individuals. And, like the linguists, we can study the processes of change in conceptual codes as well as in patterns of social behavior. (Keesing, 1974: 89)

One reason for this form of untangling is that it will allow him to deal with the difference between a collective ideational system and the psychodynamics of the individual – a problem which is at the conceptual heart of 'biculturalism'. I will come back to this later because I believe that it is not until we can understand this relationship that we can understand what it means to be bicultural. Keesing goes on to suggest that anthropologists should conceptualise culture as 'cultural competence', only within the wider concern of 'socio-cultural performance'. He concludes:

> Conceiving culture as an ideational subsystem within a vastly complex system, biological, social and symbolic, and grounding our abstract models in the concrete particularities of human social life, should make possible a continuing dialectic that yields deepening understanding. Whether in this quest the concept of culture is progressively refined, radically reinterpreted, or progressively extinguished will in the long run scarcely matter if along the way it has led us to ask strategic questions and to see connections that would otherwise have been hidden. (Keesing, 1974: 94)

[...]

What one needs to do next is to break down culture learning, i.e. C2 learning, into its component parts to see just what it is you acquire as 'cultural competence'. I shall ultimately argue that a bicultural individual – unlike a bilingual – although he can function with two sets of performances, has in fact only one set of 'cultural competence' and further that this competence is partially eclectic and shows nowhere near the same conformity between individuals as does linguistic competence.

[...]

18.3   A Digression

Bicultural status seems (almost) always to be gained as a resident in the other country or culture. As I shall discuss later, becoming bicultural is not just a cognitive process which can be carried out apart from the members of the culture. In this aspect becoming bicultural differs from becoming bilingual. It is perfectly possible to learn a foreign language from non-native speakers. As a matter of fact, I never did have an English teacher who was a native speaker. It is also possible to become bilingual without becoming bicultural, while the reverse is not true. Many, naively to my mind, claim that to become bilingual is to become bicultural; but apart from trivialities, this need not follow. [...]

I myself became fluent in French the years I lived in Morocco, but I certainly did not learn any French culture – those cultural rules I learned were Arabic even through the medium of French or Spanish. As a matter of fact, I disliked the French *colons* in Morocco and their attitudes towards the Arabs and had virtually nothing to do with them. Attitudes and perceptions are enormously important in becoming bicultural, because one does not really emulate behavior one disapproves of, at least not at any deeper level.

Of crucial importance is whether or not the process of becoming bicultural is voluntary or involuntary, whether it represents integration or forced assimilation. The topic surfaced frequently in the interviews, and it is clear that the origin of the contact situation is one reason for the fact that being bicultural means different things to different people.

Consider also the many children born of British parents who grew up in the Commonwealth. They certainly no longer belong in Kenya or the like, but nor do they feel at home in England. 'I just feel that I don't belong anywhere,' said my friend. This odd feeling of belonging nowhere is frequently reported on by people who grew up in a contact situation of two cultures.

Some have used the concept of 'third culture' to deal with the phenomena of 'the cultural patterns created, learned, and shared by members of different societies who are personally involved in relating their societies, or sections thereof, to each other' (Useem & Useem, 1967). In other words, in the contact between two cultures, a third culture becomes created, as in the American colony in India with its subgroups of missionaries, businessmen, and government officials, etc. For the purposes of my questions it is not a useful concept, as it lumps together all those factors which I would like to tease apart.

We so emphasize the notion that one culture is not better than another, only different, with the result, I think, that this mind-set obscures the process of becoming bicultural. When I lived and taught in a small rural town of some 300 families in southern Minnesota, I was always odd man out – and eventually came to accept at some subliminal level that there must be something wrong with me. And of all unlikely places, I found my bearings again in Tangier, where I felt in a sense like coming home. Tangier of course was nothing like Sweden, but it had a fairly large cosmopolitan European settlement and it was easier for me to relate to them than to puritan Minnesota. At this level it is not true that one culture is not better, or rather, perceived as better, than another – the selection of cultural traits is based on evaluation.

18.4 Becoming Bicultural

Everett Kleinjans (1975) suggests a model for learning a second culture in his 'A Question of Ethics' which provides a framework for thinking about the dimensions of (not *how* but) *what* we learn in learning a C2. The model has three categories: *cognition, affection* and *action*, and each domain has a number of levels from superficial down to profound.

Under *Cognition*, we find: information, analysis, synthesis, comprehension, insight. Cognition deals with knowing the what and why about another culture and can partially be learned outside the culture itself. Briefly, *information* deals with encyclopedia type facts; person, places, events, dates, sort of thing. (Cf. the bicultural component of the bilingual programs.) *Analysis* separates out the parts of the culture like family system, educational process, religion, art, language, etc., while *synthesis* integrates the meaningful relationship of the parts. Whereas synthesis deals with facts or existing elements, *comprehension* deals with new items 'with anticipation, extrapolation, and prediction'.

This sort of knowledge *about* other cultures is enormously important for people like us who constantly deal with persons from other cultures. Let me give you some examples. In the English Language Institute, we had a Saudi student who because of poor work, excessive absences and attitude was not allowed, according to Institute rules which he knew well, to register for the next term. Mary Bruder, our Associate Director, came to see me. 'Throw him out,' said I. 'But he promised,' said Mary. I suppose I said something like 'promises schmomises'. But Mary pointed out to me – who should have known – that when they, Arabs, promise, they usually keep their promise. So the young man was called into my office, duly raked over the coals while he piteously, and I must admit, charmingly, promised all the while. 'If you had our book here,' he said. 'It's all right,' said I most seriously, 'you may promise to Allah.' So the young man, eyes heavenward with lifted hand swore to reform his errant ways. He also signed a most solemn written agreement/promise, which Mary had composed for the occasion. My guess is that our prediction that he will shape up is accurate.[2]

Another example concerns a Peruvian student from Puno, a Quechua Indian who came to see me because he was feeling sick and nauseated, could not sleep and in fact wanted to go home, an enormous sacrifice on his part since he had a full scholarship at an American university, the chance of a lifetime. Now, Quechuas distinguish between somatic and psychosomatic illnesses, and for the latter they seek the help not of a physician but of a *curandera*, who cures by mildly magical rituals. I checked to see whether he had seen a physician which he had. 'Well,' I said, 'what you need is a *curandera*, not me,' and went on to explain to him the symptoms of culture shock. As he looked at me wide-eyed, I explained that in all likelihood at least two-thirds of his group were going through the same symptoms he had. When I added that probably he also found the food terrible and that he sorely missed rice with his meals, he clearly thought I was clairvoyant if not a *curandera*. I forbore to mention that every student we have ever had from rice-eating cultures has had that complaint. When he realized that his symptoms really were normal for his situation he went away smiling, saying 'Doctora, we have a saying that suffering is the "salsa de la vida"'. The next time I heard about him was after his first term at his university where he had amassed the respectable QPA of 3.57. Clearly, not only is it useful for us to know about other cultural rules, it also is helpful to the people we deal with.

Finally, by *insight* Kleinjans means the ability to not only look at a culture from the inside but to see the world outside as the people of that culture see it. When I told Mary about the Saudi promising to Allah we both smiled, partially I suppose out of goodwill, but more because – although at the time it was a most appropriate Arabic thing to do – it struck me, at least, as a very un-American thing to do; to call your student in and make him promise to God that he will do his homework on time just isn't the thing American professors are supposed to do. It is probably unconstitutional.

But this ability to look at the same phenomenon, or rather to be able to interpret what the same phenomenon means from the viewpoint of two cultures, I think is a hallmark of the bicultural individual. My husband sometimes says, 'What would your parents say if they saw you now?' and it is exactly this kind of bi-focal view he has in mind. Although my behavior is socially appropriate as far as he is concerned, he is teasing me for deviant behavior according to Swedish rules.

But note that all of this has only to do with the head, so to speak; none of it has anything to do with the attitudes and feelings people have towards other cultures.

Under the *Affection* domain, Kleinjans posits the following levels: perception, appreciation, reevaluation, reorientation, identification. *Perception* and *appreciation* simply refer to the coming to know and to like aspects of another culture, like food and music as well as aesthetic and moral values. It is hard for me now to think that Arabic music once just sounded like awful noise or that I thought Peruvian food was awful. Over time I learned to appreciate both. I eventually also learned to function with a different system of time but I rarely appreciated it. It is, at superficial behavior levels, perfectly possible to understand and even to be able to behave in ways one still dislikes.

Reevaluation is the process of changing one's values. 'It might mean a shift in priorities, the giving up of certain values for new ones, or an enlargement of one's value system.' *Reorientation* means changing the direction of one's life, 'spurred by values he has adopted from the second culture'. *Identification* is becoming one with the people of the other culture; 'A person changes citizenship'. At these levels I don't believe it is possible to be bicultural. When I took out US citizenship, I had to give up my Swedish citizenship; I could not have both. And so it is with conflicting cultural values; in the same way as one just can't believe in the overriding importance of consensus and conciliation of group interests at the same time as one believes in confrontation and the overriding rights of the individual in solving problems.

So what happens, I think, is that the individual picks and chooses. Some aspects of culture are beyond modification. Many Americans comment on my frankness, but Swedes never do. Now I wouldn't want to claim that Swedes lie less than Americans, but I do think there is more emphasis on the value of always telling the truth (or saying nothing) in the socialization process of Swedish children. I know some people dislike me for it, and still I don't change because I simply cannot. But many aspects of culture are within the bounds of modification; one can learn to be half an hour late and not consider it moral slackness; one can learn to eat with one's fingers and still feel like an adult. But such modifications mainly concern surface behavior, behavior one can switch back and forth.

Now, to my mind, one of the major questions which remains to be dealt with is the process of acquiring a 'cultural competence' which is based on two cultural systems. Are some patterns more salient than others, are some reinforcements stronger than others, are some values more inherently right than others?

We can find some directions for beginning to think about this problem in at first glance an unlikely source: Robert Edgerton's (1976) monograph *Deviance: A Cross-Cultural Perspective.* Now I am most specifically not claiming that being bicultural is deviant behavior, but I wonder if some of the same processes involved in deviant behavior may not also be involved in becoming bicultural.

To wit. Edgerton who is Professor of Anthropology in the Department of Psychiatry at UCLA, in his very carefully reasoned work discusses the difficulty anthropology has had in accounting for deviant behavior. All societies have cultural rules for appropriate behavior, yet all people misbehave. True, what is appropriate behavior in one culture is deviant behavior in another and vice versa; yet, all people misbehave and some more than others. Why? After a review of various theories which seek to explain deviance (social strain theory; subcultural conflict theory; psychological defense or commitment; biological defect; human nature), Edgerton considers the data of deviance from a cross-cultural perspective; data which need not concern us here, however fascinating it is. His attempt to link temperament and deviance does, however.

Individuality of temperament is a genetic predisposition to react to an environment in certain ways. Temperament as such is largely unyielding to cultural pressure, and he draws on the work of Thomas, Chess & Birch (1968) in this formulation. People *are* born with varying patterns of temperament, and these *are* relatively difficult to change. He goes on to say that societies therefore, can easily choose to define some children as bad and others as good, and he goes on to discuss deviance. But it should be equally true that individuals who are given a chance to pick and choose between two cultural systems can equally easily choose to define some cultural traits as good and some as bad and pick accordingly. I am sure that is what I have done. But what I like and dislike does not conform to any one culture; it is an idiosyncratic mixture of Swedish and American 'cultural competence' even though I am capable of appropriate 'socio-cultural performance', in Keesing's terms, in both cultures.

I think one thing that happens with or in bicultural eclecticism is that the bicultural individual becomes more impervious to sanctions he does not like. Many of the informants also said this was how they felt. For example, when a Latin American colleague tells me that I am being anal compulsive about time, I just shrug off the comment and claim Swedish status. But that does not stop me at all, when my mother hurries me because I am five minutes late, from informing her that Swedes are guilt-ridden, super-ego bound, hysterical about time, and claim American status.

An obvious difference between bilingualism and biculturalism is that when you speak Swedish or English, it is perfectly obvious which set of rules you are drawing on. But with behavior it is not necessarily clear just which cultural system your performance rules belong to. This can be a cause for problems, especially with very fluent speakers, as the addressee will fail to recognize another cultural system at work and instead merely see deviant behavior. As Virginia Allen has pointed out, it may be quite useful to keep a foreign accent.

Sometimes behavior may be deviant to both cultural systems. Occasionally on the street, by the bus stop next to my department, there are some black schoolboys who beg money for bus fare. Their mothers would have their hide, if they only knew, but friendly whites exclaim over black social conditions and pay off their collective guilt with a quarter. The boys' behavior is deviant to both cultures; the boys, however, accurately bank on whites' ignorance of acceptable black behavior and so run their game successfully. I suspect most bicultural individuals, consiciously or not, occasionally run the same sort of game where the individual claims status of the other culture when in fact his behavior is highly idiosyncratic and outside both his ideational cultural systems.

Sometimes it happens that the individual is not allowed to pick and choose between his two cultures but will have conflicting values imposed on him. The result is often some form of psychopathology. Seward (1958) in her fascinating collection of case studies documents the stress of such individuals, like the Japanese Nisei boy torn between his desire to espouse modern egalitarian values and the imposition of his father's strictly traditional Japanese values. His response to such conflict was mental breakdown, the inability (refusal?) to function with *any* cultural rules.

18.5 Implications for Education

In language teaching we are increasingly making the distinction between our teaching and the students' learning, with the emphasis on the latter. This dichotomy becomes very obvious when one is talking about biculturalism. Culture can be taught only at a cognitive level. Such information is important especially for foreign students studying in the United States. Teaching culture at this level may seem trivial, like our telling the Muslim students that as long as they buy kosher meat they need not worry about pork, but learning such rules reduces anxiety and culture shock. Such rules carry the advantage that the learning of them rarely entails approval or endorsement which is not true of cultural rules or patterns in the affective domain. Foreign students are sensitive to having foreign values imposed on them while they usually don't mind learning 'local' eccentricities which is of course how others' rules strike one. Learning cultural trivia-rules is learning to get around in another culture.

An important aspect of culture which falls under the cognitive domain is learning sociolinguistic rules or what Hymes (1972) calls 'communicative competence', the appropriate (to the target culture) social use of language. For example, it is not enough to teach the Japanese wh-questions like 'How old is your daughter?' They also need to learn that it is not appropriate to ask, as I was asked a few years ago, 'How old are you to have been promoted to Associate Professor?' (Paulston, 1974).

In bilingual/bicultural education the referent of 'bicultural' is almost invariably the mother tongue culture, the culture the children already know. One is reminded of Lado's (1957) parodical stereotype of 'Mexicans endlessly dancing around a hat' when one sees the superficial cognitive levels which passes for bicultural teaching. 'At the end of this lesson, the children will be able to correctly identify the Mexican flag' is a verbatim quotation from such a curriculum which purports to be bicultural. Apart from the confusion of nationalism with culture, the teaching of such facile, non-functional facts under the guise of 'bicultural' merely becomes a deterrent in such programs where the goals rather should be an affirmation of native values and a positive attitude towards the home culture. It should also be clear that any support of culture learning or culture maintenance in the affective domain necessitates teachers who are members of the same home culture as the children, not just bilingual in the home tongue and English.

But by the time children come to school they have already internalized a great deal of the home culture and what they very much need, if they are to succeed in school, is to learn the cultural ways of mainstream America. Susan Philips (1970) discusses this problem in her work on the Warm Springs Indian Reservation for which she uses Hymes' notion of communicative competence in accounting for the children's school failure. The children's native ways of speaking and strategies for learning are very different from those of the Anglo school's, consequently, 'Indian children fail to participate verbally in the classroom interaction because the social conditions for participation to which they have become accustomed in the Indian community are lacking'.

> Educators cannot assume that because Indian children (or children from other cultural back-
> grounds than that which is implicit in American classrooms) speak English, or are taught
> it in school, that they have also assimilated all of the sociolinguistic rules underlying inter-
> action in classrooms and other non-Indian social situations where English is spoken. (Philips,
> 1970: 95)

I think today most bilingual program personnel make no such assumption, but rather they assume that the teacher will adjust his ways, and so culture interference in the class-room will be minimized. This is exactly what some of the teachers whom Philips observed did; they adjusted their teaching to ways appropriate to Indian culture. But the ultimate result was not what they had expected. It was the very students with teachers sensitive to Indian cultures who were the first to fail out once they went to school off the reservation; this situation leads Philips to comment that:

> The teachers who make these adjustments, and not all do, are sensitive to the inclinations
> of their students and want to teach them through means to which they most readily adapt.
> However, by doing so, they are avoiding teaching the Indian children how to commun-
> icate in precisely those contexts in which they are least able, and most need to learn how
> to communicate if they are to do well in school. (Philips 1970: 88)

She ends her paper by saying that the children must be taught 'the rules for appro-priate speech usage', i.e. that they must be taught the ways of speaking, acceptable to the dominant culture. As we have seen, beyond a superficial level, culture learning entails firsthand exposure to members of the C2, and it follows, however unpalatable some will find this statement, that the children must have access to Anglo teachers, if they are to learn the rules of mainstream culture. It will be the students' choice what aspects, if any, of mainstream culture they care to incorporate into their bicultural make-up, and no school or curriculum can dictate that choice. But to deny them the opportunity of choice I find reprehensible.

It is this same opportunity of choice which necessitates not only Anglo teachers but also the home culture component in a truly bilingual/bicultural program in order to avoid the wholesale imposition of the second culture's values which occasionally results in patho-logy of the kind Seward discusses. Students in the public schools who are members of ethnic minority groups in the United States will have been exposed, albeit in varying degrees, to American mainstream culture all their lives. They will learn to become bicul-tural and they will suit themselves in the doing of it. We may say 'How typically Mexican', or 'How very Puerto Rican', but we never say 'How very typically Puerto Rican-North

American bicultural behavior' for the simple reason that being bicultural is an individual matter which does not lend itself to stereotyping. Nor can it be taught. Becoming bicultural is an eclectic process, and what a bicultural program should hope to do is to allow the student the right to pick and choose his own individual make-up as a bicultural person from the two cultures and the members of those cultures he is exposed to in the school.

Notes

This article is the written version of my TESOL presidential address in Miami, 1977. I have deliberately kept the somewhat chatty style of the original in order to underscore the speculative, non-scholarly nature of the paper. I owe thanks to the many individuals who have shared with me their own introspections and insights into the nature of biculturalism; without their contributions I could not have written the paper.

1   The following information is relevant for interpreting my comments. I was born and grew up in Sweden until I was 18 at which time I came to the United States, of which country I am now a citizen. Subsequent to 1960, I have spent some seven years living abroad in Morocco, India, Peru as well as in Sweden.
2   As this article goes to print, I reluctantly submit the following addenda. Our prediction was wrong, but not for the expected reasons. The young man subsequently succumbed to emotional distress which incapacitated him for the serious work intensive language learning is. Three of his colleagues did pull through, similarly given a second chance. The episode also illustrates how difficult it is to identify incipient disturbance cross-culturally.

References

Bock, P. (ed.) 1970, *Culture Shock: A Reader in Modern Cultural Anthropology*. New York: Alfred Knopf.

Brislin, R. W. (ed.) 1978, *Culture Learning*. Honolulu, Hawaii: University Press of Hawaii.

Brislin, R. W., Bochner, S. and Lonner, W. J. (eds.) 1975, *Cross-Cultural Perspectives on Learning*. New York: John Wiley & Sons.

Ebel, C. 1977, Can one be bilingual and not be bicultural? *BESL Reporter* 3, 1, 5–6.

Edgerton, R. B. 1973, *Deviant Behavior and Cultural Theory*. Module in Anthropology, No. 37. Menlo Park, California: Addison-Wesley.

Edgerton, R. B. 1976, *Deviance: A Cross-Cultural Perspective*. Menlo Park, California: Cummings Publishing Co.

Gordon, R. L. 1975, *Living in Latin America: A Case Study in Cross-Cultural Communication*. Skokie, Illinois: National Textbook Co.

Hymes, D. 1972, On communicative competence. In J. B. Pride and J. Holmes (eds.) *Sociolinguistics*. Harmondsworth, England: Penguin Books.

Keesing, R. 1974, Theories of culture. In B. Siegel (ed.) *Annual Review of Anthropology*, vol. 3 (pp. 73–97). Palo Alto, California.

Kleinjans, E. 1975, A question of ethics. *Exchange* X, 4, 20–5.

Lado, R. 1957, *Linguistics Across Cultures*. Ann Arbor: University of Michigan Press.

Osgood, C. E., May, W. H. and Miron, M. S. 1975, *Cross-Cultural Universals of Affective Meaning*. Urbana, Illinois: University of Illinois Press.

Paulston, C. B. 1974, Linguistic and communicative competence. *TESOL Quarterly* 8, 4.

Paulston, C. B. 1977, Research. *Bilingual Education: Current Perspectives – Linguistics*. Arlington, Virginia: Center for Applied Linguistics.

Philips, S. 1970, Acquisition of rules for appropriate speech usage. In J. Alatis (ed.) *Bilingualism and Language Contact*. 21st Annual Roundtable, Georgetown University.

Saville-Troike, M. 1976, On bilingualism and biculturalism in education. Paper presented at the Symposium on Language Development in a Bilingual Setting, Los Angeles, California.

Schneider, D. 1972, What is kinship all about? In P. Reinig (ed.) *Kinship Studies in the Morgan Memorial Year*, 32–63. Washington, D.C.: Anthropological Society.

Schneider, L. and Bonjean, C. M. (eds.) 1973, *The Idea of Culture in the Social Sciences*. Cambridge: Cambridge University Press.

Seelye, N. 1976, *Teaching Culture*. Skokie, Illinois: National Textbook Co.

Seward, G. 1958, *Clinical Studies in Culture Conflict*. New York: The Ronald Press Co.

Smalley, W. A. 1963, Culture shock, language shock, and the shock of self-discovery. *Practical Anthropology* 10, 2.

Stewart, E. C. 1971, *American Cultural Patterns: A Cross-Cultural Perspective*. Pittsburgh, Pennsylvania: Regional Council for International Education.

Thomas, E. M., Chess, S. and Birch, H. 1968, *Temperament and Behavior Disorders in Children*. New York: Holt, Rinehart and Winston.

Topics in Culture Learning, vol. 1973 – East–West Center, East–West Culture Learning Institute, Honolulu, Hawaii.

Useem, J. and Useem, R. 1967, The interfaces of a binational third culture: A study of the American community in India. *Journal of Social Issues* 23, 1, 130–43.

Discussion Questions

1. The readings in this section all discuss "identity" in one way or another. What is the difference between identity and culture? How do ways of speaking relate an individual to a culture?
2. Considering the three articles in this section, is there a difference between "biculturalism" and bilingualism? If so, what are the differences? If not, why aren't they different?
3. Do these readings challenge any of the approaches outlined in part I? How can the approaches account for speakers who learn new ways of speaking, or learn more than one way of speaking natively? Do any of the approaches have difficulty with allowing people to have more than one culture and way of speaking? Which?

Part IV

Implications

Introduction

What use does all this theoretical and at times even practical understanding and insight into culture contact have? Can it make any difference?

It should be fairly obvious to us all that if you are in international trade you want to avoid insulting your prospective buyer, however unintentionally. As a German prime minister said, if you want to buy from us, you can do it in any language you wish. But if you want to sell something to us, do it in German. Even choice of language becomes a matter of appropriate use; Hymes's concept of communicative competence can be boiled down to just that, appropriate use of language.

Television hosts sometimes insult their audience intentionally. But when Brian Gumbel reported on the Olympic Games held in Korea, he was seen on TV showing the sole of his shoe to the viewer. We doubt that an American viewer would even have noticed, but to the Koreans this gesture is a great insult. Not such a good idea for the network.

When the first President Bush arrived in Australia, stepping off the plane, he gave the Australians what he thought was a victory salute, first and second finger spread apart, the thumb on the other two fingers, only he had his hand turned wrong. Instead of show-ing the audience his palm, he showed them the back of his hand; in fact, President Bush gave the Australians in front of worldwide TV audiences the British version of what Americans call "the finger," verbalized as "Up yours." The result was worldwide ridicule of the US president, not really what we want of diplomatic missions.

These are all fairly trivial examples of fairly trivial actions, but there are three set-tings where intercultural interactions and misunderstandings can have serious and even deadly results: the educational, the legal and the medical domains. We have chosen two selections here to illustrate the serious consequences that intercultural discourse and misunderstandings can have.

The first, Susan Philips's "A comparison of Indian and Anglo communicative behavior in classroom interaction," is from her classic dissertation drawing on Hymes's framework, published in 1983 and reprinted in 1993 as *The Invisible Culture: Communication in*

Classroom and Community on the Warm Springs Indian Reservation. Paulston's "Biculturalism" (this volume, chapter 18) also discusses this work.

The second and last chapter was specifically written for this reader. Diana Eades is an Australian who has spent considerable time and work on the ethnography of speaking of Australian Aborigines and their interaction with the Australian legal system. In her "Beyond difference and domination: Intercultural communication in legal contexts" she presents shocking data to come to a shocking conclusion.

19

A Comparison of Indian and Anglo Communicative Behavior in Classroom Interaction

Susan U. Philips

The purpose of this chapter is to compare Indian and Anglo students' behavior in the classroom [. . .]. We will ask how the students differ and consider the implications of those differences for the Indian children's learning experience. Such differences are of practical concern primarily because Indian children do not seem to be learning as much in the classroom as Anglo children do.

[. . .]

19.1 Getting the Floor in the Classroom

Indian students generally make less effort than Anglo students to get the floor in classroom interaction. They compete with one another less for the teacher's attention, and make less use of the classroom interactional framework to demonstrate academic achievement. In the discussion to follow, these differences are described in detail, and related to the culturally distinctive adult organization of interaction and socialization of children [. . .].

19.1.1 Competing for the floor

In the Anglo classrooms there is a general sense that students are constantly competing for the teacher's attention which does not exist in the Indian classrooms. One reason for this is that Indian students do not make efforts to get the floor as much as Anglo students do. I have already discussed the point that Indian students do not engage in as much back channel provision of evidence that they are attending to the teacher. The

Susan Urmston Philips, "A comparison of Indian and Anglo communicative behavior in classroom interaction" from Philips's *The Invisible Culture: Communication in Classroom and Community on the Warm Springs Indian Reservation* (Long Grove, Ill.: Waveland Press, 1983), pp. 95, 108–25 (from 1993 reissue). Reprinted by permission of Waveland Press, Inc. All rights reserved.

Indian students consequently cannot be said to select themselves as the teacher's listeners as much. Thus, to the degree that a student addressed by the teacher is more likely than other students to become the next speaker, Indian students make less use of this device for selecting themselves in this way.

In addition, when the teacher reaches those junctures in her own talk where she is preparing to turn the floor over to a student by calling on one, fewer Indian students raise their hands to be called on. And they do not verbally beg to be called on in the way that Anglo students do. Indian students also much more often do not respond at all when they are called upon, even when their behavior indicates they are paying attention.

19.1.2   Talking out of turn

In addition to the Indian disinclination to select themselves as next speaker, Indian students also violate the rules for taking turns at talk less often than Anglo students. But this statement requires some clarification.

In the first grade, the Indian students take longer to learn the rules the teacher imposes to regulate their turns at talk. Especially in the early months of school, Indian children more often fail to raise their hands when directed to do so, and call out answers instead. Although the Anglo first graders adapt to the system faster, there are always some Anglo students who seem to be engaged in selective violation of the rules regulating student turns at talk – i.e., some of the time they follow the rules and some of the time they don't. They sometimes answer before the teacher has finished verbalizing a question:

8.   *Teacher*:   Do you think mother and father will play/Hide and Go Seek?/
     Student 1: /Yeh/
     Student 2: /Yeh./
     Student 3: I do.
     Teacher: Do you think so?. . . .
     [9(1) M1–770]

[. . .]

Anglo first graders more often call out answers before the teacher has called on someone. They often also answer when the teacher has called on or named someone else as the next speaker:

[. . .]

12.   *Teacher*:   Jim, what's Sally doing with the wagon?
      Student 1: Pus/hin it./
      Jim: /Pushin/ it for mother.
      [9(1) M1–828]

In addition, Anglo students, who have already had a turn to speak in a context within which the teacher has made it clear that everyone must have a turn before anyone can have a second turn, often raise their hands to be called on and even verbally beg to be called on.

The Anglo students also much more frequently initiate talk with the teacher while she is talking, when she has not explicitly ended her turn at talk, or turned the floor over to a student:

[. . .]

14.   *Teacher*:   (reading) "Then they swam up the coast of Washington." And here they are almost to the border of Canada where my finger is now.
      Student: Canada. That's where my brother is.
      Teacher: (continues reading) "Under them the ocean became twenty, then thirty, then fifty fathoms, or three hundred feet deep."

[8(2) M1–498]

In both Anglo and Indian classrooms some students violated the rules for turn taking more often than others, and certain students predictably violated the rules in certain ways and not others. Students labeled by teachers as both "leaders" and "problems" violated the rules for taking turns at talk more frequently than those children who were never spontaneously discussed by the teachers. The patterns of violation for the two labeled types were probably different, but it was difficult to record and analyze data on this source of variation in verbal behavior, so this generalization is speculative.

By the sixth grade, most types of speaking out of turn have disappeared among both Indian and Anglo students, in keeping with their generally increased skill in managing interaction. The one kind of violation that continues to be far more common among Anglo students is the interjection of comments into the middle of the teacher's talk. By this age, the Anglo students are actively engaged in attempting to exert control over teacher–student interactions, and succeed far more often in doing so than at the first-grade level. Indian students, however, do very little of this, providing further evidence of their relative lack of involvement in official classroom interactions.

The teachers' responses to students' talking out of turn vary considerably. Sometimes they ignore the violator, sometimes they scold, sometimes they simply acknowledge what has been said, and sometimes they build and elaborate upon it. There are a number of factors that affect the tactic taken by the teacher in response to violations, including the number of times the student in question, as well as other students, has already violated the rules in both the recent and distant past, the number of students talking out of turn at a given point, the amount of time the teacher has left that was allocated to complete a given lesson, and the mood of the teacher. It is consequently not easy to see clear-cut patterns in the teachers' responses to talking out of turn. It may appear from the preceding discussion that the Indian students come either to know or abide by the rules for getting the floor in the classroom better than the Anglo students, and in a rather limited sense this is true. Talking out of turn may also be viewed as another way in which a student may get the floor. As I have already indicated, some students are more successful than others at being attended to and ratified by the teacher when speaking out of turn.

In adult life too some people are more successful at getting the floor by talking out of turn. And the variable use of such means is closely tied up with Anglo organization of status differentiation. The Anglo students who talk out of turn and who are responded to variably by the teacher are learning through their exercise of turn-controlling devices when such devices will work and when they will not, when they will be accepted as appropriate, and when they will not. Because the Indian students use such devices very little, and do not go through the same trial-and-error process of discovering their acceptable use, they are less likely to develop the skills that in adulthood would enable them to use the communicative resources available for managing the Anglo system for the expression and interpretation of status differentiation.

19.1.3   Distribution of student turns at talk

In addition to this difference between Indian and Anglo students in the frequency of occurrence of talking out of turn, there is also a difference in the pattern of distribution of student responses to teachers' elicitations in the whole class and in small groups in terms of: (1) the frequency with which students raise their hands to indicate they want to be called on to answer a question; (2) the rapidity with which they raise their hands to be called on when the teacher opens the floor; and (3) the frequency with which students produce responses that are ratified by the teacher and incorporated into the discourse.

In the Anglo classrooms there is considerable variation among students in the frequency with which they come to have the floor. Some students raise their hands more than others. Some raise their hands sooner than others. And some provide responses that are more often validated by the teacher. Moreover, these three aspects of getting the floor typically function together. In other words, those students who raise their hands most often are also the students who raise their hands sooner, and who are most often ratified by the teacher. For all these reasons, these students have more turns at talk than others do.

In addition, there is a correlation between the frequency of Anglo students' turns at talk and their performance on written measures of achievement such as exercises, exams, and national tests. Generally, those who raise their hands more and faster and whose responses are more often validated by the teacher are the ones who receive higher scores on written measures of competence. One can see this pattern emerging in the first-grade classes, and at the sixth-grade level it is clear-cut.

In sum, although there are occasional interesting exceptions to this pattern, one can generally determine which students are evaluated by the teacher as good students on the basis of both their performance as speakers and the teacher's responses to their speech in teacher-structured interactions. Thus, in spite of the institutionalization of equalization of student participation through the turn systems, [. . .] participation is in fact made unequal through the joint actions of both teacher and students.

In the Indian classrooms, the situation is very different. It is generally the case that the turns at talk are more evenly distributed in Indian classrooms. At the first-grade level some Warm Springs students do raise their hands more often and sooner than others in responding to the teacher's questions. However, there is not as much variation among Indian first graders in these respects as there is among Anglo students. What variation there is is due among the Warm Springs children to the almost total nonparticipation of several students in classroom interaction structured by the teacher.

There is clearly, however, more validation by the teachers of some Warm Springs students' responses than there is of others. And there is a correlation between students' performance on written measures of achievement and validation of their responses by the teacher. Those whose responses are more often validated by the teacher are also those who perform well on written assignments. It is also the case that to some degree those who raise their hands more often and sooner score higher on written tests. However, the correlation here is not nearly as strong as it is among Anglo first graders. In the Indian classroom it was common for children who had demonstrated the ability to answer correctly a particular question in one instance to refrain from even trying to answer the same question the next time it was raised. Thus it was clear that even when they knew answers to questions they did not always try to get the floor.

At the sixth-grade level the evidence of a differentiation among Indian students in frequency of floor holding and the relation between frequency of floor holding and achievement on written tests had largely disappeared.

As was mentioned earlier, at the sixth-grade level there is much less talk to teachers by Indian students in front of their peers than at the first-grade level to begin with. With regard to what talk there is, there is little difference among the students in how often or how quickly they raise their hands, except that there are still a few who never raise their hands at all. Nor by this age are some students' responses clearly more often validated by the teacher than those of other students. Consequently, the talk of Indian sixth graders is more evenly distributed in every sense than that of Anglo students.

It should be evident from the preceding discussion that there is generally little or no relation between amount of talk ratified or unratified by Indian sixth graders and their written performances. The results of their exams indicated that the Indian sixth graders varied considerably in their comprehension of all subjects. Yet it was very difficult to predict who would do well on written assignments on the basis of verbal performance in the Indian classroom, whereas it was easy to make accurate predictions in the Anglo classroom. Nevertheless, it was apparent to the Indian students themselves who comprehended the assignments. The students who were getting good grades were approached much more often than others by their peers for help with assignments during periods when they were working alone at their desks.

In the Anglo classrooms, then, students are differentiated in the frequency of their responses to the teacher, and those who have the floor more often are also evaluated more highly on written assignments. By contrast, in the Indian classrooms, students are not differentiated in terms of their frequency of response to the teacher, and amount of talk cannot be correlated with performance on written assignments.

It will be useful at this point to summarize the ways in which the participation of Indian and Anglo students as speakers differs. First, Indian students generally participate less as speakers. Second, they do not select themselves as next speakers as much: they do not behave in ways that indicate to the teacher that they wish to speak. Third, Indian students do not as often respond when they are explicitly asked to speak by the teacher. Fourth, while the Indian students are slower to learn the rules for regulating turns at talk in the classroom, once they have acquired them they don't violate them as often by talking out of turn. To put it another way, the Indian students do not as often use interruption and speaking when another has been addressed as devices for getting the floor. Finally, talk is more evenly distributed among Indian students so that a greater frequency of turns at talk is not correlated with better performance on written assignments as it is in the Anglo classrooms.

19.1.4   A cultural account

In attempting to account for the differences between Anglo and Indian students' behavior as addressors, a number of possible sources or causes of such differences can be
plausibly invoked within a framework that emphasizes cultural differences. Here I will
argue that the differences which have been discussed are due primarily, although not
entirely, to an incompatibility between Indian and Anglo systems for the regulation of
turns at talk. For the Indian students, getting the floor in classroom encounters regulated in Anglo fashion requires them to behave in ways that run counter to expectations
of socially appropriate behavior in the Warm Springs Indian community.

It will be useful at this point to review the discussion of the ways in which Indian
and Anglo regulation of speaker change differ, and to highlight the senses in which the
regulation of turns at talk in the classroom are characteristic of Anglo organization of
interaction.

Indian organization of interaction can be characterized as maximizing the control that
an individual has over his or her own turn at talk, and as minimizing the control that a
given individual has over the turns of others. This system of control is largely accomplished through three aspects of turn taking. First, address by a speaker is more often
general, rather than focused on a particular individual. This minimizes the possibility that any single addressee can or will deprive the speaker of a floor by withdrawing
attention. In addition, to the degree that focused address increases the likelihood
that the person the speaker seeks as a listener will be the next speaker, general address
eliminates this possibility.

Second, in Indian interaction an immediate response to what a speaker has said is not
always necessary, but may be delayed. Long pauses between speakers' turns at talk are
common, as are responses that occur after other topics have been pursued. This provides the potential respondent with more control in determining when to speak and
whether to speak at all.

Finally, Indian speakers control the ends of their own turns; they are not interrupted
by others.

Such features that maximize the speakers' control over their own turn at talk also allow
for the potential abuse of the system, so that in theory a given speaker could run on
and on without interruption. But in practice, talk is usually distributed equally among
Indian parties to an encounter. In a given encounter some people may not talk at all,
but the turns of those who *do* speak vary little in length and frequency.

By contrast, Anglo interaction may be characterized as involving greater exercise on
the part of speakers and hearers of control over the turns of others. While address is
by no means always directed to a single listener, focused address is much more common in Anglo interaction than in Indian interaction. Focused address allows the person
addressed to control the speaker's turn by choosing to provide or withdraw attention.
Because an addressed recipient is more likely to be the next speaker, focused address
gives the speaker some control over who will speak next. Anglo interaction also normally entails the assumption that if a response to a speaker is going to occur, it will
immediately follow the end of that speaker's turn at talk. This means the respondent
has little control over the point at which she or he will reply. Finally, Anglo interaction
is characterized by interruption of speakers that results in the ends of their turns being

controlled by others. Moreover, it is not uncommon for two people to begin speaking at once in Anglo interactions, which in turn seems related to the absence of pause between speakers' turns at talk. While one speaker may defer to another, this event often allows those sought as listeners to choose between speakers through their allocation of attention.

In Anglo conversation where there is no institutionalized system for allocating turns at talk as there is in the classroom, all participants theoretically have access to the means for controlling the talk of others. In practice, however, it is common for some individuals to attempt to exert more control than others do, and for some individuals to be allowed or given more control than others, so that parties to an interaction are differentiated in the extent to which they control the talk.

In bureaucratized settings where many people become involved in sustaining a single focused interaction – e.g., courtrooms, classrooms, business meetings – talk usually is regulated by a system that explicitly allocates various types of control over turns at talk according to the social identities or roles of the participants. In the classroom the allocation of means for controlling turns at talk is asymmetrical, so that the person to whom the social identity of teacher is given has the right to make use of all forms of control, while those to whom the social identity of student has been assigned have few or none.

More specifically, the teacher determines who will speak next, and because a student must respond when called on, or not at all, the teacher also determines when a student will speak. This determination of who will speak next is not accomplished so much through focused address as through naming the next speaker. But it is also accomplished by virtue of the teacher's position as the only validating addressed recipient of student talk. Whomever the teacher focuses attention on has the floor, and whenever the teacher withdraws that attention, the student no longer has the floor.

It is this same position as sole validating addressed recipient that provides the teacher with control over the ends of students' turns at talk. While it is understood that teachers can interrupt them with their own talk, which they do not allow students to do to one another or to them, it is still generally not appropriate for teachers to do so once they have given students the floor. But it is common for teachers to have their attention focused on a student who is speaking, and to then have their attention drawn to the actions of another student, which effectively cuts off the speech of the first student.

In these ways then, the means for controlling turns at talk available in Anglo interaction are associated with the social identity of teacher in the classroom. Thus the differentiation of speakers in the extent of their use of such means, which normally emerges in the course of conversation and usually involves an association between higher status and greater control, is crystallized and institutionalized in the classroom.

The Warm Springs community patterns of interactional organization suggest that Warm Springs Indians are not accustomed to having to appeal to a single individual for permission to speak but rather to determining for themselves whether they will speak. Nor are they accustomed to having only one individual (the teacher) as their sole addressed recipient, but rather to more general address. And in the classroom, the teacher who has this control is not a familiar member of the community, but an outsider whose behavior is strange and unpredictable in many respects.

The Indian children are also not accustomed to a system for regulating turns at talk that always requires them to respond immediately if they are to respond at all. The teacher does not function within a framework that allows for the longer pauses between speakers' turns at talk that the Indian children observe in large-scale community events. The teacher is likely to allow too little time for a response before calling on another student or asking another question. The possibility that a child might respond to the question somewhat later in the sequential development of a class discussion is not likely to occur to the teacher. Such a response would in all likelihood not even be recognized as meaningful.

The system for regulating talk that is maintained in the classroom is also not compatible with many of the socialization practices within the Warm Springs community [. . .]. The children are not oriented toward a single adult authority, being cared for by a number of adults and older children as they are. Partly because of this, Warm Springs children do not compete with one another for parental attention. They are expected to become more self-sufficient at younger ages, and to cooperate with older brothers and sisters and cousins in providing mutual companionship and care. For all of these reasons Warm Springs Indian children are less likely than Anglo children to be motivated to compete with one another for the teacher's attention.

And finally, the children are raised in an environment that discourages drawing attention to oneself by acting as though one is better than another. The efforts children are expected to make to get the teacher's attention to be given a turn at talk require them to draw attention to themselves, to lay claim to knowing more than their peers, and to demonstrate a desire to display that knowledge, all of which is unseemly by Indian adult standards for behavior.

For all of the above reasons, talking out of turn is also incompatible with Indian community norms, so it is not surprising that Indian students interrupt less often and do not attempt to speak when another student has been given a turn. Such actions are inconsistent with the tendency to allow individuals control over their own turns, and over their own behavior generally. The Indian children do not see others talking out of turn in the Warm Springs community. Furthermore, such violations also draw attention to the violator, just as other efforts to get the floor do, and as I have indicated, most Warm Springs Indians do not feel comfortable drawing attention to themselves.

Finally, the relatively more equal distribution of turns at talk among Indian students is also in keeping with behavior in the Indian community. This is what the children see in adult interactions. Talking too frequently or for too long is again likely to be seen as drawing attention to oneself and acting as though one is better than others, particularly in a young person. Raising one's hand quickly and often to indicate one knows the answer, which in turn leads to talking more, is associated with academic excellence among Anglos. But among Indian students such behavior is also interpreted as putting oneself above others.

19.1.5   Participant structures

Thus far I have argued that Indian students withdraw from classroom interaction because it requires them to behave in ways that are incompatible with Warm Springs community members' notions of socially appropriate behavior. And I have tried to show how Indian behavior in the classroom is consistent with both Warm Springs adult behavior in face-to-face interaction, and the ways in which Warm Springs children are socialized in the community.

Most of the discussion of students as speakers that has been presented so far is drawn from encounters where the teacher is engaged in interaction with the whole class or a small group. But [. . .] these are only two of several ways of organizing interaction that have been referred to as participant structures.

When a comparison of Indian and Anglo behavior is made across the various participant structures used for organizing interaction, it is possible to see that the Indian students participate more actively in some than in others. They pay more attention and talk more in those participant structures that minimize the features identified as typical of Anglo interaction and that maximize the possibility of regulating talk in a manner more characteristic of Warm Springs Indian interaction.

Indian students participate much less than Anglo students when the whole class is engaged in interaction with the teacher. Indian first graders are most reluctant to speak when they must assume the teacher's position to do so by standing up in front of and facing their peers, and, in some cases, fielding questions from them. The main opportunity for assuming the central position at the first-grade level occurs in the activity of Show and Tell. Most Anglo children at this age are at least a little shy about getting up before the class. But the Indian first graders are so reluctant to volunteer for Show and Tell that one teacher reported having dropped it altogether after several years of no success with it.

At the sixth-grade level, the Show and Tell format is used for individual reports as well as for activities resembling Show and Tell in which, for example, students might bring interesting newspaper articles to tell the class about. While this format was used frequently in the Anglo sixth-grade classroom, it was not used at all in the Indian sixth-grade classroom, again because the teacher had so little success with it.

The small group participant structure, in which the teacher engages in interaction with a small number of students, also meets with little enthusiasm among the Indian students. Here, too, the Indian students participate much less than the non-Indian students. [. . .] It is in the use of this participant structure that one most often sees students being called on one after another, regardless of whether they have raised their hands to indicate they wish to respond. When turn taking is handled in this way, Indian students much more often than Anglo students simply do not respond at all.

In the variant of the small group participant structure at the sixth-grade level, namely the group project, Indian students respond very differently. Here they are given the opportunity to control their own interaction. The group project is not normally used at the first-grade level, presumably because it is assumed that the children are not yet capable of sustaining a focused encounter by themselves, particularly one involving the coordination of six or seven students' actions in carrying out a task. But at my request, the first-grade teachers in whose classes I observed did arrange such encounters on a one-time basis, so I had the opportunity to compare the six-year-olds engaged in group projects. At the sixth-grade level the group project is used for a variety of activities ranging from creating murals, to production of a class newspaper, to the construction of battery-run motors.

The Indian student verbal participation in group projects was not only much greater than in either whole-class or small-groups encounters, but also qualitatively different. As a rule, one could not determine who had been appointed as leaders of the Indian groups on the basis of the organization of interaction, and when the students were asked to pick a leader, they usually ignored that instruction and got on with the task at hand. In essence, they transformed the group-project organizational format so that it could no longer even be said to be a variant of the small-group participant structure. There was never any conflict over who should be directing activity or over who should be carrying out what task. Suggestions were either ignored or supported verbally and carried out. The students worked quickly and effectively, and completed their tasks without intervention from the teacher. They often turned the activity into a competition between the groups, verbalizing their desire to finish what they were doing ahead of other groups.

The Anglo students' behavior in group-project activities was quite different. Their leaders were readily identifiable by their manner of attempting to control the turns at talk and the actions of the others. When asked to select leaders they took the assignment to heart, but had difficulty in agreeing on how to accomplish this. They often disagreed about how to carry out their tasks and the leaders often had difficulty maintaining their authority. The Anglo students occasionally found it necessary to ask the teacher to intervene in their disputes, if the teacher had not already done so. Invariably, for any given task, some groups would not have completed the task in the time allotted by the teacher. The Anglo students took interest in the activities of groups other than their own, and were obviously observing them to compare their work with their own, but there was not the sort of open and explicit competition between groups that was initiated by the Indian students.

Perhaps the most striking differences between the Anglo and Indian students in their involvement in and use of the various participant structures was in relation to the one-to-one encounters between the teacher and individual students through which students were given help with their schoolwork. These encounters typically occurred while the students were working at their desks on reading or writing assignments. Students usually initiated such encounters by approaching the teacher at the teacher's desk, or raising their hands to signal to the teacher that they wished the teacher to approach. The Indian students at both the first- and sixth-grade levels made much more use of this optional encounter than did the Anglo students. It was almost as if they were attempting to compensate for their lack of communication with the teacher when the whole class or small groups met with her. In sum, then, the Warm Springs Indian children participated much more actively in one-to-one encounters and in group projects than in lessons where the teacher met with the whole class or in small groups.

In encounters between the teacher and the whole class or a small group, those features which have been identified as distinctive to Anglo organization of interaction are most in evidence. It is in these participant structures that the teacher exercises greatest control over who will talk, when they will talk, and what they will talk about. In these arrangements the children have the least control over their own turns at talk. In the Show and Tell variant of the whole-class participant structure the children themselves are being asked to learn to assume the controlling position that the teacher normally occupies. These participant structures, then, are the least compatible with Warm Springs' ways of organizing interaction, and it is accordingly understandable that the Indian children participate in them as little as they do.

In the group-project variant of the small-group participant structure, by contrast, the Indian students have an opportunity to regulate their own turns at talk as they wish. In this context they make little use of leaders, so that students are able to control their turns at talk, and avoid attempting to control the talk of others. The Indian children's high degree of involvement in group projects is due, then, to the opportunity there to regulate interaction in a manner to which they are accustomed in the Warm Springs community.

The one-to-one encounters between teacher and student similarly allow students greater control over their contribution to the interaction. Students are able to determine to some degree the point at which such encounters will take place, and the specific topical concern that will be taken up. In these involvements the child is the only other possible speaker besides the teacher and does not have to compete with other students to get the teacher's attention. And children in one-to-one encounters with the teacher need not be concerned with avoiding drawing attention to themselves by talking more than others. In sum, it is evident that the Indian children participate most actively in those participant structures which allow them to approximate the modes of interaction that are most familiar to them from their experiences in the Warm Springs community.

One can see these same preferences expressed in the children's playground activities during recess periods, and before and after school.

At the first-grade level one of the two recess periods is regularly devoted to physical activities supervised by the teacher, ranging from exercises on the jungle gym to organized games. In contrast to the Anglo children, the Warm Springs Indian children demonstrate a strong preference for team games and races, engaging in them with enthusiasm. But they show reluctance to function as leaders in games that require one person to control the activities of others, as in Farmer in the Dell and Follow the Leader. It is interesting to note that games requiring such control provide children with practice in singly exerting authority over others, just as Show and Tell and group projects with leaders do in the classroom. Anglo children engage in these games with enthusiasm, and during free periods are sometimes seen playing school, where one child assumes the role of teacher, a game the Indian children do not play.

During free recess periods, Indian children play more team games than Anglo children. There is more mingling of children of different ages and grades on the Indian playground as well. This is largely due to the fact that most of the children have siblings and cousins in the other grades who are accustomed to playing together at one another's homes. The Indian children are also able to sustain interactions involving more children for longer periods of time than the Anglo children of this age. This may be due in part to their greater degree of involvement with older children.

At the sixth-grade level there are regular physical education periods instead of physical activities controlled by the classroom teachers. The sixth-grade Indian students' behavior during recess periods differs from that of the Anglo students in a manner similar to that of the first graders. By the time they reach this age, the Indian students regularly engage in team sports and spend more of their time in such activities than the Anglo students. In keeping with the seasonal cycle of the most popular team sports, the males play football constantly in the fall months, and both males and females play basketball and baseball in the months that follow. Once again, the Indian students are capable of sustaining such team activities with more children involved for longer periods of time.

This preference for team acitivity and success in sustaining interaction without adult supervision is expressed largely through physical activity monitored in the visual channel when it occurs on the playground. But analogous behavior is expressed in both the visual and the auditory channels in classroom infrastructure activity.

The greater involvement of Indian students in the interaction between peers that flourishes covertly around the activities of the official structure organized by the teacher has already been discussed in the section on paying attention. What is relevant here is that in Indian classrooms the lines of infrastructure communication are more equally distributed. All of the Indian children were involved in talking to one another, whereas in the Anglo classrooms there were always one or two students who were clearly peripheral to peer interaction and rarely talked to anyone.

In addition, in the Anglo classrooms, particularly at the sixth-grade level, most of the communication of most children was with two or three other students who were usually seated close by. And during recess periods these students were usually seen with one or two of those they usually talked to in the classroom. By contrast, the Indian students each engaged in communication with a greater number of students, and did not limit themselves to those seated close by. The Indian students' greater range was very much facilitated by their greater use of nonverbal communication in the visual channel discussed earlier.

Nor could the more equal distribution of connections in the Indian students' interactional network be attributed to the teacher's seating plan, for in both Indian and Anglo sixth-grade classrooms the teachers allowed the students preferential seating, so they were able to sit next to those they chose.

There is one qualification to this general pattern, however, that should be noted. At both the first- and sixth-grade levels, Indian students' infrastructure encounters were more sexually segregated, in that they less often communicated with members of the opposite sex. While such segregation is usual among Anglo children also, it was still manifest in a more extreme form in the Indian peer interactions. On the playground, in the cafeteria, and even in choosing seats in the music room, greater sexual segregation was observed among Indian students. Such segregation is also the norm in large-scale public events within the community, where husbands and wives who come together more often than not separate upon arrival to join kinsmen of the same sex. And it is manifest in ritual as well, where roles are sex-specific and spatially separated.

Thus the more equal distribution of peer exchanges among the Indian students is primarily in reference to the same sex. Yet even in regard to attention directed to the opposite sex, the Indian children were more likely to have contact with a greater number of classroom members.

And finally as was the case in group projects and playground activities, the Indian students were able to sustain infrastructure interactions involving more students for a longer time without the interaction breaking down because of conflict or too many people attempting to control the talk.

Earlier in this discussion on the behavior of students as speakers, it was argued that the use of devices for controlling the turns at talk of others are incompatible with the Warm Springs Indian preference for minimization of control over the turns at talk of others. Because such control over others' talk is allocated to the teacher in the classroom to varying degrees, Indian students withdraw from participant structures in which the exercise of such control is most in evidence, preferring neither to be controlled by the teacher nor to be put in the leadership position of controlling others. On the playground at recesses, one finds a similar preference among Indian children for activities that do not involve one person controlling the activities of others.

Related to these preferences is the greater competence the Indian students demonstrate in maintaining interaction among a greater number of children for longer periods of time without the supervision of a leader. This ability is apparent not only in the group-project activities set up by the teacher as part of official classroom interaction, but also in the children's play at recess and in the infrastructure encounters in the classroom.

The Indian children's tendency to distribute their infrastructure involvements among a greater number of children than Anglo children also facilitates their ability to maintain interactions in this way, as does their experience in play with older kinsmen at home, where the children as a group are held collectively responsible for their actions. All in all, they have a great deal of practice in interaction that does not involve control by a single individual, so that their experience in any one of the situations described increases their ability to maintain interaction in the other situations.

The Anglo children, by contrast, have more difficulty regulating interaction among more than three or four children in all of the contexts discussed. However, they learn to use leaders to regulate interaction in games with leaders, and in the classroom interactions. This in turn prepares them for the hierarchically organized interactions of the occupational worlds they will enter. Thus while there is continuity and consistency among the various spheres of activity through which the Anglo children are socialized, and between their socializing experiences and the adult world of work they will enter, for the Warm Springs Indian children this is not the case. The Indian children instead experience conflict between their community socializing experiences and classroom socialization – a conflict that continues into adult life.

20

Beyond Difference and Domination? Intercultural Communication in Legal Contexts

Diana Eades

20.1 Aboriginal English and the Legal Process

This chapter discusses intercultural communication in the legal system, an institutional context where the exercise of power through the manipulation of language is central.[1] It examines the way that an understanding of differences between Aboriginal English and standard Australian English has been used in an initiative aimed at improving intercultural communication in the legal system. But it goes on to show some problems with the assumptions underlying this approach, problems which are highlighted in a particularly shocking court case in 1995. The discussion of this case points to the need for a new approach to intercultural communication in the legal process.

The Aboriginal population comprises approximately two percent of the total of nearly 20 million Australians. Like dispossessed indigenous people the world over, Aboriginal people are the most disadvantaged ethnic group in the country in terms of poverty, ill health, discrimination, mortality rates, unemployment, and inadequate housing. They are also grossly overrepresented in police custody and prisons.

The first language of most Aboriginal people is either Aboriginal English, or one of the English-lexified creoles, Kriol or Torres Strait Creole, although in the remote northern and central areas of Australia there are still a number of people speaking "traditional" languages. In their dealings with the law most Aboriginal people speak a variety of Aboriginal English or a second language variety of English.

Aboriginal English (AE) is the name given to dialects of English spoken by Aboriginal people throughout Australia, which differ from standard Australian English (SE) in systematic ways. There is considerable variation in the varieties of AE spoken, with the heaviest (or furthest from SE) varieties being spoken most in more remote areas, and the lightest (or closest to SE) being spoken most in urban and metropolitan areas.

In the populated eastern seaboard of Australia, most Aboriginal people are of mixed descent, but there are strong cultural continuities with earlier pre-invasion

Diana Eades, "Beyond difference and domination?: Intercultural communication in legal contexts." © 2004 by Blackwell Publishing Ltd. This essay was specially commissioned for this volume.

Aboriginal societies. Many non-Aboriginal Australians are ignorant of the Aboriginality of contemporary Aboriginal people who live in cities and towns, in lifestyles that appear to be very similar to that of other Australians of similar socioeconomic status. An important aspect of ongoing Aboriginal values and ways of acting concerns communication patterns, often termed pragmatics, even where people are using varieties of English.

My work over more than a decade has shown that even where the grammatical differences between SE and AE are not great, there are significant pragmatic differences, which have implications for intercultural communication (e.g. Eades 1988, 1991, 1994). While most of this research and applied work has been carried out in the state of Queensland, there is reason to believe that similar situations exist in other parts of Australia (see for example Mildren 1999). The general point made over 20 years ago by Gumperz and Cook-Gumperz (1982: 13) is still pertinent to much intercultural communication in Australia:

> Speakers may have similar lifestyles, speak closely related dialects of the same language, and yet regularly fail to communicate.

The most relevant aspect of Aboriginal communication to the legal process relates to the cultural assumptions and linguistic strategies used in finding out information, and the ways in which these contrast with the assumptions and strategies used in interviews. The interview is a speech event specific to western societies. The use of interviewing strategies in Aboriginal societies often results in behavior that is culturally inappropriate, bad manners, and ineffective. For example, as Philips (this volume, chapter 19) and others have explained for Native Americans, Aboriginal people use and interpret silence quite differently from non-Aboriginal societies. Aboriginal people often do not see silence in an interaction as an indication that communication has broken down. People often like to sit in silence while enjoying the company of others, or while thinking about serious matters.

Another important pragmatic difference relates to responses to questioning, which is central to information seeking in western societies. As Aboriginal people use a number of indirect strategies in much of their information seeking, direct questions are not so important. Further, many Aboriginal English speakers, like speakers of traditional Aboriginal languages, have a tendency to freely agree to questions, regardless of whether they actually agree with the proposition, or even whether they understand it. This pragmatic pattern, referred to as "gratuitous concurrence," has been found to be problematic in legal contexts. Once a person has agreed to a proposition in certain legal contexts, such as a police interview or a courtroom hearing, the consequences can be very serious, as we will see.

In the 1990s, a growing realization of the significance for the legal process of such differences between Aboriginal English and standard English came at the same time as increasing concern about the shocking overrepresentation of Aboriginal people in custody and prisons. In response to this realization, the Law Society of Queensland undertook an initiative to provide sociolinguistic information for legal professionals, by publishing a handbook for lawyers in Queensland titled *Aboriginal English and the Law* (Eades 1992, hereafter LH).

20.2   Language Awareness for Legal Professionals: The Lawyers' Handbook (LH)

The handbook had the general aim of putting Aboriginal English "on the map," as it were, for the legal profession particularly. Aboriginal English is presented in a general introductory sociolinguistic framework for understanding concepts such as language socialization, dialect difference, communicative style, bicultural competence, cultural continuity, and dialect continuum. Related to this general aim was the specific goal of explaining particular features of Aboriginal English which seemed relevant to communication with speakers of this dialect in legal contexts, particularly in the courtroom. These features included ways of seeking substantial information which avoid direct questions, the use of silence, and the tendency to use gratuitous concurrence. There were also sections on Aboriginal English pronunciation, grammar and vocabulary. It was my hope that the handbook would "help lawyers communicate more effectively with Aboriginal English speaking clients" (p. 1). An important aspect which addressed this goal was the practical strategies "which can help accommodate relevant cultural differences in the legal system" (p. 32), such as:

> Do not interpret silence as an Aboriginal speaker's admission of guilt or ignorance, or even as evidence of a communication breakdown. Remember that silence is often used positively by Aboriginal people to think about things and to get comfortable with the social situation. (p. 46)

In presenting this kind of information in the LH, I was following the work of Gumperz (e.g. 1982a, 1982b, this volume, chapter 3), who made a powerful case for the central role of the interactional sociolinguistic analysis of communicative differences in addressing problems of intercultural communication. This approach was also taken up by the state Attorney General, who launched the LH, saying that "it is the responsibility of those involved in the [legal] system to be aware of the cross-cultural difficulties and to do everything in their power to overcome them" (Gagliardi 1992). The LH received considerable newspaper publicity, and it is reportedly widely used, in law schools and in offices of Aboriginal Legal Services and other lawyers who work with Aboriginal clients. It has been cited in judgments and drawn on (at times quite extensively) in government reports and manuals. Although based on Queensland research, and written for legal practitioners in that state, it has been cited as helpful and relevant to lawyers in other parts of the country.

20.3   Criticisms of the Difference Approach

A major theme of the handbook related to my belief that "Aboriginal people are seriously disadvantaged in those formal situations where success in an interview is crucial to an individual's rights and benefits" (p. 30). I saw the handbook as one way to address Aboriginal disadvantage in the legal system and thus promote justice, by increasing awareness about language difference. The assumptions underlying this initiative are those found in what is often termed a "difference approach" to language diversity. This approach sees all language varieties as equal, or in Rampton's (2001: 261) terms "emphasises the integrity and autonomy of the language and culture of subordinate groups, and the need for institutions to be hospitable to diversity." Inspiration within this difference approach has been provided by the work of interactional sociolinguists, such as Gumperz (e.g. 1982a, 1982b), whose work focuses on intercultural communication in gate-keeping encounters in post-industrial societies, and Tannen (e.g. 1994) whose use of this approach is best known in the explanation of male–female communication.

A major criticism of this difference approach is that it ignores the "social inequality and power relations present in intercultural encounters" (Meeuwis and Sarangi 1994: 310). A good example of this criticism is found in chapter 4 of this volume (Singh, Lele, and Martohardjono). However, sociolinguists working within the difference approach have disputed the criticism that they have ignored power relations. Tannen points out that "societally determined power differences are an inextricable element of cultural differ-ence theory and research" (1994: 8). Arguing against the "unfortunate dichotomy" between the "cultural difference" and the "power" or "dominance" approaches (p. 9), she says that "the cultural difference framework provides a model for explaining how dominance can be created in face-to-face interaction" (p. 10). But the fact remains that in socio-linguistic studies within the difference approach, there is no *analysis* of societal power relations beyond the immediate contexts (see for example Roberts, Davies, and Jupp 1992).

In the LH there is no discussion, let alone analysis, of power relations. The LH sim-ply presents a descriptive account of features of Aboriginal English pragmatics, gram-mar, lexicon and pronunciation, highlighting possible areas of miscommunication for speakers of standard English communicating with Aboriginal English speakers in legal contexts. In its focus on the seemingly neutral goal of "effective communication," the LH avoids any discussion of domination, power relations, or broader structural issues.

But in focusing on differences, and ignoring the role of power in the way that Aboriginal people participate in the legal system, the LH did not take into account the work of key Australian socio-legal scholars. As early as 1976, Eggleston's groundbreaking analysis of Aborigines in the criminal justice system pointed to political and structural inequality. In 1991, a fairly comprehensive textbook titled *Aboriginal Legal Issues* put the point forcefully:

> Far from providing Indigenous Australians with a just and respected means of social con-trol and protection, appropriate to their needs, the Australian criminal justice system remains an alien and discriminatory instrument of oppression, through which Indigenous people are harassed, subjected to unfair legal procedures, needlessly gaoled and all too often die whilst in legal custody. (McRae, Nettheim and Beacroft 1991: 238, also in 1997 edn: 342)

The socio-legal scholars do not generally deal with language issues, and their ana-lysis of Aboriginal inequality in the legal process is not about cultural difference. Their analysis is situated within structural and historical contexts, and power is central. This approach is the "domination" approach (or as it is generally called in language and gen-der studies, the "dominance" approach; see Freed 1995). In this approach, "the focus shifts to larger structures of *domination*, and the need is stressed for institutions to combat the institutional processes and ideologies that reproduce the oppression of sub-ordinate groups" (Rampton 2001: 260, emphasis in original).

Of course, it may be unfair in some ways to compare the LH with scholarly publications, as the LH is unique in being a lawyers' handbook, intended as an easily accessible "how-to" book, that would help lawyers towards more effective communication. As such, it was based on ethnography of communication and interactional sociolinguistic research, but it was not intended to be a scholarly work. However, scholarly writing about Aboriginal English and the law also typically ignores power relations in the involvement of Aboriginal people. If such issues are raised at all, they are only briefly mentioned. For example, Eades (1994: 235) mentions "racism towards Aboriginal people by the community generally, and by people within the police force and judiciary specifically," as well as "the fundamental problem" that has resulted from the dispossession and colonization of Aboriginal people. The philosophy is that such socio-political issues are separate from the sociolinguistic issues, and the focus is on the way that Aboriginal people are disadvantaged in the legal system by "the culturally different approach to information seeking" (Eades 1992: 40).

20.4   The Pinkenba Case: The Failure of the Difference Approach

The explanatory inadequacy of this difference approach to understanding Aboriginal English in the legal system, ignoring socio-political issues as it does, was revealed in no uncertain terms in a 1995 case in the city of Brisbane, known as the Pinkenba case. Before discussing this inadequacy, a short summary of the case is required:

> Some time after midnight on 10 May 1994, three Aboriginal boys aged 12, 13 and 14 were walking around a shopping mall near the Brisbane downtown area. The boys were approached by six armed police officers who told them to get into three separate vehicles. They were then driven 14 kilometers out of town and abandoned in an industrial wasteland in Pinkenba near the mouth of the Brisbane River, from where they had to find their own way back.
>
> The boys were not charged with any offence, nor were they taken to any police station. According to police, the young people were "taken down to Pinkenba to reflect on their misdemeanours" (ABC *Four Corners*, 8 March 1996). Following the boys' complaint to the Aboriginal Legal Service, an investigation was conducted by the Criminal Justice Commission. This investigation recommended that criminal charges be laid against the six police officers. As a result, the police officers were charged that they had unlawfully deprived each of the boys of "his personal liberty by carrying him away in a motor vehicle against his will."
>
> In February 1995, the boys were prosecution witnesses in the committal hearing, which was the first stage in the trial process against the police officers. Most of the four-day hearing consisted of evidence from the three boys, which included lengthy cross-examination by each of the two defense counsel who represented three of the police officers. The case centered on the issue of whether or not the boys had got into and traveled in the police cars against their will: no doubt was ever raised that they were approached and told to get in the police cars, and that they were taken to the industrial wasteland and abandoned there. The defense case was that the boys "gave up their liberty" and that "there's no offence of allowing a person to give up his liberty."

The cross-examination of the boys was devastating: these three young Aboriginal part-time street kids, with minimal successful participation in mainstream Australian institutions, such as education, were pitted against the two most highly paid and experienced criminal barristers in the state. It is hardly surprising that the boys were unable to maintain a consistent story under the barrage of cross-examination, which involved so much shouting at times that many legal professionals in the public gallery were amazed that the lawyers were not restrained or disallowed from using this haranguing behavior. Elsewhere (Eades 2002, 2003a), I have written about the linguistic strategies used by these two defense counsel to manipulate and construe the evidence of the three boys. These strategies resulted in the magistrate accepting defense counsel's construction of these victim–witnesses as criminals with "no regard for the community," and the reinterpretation of the alleged abduction as the boys voluntarily giving up their liberty while the police took them for a ride (both literally and metaphorically). As a result, the charges against the police officers were dropped.

As I explain in the works cited above, the manipulation of Aboriginal ways of using English was central to this defense strategy, particularly the use of silence and gratuitous concurrence. Let us examine one example of the lawyers' exploitation of the Aboriginal tendency to gratuitous concurrence. This example is part of the successful strategy of constructing Barry (a pseudonym) as an unreliable witness, as a result of his being easily and skilfully pressured into conflicting answers by defense counsel (DC) on the central point of the whole hearing.[2]

1. DC: And you <u>knew</u> (1.4) when you spoke to these six police in the Valley that you didn't have to go anywhere with them if you didn't want to, didn't you?

2. BARRY: (1.3) No.

3. DC: You <u>knew</u> that, Mr (1.2) Coley I'd suggest to you, PLEASE DO NOT LIE. YOU KNEW THAT YOU DIDN'T HAVE TO GO ANYWHERE if you didn't want to, didn't you? (2.2) DIDN'T YOU? (2.2) DIDN'T YOU, MR COLEY?

4. BARRY: (1.3) Yeh.

5. DC: WHY DID YOU JUST LIE TO ME? WHY DID YOU JUST SAY "NO" MR COLEY (4.4)? YOU WANT ME TO SUGGEST A REASON TO YOU MR COLEY? THE REASON WAS THIS, THAT YOU WANTED THIS COURT TO <u>BELIEVE</u> (2.1) THAT YOU THOUGHT YOU HAD TO <u>GO</u> WITH POLICE, ISN'T THAT SO?

6. BARRY: (1.2) Yeh.

7. DC: AND YOU <u>LIED</u> TO THE COURT, TRYING TO, TO (1.2) YOU <u>LIED</u> TO THE COURT TRYING TO PUT ONE <u>OVER</u> THE COURT, DIDN'T YOU?

8. BARRY: (1.8) (p) No.

9. DC: THAT WAS YOUR REASON, MR COLEY WASN'T IT? (3.1) WASN'T IT? (3.2) WASN'T IT, MR COLEY?

10. BARRY: (1.9) Yeh=

11. DC: =YES. (2.9) BECAUSE YOU WANTED THE <u>COURT</u> TO <u>THINK</u> THAT <u>YOU</u> DIDN'T KNOW THAT YOU COULD TELL THESE POLICE YOU WEREN'T GOING <u>ANY</u>WHERE WITH THEM. THAT WAS THE REASON, WASN'T IT? (1.5) WASN'T IT?

12. BARRY: (0.6) Yes=

13. DC: =Yes.

This excerpt occurs after Barry (who is sarcastically addressed by this defense counsel as 'Mr Coley') has been on the witness stand for over 90 minutes on two consecutive days, most of it being cross-examination. Turn 1 in this example puts the proposition central to the defense argument: that the witness knew he did not have to go in the police car. The witness's answer of "No" (Turn 2) is not accepted by defense counsel, so he is harassed in Turn 3 until he does agree (in Turn 4). Of course, we cannot know what is in the witness's mind, but we can see the ideal situation for gratuitous concurrence, increased when defense counsel begins shouting angrily in Turn 3. The contradictory answers given by the witness in Turns 2 and 8 on the one hand, and Turns 4, 6, 10 and 12 on the other hand, are interpreted literally by defense counsel, to provide clear evidence that the witness is a liar (emphasized for the court with the theme of "Why did you lie?", a frequently repeated 'chorus' throughout the cross-examination of all three boys).

However, an understanding of Aboriginal English background assumptions and ways of speaking might well lead to a situated inference indicating that the answer of "Yeh" in Turns 4, 6, 10 and 12 are answers of gratuitous concurrence – indicating the witness's realization that he will be harassed until he gives the answer required by his interrogator. It is clear that we cannot with confidence assume that Barry intends to agree with the proposition of the question. Indeed, there are compelling reasons which would caution against such a literal interpretation, suggesting a strong possibility of gratuitous concurrence. Further, the question in Turn 11 contains four clauses embedded in the main clause, a sentence structure which would confuse many witnesses, regardless of age, sociolinguistic background, and experience with interviews.

The example gives an indication of the way in which the knowledge of the Aboriginal English use of gratuitous concurrence was used by defense counsel to lead the boys to agree to conflicting propositions, and thus appear to be unreliable and untrustworthy witnesses. Given the highly adversarial nature of the hearing and the fact that the two defense counsel were among the top criminal lawyers in the state, it would be safe to assume that such strategies were deliberately used to destroy the credibility of the witnesses (which is, after all, the major aim of cross-examination). It was disturbing to find out that the two defense counsel had at the Bar table a copy of the LH. So it appeared that the handbook which had been written to bring about more effective communication between lawyers and Aboriginal witnesses was being used in this case to achieve *less* effective communication, and even to subvert the witnesses' attempts at communication. And indeed it was very successful in that purpose.

From the outset, I had been concerned about what might happen in particular cases, if communication strategies became so easily identified and understood that they could be used for *less* effective communication. When I had raised this concern with legal professionals before writing the LH, they had reassured me that in the adversarial legal system, this possible danger was mitigated by the balance inherent in having opposing counsel. They had argued that, as the handbook was to be made widely available to legal professionals throughout the state, any lawyer attempting to use information in it to achieve less effective communication would be countered by that witness's lawyer recognizing the strategy, and countering it, in true adversarial style. But the Pinkenba case showed that it is not that straightforward.

The realization of the "effectiveness" of the LH in subverting intercultural communication in this case marked a turning point in my approach to understanding issues involving Aboriginal English in legal contexts. The difference approach to language inequality cannot explain what was going on in the cross-examination of these three boys: it was clearly not a situation in which there was misunderstanding of cultural differences in the use of English. Elsewhere (Eades 2003a), I have explored the important question of why there was no adversarial balance in this case (such as had been "promised" to me by legal professionals when I was writing the LH).

Of course, it can be argued that this was an extreme case, and certainly I have never seen cross-examination like it, either before or since. But the important point is that it happened, and it was allowed to happen. The cross-examination was so successful that the magistrate decided to drop the charges against the police officers. When the families of the boys complained, an appeal was launched against this decision. This resulted in a judge reviewing the magistrate's decision; and dismissing the appeal. So, it is clear that while the cross-examination of the three boys in this case may have been an aberration, it was still widely taken as "due process" and the proper functioning of the justice system, and indeed legitimized by the judicial review.

20.5 Beyond Difference and Domination to Discourse

An examination of the Pinkenba case points to problems with both the "difference" and the "domination" perspectives on inequality. Firstly, let's consider the "difference" perspective: Simply describing cultural differences between Aboriginal and mainstream ways of using English from a liberal pluralist position ignores wider political structures and processes that play an essential role in the ways in which Aboriginal people participate in the legal system. The difference approach assumes that language awareness can lead to justice, but in the Pinkenba case, this clearly evident language awareness was unfairly used to subvert the evidence of the Aboriginal witnesses. Awareness of cultural difference is not sufficient to promote justice in the adversarial system (despite earlier optimism by several legal professionals that it would be). But it goes further than this: there is good evidence that the descriptive account of Aboriginal ways of communicating provided in the LH became a powerful instrument in the denial of justice in this case. This shows that despite the apolitical and attempted neutral stance of the difference approach (Rampton 2001: 263), such neutrality is unachievable.

A reading of the criminological literature would suggest that it is indeed naive for sociolinguists to assume that an understanding of cultural and linguistic difference can substantially alter the participation of Aboriginal people in the criminal justice system. Nothing short of change in the key elements of the system is required, including all levels of police and judicial work: recruiting, training, practice, supervision and regulation. This seems to suggest that a domination perspective on inequality would have much greater explanatory power than the difference approach to account for what was happening in the Pinkenba case.

In Rampton's (2001: 260) terms, discussed above, in this approach we have a shift of focus to larger structures of domination. But, as we think about the domination perspective on the participation of Aboriginal people in the criminal justice system, a sense of overwhelming fatalism can easily develop. If the Pinkenba hearing can be legitimized by the legal system, what hope is there for change to the position of Aboriginal people in the criminal justice system? What hope is there for an oppressed minority group to change its participation in this "apparatus of state coercive power" (in Gramsci's terms, 1971: 12)? How can the criminalization of Aboriginal young people (in Cunneen's 2001 terms) be recognized and challenged? How can police powers, which include the removal of Aboriginal children, be controlled? How can the legal system be moved to a position where the rules of courtroom evidence become subordinated to the delivery of justice? And the obvious question for the sociolinguist to ask is: can any contribution be made by the sociolinguistic analysis of courtroom language practices?

In order to answer these questions, we need to understand the major criticism of the domination perspective, voiced in the field of applied linguistics and sociolinguistics by scholars such as Rampton (2001) and Pennycook (2001),[3] who draw on contemporary poststructural theory. Also central to their criticism is the work of the sociologist Giddens (e.g. 1987), who argues that we have to examine both structure and agency in the ana-lysis of society. Thus, the domination perspective is criticized for deterministically situating the basis of inequality in social structures, and leaving little room for human agency. In its focus on static power structures, this perspective ignores the way that indi-viduals actively work both for and against the actual processes of domination. Language is central to this active work, or agency, and hence Rampton uses the term "discourse" approach for this approach to linguistic and cultural diversity and inequality. What is important in this approach is "viewing language as inherently political" and "understand-ing power more in terms of its micro operations in relation to questions of class, race, gender, ethnicity, sexuality, and so on" (Pennycook 2001: 167). With relevance to the theme of this paper, Pennycook points out (p. 168) that such an approach is also "skeptical about the notion that awareness can lead to emancipation" (ibid.).

What does this mean for the analysis of intercultural communication in the legal pro-cess? Adopting this "discourse" approach requires us to examine socio-political struc-tures of domination, not in a deterministic static way, but in terms of the ways in which this domination is constantly being worked for (Matoesian 1993: 208) and worked against (or resisted). That is, in this approach, there is no static dominant group whose power is assured. There is always some kind of struggle or work involved in retaining power, and there are always ways in which the dominated groups or individuals resist the power of the dominant group. Pennycook (2001: 90) draws attention to Foucault's (1991: 148) insistence that power needs to be explained, and argues that this approach leads us to "analyses of discourse [which] aim to explore how power may operate, rather than to demonstrate its existence" (p. 93). As Conley and O'Barr argue in their book *Just Words: Law, Language and Power*, sociolinguistic micro-analysis has a powerful role to play, by "exposing the mechanisms that produce . . . inequalities" (1998: 13).

20.6   Intercultural Communication in the Pinkenba Case Re-examined

Coming back to the Pinkenba case then, how can sociolinguistics account for the inter-cultural communication in the courtroom? What happened to the "adversarial balance" in this hearing? Why did the magistrate not use the rules of evidence which would have allowed him to override the harassment and haranguing during cross-examination? Why did the prosecutor make very few objections? Why did the magistrate place so much weight on a literal interpretation of the boys' answers? And why did the review judge uphold the magistrate's decision?

It has become clear (e.g. Eades 2002, 2003a) that this case cannot be adequately explained by limiting the focus to the analysis of power *within* the discourse. Several scholars whose work is in the perspective which Rampton calls the "discourse" perspective exemplify the way that the analysis of power *behind* the discourse (in Fairclough's 1989 terms) can be essential to the analysis of courtroom language (e.g. Matoesian 1993, Philips 1998, Ehrlich 2001). For example, Matoesian's (1993) conversation analysis of the language of rape trials presents a powerful argument for the need to examine both structure (e.g. the patriarchal structure of society generally, and the trial process specifically) and agency (the specific ways in which participants in the rape trial struggle over contested meanings and ideologies). Matoesian's work is a good example of a study which illustrates Giddens's important point mentioned above, namely that understanding society requires the examination of social structures (such as the legal process) as well as of the agency of individuals. Matoesian shows the important role that sociolinguistics can play in such analysis.

Another way of thinking about the relationship between structure and agency in the explanation of society, is to see that analysis is required on both macro and micro levels (Sarangi 1994, Meeuwis 1994). However, Pennycook cautions that what is required is not merely to map micro and macro relations, but "to understand in much more subtle ways how power circulates at multiple levels" (2001: 114–15). He says (p. 172) that "in our search for an understanding of language and power it is important that we do not seek closure too quickly by assuming a given structure of power and then trying to map language onto it."

In order to understand this circulation of power in the Pinkenba case, we need to draw substantially on the work of socio-legal scholars. This case needs to be understood in the light of ongoing police control over the movements of Queensland Aboriginal people in various ways, since British invasion and settlement in the early nineteenth century. Central to this control have been two processes: (1) the "pivotal role" of police in the removal of Aboriginal children from their families and kinship groups under "protective" legislation from the 1860s for over a century (HREOC 1997: 44), and (2) the current "overpolicing" of Aboriginal young people in public places, which has resulted in their being 41 times more likely to be in juvenile correctional institutions than a non-indigenous young person, and 26 times more likely to be in police custody (HREOC, based on 1995 statistics).

It is not difficult to see this extreme overrepresentation of indigenous young people in police custody and detention as an extension of the earlier official removal policies and practices. Cunneen (e.g. 2001) argues that this process of criminalization, which clearly discriminates against Aboriginal young people, results to a considerable extent from the way in which police continue to exercise their discretionary power (e.g. deciding whether to arrest, use diversionary measures, or to issue a caution).

Not surprisingly, Aboriginal people do not accept this situation, and there is an ongoing struggle between police and Aboriginal people. In the Pinkenba incident, yet again Aboriginal young people in a public place were being singled out for police attention, and yet again Aboriginal young people were removed by police. But unlike so many of the earlier occurrences, Aboriginal complaints about this police action were not ignored: through the Aboriginal Legal Service and the Criminal Justice Commission these complaints were heard and investigated. The struggle between Aboriginal people and the police moved from the streets into the courtroom, where the major weapon is undoubtedly language.

What was happening during the cross-examination of the three Aboriginal boys was not simply a situational struggle in which defense counsel were using their power as "leading barristers" cross-examining Aboriginal child witnesses. This cross-examination needs to be understood as a speech event firmly embedded in the ongoing struggle, both institutional and societal (in Fairclough's 1989 terms), about state control over the freedoms of Aboriginal young people. It was not just that the police took the boys for a ride in circumstances where it is ludicrous to claim that they could have exercised their legal right to refuse. But the whole criminal justice system worked to legitimize the actions of the police officers. In this way, the boys' claims to freedom from police harassment were denied through so-called "due process."

In conclusion, the Pinkenba case teaches us an important lesson about the analysis of intercultural communication: it demonstrates how the difference approach within sociolinguistics can be inadequate, particularly in legal settings, where issues of domination and control are so pertinent. Further, this case provides a telling example of the consequences of sociolinguistic "naiveté about social theory" (Rampton 2001: 262). In understanding Aboriginal English in the legal system, we certainly need to understand cultural and linguistic features that are involved in conversational inferencing, and this is the area in which we have made some headway already. We also need to examine the larger historical and political forces in Australian society that are integral to the ongoing neocolonial control of the criminal justice system over Aboriginal people (in Cunneen's 2001 terms). But we need to go beyond both the dominance and the difference perspective, and critically examine the details of what is actually happening when Aboriginal people participate in the legal system. An important feature of this "discourse" approach is "the need to understand how people resist and appropriate forms of language oppression" (Pennycook 2001: 167). As long as sociolinguistic examinations of Aboriginal people in the legal system confine analysis to the courtroom, these resistances and appropriations will be very hard to find. The ways in which Aboriginal people are claiming agency are revealed in the wider power struggles within which trials are situated, such as complaints about the Pinkenba incident which resulted in the charges against the police officers, and in demonstrations and street riots (see Eades 2003a).

Thus, in order to account for the intercultural communication and miscommunication that affects the participation of Aboriginal English speakers in the legal process, we need sociolinguistic micro-analysis of courtroom interactions undertaken in conjunction with the analysis of the wider power struggles that involve the criminalization of Aboriginal young people, and the ongoing police control over their movements, as well as Aboriginal resistance to these processes.

Notes

I am grateful to Michael Cooke for many discussions about issues of language and power in the legal system, and to him, as well as Jeff Siegel and Janet Holmes for helpful comments on the draft. I take sole responsibility for this paper.

1   This paper is drawn from Eades (2002, 2003a, 2003b). Readers are referred to these publications for further details and fuller bibliographic references.
2   I use the following standard transcription conventions:

underlining indicates utterance emphasis
SMALL CAPITALS indicate raised volume
(p) before an utterance indicates that it is spoken in a low volume
= indicates latched utterances, i.e. no pause between the end of one utterance and the start of the next
a number in parentheses indicates the length of a pause in seconds, e.g. (3.2)
the following abbreviations are also used in the transcripts: DC = defense counsel; M = magistrate; P = prosecutor; W = witness.

All personal names in this paper are pseudonyms.
3   Pennycook (2001) uses the term "emancipatory modernism" in the way that Rampton uses "domination" perspective.

References

Australian Broadcasting Commission (ABC). 1996. *Black and Blue*. Four Corners TV documentary 8 March.

Conley, J. and W. O'Barr. 1998. *Just Words: Law, Language and Power*. Chicago: University of Chicago Press.

Cunneen, C. 2001. *Conflict, Politics and Crime: Aboriginal Communities and the Police*. Sydney: Allen and Unwin.

Eades, D. 1988. "They don't speak an Aboriginal language, or do they?" In I. Keen (ed.), *Being Black: Aboriginal Cultures in Settled Australia*. Canberra: Aboriginal Studies Press, pp. 97–117.

Eades, D. 1991. Communicative strategies in Aboriginal English. In S. Romaine (ed.), *Language in Australia*. Cambridge: Cambridge University Press, pp. 84–93.

Eades, D. 1992. *Aboriginal English and the Law: Communicating with Aboriginal English Speaking Clients: A Handbook for Legal Practitioners*. Brisbane: Queensland Law Society.

Eades, D. 1994. A case of communicative clash: Aboriginal English and the legal system. In J. Gibbons (ed.), *Language and the Law*. London: Longman, pp. 234–64.

Eades, D. 2002. "Evidence given in unequivocal terms": Gaining consent of Aboriginal kids in court. In J. Cotterill (ed.), *Language in the Legal Process*. Basingstoke: Palgrave, pp. 162–79.

Eades, D. 2003a. The politics of misunderstanding in the legal process: Aboriginal English in Queensland. In J. House, G. Kasper and S. Ross (eds.), *Misunderstanding in Spoken Discourse*. London: Longman.

Eades, D. 2003b. Understanding Aboriginal English in the legal system: A critical sociolinguistics approach. MS.

Eggleston, E. 1976. *Fear, Favour or Affection: Aborigines and the Criminal Law in Victoria, South Australia and Western Australia*. Canberra: Australian National University Press.

Ehrlich, S. 2001. *Representing Rape: Language and Sexual Consent*. London: Routledge.

Fairclough, N. 1989. *Language and Power*. London: Longman.

Foucault, M. 1991. *Remarks on Marx*. New York: Semiotext(e).

Freed, A. 1995. Language and gender. *Annual Review of Applied Linguistics* 15, 3–22.

Gagliardi, J. 1992. 'Law group sees black injustice: Handbook outlines language problems.' *Brisbane Courier Mail*, April 13, 1992.

Giddens, A. 1987. *Social Theory and Modern Sociology*. Cambridge: Polity Press.

Gramsci, A. 1971. *Selections from the Prison Notebooks of Antonio Gramsci*, ed. and trans. by Q. Hoare and G. Nowell Smith. London: Laurence and Wishart.

Gumperz, J. 1982a. *Discourse Strategies*. Cambridge: Cambridge University Press.

Gumperz, J. (ed.) 1982b. *Language and Social Identity*. Cambridge: Cambridge University Press.

Gumperz, J. and J. Cook-Gumperz. 1982. Introduction: language and the communication of social identity. In J. Gumperz (ed.), pp. 1–21.

HREOC (Human Rights and Equal Opportunity Commission). 1997. *Bringing them Home: National Inquiry into the Separation of Aboriginal and Torres Strait Islander Children from their Families*. Sydney: Commonwealth of Australia.

McRae, H., G. Nettheim, and L. Beacroft. 1991. *Aboriginal Legal Issues: Commentary and Materials*. Sydney: Law Book Company. (2nd edn 1997 titled *Indigenous Legal Issues*.)

Matoesian, G. 1993. *Reproducing Rape: Domination through Talk in the Courtroom*. Chicago: The University of Chicago Press.

Meeuwis, M. 1994. Leniency and testiness in intercultural communication: Remarks on ideology and context in interactional sociolinguistics. *Pragmatics* 4(3), 391–408.

Meeuwis, M. and S. Sarangi. 1994. Perspectives on intercultural communication: A critical reading. *Pragmatics* 4(3), 309–14.

Mildren, D. 1999. Redressing the imbalance: Aboriginal people in the criminal justice system. *Forensic Linguistics* 6(1), 137–60.

Pennycook, A. 2001. *Critical Applied Linguistics: A Critical Introduction*. Mahwah, NJ: Lawrence Erlbaum Associates.

Philips, S. 1998. *Ideology in the Language of Judges: How Judges Practice Law, Politics and Courtroom Control*. New York: Oxford University Press.

Rampton, B. (2001). Language crossing, cross-talk and cross-disciplinarity in sociolinguistics. In N. Coupland, S. Sarangi and C. Candlin (eds.): *Sociolinguistics and Social Theory*. London: Pearson Education Limited, pp. 261–96.

Roberts, C., E. Davies, and T. Jupp. 1992. *Language and Discrimination*. London: Longman.

Sarangi, S. 1994. Intercultural or not? Beyond celebration of cultural differences in miscommunication analysis. *Pragmatics* 4(3), 409–28.

Tannen, D. 1994. *Gender and Discourse*. Oxford: Oxford University Press.

Discussion Questions

For these questions, choose a minority group in your culture, such as African Americans in the US, Maoris in New Zealand, or South Asians in the UK, to compare with the articles presented in this part.

1. Are there parallels between a minority group in your culture and Aboriginal Australians in terms of their relationship with the "mainstream" culture? What are they?
2. What interactional differences have you noticed between the so-called "mainstream" culture and the minority (sub)culture? For example, what directive forms are used in families and schools? Is one subculture more or less direct than the other? Which? Can you describe differences in terms of speech events, contextualization cues, or politeness?
3. Do these differences help perpetuate the inequality between minority and majority cultures in the country under consideration? If so, how?
4. Is it enough to *understand* these differences, or do our subcultures need to work to *accommodate*? Should the majority or the minority accommodate more?
5. To what extent do you think training programs and/or affirmative action and school integration help with appreciating, understanding, and even accommodating to different cultures?

Index

Lightning Source UK Ltd.
Milton Keynes UK
UKOW022057230613

212659UK00001B/1/P